FISHING'S *Best*
SHORT STORIES

FISHING'S *Best*
SHORT STORIES

Edited by Paul D. Staudohar

CHICAGO
REVIEW
PRESS

Library of Congress Cataloging-in-Publication Data

Fishing's best short stories / edited by Paul D. Staudohar.
   p. cm.
   Contents: Opening day / Jack Gilchrist—Light Tackle / Philip
Wylie—The big brown trout / Robert Travers—Squirrelly's grouper/
Bob Shacochis.
   ISBN 1-55652-403-X
   1. Fishing stories, American. 1. Staudohar, Paul D.
PS648.F57 F57 2000
813'.0108355—dc21

00–025135

Published by Chicago Review Press, Incorporated
814 North Franklin Street
Chicago, Illinois 60610
ISBN 1-55652-403-X

Printed in the United States of America
5 4 3 2 1

CONTENTS

ACKNOWLEDGMENTS

The editor is grateful to numerous people whose time and effort made this book possible. Publisher Linda Matthews and executive editor Cynthia Sherry of Chicago Review Press were important contributors, as they have been with other books in this series. Thanks also to librarians and archivists who helped me unearth material. These included Kathy Bryant of the Catskill Fly Fishing Center and Museum in Livingston Manor, New York; Gail M. Morchower of the International Game Fish Association in Pompano Beach, Florida; and Michael Salmon of the Amateur Athletic Association in Los Angeles. At California State University, Hayward, valuable library resource assistance was provided by Lynne LeFleur, Kristin Ramsdell, and Douglas K. Ferguson. Florence Bongard of Cal State was a versatile secretary, in association with Linda Wickwire. Professor Milton Kessler and Ruth Stanek, from the English department at State University of New York at Binghamton, deserve credit. Editors and staff at distinguished magazines provided advice, including Robert Scheffler at *Esquire*, Alice K. Turner at *Playboy*, Melissa DeMeo at the *New Yorker*, Susannah Meadows at *Gentlemen's Quarterly*, Slaton White and Carolee Green at *Field and Stream*, and Monte Burke and Paul Ghiotto at *Sports Afield*. Gerilee Hundt and Drew Hamrick of Chicago Review Press were helpful in producing the manuscript. Thanks also to Julie Cohen, Professor Donald Wort, and my fishing buddies, Gary Stearns and Len Vereecken. This book is dedicated to my longtime friends, Al and Suzy Pakkala.

—Paul D. Staudohar

ACKNOWLEDGMENTS

INTRODUCTION

Fishing's Best Short Stories and its companion, *Hunting's Best Short Stories,* continue a series that began with a collection of baseball short stories published in 1995. Throughout the series, which includes golf (1997), football (1998), and boxing (1999), the goal has remained the same: to present the very best short fiction on favorite sports.

This book contains twenty-five outstanding stories about fishing that can be enjoyed by serious sportsmen and by people who have never dropped a line. Three are treasures from the nineteenth century and the rest come from the twentieth, pretty evenly distributed among the decades. Classic tales by the German brothers Grimm and the French master Guy de Maupassant join offerings by Americans Stephen Vincent Benét, Philip Wylie, and Robert Traver, who were also distinguished novelists. Contemporary writers from the front rank include Stephen King, E. Annie Proulx, P. J. O'Rourke, and Bob Shacochis, among others. The two great outdoor magazines *Field and Stream* and *Sports Afield* are represented, as is the former adventure magazine *Argosy.* Several stories were originally published in fine literary sources like the *New Yorker, Esquire, Saturday Evening Post,* and *Playboy.*

The stories themselves resonate with superb plotting, love and skill for the sport, surprise endings, humor, chicanery, and other pleasures. They portray a tantalizing selection of the many worlds fish inhabit: roiling oceans, still ponds, swift rivers, and bubbling brooks. And they introduce a nice variety of our piscatorial friends. Dominating the collection is the noble trout, but salmon, tarpon, bass, dolphin, permit, flounder, grouper, weakfish, northern pike, and even a sea monster appear in these pages.

Of course, fishing originated in the depths of human prehistory as a means of survival, but it must quickly have become a favorite occupation and a campfire storyteller's delight. The first English-language description of fishing as sport is "The Treatise on Fishing with an Angle," which appears in the second *Book of St. Albans* (1496). Although its authorship is something of a mystery, it is usually attributed to Dame Juliana Berners, an English noblewoman and outdoors writer "endowed with excellent gifts of both body and mind."

Perhaps the most famous essayist on fishing is another Englander, Izaak Walton (1593–1683). His book *The Compleat Angler* has been published in over four hundred editions, more than any other work in English except the Bible. Walton's quaint but eloquent prose remains vibrant today, in describing the trout, for instance: "Gesner says his name is of a German offspring, and says he is a fish that feeds clean and purely, in the swiftest streams, and on the hardest gravel; and that he may justly contend with all freshwater fish. . . ."

The most important early American fishing writer is Theodore Gordon (1854–1915). Gordon was the "father" of the American dry fly. He created the famous Quill Gordon and is distinguished for designing other flies that severed American reliance on British styles. Gordon's writing for popular magazines such as *Forest and Stream* (predecessor of *Field and Stream*) spawned the modern era in fly-fishing.

Several United States presidents were avid anglers, none more than Grover Cleveland and Herbert Hoover. Cleveland, who hooked many a small-mouthed bass, wrote a delightful book called *Fishing and Hunting Sketches*. Hoover's *Fishing for Fun* recalls his quests for trout on the Brule River in Wisconsin. But the sport's alluring literary tradition is especially on display in Ernest Hemingway's great novel *The Old Man and the Sea*, and in Norman Maclean's *A River Runs Through It*. Both books were made into successful movies, and Maclean's sparked a fly-fishing boom in the 1990s.

Why the attraction of big-time writers to fishing? Simply, it's a wonderful activity. Unlike spectator sports, it gets us out into nature's beauty for fresh air and exercise. People of all ages and abilities enjoy it, everywhere in the world. It can be expensive and complex or cheap and easy. A fisherman can spend thousands on a good bass boat or practice fly-fishing for years to achieve perfection—or he can attach a string with a hook to a bamboo pole and drop a worm into the water. Eating one's catch at the end of the day is a culinary treat. Though it can be loved as a solitary recreation, fishing often brings family and friends together in adventures that form lasting memories.

And fishermen are endearing folk, quick with a yarn, eager to help a novice, able to enjoy their day even if the fish aren't biting. They have a wry sense of humor and a talent for exaggeration. If a fish gets away, it is always a leviathan of the species. The fishing is never as good as it was yesterday, or last season, or a decade ago. They especially applaud and repeat all tales told over strong drink. They are ideal characters for stories of every stripe.

The stories in this book can't replace the real thing, fishing in the great outdoors. But they're more accessible and much less time-consuming. Fisherfolk like to hear and tell stories. Lovers of top-notch literature will find an abundance of great yarns here. The adventure is vicarious, but there's plenty to chew on and savor. Bon appétit!

As the trout season begins, a determined angler makes his way to a favorite spot where a big rainbow has twice before eluded him. There is a purity about this story—the pristine grandeur of nature, the deft use of fly rod by a skilled practitioner, the courage and beauty of the great fish. While the tale has the high polish of work from a veteran storyteller, it is actually the author's first attempt at fiction. Originally published in the Georgia Review, *it was included in* The Best American Short Stories 1965.

Jack Gilchrist

OPENING DAY (1964)

THE AIR HUNG HEAVY WITH the chilly dampness of a frosty spring morning. Light of another day played tag with shadows of the forest and wisps of fog resembling miniature cyclones curled up slowly from quiet spots on the face of the stream.

The man in the water crouched low as if hiding. Chest high rubber waders protected him from the dampness. The khaki shirt he wore blended almost perfectly with the color of the waders and a wide-brimmed hat of almost the same neutral tan shielded a face that bore the pallor of indoor confinement and office employment. A willow creel hung at his left side and in his right hand he carried the slender, flexible length of a fly rod.

Progressing gently, the stranger placed each foot forward with care as he waded silently and steadily upstream in the shallow water. Slowly and ever so quietly, his eyes focused on a bend in the stream ahead, he moved in his creeping crouch, pausing occasionally for long moments as if time were endless and this day forever.

Gaining his objective, the bend in the stream, the wilderness intruder straightened behind the concealing screen of a rhododendron bush. Carefully, as if fingering the delicate web of a spider, he parted two frost laden branches of green and peered through to survey a deep wide pocket of water that escaped silently but swiftly from the churning base of a crashing waterfall. Nothing missed his scrutiny as he surveyed the pool . . . his attention eventually focusing on a large boulder that rose from the water near the head of the pool but some fifty feet to his right of the falls.

Estimating his distance from the boulder the man's experienced eye judged what needed to be done to accomplish the mission that had brought him some 150 miles during the early hours of predawn darkness. His objective was a fish. Not just any fish but one single, solitary fish; to him the only fish in the world. A beautiful creature of iridescent colors with a blood-red band lining each side. A trout. A rainbow trout. The largest he had ever seen and the largest he could ever hope to catch.

Thoughts of the fish filled him with impatience and a burning desire to get on with the job at hand. But thoughts of two previous meetings with the beautiful creature of the hidden pool filled him with a wariness and a caution. Twice before, during his first two years of fly-fishing apprenticeship, he had hung this wonderful fish. Twice before, in the early part of the two past seasons, before warming weather brought out novice fishermen to tramp the tender fern on the banks of the stream and muddy the quiet pools, he had met the fish in combat. And in his inexperience he twice had lost. Now for the third time and in the third season he would try again.

Crawling silently beneath trailing branches of the rhododendron bush, he waded cautiously into the shallow end of the pool barely disturbing its surface. Still crouching and pausing long moments between each step he moved so slowly that the surface of the water softly hugged his rubber clothed legs and finally his waist as the ocean of morning mist hugged the tops of the Georgia mountains towering to either side. After many long minutes he had moved less than fifteen feet from the bend in the stream and the concealing screen of rhododendron that had guarded his approach to the pool.

Eventually reaching a location he deemed suitable for his work, the fisherman paused there for a long moment and then, turning, carefully appraised the terrain to his rear to make certain his back cast would not flick a leaf or nick a twig. Satisfied he quietly committed himself to the moment. Breathing deeply he summoned all his skill, all his planning and all his patience to the meticulous task of placing the delicate fly lightly on the water in an exact spot some thirty feet away and not more than two feet past the boulder.

Lengthening several feet of leader and line through the guides of the wispy rod the fisherman stretched the bamboo before him and then raised it sharply but smoothly, sending the line backward in one long continuous flow. As it straightened, he flicked the rod forward changing the direction of the line 180 degrees while feeding excess line through the guides with his left hand to get more distance. As the line completed its first roll before him he brought his right forearm back a second time, reversing the direction of the line again, and as the added length completed an arc and tugged gently with its backward motion, he drove the rod forward for the last time, with power and yet grace in the movement.

The lengthening line shot forward. As it straightened and flew past the boulder, he lowered the rod tip slightly and then raised it deftly to settle the fly on the surface of the water with the barest whisper of disturbance.

Completely absorbed in the rhythmic ritual, the fisherman noted with satisfaction the location of the fly some few inches short of its goal but sufficiently past the lair of the trout to insure a proper float. The muscles of his arms and shoulders tensed expectantly as the bit of camouflaged steel swirled gently in a slight cross current then began the journey that would carry it to the base of the boulder.

Although it took only a moment for the short drift it seemed to the fisherman an endless moment. His brow furrowed and crowfoot wrinkles of concentration deepened at the corners of his eyes as he projected himself thoughtfully to the drifting fly and the creature that lay watching from the depths of the pool below.

The artificial insect sailed lazily toward its destiny, then brushed the face of the boulder, and the surface of the water dimpled deeply as the trout took.

The fisherman's strike came at the same instant . . . so quickly and efficiently and yet so gently that any casual onlooker would have sworn the fisherman could see the fish and thus know the exact moment it sucked the fly into its mouth.

At the first solid tug of resistance the fisherman struck a second time but with more power and less delicacy. As the point of the hook followed by its sharp engaging barb dug into the jaw of the trout the surface of the quiet pool shattered like a breaking mirror and with a mighty surge the great fish began its fight for life.

The trout dived for its hideaway beneath the boulder and the fisherman raised his rod to apply firm line pressure and halt the surge. Fearful of abrasion from the rock that could easily weaken the delicate leader but mindful of the power in his adversary, he fought to keep the fish away from the rock and in open water.

Responding to the pressure the fish jumped again, leaving a momentary spray-filled hole in the middle of the pool. Then as its strong sleek body crashed back into the water the trout propelled itself across the pool toward the boiling froth at the foot of the falls seeking refuge and help in the cascading force.

Once again the fisherman raised the rod and applied line pressure to turn the fish, but he had underestimated its strength and before he could turn it, the trout reached the churning water. Suddenly tautness left the line and a sickening feeling clawed at the heart of the man in the pool.

Had the great fish escaped? Had its strength, aided by the thundering water, torn the hook from its mouth? Quickly the fisherman raised the slender bamboo higher with arms reaching skyward and stepped back to get better leverage on the rod. Then again he felt the resistance, the power and the strength that would test his own, and panic subsided as thoughts once again turned to his strategy for the battle that still lay ahead.

He did not try to sting the fish into moving out from under the falls immediately. Knowing that the buffeting water was forcing the fish to exert itself against the tension of the rod, he was satisfied to keep pressure on and let the fish sap its own strength.

Gradually the great trout began to yield. Its continued pull against the strength of the line and the tension of the rod began to lessen. With pectoral fins fanning gracefully, the fish floated out from under the falls slowly as if undecided what action to take next. Gradually it began to move rapidly. It exploded on the surface for a third time and then began circling the pool as if seeking a watery side door through which to escape. For better than ten minutes the fish canvassed the pool as if caged in a strange and unknown world.

Finally, with ebbing strength and in fearful panic of approaching death, the trout made one last great effort to get away. Sweeping across the pool in a renewed surge of action it turned sharply and directly toward the fisherman, seeking access to the stream that flowed from the trail of the pool. Borne on the wings of fright it shot toward the shallow water as if to crash through the legs of its tormentor and into the neck of the stream by force. The bullet shaped missile of color sped toward the freedom gate, and for the first time since it had taken the fly the fish was free from the pressure of the rod and line.

The sudden and increasing slackness in the line as the fish approached made it impossible for the fisherman to force line pressure control on his adversary. Once again panic gripped his mind and fear crawled through the alley of his imagination as thoughts of losing the fish spurred him to action. Abandoning caution in a desperate attempt to halt the rush of his quarry and turn it back into deeper water, he knelt and then sprawled his length across the mouth of the small stream, blocking exit from the pool.

Frightened by the disturbance in the shallow water and finding its escape path blocked the great trout turned and bore back toward its lair under the boulder. The fisherman struggled quickly to his feet and rapidly gathered slack line until he could once again feel the tautness of the connection between himself and his opponent. Wet, with waders full of water and hat floating out of sight down stream, he was oblivious to all but the soul-satisfying thought that now he had the battle nearly won.

The fisherman continued to play the fish gently, feeling its strength and power bleed slowly through the line and rod. The growing weakness of the fish served as a transfusion of strength to him, and his growing confidence lifted him on wings of exhilaration.

What a stir he would create at home. This should rank as one of the finest trout killed in the state in years. He could envision the shine of enchantment in the eyes of his nine-year-old son at the telling of the story of the fight, and in his imaginings he could picture the creature mounted in a curving leap, positioned on a rustic plaque and hanging on a wall at the office.

Now the job was done. The dark broad band of red lay exposed on the face of the pool as the spent creature floated on its side almost as motionless as the misty dampness that hung suspended in the air of the close mountain valley. Firmly but with great care the victor steadily drew line in through the guides of the rod and as he did so the lifeless bulk gradually approached. He had done his job well. As he quit gathering line and raised the rod to float the fish into the shallow water at his feet, the creature came in with hardly a stir, its gills pumping gulps of oxygenated water but its broad, powerful tail virtually motionless.

Stooping quickly the fisherman inserted his thumb into the mouth of the big trout grasping the lower jaw firmly between thumb and fore finger. Rising he lifted his arm up and forward and in almost unbelieving awe inspected his prize. Never could he have imagined capturing such a trout.

Suddenly, as if on command, a bolt of sunshine pierced the gray mist of early morning and focused itself on the drama. The red band extending full length on each side of the great fish captured the bright ray to glow like wired neon tubing, and speckled blotches of color that bordered its back and sides flickered and glimmered with the fire of diamonds, rubies, and emeralds. As if imitating the beauty of the trout, a rainbow formed in the waterfall beyond, and as the sun's rays fought through the fog of morning, its reflection danced on the surface of the pool.

The fisherman stood briefly as a frown of contemplation replaced the smile of victory on his face and then suddenly, as if obeying an order he could not refuse from a voice he could not deny, he knelt in the shadows and lowered the trout into the pool. With a firm but gentle grip he released the barb from its lip, and holding the creature upright, moved it to and fro in the water until its gills stroked firmly. He then released his hold, and with a weak wavering motion of its broad tail the fish moved slowly away from him until it disappeared beneath the sunlit surface of the pool.

For a long, long time the fisherman knelt there in the shallow water and the warm sunshine and gazed into the heart of the pool where the great trout had disappeared.

One of the great masters of saltwater fishing stories is Philip Wylie (1902–1971). His yarns about Crunch and Des, operators of the Miami charter boat Poseidon, *enchanted readers of the* Saturday Evening Post *for nearly two decades. Of his many wonderful stories, two were chosen for this book. In this one, a motley crew of anglers, including a pretty woman, pursue barracuda, amberjack, tarpon, and other denizens of the deep. Wylie's wit and fishing knowledge are well represented here, along with his poignant characterization.*

Philip Wylie

LIGHT TACKLE (1940)

MISS JONES REACHED HER FAVORITE "spot" on the County Causeway after supper but before all the color had gone from the sky. The tide was coming in, which was good, and the breeze was dropping. Unmindful of the trucks, the squealing trolleys and the horde of automobiles which streamed from Miami to Miami Beach and from the beach to the mainland, she unwrapped a paper bundle, took out a neatly wound hand line which was equipped with a sinker, a short wire leader, and a hook, and she carefully pressed the hook into the body of a dead, rather overdead, shrimp. She threw the assemblage into the flowing salt water, watched it drift out from the masonry that supported the bridge, and felt the lead touch bottom. She began her wait.

The sky flamed and bleached itself. The drawbridge lifted and settled ponderously many times—to the impatient accompaniment of the horns and voices of motorists. Ranged along the cement railing beside Miss Jones were scores of other fishermen—old men and young, women and children; some with rods and reels and pails of live bait, but most with less ostentatious gear: hand lines, or bamboo poles innocent of reels. Miss Jones fished hopefully, but without success.

It was dark and the distant beach had turned on the full glamour of its neon skyline when she noticed that the man nearest her was catching quite a few fish. Grunts and sand perch and an occasional snapper. He, too, was using a hand line, but he threw it farther than she could and in a diagonal direction. His bait was different. His manner of waiting after a nibble, and striking hard, was not the technique she had used. At last, though the act was unprecedented for her, she decided to speak to him; he was not well-dressed, but he looked nice.

"I guess," she said, "you're having the luck for the whole causeway." She smiled while she spoke—a little ruefully.

Crunch Adams had not even noticed his neighbor. Now, in the light of the street lamp, he could see a pretty girl, maybe twenty-three or -four, a bit thin; a girl with a mighty nice voice—sincere and curiously vibrant. Miss Jones was further illuminated by the headlight of a passing car. A blonde, Crunch perceived; one of the maple-fudge kind, and with gray eyes. No man—not even a happily married man—wantonly rebuffs the Miss Joneses of this world.

"The people," Crunch began, "who fish the causeways hardly ever bother to think about the bottom. But it's the bottom that determines where the fish are. If you come up here at slack tide on a calm day you can see that right where I'm throwing my rig there's a mess of rock. A barge sank there during the '26 blow. Here!"

The word meant that he had reached out for her line. She yielded it without a word and let him throw. He handed it back to her. She thanked him—and waited—and presently she felt a jiggle.

"Let him run with it a second," Crunch said, watching critically. "Now! Yank!"

The girl yanked. A yank answered her. The fish ran through the careening tide and the line slid through her fingers. She caught it up and pulled in, hand over hand. There was a white splash far below. She felt the fish wriggling in the air. Then Crunch reached down and tossed it onto the sidewalk, where it began to spring into the air. "Snapper," he said. "Nice one, too. Ought to go a pound and a half."

Miss Jones looked at the fish with shining eyes. "Would you . . . would you . . . kill it for me? Before it gets under somebody's car?"

Crunch picked up the fish, carefully avoiding its clicking teeth, and he dispatched it. He regarded Miss Jones's excitement with understanding, and threw his own line.

"Snappers are so darned good to eat," she said, wrapping the fish in paper.

"You bet they are. And people leave 'em lying around here to rot, sometimes." Crunch jerked his line, brought up a grunt, and dropped it–alive–into a pail of water.

"Once, right here," Miss Jones continued, "I got a grouper. Quite a big one." Success seemed to have made her talkative. "Two pounds, the man at the bait place said. I made chowder out of him–and it was simply delicious! Tasted like cinnamon." She began winding up her line. "And once I caught a jack–but he wasn't very good."

Crunch baited again–with a cubical chunk of purple meat cut from a bonita. It occurred to him that the young lady was more interested in her catch from the gastronomic standpoint than from the aspect of sport. He peered through the night. She was pretty thin–although not that thin. "You better keep right on fishing," he said. "We ought to be able to get you a dozen of those."

She shook her head. "I haven't any place to keep 'em. I–well–I sort of get 'em as I need 'em. *If* I'm lucky, that is." She looked into his bucket, where six or eight fish were swimming and panting. "They wouldn't keep–like that–I mean for days, would they?"

He was thinking about her–a pretty girl, a nice one, who fished for food and didn't even have an icebox to preserve her catch. He answered rather absently. "In a pail? I'm afraid not. Die in an hour or two. My mate'll be along to get these soon—and put 'em in our live well. They're for bait. We've got an open party slated to fish amberjack tomorrow." His line tugged, and that kept him from seeing her face.

But her voice turned him around. It was stunned. "You mean—you're a charter-boat captain?"

"Uh-uh."

"Which one?"

"The *Poseidon*."

"Then—" she swallowed—"then . . . you're Crunch Adams! Last winter I used to go down to buy fish from the boatmen. Mackerel—and pieces of kingfish—and dolphin—and I've often seen your boat come in!"

Crunch knew what it was like to be poor. He also knew what it was like to be proud. But he took a chance. "You're kind of—stranded down here—Miss—?"

The girl supplied her name quietly. She finished wrapping her fish and her line in newspaper before she continued. She had been thinking it over. It was all right for her to tell him. Everybody knew that Crunch Adams was a perfectly swell person. And you had to talk to somebody—sometimes. "Not exactly," she said at last. "I—I've got my rent paid for all summer. And a little money—if I stretch it. I've been looking for a job, but things kind of drop off here in the spring. I've got one promised—if I can wait till fall. You see . . . I'm a librarian. That is, I was—up north. I got arthritis and came down here for two months. I was fine—but when I went back, I got sick again. So . . ."

Desperate came along the causeway with a fresh pail of water. Not realizing that his skipper was engaged in conversation, he broached the only subject on his mind at the moment: "I got one more guy for tomorrow. That makes three. And guess who? Thornton Denby, no less! Wanted to weasel in for five bucks, as usual, but I made him pay six. He also wanted to fish the stream—but I said it was the reef or no dice."

Somewhat to Desperate's surprise, a response came from a lady standing beside Crunch. "You mean—you mean people can actually go out in a charter boat for as little as six dollars?"

Scenting a customer, Desperate lost no time. "Sure! When business is slack we split the summer price four ways and get four people to go. Twenty-five bucks divided by four is six and a quarter—and we knock off the two bits for luck."

"Could I be the fourth? Do you take—women? I've been absolutely out of my mind to go fishing on one of those boats ever since I got here!"

Crunch, upon seeing Miss Jones about to spend six dollars she couldn't conceivably afford, tried to think of something. The best idea—which he voiced—was hardly polite. "We can't take a dame—a woman. We don't know the first two guys very well—and this Denby is the stickiest fishing man in Florida. Besides—"

"We took that Mrs. Hoag with three men," Des countered, "and she caught a tuna!" His only alert instinct at the moment was the instinct for trade and commerce. "Crunch and I can look out for you. If you've got six bucks handy? . . ."

The *Poseidon*'s skipper was stammering. Miss Jones hesitated and then produced a small pocketbook. Crunch heard her murmur, "I shouldn't do it! But I've just got to!" He didn't interfere, because his mate, with a smirk of triumph, was reaching for the money. Instead, he began to think of how he could return the six dollars to the girl.

Des glanced at the fish in the pail and said, "We'll need that many more, easy." He started off with them, giving Crunch a wink to indicate it took a go-getter to nail the business. "Be at the dock at eight," he said to Miss Jones. "This Denby likes to start early."

Crunch and Miss Jones were left alone—except for the noisily passing thousands. "You shouldn't have done that," he said.

She nodded. "I know it. But a time comes in your life when you've got to do at least something rash!" She began to unwrap her line. "I might as well help, now, hadn't I, since I'm going to use some of that live bait? Golly! Can you imagine *me* in a charter boat!"

The morning was halcyon—soft as the spring always is in south Florida; sun-drenched, cloud-shaded, perfumed. A light breeze shattered the water outside the jetties into millions of bright facets; the sharp bow of the *Poseidon* divided a moving pattern of foam that was like etching on glass.

Miss Jones—she had been reticent about her first name—lay on the warm canvas deck forward, where Crunch had put her so that the men could get acquainted, tell their jokes, and pass around an eye opener if they wished. She watched the changing blues of the bottom under the ship's keel—the light blue made by the sand and the dark patches where the rocks were. She watched the hawks tower and the gulls dive and the pelicans volplane. Inside her mind, she talked to herself.

I shouldn't have come, she thought. Those two men—Mr. Porter and Mr. Welch—didn't want me much. And Mr. Denby didn't want me at all! I never saw such a fussy person! A bachelor, I'll bet! All that tackle! And all that talk! You'd think fishing was as important and as difficult as a surgical operation! Mr. Porter and Mr. Welch didn't seem to like him much. Which makes things just lovely! And I can afford six bucks about as well as I can afford platinum shoes!

Crunch came and sat down beside her. She was wearing the same slacks—pink—purchased, no doubt, when she'd still had that librarian's job. Her pink and blue scarf fluttered in the air. Her eyes were dark gray; only, the water made them seem blue. And her hair, although of a maple-fudge blondness, had lemon-colored glints in it. "I'm sorry my mate hooked you for that money," Crunch began. "I'd have been darned glad—in your case—to take you out . . ."

Miss Jones flushed. "I wouldn't think of going any other way!"

"Yeah. I suppose not." He, also, flushed a little. "Those guys weren't rude to you when we started, were they? I had to be on top . . ."

The girl grimaced a little. "They weren't overjoyed at the prospect of a woman being along."

Crunch nodded. "Welch and Porter work in town—and have families. They can only afford to go out this way—once in a while—in the summer. They're both pretty good guys, really. As for Denby—he has plenty of dough. Stays here year around. Owns a house on the beach. He fishes light tackle—he's an expert at it—but he's stingy."

"A bachelor, I bet," she said.

Crunch chuckled. "For reasons too numerous to mention! Tell you what. He'll fish on top—always does. I'll put Porter up here, too. You and

Mr. Welch can sit below. Ask him about his kids—he has five and he's proud of 'em all—and he'll be your friend."

"You're sweet," Miss Jones said gratefully. "I'll go through his kids from infant diseases to marks in arithmetic!"

So they began to fish. In the lazy morning, with Mr. Welch pouring out proud-parent anecdotes and beginning to think that the female passenger was not altogether a washout. Overhead, Mr. Porter was silent, sitting in a little chair on the edge of the canopy. Miss Jones held her rod tremblingly and watched the water. But Mr. Denby really provided the thematic monologue for the trip. He would have had a pleasant voice, she thought, if he had not kept it high and penetrating. He might have had pleasant manners, too—but fishing seemed to make manners inaccessible to him.

"Crunch," he said loudly, "you missed some rather good weeds about a hundred yards off the port quarter! . . . There's a rock bed just off the lighthouse that you completely overlooked! . . . Don't see how you fellows take any pleasure in fishing with that rope . . . Look at my gear: a four-ounce tip—a six-thread line that breaks with a strain of eighteen or twenty pounds—and a hook with the barb filed off! Now—that's what I call fishing! Give the fish a chance! . . . Most men don't realize that even with reef fish there's often the problem of a drop back—very slight, mind you, but real. You do it with your rod, and everything depends on feel. Though I can't see why anybody wants to fish the reef. Let me show you, Porter. . . . Crunch! Don't you think we're going about half a knot too fast? And look at that bait! It turned over three times while I was letting it back! It'll unwind my whole line, if you don't trim it! I tell you, nobody knows how to cut a bait out here. . . . Now here's another thing, Porter. You fish a number ten hook and a 6/0 reel. It's a crime, actually! Take a squint at this 3/0 of mine. Had it built specially. Isn't geared up like that thing of yours. Winds in a ratio of 1 to 1. The reason for that . . ."

"That guy," Mr. Welch murmured to Miss Jones, "knows all about fishing. *He* knows he knows it. And *we* know he knows. Why in hell doesn't he shut up?"

Miss Jones giggled. Then she had a strike.

For months she had watched them bring in the "big ones." Months of living alone in a one-room apartment with a bed that folded into the wall and an electric plate for cooking. Months of being lonely. Of going to "free" things—concerts and lectures and the fishing docks. Months of being ill—and then better—but always poorer and more worried. Now—a "big one" had hit her line. She could see the welter in the ocean, feel the jerk in her arms, hear the reel's unforgettable sound as the fish ran—a harsh and heady whir. She had always imagined that it would be exciting; she had never guessed that it would have that particular quality of thrill—of wildness, violence, fury and fight.

She became aware of Crunch beside her. "Barracuda," he said quietly. Then she heard Mr. Denby's voice. It was an anxious staccato of advice. His heart was in it—and his whole nervous system—as if he were catching the fish by talk: "Keep the rod tip up, Miss Jones! But not too high! That's it! Now! Reel! He's going to broach! Bad! Very bad! You gave him slack! Better tighten the drag, Crunch. With a telegraph pole like that, she can stand more strain! Besides—she's keeping the rest of us from fishing! Come on! Wind, woman! Drop the tip and pick up what you gain that way! Then back—and do it over!"

Crunch cast toward his passenger a glance around which were invisible brass knuckles. Denby did not even notice. But Miss Jones was aware of his words, and consciously or not, she began to follow each suggestion. Almost to her annoyance, she observed a change in his tone: "Fine! That's right! Never saw a man who could get the idea so quickly!"

In a few minutes, Crunch made a swoop with a big gaff—although Denby protested at gaffing a 'cuda—and brought aboard a silver fish about four feet long. It was mottled with black and Crunch spread its jaws with pliers for the girl to see. "Teeth like a wolf," he said. "Look!"

Miss Jones was panting delicately. Tendrils of her hair were stuck upon her brow. Her eyes were dilated. "Imagine," she whispered. "*Me!* I caught it! *Think of it!*"

Mr. Porter spoke rather petulantly: "Let's go fishing."

Des gunned the motors. The *Poseidon* moved along again. "On six-thread," Mr. Denby said good-humoredly, "that would have been quite a little scrap."

There are many sorts of fishing along the Florida coast. Trolling in the Gulf Stream is one. Trolling on the "reef" is another. The "reef" is a generic name for the shoal water along that edge of the Atlantic. It is clear water—green, sometimes, more often pale blue—and it varies in depth from coral emergences to more than a hundred feet. In that relatively shallow territory lie thousands of square miles of underwater wilderness—forests of coral, caverns, blind valleys, stone flowers and stone trees; and hundreds of square miles of submarine desert—regions of bare sand, rippled and duned, like the Sahara. There are lunar places in it—plains and abysses of raw rock—and places where colored vegetation grows in weird, uncouth jungles.

The reef is to fish what the primeval forest is to mammalian game. Not the streamlined, purple creatures of the gulf current live there—not sailfish and marlin and tunas and dolphins—but other fish which are strong, more numerous, and also, perhaps, hungrier. Jacks inhabit that fantastic land, and the groupers, which are bass, the many snappers, parrots, yellowtail, ordinary mackerel, triggers, countless small fish that travel in butterfly-bright schools, 'cudas, and, of course, all the rays together with a large variety of sharks. More fish are caught, as a rule, on a given day on the reef than are caught in a day on the Stream.

The *Poseidon*'s mixed party began to catch fish. Mr. Porter boated a twenty-pound grouper. Mr. Welch hung and lost a hard-running fish of uncertain identity. Miss Jones caught another barracuda. Mr. Denby managed to bring to gaff a small jack after a battle; he stood on his feet, with his light rod bowed in a U, and kept his line taut with a skill that was admired even by Crunch.

Then Miss Jones hung a small mackerel and when she had it close to the boat, something tore it from her hook. For a moment line ripped from the reel. Then it went slack in the water.

Crunch, who had been at her side, acted swiftly. "An amberjack took that fish," he said. "Let's go!" He lifted the cover from the live-bait well. With a dip net, he took out one of the fish he had caught on the night before. Quickly he fixed it to a hook—with string. He chose the handiest hook—which was Mr. Welch's. He threw the fish overboard. "Watch it," he said to Miss Jones. "Watch it as long as you can."

So she stood up and leaned over the stern. The *Poseidon* was drifting, her motors stopped. She could see the little fish swim down in spirals, carrying the shiny leader. Then she saw something else. Around it loomed shapes—big, tan-colored shapes—and one of them shot toward it. She could actually see the big fish grab the little one and she bit the back of her hand. "He's got it!" she said sharply. "There's a dozen of them down there!"

"Let him run till he swallows it!" Crunch advised Mr. Welch. "All right! Sock him!"

Mr. Welch "socked." His reel wailed. Miss Jones sat back in her chair. She watched him hang on while the fish ran, watched him pump and perspire when the amberjack paused to consider, listened to him swear when the fish took off again, and looked at the expression in his face—an expression of concentration, jubilation, and anxiety which would have been funny if she had not shared every second of that mood. After fifteen minutes the fish was close to the boat. She saw that Crunch had gone to the bait well. He had another grunt in his hand. He peered up to the canopy. "Mr. Denby! Like to try one on light tackle? They're pretty big in this school."

Miss Jones hadn't guessed that there would be another chance. But now, looking into the water, she could see Mr. Welch's fish being hoisted to the surface, inch by inch, and around it was the school to which it had belonged. Big, shooting shapes following along beside their hooked companion, trying from time to time to make a grab at whatever it had in its mouth.

The small fish on Mr. Denby's line swam down toward what would obviously be a horrid reception, and while Miss Jones still looked, she saw one of the big fish spot the new arrival, wheel, and torpedo toward it. Then she heard Mr. Denby's reel purr interminably. She wondered how such a thin line could hold so huge a fish.

For a while she forgot Mr. Denby. They boated Mr. Welch's fish. "Go sixty, easy," Des said, grinning. But Miss Jones just stared. She'd only seen dead big fish until then. It was a beautiful thing alive: opalescent, silver, bronze—from that color came its name—and full of dazzling, almost tangible vitality.

Mr. Denby called attention to himself, presently: "Crunch! This devil's got nearly all my line! Guess you better head around!"

So Crunch ran to the controls and started the boat. He chased the amberjack while the angler gathered back line on his little reel. That was the beginning of a long session. Very long, as Mr. Porter and Mr. Welch began to hint. A half hour; then an hour. And it was Denby, they said in guarded tones, who had complained that Miss Jones was taking so long to get in her fish!

When an hour and a half had passed and Mr. Denby was still battling—still reeling with rapid endurance—still bracing himself against the hurtling runs of his quarry, Mr. Porter's patience snapped. "Really, man," he said in a tone of suppressed anger, "you're taking up our day! You shouldn't have used that light rig! It's not fair!"

But Denby fished on as if he had not heard.

Miss Jones began to look, not at the water and the thin line cutting through it, but at the man on the canopy. He wasn't exactly selfish, consciously. He was just determined. Terribly determined. He fought his fish as if he were fighting something much more important. She wondered about that. And when, after nearly two hours, Denby's line broke, she did not feel furious, like the other two men. She felt sad. She looked at Denby to see how he was taking it. For a minute—a short part of a minute—she thought he was going to cry. But, then, he smiled. He smiled distinctly. "Part of the game," he said quietly. "Must have been a whopper. Sorry I held you up so long, fellows."

That was all he did say. Miss Jones felt like crying herself. She caught Crunch staring up at his finicky passenger and in Crunch's startling blue eyes there was a gleam; the kind of gleam anybody would like to be responsible for. But Mr. Denby didn't seem to see that either.

They came in late that afternoon, when the sun was shooting bars of radiance halfway to the zenith. Miss Jones was on the forward deck again. She had been there ever since the fish had been lost. She'd protested that

PHILIP WYLIE

she was tired—though she wasn't. And Crunch had supplied her with an abundant lunch, having suspected that she would not know it was the duty of the passengers to bring lunch for the ship's crew. Somehow, she hadn't wanted to fish any more that day—partly for fear that she would hang a big one and annoy the others by taking too long, and partly for some inner reason she couldn't analyze.

By and by—to her surprise—Mr. Denby came up and sat beside her. "I never quit until we get in past the bell buoy," he said. "Sorry I wasn't more sociable today. Your first trip? Thought so. You did well."

She thanked him. At close range, he looked different. He had direct, hazel eyes and a high forehead. His skin was sunburned a rather silly pink but, near to, that didn't matter. And his voice, when he lowered it, was shy. "It's too bad," she said, "you lost that big amberjack. I saw him take the bait, and he surely was a monster."

The two men in the cockpit invited them to have a drink, but Miss Jones's companion said he never touched the stuff, and, evidently, he assumed that she didn't either.

"I . . ." he began presently—and was not satisfied with whatever opener he had in mind. "You see, Miss Jones—I'm a fanatic about fishing. I wasn't athletic in school or college. Quite the reverse. Kind of a—a coward. But after I grew up I got the idea that someday I could hang up a light-tackle record fishing—if I stuck to it. I love to fish, you know. I release most of the ones I get. Hate a meat hog."

She understood the look in his eye—then. The frantic determination. He had been fighting—not a fish, but himself. Old wounds, old feelings of inferiority. "Did you ever break a record?" she asked.

He smiled, a crinkly smile, as if he were looking into the future and seeing himself with the record broken. "Not yet. But—of course—I've only been after one for twelve years."

Then they were nearing the dock. Mr. Denby tried to seem offhand. "Well . . . another time! I hope you'll be a member of some party that I'm on one of these days." He was earnest and worried, as if he wanted to say more and did not know how.

Miss Jones looked at him and smiled. "Thanks. I'm afraid not, though.

20

It's a bit too expensive for me. I'm strictly a causeway Waltonian, and this was just a . . ."

"A binge?" He was chuckling sympathetically.

"Yes. For me—a binge. But I did enjoy it. And I think you're a terribly good sport."

They were throwing the stern lines aboard the *Poseidon* then. People on the dock crowded through the vermillion sunlight to see what wonders had been wrenched from the sea that day. Miss Jones made ready to go ashore. And Crunch came up to her. He was uncomfortable. "Look," he said. "One thing—I mean . . . Well . . ." He tried to thrust six dollars into her hand. But she stepped lightly on the fish box, laughed at him, smiled at Mr. Denby, and was gone.

Some nights later, just as Miss Jones was on the point of throwing her rig into the running tide, Crunch came along the luminous, thunderous causeway. He had a rod in his hand—a rod with a shiny reel and agate-lined guides. "Hello," he said.

Miss Jones grinned. "After more bait? You know, I still dream about my day at sea! It was just gorgeous! And I was probably an awful nuisance!"

"Not to one man," Crunch answered. "You made quite a hit with Denby, I guess. He's been hanging around for days—and I didn't know why until this afternoon. He came down with this rod. For you. He said it was an old one that he didn't use any more."

She was embarrassed—and touched. "I couldn't think of taking it!"

"Why not? He can afford it. You're fishing for serious out here—and I know what that's like. This rod'll help you. You can cast a mile with it—after a little practice. Look."

Crunch whipped the rod in an arc. The reel sang. The bait went flying through the twilight like a driven golf ball. It splashed far out beyond the other lines that sagged down from the causeway. "He was afraid you'd refuse," Crunch continued. "So he made me take it to you. The old hundred-percenter had a barbless hook and three-thread line on it. I changed the three-thread to twelve—you can't handle that fine stuff on a rocky bottom. But it's a nice rig. I'd take it."

"He's kind of a cute guy," she said.

Crunch eyed her as he handed over the rod. "I bet you didn't talk that way in the library!"

"Even a librarian," she answered, with an assumption of mock dignity, "has access to the vernacular."

"Denby said—if you ever got anything good—to let him know."

"Oh?" She pursed her lips. "A string attached, hunh? Well—I must say—that if I were going to sell my soul—I think deep-sea fishing whenever you wanted to go, would be a fair price. I loved it!"

He stood beside her for a while. A hell of a nice girl, he thought; if she were a boy I could get her a job as a mate; she'd be a crackerjack, I'll bet. He knew how it was to want things and not have them. He could imagine her "efficiency" apartment, her regular diet of fish, and her feelings, when she watched the fishing fleet go out and come in.

She reeled in and was getting ready to cast. He showed her how to thumb the reel, how to use her wrists, and, a moment later, how to pick out a backlash when you did it wrong. After a dozen tries, she had grasped the fundamentals. Maybe, Crunch began thinking, Sari could do something about her.

His eyes were fixed on the dark waters of the bay—somberly—because his thoughts made him unhappy. Then his eyes flickered and focused. There had been a roll—a shimmer—a silhouette of a fin—out on the inky surface. He knew what that was. If he could get it—or them—to hit, that would be another happy experience for Miss Jones. But he had no plug. They came through often—under the arches of the causeway—in the spring. Sometimes they wouldn't strike a diamond brooch, but sometimes they would take anything.

At Miss Jones's feet was the newspaper that contained her shrimp, and the string that had been around it. The paper was white and it would stay white in the water for a while. He tore off several strips and picked up the string. "Wind in," he said. "Let me have that hook for a second!"

Puzzled, she obeyed. Crunch fixed the strips of paper around the hook as much as possible in imitation of a feather lure. Then he scanned the water again. "Now," he said. "Yonder—just in line with the bow of that yacht! Cast as far as you can and don't let it sink! Instead, reel in slowly and jerk your rod a bit. If anything hits, hit back as hard as you can—and fast!"

She caught the excitement in his voice. "But—did you see something?"

"Go ahead! Cast! Exactly the way I said!"

Doubtfully, she cast the impromptu bait. It arced through the evening and hit the water. Crunch could see it there—a white dot. He saw it start to wiggle toward them. "That's it!" Then he saw the heavy surge under the paper lure.

Miss Jones struck. She pressed on the thumbstall hard. But something—something like lightning—was on that line. It ran as if she had hooked into a passing automobile. Then it stopped. "Wind!" Crunch yelled. "Wind as you never did in your life! It's going to jump!"

"But what is it?" she gasped.

"Look!"

She was barely able to manage her rod and to look. Out in the light of the electric signs and the buildings and the radiance from the causeway she saw a silverish-white fish crash up into the air, hang for a second, somersault completely, and vanish. "Oh, my," she murmured.

"Tarpon!" he yelled. "A beauty! If you get him—you'll really have something!" He raced along the sidewalk past the other fishermen. He bawled at the top of his lungs. "Pull in your lines, everybody, please! We've hung a big tarpon here! Hey! You with the big stomach! Pull in that line! That lady'll foul you if you don't!" His voice changed to an ominous roar: "And if you don't think I can make you, wise guy! . . . Well . . . that's better!"

He ran back to Miss Jones. "Keep the line tight! After we wear him down, we'll lead him along the causeway to shore and beach him! Boy! That's it!" He ran off to warn more distant anglers.

Miss Jones was thinking. Thinking of the fish she had promised to bring to her neighbors the day she had gone out to sea. Fish she had not provided because she had caught only two barracudas. She was thinking of the size of the tarpon, and of poor old Mrs. Wilmot, and of Mr. Treelman who was out of work, and the Berkimer kids. She also thought, for a flash, of Mr. Denby and his tragic desire to break a record. Then she had no more time for thinking. The tarpon ran under the causeway and shot out—miraculously without cutting the line—and it began to leap and pinwheel in the air.

Around Miss Jones the other causeway fishermen gathered, but she did not notice them. She did not hear their shouts of advice. Behind her, a car stopped and a man in a white dinner jacket hopped out to look. He hurried back to a woman in the car and said rather dazedly, "Some girl has hung a walloping big tarpon on a casting outfit! Let's watch!" He helped from the car a woman in evening clothes. Behind them, another car stopped. A truck driver headed for the beach peered, slowed, and pulled up his brake. Horns began to blow. The crowd bulged out on the street. From Miami, a motorcycle policeman cut through the snarl with a braying siren and began to yell questions: "What's going on? Where's the accident? Did some half-wit go through the railing?"

Then, he too, saw the great silver king plunging in the night, and because many—perhaps most—of the people of Miami are fishermen, he forgot his duty, pushed to the rail, and bellowed, "Lady, you better watch out on those jumps! Come back farther with the rod!"

Miss Jones didn't notice him. But she did notice that the thumbstall—rotten by long sitting in Mr. Denby's tackle closet—was wearing thin. Her finger became hot. A chunk of leather tore away. Her bare thumb hit the wet and racing spool. She shut her jaws. When pain shot into her arms, she used the other thumb, although it was awkward. Then she found that by pressing against the metal side of the spinning spool, less heat was generated. When her left thumb grew slippery, she knew it was bleeding. But she did not care. The tarpon was not leaping quite as high or quite as often. Crunch had cleared away all the dangling lines and was beside her again.

The fish sank below the surface and she could feel the slow, steady beat of its tail.

"Sulking," Crunch said. "Let's start leading him. Every time you come to a post, get all set and pass the rod around it from your left hand to your right. If he starts to leap or run—stop and fight him!"

24

So they began to move along the causeway. Miss Jones passed the rod around obstructions. Crunch followed, coaching. And the crowed followed, too, yelling, encouraging and voicing envy. Traffic behind them was a hopeless tangle and traffic was piling up ahead. From one of the stalled cars came a man with a camera to which was attached a bulb. Its soundless light broke over the mob.

Miss Jones found that by pulling steadily, she could tow the tarpon in the desired direction. Her fingers bled. Her wrists ached. Her shoulder joints felt separated. But she kept on. When they came around the end of the causeway, she was groggy. She tripped on some weeds and stumbled over a pile of rubble. The crowed stayed above her, looking down, and the man with the camera kept shooting pictures. But Crunch was at her side.

"Just get out there on that bare spot—and pump," he said. "The way you did the 'cudas."

So she pumped. She was out of breath and wet with perspiration. But she kept pulling. And suddenly, to her vague amazement, Crunch waded into the water. He bent over. He groped. Then he half threw up on the land a prodigious, glittering fish which flopped heavily in the red glare of a big electric sign. "Got it," Crunch said.

Miss Jones didn't exactly faint, but her knees gave way and she sat down.

Twenty minutes later she was ensconced in the stern of the *Poseidon*. Traffic had been restored on the causeway. There was only a small crowd on the Gulf Stream Dock—perhaps a couple of hundred people—and out of it came the fishing editor of the *Dispatch* to interview her. The tarpon was hanging on the rack. He stopped to look at it. He whistled. Then he said, "You're Miss Jones?"

She was about to reply. But another person broke through the awed spectators. It was Mr. Denby—without a hat—with staring eyes. He charged up to the fishing editor. "On three-thread!" he yelled. "Three-thread, old man! A world's record!"

Miss Jones, who had felt her heart bounce at the sight of Mr. Denby, now felt that same organ wither and grow ashamed. "On twelve-thread," she said quietly. "Crunch changed it. I'm afraid, Mr. Denby, we're still as far from that record as ever."

The skipper came up from below in dry shoes and trousers. He heard her words and took in the disappointment on the expert's face. "Yeah," he said slowly. "She couldn't handle three-thread on that bottom, Denby. Another thing—your thumbstall wore out and she's torn her fingers all up. Maybe it wasn't a world's record—but it's a new high for grit!"

Mr. Denby still seemed bogged in disappointment.

"Anyway," Miss Jones said sorrowfully, "it'll make up for the meal I promised the Wilmots and the Treelmans and the Berkimers. Not to mention myself. I've got the use of an icebox now."

Crunch gulped.

Mr. Denby stared.

"But," the fishing editor said, "tarpon are no good to eat! They're muddy."

Denby grabbed Crunch's arm and pulled him aside. "You mean to say—a lovely girl like that—fishes because she needs food?"

"Lots of people do," Crunch replied laconically. "Nice people."

Denby gulped.

"Our cameraman happened to be going over the causeway—" the fishing editor felt compelled to lighten a pall he could not fathom—"and he says he got some elegant stuff! We'll give you a spread on the sports page! . . ."

He went on talking. But the situation was not relieved then. Not wholly relieved later—when Mr. Denby insisted that as soon as Miss Jones's hands were healed she should be his guest for a day "outside."

It is that day which changed everything.

A day like all the other days of spring on the Florida coast. The *Poseidon* was moving smoothly out toward the purple edge of the Gulf Stream. Desperate was at the controls. Crunch was rigging up Mr. Denby's four-six outfit. And Mr. Denby detached himself from an animated conversation with Miss Jones. "Not the light outfit, Crunch!" he said in a low voice. "Give me the heaviest stuff you have. Thirty-nine thread, if you've got it. And tell Des not to head for the Stream. I want to fish the reef."

Crunch was startled. "Thought you hated the reef?"

Mr. Denby's mouth was firm. "We're fishing for groupers, today. Groupers for the Wilmots and the Treelmans and those other people. Big, delicious groupers. Dozens of them! I don't want to take a chance on losing anything we hang."

Crunch put down the light outfit. There was written on his face a masterpiece of mixed moods. Surely, he reflected, Denby has changed. Maybe Miss Jones was right. Maybe he was at bottom a good egg. "Head for Fowey Rock," he yelled to Des. He fixed two big rigs.

Mr. Denby had returned to the cockpit with a pillow. "This," he said, "will make you more comfortable–ah–Miss Jones. I wish I knew your first name."

"If I told you you'd be shocked. My mother had imagination, she was practically reckless."

There was amusement in his eyes–and affection. "I'll find out," he said. "You only gave your initials in the newspaper story. But I'm a determined man. Very determined!"

"Yes. I know." She said that earnestly.

"My own," he continued, "is Thornton. Does that give you courage?"

Miss Jones blushed. "You won't believe it–but it's Scheherazade."

Mr. Denby peered at the radiant sea. "It's beautiful," he murmured.

Crunch gazed at Mr. Denby and Miss Jones. Then he ducked out through a window and joined Desperate.

The mate started below to replace him, but Crunch caught his arm. "As much as possible," he said, "I think we'll both stay up on top today. We may get some fish–but mostly, we're just a gondola."

Des thought that over and understood. "I hope she'll teach him not to tell everybody how to fish," he finally said.

At that instant, Mr. Denby called, "I've got a strike! Nope! Missed him!"

Crunch leaned over the canopy edge.

"You hit too hard," Scheherazade said sweetly but firmly.

There was utter devotion in Thornton's response. "So I did! Much too hard."

In this story, infantry buddies from the Korean War reunite. One has become a simple dairy farmer, the other a high-flying corporate tycoon. But they share a common past and interest in fishing. Massachusetts native Robert Travers has edited and written newspapers and magazines. He has published two novels and a collection of stories. This story initially appeared in Argosy, *and was honored by inclusion in* The Best American Short Stories 1967.

Robert Travers

THE BIG BROWN TROUT (1966)

CLAY MILLER LEANED AGAINST THE SLOPE of his spring-green pasture and watched the Co-op milk truck spiraling down the road toward the city. The city was a long way from the Schoharie hills; it was at the faraway end of the truck route. And that's the way Clay Miller wanted it. At this end of the route—Clay's end—was the farm. The farm was the way he wanted it, too.

Turning toward the higher acres, he saw his spread of Ayrshires drifting away from the patches of early morning sun. By noon, they would be under the maples, hunched together in the shade. The late afternoon would nudge them easterly again toward the high red barn and the milking stalls. The Ayrshires moved with the sun and the seasons, and Clay Miller moved with them.

Near the barn was the hundred-year-old house he had restored with his own hands and his own tools. It was operated on the time of sun and season. Right now, Clay knew, his wife would be in the kitchen, pushing the buttons on the electric stove. The boys, both of them towheads, would be coming down for breakfast; they'd eat and run for the school bus. Then the chores, the orderly pattern of the day's labor, until the sun moved all the way across the sky.

To Clay Miller, there was nothing more important than the routine of house and farm. He didn't have time left over for the city or for the world, either. In politics, he supported the objectives and the involvements of the free world without paying too much attention to what was going on in Vietnam or in Cuba. He was a dairy farmer. His world was enclosed by the rim of the Schoharie hills. As he headed for the house, he was thinking about the things that were closest to him, things such as bacon and eggs and, after a couple of cups of coffee, the repairs to be made on one of the milking machines.

His wife, Helen—she was as towheaded and blue-eyed as the two boys—met him at the kitchen door. "They phoned a telegram from town," she said.

"Those tractor parts finally arrived?" he asked.

"No. It's signed 'Sergeant Sales.'" Then she read the words she had scribbled on the telephone pad: "In New York for a sales conference. Any chance for a weekend reunion with Corporal Hayfoot? How is the fishing up there?"

"That's Harry Larkin!" Clay said. And just saying the name took him back a long, long time. Clay and Harry had been in the same infantry company, in the same squad and often in the same foxhole throughout the Korean War. They were young then, perhaps too young to understand what it was all about. They concentrated, instead, on survival. Clayton Miller, from upstate New York, and Chicago-born Harry Larkin were tossed together in a bleak village in southern Korea, and they learned how to stay alive as they moved north over the alien plains and rocky steeps.

After the truce, Clay returned to Albany and tried to readjust to civilian life. It wasn't easy; he had no goal or direction. What he did have, though, was a small legacy left by his father and a driving need to make his own, and separate, peace. He finally found the place he was looking for—an old farmhouse surrounded by eighty grassy acres in the Schoharie hills. His inheritance covered the down payment, with a little left over for enough Ayrshires to build a herd. Then, starting along the way he wanted to go, he married the girl he'd known before Korea. They settled on the land, and Clay learned dairy farming the hard way.

Harry Larkin went back to Chicago, joined a high-powered manufacturing firm and lit into his new job as if he were still fighting a war. After five years, he was sales manager and, after three more, vice-president in charge of sales. He was smart and ambitious. He got around. His Christmas cards, expensively engraved, and the occasional letters were postmarked from every industrial city west of the Mississippi. Now, for the first time in almost twelve years, he had come this close to the Army buddy he used to call Corporal Hayfoot.

"I've told you about him," Clay said to his wife. "We were in Korea."

While she put his breakfast on the table, he phoned a telegram to Harry Larkin's hotel: TAKE ROUTE 145 TO SCHOHARIE. GET DIRECTIONS TO OUR PLACE AT FEED STORE THERE. HAVE SET OUT THE JUG, AND THE FISH ARE BITING IN THE CREEK.

Harry Larkin arrived at the farm the following Friday evening in a Cadillac, bringing with him a cowhide traveling bag and a handful of beat-up fly rods. He was older, of course; the gray was starting to show around his temples. But he still looked strong and very sure of himself.

Harry took one look at Helen Miller, grinned, and said something about old Corporal Hayfoot being a lucky guy. Helen liked him; when she went out to the kitchen, Clay could tell she was going to dig the best steaks out of the freezer. The boys liked him, too.

Later, when Clay and Harry were alone with a bottle between them and the quiet house like some kind of a cover around them, they talked about the Army. It was nostalgic talk. They didn't recall any of the tough times; they remembered only the sunny days. Soon, since there hadn't been many sunny days in Korea, they were talking about their peacetime careers.

"Old Corporal Hayfoot," Harry said, grinning. "I was afraid you'd end up pushing a plow. What happened to you?"

"Happened?" Clay asked. "What do you mean? Man, I've got it made!"

Harry wasn't so sure about that. "I thought you were going into electronics. You had the head for it."

"I changed my head."

Harry laughed. "I guess a real campaigner can get used to anything."

"Depends on what you want to get used to," Clay said.

"Well . . ." Harry glanced around the living room. There was a stack of magazines, farming and animal husbandry journals, on the table. Also, a few books and a country newspaper, creased and unread.

"It's kind of quiet," he remarked. He let it go at that and shifted to a discussion of what was going on in the world. But, on that subject, Clay didn't have much to say.

"I'm not getting to you," Harry said.

"I'm not a debater," Clay replied. "I'm a farmer."

"And that's enough for you?"

"Sure is. Tomorrow, I'll show you around the place. You'll see what I mean."

"Okay," Harry said. "After I get back from the creek."

Harry left right after breakfast the next morning, wearing grimy flannels, a felt hat decorated with hand-tied flies and a nicely blackened briar pipe. The older Miller boy, ten-year-old Tommy, went with him.

Clay called after them: "Good luck!"

Harry signaled the all-okay sign. As he swung the Cadillac around, he shouted: "Tell Helen we'll bring fish for supper."

They did get back in time for supper, but Harry didn't have any fish.

"I thought Schoharie Creek was a real trout stream," he said. "There's nothing in it bigger than your hand!" He glanced at Tommy. "Even an experienced guide, the best one I ever had, couldn't get me a good strike."

Tommy grinned. He'd had a fine day; he learned something about fly-casting and heard a lot of good stories. But Clay could see that Harry was disappointed. To Harry, taking a fish would be like landing a new account. He'd hate to lose.

"You can try it again tomorrow," Clay told him. "You luck will change."

Harry shook his head. "It's not luck. The water's too high; the big ones just aren't hitting."

Later on, as the sun was starting to touch the top of the hills, Clay took Harry out to the barn and showed him the gleaming equipment racked up under massive oak beams. They inspected the milking stalls, the feed bins, the cooling room. Finally, they went up the back path and looked at the Ayrshires standing philosophically in the dusk. There was a breeze with the new-grass smell in it, and the birds were as busy and noisy as they always were just before sundown.

"It's peaceful," Harry admitted. "But what the hell, Clay. You're cut out for more action."

"What kind of action?" Clay asked.

"There's a job opening with my outfit. On the management side. You'd be good at it. You'd save more in a year than you'll make here in ten. And you'd be *doing* something."

"I *am* doing something," Clay pointed out. He couldn't quite find the words for the way he felt about his eighty acres. He kicked out a bit of pasture dirt. "This is my land," he said. "I'm working it."

Harry wasn't convinced. "I'm not just talking about a job," he said. "Or about money. Things are going on, Clay. Over in the Pacific. In the Caribbean. Even in Europe. The people in Washington, the ones who know the score, are saying we're in a fight for our lives. You know—our national lives. We're fighting for everything we are, everything we stand for. It's a lot bigger than Korea ever was. A lot bigger. And everything we have depends on how it turns out."

"I know it," Clay said.

"Sure, you know it." Harry was talking fast, like a salesman selling something he really believed in. "But you're not in it. You're way back in the hills. You're ducking away from the front lines—something you never did before."

"That's kind of rough talk," Clay said.

"It's straight talk," Harry said.

Clay looked at him. They were friends, good friends; they had covered a lot of ground together. In Korea, they had talked bluntly about what they thought and believed. They were still talking that way—as though the time between this hour and the hours in Korea hadn't changed anything at all.

"See if you can get this through your head," Clay said. "Right here is the front lines for me."

"No," Harry said. "You're on the sidelines; you're sitting it out."

"What does your company make?" Clay asked. "Machine parts?"

"Right."

"And that's more important than running a dairy farm?"

"It might be," Harry said. "We're ready to convert to essentials, to weapons, in twelve hours. But that's still not what I mean. I mean the thinking part of it. You're . . . well, you're isolated. You're not part of what's going on."

"You think what I'm doing doesn't count?" Clay asked.

"It's not just doing something, Clay. Plenty of people aren't doing anything. I mean, they're not up in the front lines. But they're *still* involved. Even in just thinking. They're part of what's going on."

Clay used one of the phrases they had tossed around in Korea. "You figure I've been brainwashed?"

"Something like that," Harry said.

"Let me tell *you* something," Clay said. "All this is part of what's going on, too." He motioned toward the darkening stretch of his acres. "The land is what the shooting is all about in the first place. It gives men something to fight for. Don't you see that?" There was passion in his voice. "This farm went through the Revolution. And the Civil War. And all the rest of them. And the people on the land went through those wars. They were in them just staying here, just *being* here. That meant as much, in the long run, as joining up with a regiment." He paused. "The land is in the war. In any war, a cold war or a hot one. Remember how we held those hills in Korea? Now I'm holding these hills. The way the families living here before us held them. You understand what I mean?"

"Let me think about it," Harry said. He was starting to turn away. "Anyway, we better knock it off for awhile—before we start slugging."

They didn't talk any more as they crossed the meadow. The evening was quiet, too. They could hear the water tinkling in the pool long before they elbowed through the fringe of laurel.

When Clay Miller bought his eighty acres, the pool wasn't much more than a trickle of water coursing along an old stream bed. But after the house and barn were in shape, he found time to build a timber dam along the downgrade end of a little valley. Thereafter, the mud of several Aprils and the leaves of October chinked the dam. It became as solid as stone; the water, flowing steadily from a hillside spring, collected and spread out against it and deepened into a broad pool. There was a screen of laurel around it, and the birches had grown and leaned their branches toward the water.

Harry had forgotten his salesman's pitch about the cold war. He was looking at the pool with a fisherman's eye. "Nice," he said. "Ever think of stocking it?"

"There's some bluegills in it," Clay said. "And a few perch."

"I mean *fish*," Harry said.

As he spoke, the big brown trout—which Clay Miller knew was also in the pool—started to feed. There was a dimpling of the darker water near the dam as he rolled over lazily and scooped up a hatch of insects. Then he broke water, leaping, throwing a lot of spray.

"That's a trout!" Harry shouted.

Clay didn't say anything.

"How'd a buster like that get in there?" Harry asked. He was excited.

"I don't know," Clay said.

That was a fact. Clay didn't know where the big brown trout came from. Perhaps when he was a fingerling, he was washed down in the flood waters following a late winter thaw. Perhaps some bird picked him up out of the creek and, on the way to his nest, dropped him into the widening pool. There were a lot of possibilities. But who could tell now where the trout came from? And what difference did it make? He was there.

Clay Miller first saw the trout two years after the dam was built. During the following years, he watched him grow, and he developed a real feeling, a kinship, for him. Sometimes, in the summery dusk, he stood by the pool and heard the trout finning near a submerged root. It occurred to Clay that the fish lived in water which was as calm, on its surface anyway, as the farm. You wouldn't expect to find so big a fish in such a placid pool. And you wouldn't believe he'd be content to stay there— he had a heritage linked to the freedom of a running stream. But there he was; he had adapted to the backwaters. Even so, he was still close to his origins. The water the trout lived in came down from the hills. Before that, it came from a river. And, before that, from the sky.

Harry was saying: "Nothing to match him in the Schoharie."

"I suppose not," Clay said.

"You ever cast for him?"

Clay shook his head.

The trout jumped again. After a moment, Harry said, "I'd sure like to try a couple a' lures on him."

Clay hesitated. Then, as heartily as he could, he said, "It's okay with me. I'll give you an early call."

Sunday was Harry's last day. He was up, dressed and at the pool by sunrise. Clay took a lot of time over a cup of coffee and then joined him there.

Harry cast and retrieved skillfully, until the sun was an hour high. Handling the four-ounce rod as though he'd been born with it, he worked the sides and then the center of the pool. He showed more patience than one might suspect he had. He was surely a match for the big brown trout. They both were wise and wary. And they both could play the old waiting game.

Clay watched and said nothing. He knew the trout did most of his feeding in late afternoon. Harry must have realized it, too. "I'll try again," he said. "Later."

It was a pleasant day, but neither Clay nor Harry were with it. They were thinking, in different ways, about the pool. And, at five o'clock, they were back there.

"This is it," Harry said. "Last round."

After he cast a fly into the center of the pool, Clay sat down, put his shoulders against one of the birches and took it easy. He wasn't worrying much. He knew Harry would never catch the trout that way.

Harry switched to a silver-colored streamer, a Gray Drake, and then to one of the flies he had tied himself. But nothing happened.

"Other side may be better," he decided.

Sitting silently, facing into the last slants of the sun, Clay watched Harry cross the log dam. Standing well back from the opposite shore, he cast again into the center of the pool.

Clay got out a cigarette and struck a match. There was less than half an hour's fishing time left, and he was beginning to think the big brown trout was safe because he never fed in the center of the pool. He stayed close to a deep hole at the base of the dam, and even the most expert angler probably couldn't coax him away from it. That was one thing Harry didn't know. And Clay didn't tell him. He was neutral. He was giving both Harry and the trout an even break. He leaned against the birch, waiting to see what would happen.

As he watched the smooth cast and retrieve, cast and retrieve, Clay's thoughts wandered back to a particular night in Korea. In a darkness torn with flares and shell bursts, they were starting the long journey to the crest of some nameless ridge. It was a position they had taken and lost, and taken and lost again. This time, they had to go up and stay there. And they went up, and they did stay there. But not all of them made it all the way. Clay Miller was one of them. A few crouching steps from the top, he stumbled into a blinding flash that was half hit and half concussion. Panic and fear flooded into every part of his mind. He retreated away from it into something even darker than the night. Then, Harry Larkin was bending over him, pulling him back to consciousness. As he got his eyes open, he heard Harry talking, telling him to hang on until the medics came.

During the next half hour, Harry kept talking, talking and holding onto him. And when he couldn't think of anything else to say, he talked about a trout stream he had fished years before he ever heard of Korea. He told Clay how it felt to wade in the stream and cast and get a strike. He described the water, the cool feel of it, the warmth of the sun, the sound of a breeze in the weeds along the shore.

That's how Clay Miller first learned Harry was a fisherman. He was a good deal more than that, of course. He had ideas about how to get through a war and what to do afterward. Maybe he had different notions about things. Maybe there were some things, such as a feeling for eighty acres and a remote farmhouse, which he didn't understand. But he *was* a fisherman. More than that, he was a friend.

Clay rubbed his cigarette out and stood up. He looked at Harry, still on the far side of the pool. There wasn't much light left. "Come on back over here," he called.

Harry made a fast retrieve and crossed the dam.

"You see that snag over there?" Clay said, when Harry was standing beside him. He was pointing to the spot above the deep hole, where he knew the big brown trout lived.

Harry nodded.

"That's the best place," Clay said. "There's some old roots down there. If you drop a fly easy, you might raise him."

Harry was glancing at Clay and smiling a little—a good smile, a warm one. "I noticed that spot myself," he said. He hesitated a moment. "But I figured I better stay away from it. Just casting is sport, too." He hesitated again. "I'll tell you the truth. I get the idea you don't want anyone to take that trout."

"You're crazy!" Clay said gruffly. "Work around that snag. Go ahead!"

Harry cast deftly, in exactly the right place. On the third delicate, tantalizing retrieve, the fly disappeared in a sudden scoop of water. Harry flipped up the rod, bending it almost double, and set the hook. The brown trout reacted like lightning. He came out of the water in an explosive leap.

The reel zipped. Harry let it go, just for a few seconds, and then put on the pressure. If the trout got enough line, he'd wrap it around half a dozen roots and rocks and snap it like cotton thread. He was feeling the drag now, and he fought it, breaking out again, curving and twisting, and then running back toward the base of the dam. But Harry judged the run nicely and checked it, gaining a few feet of line. The trout's next leap wasn't as high. He arched slowly, showing his full length, the streamline form, the spotted sides, the wild head shaking in a frantic effort to throw the barb.

"A four-pounder!" Harry shouted. "A real fighter! Look at him!"

Clay looked. He was a fighter, all right. Harry was a fighter too. It took him ten pulse-pounding minutes to work the trout close to the bank. He worked carefully, gaining slowly and steadily, wearing the trout down until he couldn't surge any more, until he was quiet and beat at the end of the line.

Harry held up the rod tip. He was stepping into the shallows. The trout made a final, stout-hearted run, and Harry yielded some line. "Still game," he said admittedly. He won the line back and led the trout closer, bringing him in under the shadow of the trees.

There was a landing net swinging on Harry's belt. He groped for it with his right hand and started to unhook it. His fingers stopped moving, though, before the net was clear. He was remembering the trout's final run, and then he was glancing back over his shoulder at Clay. Since Harry was a fisherman, he understood—and respected—the trout. And he could understand, now, some of the same things about Clay. He could express it best in angler's language: the fish, in a way, was part of the fisherman, but this trout had a stronger bond to the pool. It was the same kind of deep-going, fiercely loyal bond that held Clay to his land.

Clay watched, surprised, as Harry turned back toward the pool. He hadn't unhooked the net. Instead, he clamped the handle of the rod under his arm and leaned over to wet his hands in the pool. "This way it won't harm the scales," he said.

"Use your net!" Clay told him. "That's what it's for!"

Harry reached toward the water. Swiftly, with a sure touch, he held the trout for a flailing instant and backed the hook out of his lip.

There was a moment when nothing happened, a complete stop, with Harry still bending over, hands outstretched, and the trout motionless beyond his fingers. Then, action again; a new start. Harry straightened up. The big brown trout moved, too. He rolled, steadied and finned away, heading back toward the deep hole by the dam. His shadow, blurred by the water, went deeper. Then he was gone.

"Why didn't you take him?" Clay said. "He was yours! You had him!" His voice was strained. He hadn't said anything while Harry played the trout, but his throat felt as though he had been shouting.

Harry was staring after the fish. "Be a long time before he strikes another hook," he said. "A long time."

"Why didn't you take him!"

"Remember what you were telling me last night?" Harry said. "About the land?" He was smiling. "I see what you mean. That trout belongs here. The same as you."

Clay swung away. He didn't want Harry to see his eyes. "We better go up to the house and get some coffee," he said. "You got some miles ahead of you."

"We both have," Harry said, coming along after him, unjointing his fly rod. "You stay here and hold onto these hills." He added, "Sure. You're right. This is important, too. And as long as you don't let anyone talk you out of it, I guess everything will turn out okay."

"Squirrelly" is a commercial fisherman in Hatteras, a long barrier island off the coast of North Carolina. He catches an enormous grouper, which leads to un-expected consequences and a surprise ending. The story originally appeared in Playboy. *Author Bob Shacochis is a winner of the American Book Award for his fiction. Among his books are* Easy in the Islands *(1985) and* The Next New World *(1989). In 1999 Shacochis published a nonfiction book called* The Im-maculate Invasion, *about the U.S. incursion into Haiti in the mid-1990s. He spent eighteen months in the field there as a noncombatant with Special Forces commandos.*

Bob Shacochis

SQUIRRELLY'S GROUPER (1989)

A FISH STORY IS LIKE ANY other, never about a fish but always about a man and a place. I wouldn't even mention it if I thought every-body knew. When you cut down to the bone of the matter, a fish is just Pleasure with a capital P. Rule of thumb—the bigger the fish, the bigger the pleasure. That's one side of the coin of fishing, the personal best and finest, but this is Hatteras, and there's that other side. On the Outer Banks of North Carolina, you can't pitch a rock in the air in the morn-ing without rock-throwing becoming widespread ruthless competition by the time the sun goes down over Pamlico Sound, and that is because we go to sea for our living, and because commercial fisherman think they are God's own image of male perfection. I've seen it go on all my life here on the coast, each generation afflicted with the same desire to lord, bully, and triumph; doesn't even matter where they come from once they're here, north or south or bumbled in from Ohio and beyond like Willie Striker. So that's the other side, where size counts, wakes the sleepyheads right up, subdues the swollen-head gang, and becomes everybody's business.

We saw the boats off that morning like we always do, and near an hour later Mrs. Mitty Terbill came in the marina store to post a sign she had made, a little gray cardboard square she had scissored from the back of a cereal box. It said: LOST DOG, YORKSHIRE TERRIER. NAME—PRINCE ED, MY SOLE COMPANION. REWARD, and then a number to reach her at.

"What's the reward, Mitty?" I asked. It was five dollars, which is about right for a Yorkie, measured by appeal per pound. Mitty Terbill is not an upright-standing woman, but then considerable woe has befallen her and keeps her squashed into her pumpkin self, allowing for only brief religious ascension. She spent that much plus tax on a twelve-pack and trudged back out the door, foot-heavy in her fishwife's boots, going back to her empty house on the beach to sit by the phone. Well, this story's not about the widow Terbill, though plenty of stories are since she lost her old man and her dope-pirate offspring two Januarys ago when they ran into weather off Cape May, up there flounder fishing I believe it was. That's just how I remember the day settling down after the dawn rush, with Mitty coming in, some of the fellows cracking jokes about how one of the boys must have mistook Prince Ed for bait and gone out for shark, and although Mitty likes her opinions to be known and gets the last word in on most events, let me please go on.

Life is slack at a marina between the time the boats go out early and vacationers get burnt off the beach about noon and come round to browse; then in the afternoons all hell breaks when the boats return. Anyway, after Mitty stopped in, Junior left to pull crab pots; Buddy said he's driving out to Cape Point to see if the red drum are in on the shoals with the tide change; Vickilee took a biscuit breakfast over to her cousins at the firehouse; Albert went down to the Coast Guard station to ingratiate himself to uniformed men; Brainless was out at the pumps refueling his uncle's trawler so he could get back to the shrimp wars, which left just me, my manager Emory Plum, and my two sacked-out Bay Retrievers in the place when I hear what might be an emergency broadcast on the citizen's band, because it's old grouch Striker calling J. B. on channel seventeen. Willie Striker has been one to spurn the advancement of radio and the charity of fellow captains, not like the other jackers out there bounced wave to wave on the ocean. They yammer the livelong day, going on like a team of evangelical auctioneers about where the fish aren't to be found, lying about how they barely filled a hundred-pound box, complaining how there's too many boats these days on the Banks and too many Yankees on land, in a rage because the boys up in Manteo are fetching a nickel more for yellowfin, and who messed with who, and who's been reborn in Christ, and who knows that college girl's name from Rodanthe, and who's going to get theirs if they don't watch it. Willie Striker has something to say himself, but you wouldn't find him reaching out. He kept to himself and preferred to talk that way, to himself, unless he had a word for his wife, Issabell. Keeping to himself was no accident, and I'll tell you why if you just hold on.

J.B.J.B. . . . come in, Tarbaby, I hear, and even though an individual's voice coming through the squawk box fizzes like buggy tires on a flooded road, you know it's Willie Striker transmitting because his words had the added weight of an accent, nothing much, just a low spin or bite on some words. Like mullet, Willie Striker would say, *maul-*it.

Tarbaby Tarbaby . . . come in. That was the name of J. B.'s workboat.

I was restocking baits, ballyhoo and chum, my head bent into the freezer locker, and Emory, he was back behind the counter studying delinquent accounts. "Turn her up a bit there, Emory," I told him, "if you please."

He didn't need to look to do it, he's done it so many times. He just reached behind and spun the dial to volume nine, put a hailstorm and a fifty-knot blow between us and the boats. "Well, who's that we're listening to?" Emory yelled out. "That's not our Mr. Squirrel, is it?"

Some twenty-five years it'd been I guess that Willie Striker had lived among us, married Issabell Preddy, one of our own, came south it was said sick and tired of Dayton and a factory job, and from the day he showed his jumpy self at Old Christmas in Salvo, folks called Striker Squirrelly. If you've seen his picture in the paper, you might think you know why. Squirrelly's got a small shrewd but skittish face with darting, then locking, eyes, a chin that never grew, some skinny teeth right out in the front of his mouth, and his upper lip was short, tight, some called it a sneer. The top of his head was ball-round and bald up to the crown, then silver hair spread smooth like fur. But like any good made-up name that fits and stays, there was more to it than manner of appearance.

Way-of-life on Hatteras Island has long been settled, that's just the way it is. A couple dozen families like mine, we lived together close back to Indian times, wreckers and victims of wrecks, freebooters and lifesavers, outcasts and hermits, beachcombers and pound netters and cargo ferry-men, scoundrels and tired saintly women, until they put the bridge across Oregon Inlet not long after Willie moved down. Outsiders meant complications to us one way or another; the truth is we don't take to them very well—which used to have significance but doesn't anymore, not since the herd stampeded in the last ten years to buy up the dunes and then bulldoze the aquifer. That's the island mascot these days, the yellow bulldozer, and the Park Service rules the beach like communists. That's one thing, but the fact is Willie Striker wouldn't care and never did if a Midgett or a Burrus or a Foster ever said, "Fine day, iddn't Skipper" to him or not. He wasn't that type of man, and we weren't that type of community to look twice at anything unless it had our blood and our history, but Issabell Preddy was the type of woman inwardly endeared to signs of acceptance, which you could say was the result of having a drunkard father and a drunkard mother. Issabell and her brothers went to live with their Aunt Betty in Salvo until they finished school, but Betty had seven children of her own, a husband who wouldn't get off the water, and no time to love them all. I went to school with Issabell and have always known her to be sweet in a motionless way, and not the first on anybody's list. She had one eye floating and purblind from when her daddy socked her when she was small, wore hand-down boys' clothes or sack dresses on Sundays, her fuzzy red hair always had a chewed-on aspect about it, and her skin was such thin milk you never saw her outside all summer unless she was swaddled like an Arab. Back then something inside Issabell made her afraid of a good time, which made her the only Preddy in existence with a docile nature, and the truth is a quiet girl who is no beauty is like a ghost ship or a desert isle to the eyes of young and active men: No matter how curious you are you don't want to be stuck on it.

One by one Issabell's brothers quit school and took off, joined the Navy and the Merchant Marines, and Issabell herself moved back down the road to Hatteras, rented the apartment above the fishhouse and got employed packing trout, prospered modestly on the modest fringe, didn't hide herself exactly but wouldn't so much as sneeze in company without written invitation. The charter fleet was something new back then; there were not-unfriendly rumors that Issabell upon occasion would entertain a first mate or two during the season. These rumors were not so bad for her reputation as you might expect in a Christian village except none of us really believed them, and it would have come as no surprise if sooner or later one of our crowd got around to marrying Issabell Preddy, but the island had temporarily run out of eligible men by the time Terry Newman met Willie Striker in a Norfolk juke joint and brought him back with him for Old Christmas in Salvo. Old Christmas all the long-time families come together to feast by day, to game and make music and catch up with the facts of the year; by night we loudly take issue with one another and drink like only folks in a dry county can, and of course we fistfight—brother and cousin and father and godfather and grandfather and in-law; the whole bunch—and kid about it for three hundred sixty-five days until we can do it again. A few years back a lady from a city magazine came to write about our Old Christmas, called it culture, and I told her call it what the hell you want but it's still just a bust-loose party, gal, and when the night fell and the fur started to fly she jumped up on a table above the ruckus, took flashbulb pictures, and asked me afterward why Hatterasmen liked to brawl. I told her there's nothing to explain, we all think we're twelve years old, and if it was real fighting somebody'd be dead. Anyway, Terry Newman showed up that January with his twenty-four-hour buddy, Willie Striker, and it was the year that Terry's brother Bull Newman decided Terry was good-for-nothing and needed to be taught a lesson. One minute Bull had his arm across Terry's shoulder laughing, and the next he had knocked him down and out cold, continued through the room rapping heads of all he perceived to have exercised bad influence on his younger brother, including the skull of his own daddy, until he arrived at Willie, nursing a bottle of beer off by himself at a table in the corner. Bull was a huge man but dim; Willie Striker was no young buck but was given to juvenile movements the eye couldn't properly follow—twitches and shoulder jerks and sudden frightening turns—so even as he sat there holding his beer he seemed capable of attack. Bull towered over him with an unsure expression, a doglike concern, trying to determine who this person was and if he was someone he held an identifiable grudge against or someone he was going to hit on principle alone, and when he swung Willie dodged and lunged, laid Bull's nose flat with his beer bottle without breaking the glass, threw open the window at his back, and scrambled out.

"That'll teach you to go messin' with squirrels," someone said to Bull.

No one saw Willie Striker again until a week later, raking scallops in the Sound with Issabell Preddy. The way I heard it was, Willie got to the road that night about the same time Issabell was headed back to Hatteras from her visit with her Aunt Betty, driving a fifty-dollar Ford truck she had bought off Albert James, her Christmas present to herself, and even though Willie was hitching back north, she stopped and he got in anyway and went with her south, neither of them, the story goes, exchanging a word until they passed the lighthouse and got to the village, everything shut down dark and locked up, not a soul in sight of course, and Issabell said to him, so the story goes, that he could sleep in the truck if he wanted, or if he was going to be around for the week he could come upstairs and have the couch for thirty cents a night, or if he had plans to stay longer he could give her bed a try. Willie went the whole route: truck, couch, Issabell Preddy's lonely single bed.

In those days scalloping was women's work, so it was hard to raise any sort of positive opinion about Willie. He was a mainlander, and worse, some brand of foreigner; out there wading in the Sound it appeared he had come to work, but not work seriously, not do man's work; he had moved into Issabell's apartment above the firehouse and burdened her social load with scandal; and he had clobbered Bull Newman, which was all right by itself, but he hadn't held his ground to take licks in kind. He had run away.

The following Old Christmas Willie wedded Issabell Preddy in her Aunt Betty's kitchen, though for her sake I'm ashamed to say the ceremony was not well-attended. She wanted kids, I heard, but there was talk among the wives that Willie Striker had been made unfit for planting seed due to unspecified wounds. For a few years there he went from one boat to another, close-mouthed and sore-fingered, every captain and crew's back-up boy, and Issabell scalloped and packed fish and picked crabs until they together had saved enough for a down payment on the *Sea Eagle.* Since that day he had bottom-fished by himself, on the reefs and sunken wrecks, at the edge of the Stream or off the shoals, got himself electric reels a couple of years ago, wouldn't drop a line until the fleet was out of sight, wouldn't share Loran numbers, hoarded whatever fell into his hands so he wouldn't have to borrow when the fish weren't there, growled to himself and was all-around gumptious, a squirrel-hearted stand-alone, forever on guard against invasion of self, and in that sense he ended up where he belonged, maybe, because nobody interfered with Willie Striker, we let him be, and as far as I know no one had the gall to look him straight in his jumpy eyes and call him Squirrelly, though he knew that's what he was called behind his back. Whatever world Willie had fallen from at mid-life, he wound up in the right place with the right woman to bury it. Maybe he had fallen from a great height, and if the plunge made him a loon, it also made him a man of uncommon independence, and so in our minds he was not fully without virtue.

Squirrelly finally connected with J. B., who bottom-fished as well, not possessing the craft or the personal etiquette—that is to say, willingness to baby the drunken or fish-crazed rich—to charter out for sport. Like-wise, he was a mainlander, a West Virginian with a fancy for the rough peace of the sea, and for these reasons Willie, I suspect, was not loathe to chance his debt. They switched radio channels to twenty-two in order to gain privacy and I asked Emory to follow them over. Up at their trailer in Trent, Issabell had been listening in too; hers was the first voice we found when we transferred. She questioned Willie about what was wrong; he asked her to pipe down.

"What you need there, *Sea Eagle*?" J. B. squawked. After a moment Willie came back on; hard to tell through the greasy sizzle, but he sounded apologetic.

"*Tarbaby*," he said, "(something . . . something) . . . require assistance. Can you . . .?"

"What's he say was the trouble?" Emory bellowed. "I couldn't tell, could you?"

"Roger, *Sea Eagle*," J. B. answered. "Broke down, are you, Captain?" Willie failed to respond, though J. B. assumed he did. "I didn't get that, Willie," he said. "Where the hell are you? Gimme your numbers and I'll come rescue your sorry ass."

"Negative," we heard Willie say. "Report your numbers and I come to you."

So that's how it went, Striker ignoring his Issabell's pleas to divulge the nature of his trouble, J. B. staying at location while the *Sea Eagle* slowly motored through three-foot seas to find him while we sat around the marina, trying to figure out what it meant. Squirrelly had a problem, but it didn't seem to be with his boat; he needed help, but he would come to it rather than have it go to him. J. B. was about twenty miles out southeast of the shoals, tile fishing; likely Willie was farther east, sitting over one of his secret spots, a hundred fathoms at the brink of the con-tinental shelf. We heard no further radio contact except once, more than an hour later, when Striker advised J. B. he had the *Tarbaby* in sight and would come up on his starboard side. Back at the marina the Parcel Ser-vice man lugged in eighteen cartons of merchandise and we were fairly occupied. Then past twelve J. B. called into us, jigging the news.

"Diamond Shoals Marina," J. B. crowed, "y'all come in. Dillon," he said to me, "better clean up things around there and get ready for a fuss. Squirrelly caught himself a fat bejesus."

I picked up the transmitter and asked for more information but J. B. declined, claiming he would not be responsible for spoiling the suspense. I slid over to channel twenty-two, waited for Issabell to stop badgering Willie, and asked him what was up.

"*Up?*" he spit into the microphone. "I tell you *up!* Up come victory, by God. Up come justice . . . Going to seventeen," he muttered, and I flipped channels to hear him advertise his fortune to a wider audience. "Ya-ha-ha," we all heard him cackle. "Cover your goddamn eyes, sons of bitches. Hang your heads. Age of Squirrelly has come . . ."

We had never heard him express himself at such provocative length.

The island's like one small room of gossip-starved biddys when something like this happens. People commenced telephoning the marina, took no more than five minutes for the noise to travel sixty miles, south to north to Nags Head, then jump Albemarle Sound to Manteo and the mainland. "Don't know a thing more than you," Emory told each and every caller. "Best get down here to see for yourself when he comes in around three." I took a handcart to the stockroom and loaded the coolers with Coca-Cola and beer.

Now, there are three types of beast brought in to the dock. First kind are useless except as a sight to see, tourists gather round and take snapshots, Miss Luelle brings her day-care kids down to pee their pants, old stories of similar beasts caught or seen are told once more, then when the beast gets rank somebody kicks it back into the water and that's that. I'm talking sharks or anything big, boney, red-meated, and weird. Second style of beast is your sport beast: marlins, tuna, wahoo, barracuda, etcetera, but primarily billfish, the stallions of wide-open blue water. This class of beast prompts tourists to sign up for the Stream, but Miss Luelle and her children stay home, as do the rest of the locals unless a record's shattered, because these are regular beasts on the Outer Banks, at least for a few more years until they are gone forever, and after the captain and the angler quit swaggering around thinking they're movie stars, I send Brainless out to cut down that poor dead and stinking hero-fish and tow it into the Sound for the crabs and eels, and that's that too. The third style of beast is kidnapped from the bottom of the world and is worth a ransom, and that's what Striker would have. He wouldn't bring anything in for its freak value, he was the last man on earth to recognize sport—all he did day in day out was labor for a living, like most but not all of us out here—so I figured he hooked himself a windfall beast destined for finer restaurants, he'd weigh it and set it on ice for brief display, then haul it to the fishhouse, exchange beast for cash and steer home to Issabell for supper and his bottle of beer, go to bed and rise before dawn and be down here at his slip getting rigged, then on the water before the sun was up.

First in was J. B. on the *Tarbaby*, which is a Wanchese boat and faster than most; J. B. likes to steam up a wake anyway, put spray in the air. Already the multitudes converged in the parking lot and out on the porch, elbowing in to the store. Vickilee came back across the street with her cousins from the fishhouse to start her second shift; Buddy led a caravan of four-wheelers down the beach from Cape Point. Packers and pickers and shuckers shuffled drag-ass from inside the fishhouse, gas station geniuses sauntered over from the garage. Coast Guard swabs drove up in a van, the girls from Bubba's Barbecue, Barris from Scales and Tales, Geegee from the video rental, Cornbread from the surf shop, Sheriff Spine, Sam and Maggie from over at the deli, the tellers from the bank, Daddy Wiss leading a pack of skeptical elders, and tourists galore drawn by the scent of photo opportunity and fish history. Before three all Hatteras had closed and come down, appetites inflamed, wondering what the devil Willie Striker was bringing in from the ocean floor that was so humongous he had to defy his own personal code and ask for help.

J. B.'s mate tossed a bowline to Brainless; took him in the face as usual because the poor boy can't catch. J. B. stepped ashore in his yellow oilskins and scale-smeared boots, saying, "I can't take credit for anything, but damn if I can't tell my grandkids I was there to lend a hand." Without further elaboration he walked directly up the steps to the store, went to the glass cooler, and purchased one of the bottles of French champagne we stock for high-rollers and unequaled luck. Paid twenty-eight dollars, and he bought a case of ice-colds too for his crew, went back out to the *Tarbaby* with it under his arm, going to clean tile fish.

"Well, come on, J. B.," the crowd begged, making way for him, "tell us what old Squirrelly yanked from the deep." But J. B. knew the game, he knew fishing by now and what it was about when it wasn't about paying rent, and kept his mouth glued shut, grinning up at the throng from the deck, all hillbilly charm, as he flung guts to the pelicans.

Someone shouted, *He just come through the inlet!* The crowd buzzed. Someone else said, *I heard tell it's only a mako shark.* Another shouted, *I heard it was a tiger!* Then, *No sir, a great white's what I hear. Hell it is,* said another boy, *it's a dang big tuttie. Them's illegal,* says his friend, *take your butt right to jail.* One of our more God-fearing citizens maneuvered to take advantage of the gathering. I wasn't going to have that. I stepped back off the porch and switched on the public address system. *Jerry Stubbs,* I announced in the lot, *this ain't Sunday and this property you're on ain't church. I don't want to see nobody speaking in tongues and rolling on the asphalt out there,* I said. *This is a nonreligious, nondenominational event.* You have to take things in hand before they twist out of control, and I run the business on a family standard.

Here he comes now, someone hollered. We all craned our necks to look as the *Sea Eagle* rounded the buoy into harbor waters and a rebel cheer was given. Cars parked in the street, fouling traffic. The rescue squad came with lights flashing for a fainted woman. I went and got my binoculars from under the counter and muscled back out among the porch rats to the rail, focused in as Willie throttled down at the bend in the cut. I could see through the glasses that this old man without kindness or neighborly acts, who neither gave nor received, had the look of newfound leverage to the set of his jaw. You just can't tell what a prize fish is going to do to the insides of a man, the way it will turn on the bulb over his head and shape how he wants himself seen.

I went back inside to help Emory at the register. Issabell Striker was in there, arguing politely with Vickilee, who threw up her hands. Emory shot me a dirty look. Issabell was being very serious—not upset, exactly, just serious. "Mister Aldie," she declared, "you must make everyone go away."

"No problem, Mizz Striker," I said, and grabbed the microphone to the P.A. *Y'all go home now, get,* I said. I shrugged my shoulders and looked at this awkward lonesome woman, her floppy straw hat wrapped with a lime-green scarf to shade her delicate face, swoops of frosty strawberry hair poking out, her skin unpainted and pinkish, that loose eye drifting, and Issabell just not familiar enough with people to be used to making sense. "Didn't work."

Her expression was firm in innocence; she had her mind set on results but little idea how to influence an outcome. "Issabell," I said to her, "what's wrong, hon?" The thought that she might have to assert herself against the many made her weak, but finally it came out. She had spent the last hours calling television stations. When she came down to the water and saw the traffic tie-up and gobs of people, her worry was that the reporter men and cameramen wouldn't get through, and she wanted them to get through with all her sheltered heart, for Willie's sake, so he could get the recognition he deserved, which he couldn't get any other way on earth, given the nature of Hatteras and the nature of her husband.

Issabell had changed some but not much in all the years she had been paired with Squirrelly in a plain but honest life. She still held herself apart, but not as far. Not because she believed herself better; it never crossed our minds to think so. Her brothers had all turned out bad, and I believe she felt the pull of a family deficiency that would sweep her away were she not on guard.

Her hands had curled up from working at the fishhouse. Striker brought her a set of Jack Russell terriers and she began to breed them for sale, and on weekends during the season she'd have a little roadside flea market out in front of their place, and then of course there was being wife to a waterman, but what I'm saying is she had spare time and she used it for the quiet good of others, baking for the church, attending environmental meetings even though she sat in the back of the school auditorium and never spoke a word, babysitting for kids when someone died. Once I even saw her dance when Buddy's daughter got married, but it wasn't with Willie she danced because Willie went to sea or Willie stayed home, and that was that. I don't think she ever pushed him; she knew how things were. The only difference between the two of them was that she had an ever-strengthening ray of faith that convinced her that someday life would change and she'd fit in right; Willie had faith that the life he'd found in Hatteras was set in concrete. The man was providing, you know, just providing, bending his spine and risking his neck to pay bills the way he knew how, and all he asked in return was for folks to let him be. All right, I say, but if he didn't want excitement he should've reconsidered before he chose the life of a waterman and flirted with the beauty of the unknown, as we have it here.

"Mizz Striker, don't worry," I comforted the woman. Besides, a big fish is about the best advertisement a marina can have. "Any TV people come round here, I'll make it my business they get what they want."

"Every man needs a little attention now and then," she said, but her own opinion made her shy. She lowered her eyes and blushed, tender soul. "Is that not right, Dillon?" she questioned. "If he's done something to make us all proud?"

Out on the bayside window we could watch the *Sea Eagle* angling to dock, come alongside the block and tackle hoist, the mob pressing forward to gape in the stern, children riding high on their daddies' shoulders. Willie stood in the wheelhouse easing her in, his face enclosed by the bill of his cap and sunglasses, and when he shut down the engines I saw his head jerk around, a smile of satisfaction form and vanish. He pinched his nose with his left hand and batted the air with the other, surveying the army of folks, then he looked up toward me and his wife. You could read his lips saying *Phooey*.

"What in tarnation did he catch anyway?" I said, nudging Issabell.

"All he told me was 'a big one,'" she admitted.

One of the porch layabouts had clambered down dockside and back, bursting through the screen door with a report. "I only got close enough to see its tail," he hooted.

"*What in the devil is it?*" Emory said. "I'm tired of waitin' to find out."

"Warsaw grouper," said the porch rat. "Size of an Oldsmobile, I'm told."

"Record buster, is she?"

"Does a whale have tits?" said the rat. "'Scuse me, Mizz Striker."

You can't buy publicity like that for an outfit or even an entire state, and taking the record on a grouper is enough to make the angler a famous and well-thought-of man. I looked back out the bayside window. Squirrelly was above the congregation on the lid of his fishbox, J. B. next to him. Squirrelly had his arms outstretched like Preacher exhorting his flock. J. B. had whisked off the old man's cap. Willie's tongue was hanging out, lapping at a baptism of foamy champagne.

"Old Squirrel come out of his nest," Emory remarked. I fixed him with a sour look for speaking that way in front of Issabell. "Old Squirrelly's on top of the world."

Issabell's pale eyes glistened. "Squirrelly," she repeated, strangely pleased. "That's what y'all call Willie, isn't it." She took for herself a deep and surprising breath of gratitude. "I just think it's so nice of y'all to give him a pet name like that."

The crowd multiplied; a state trooper came to try to clear a lane on Highway Twelve. At intervals boats from the charter fleet arrived back from the Gulf Stream, captains and crew saluting Squirrelly from the bridge. Issabell went down to be with her champion. Emory and I and Vickilee had all we could do to handle customers, sold out of camera film in nothing flat, moved thirty-eight cases of beer mostly by the can. I figured it was time I went down and congratulated Willie, verify if he had made himself newsworthy or was just being a stinker. First thing though, I placed a call to Fort Lauderdale and got educated on the state, national, and world records for said variety of beast so at least there'd be one of us on the dock knew what he was talking about.

To avoid the crowd I untied my outboard runabout over at the top of the slips and puttered down the harbor, tied up on the stern of the *Sea Eagle*, and J. B. gave me a hand aboard. For the first time I saw that awesome fish, had to hike over it in fact. Let me just say this: you live on the Outer Banks all your life and you're destined to have your run-ins with leviathans, you're bound to see things and be called on to believe things that others elsewhere wouldn't, wonders that are in a class by themselves, gruesome creatures, underwater shocks and marvels, fearsome life forms, finned shapes vicious as jaguars, quick and pretty as racehorses, sleek as guided missiles and exploding with power, and the more damn sights you see the more you never know what to expect next. Only a dead man would take what's below the surface for granted, and so when I looked upon Squirrelly's grouper I confess my legs lost strength and my eyes bugged, it was as though Preacher had taken grip on my thoughts, and I said to myself, *Monster and miracle greater than me, darkness which may be felt.*

J. B. revered the beast. "Fattest damn unprecedented jumbo specimen of Mongolian sea pig known to man," he said (he could be an eloquent fool). "St. Gompus, king of terrors, immortal till this day." He leaned into me, whispering, fairly snockered by now, which was proper for the occasion. "Dillon," he confided, "don't think I'm queer." He wanted to crawl down the beast's throat and see what it felt like inside, have his picture taken with his tootsies sticking out the maw.

"Stay out of the fish," I warned J. B. "I don't have insurance for that sort of stunt."

A big fish is naturally a source of crude and pagan inspirations. I knew what J. B. had in mind: get my marina photographer to snap his picture being swallowed and make a bundle selling copies, print the image on T-shirts and posters too. He could snuggle in there, no doubt, take his wife and three kids with him, there was room. The fish had a mouth wide as a bicycle tire, with lips as black and hard, and you could look past the rigid shovel of tongue in as far as the puckered folds of the gullet, the red spikey scythes of gills, and shudder at the notion of being suckered through that portal, wolfed down in one screaming piece into the dungeon of its gut. Don't for a minute think it hasn't happened before.

Willie wasn't in sight, I noticed. I asked J. B. where the old man had put himself, it being high time to hang the beast and weigh it, see where we stood on the record, have the photographer take pictures, let tourists view the creature so we could move traffic and give the other fishermen space to go about their daily business, lay the beast on ice while Willie planned what he wanted to do.

"He's up there in the cuddy cabin with Issabell," J. B. said, nodding sideways. "Something's gotten into him, don't ask me what." Vacationers shouted inquiries our way; J. B. squared his shoulders to respond to an imprudent gal in a string bikini. "Well ma'am," he bragged, "this kind of fish is a hippocampus grumpus. People round here call 'em *wads*. This one's a damn big wad, iddn't it." As I walked forward I heard her ask if she could step aboard and touch it, and there was beast worship in her voice.

I opened the door to the wheelhouse; ahead past the step-down there was Willie Striker, his scrawny behind on a five-gallon bucket, the salty bill of his cap tugged down to the radish of his pug nose, hunched elbows on threadbare knees, with a pint of mint schnapps clutched in his hands. If you've seen a man who's been skunked seven days running and towed back to port by his worst enemy, you know how Willie looked when I found him in there. Issabell was scooched on the gallery bench, her hands in front of her on the chart. She was baffled and cheerless, casting glances at Willie but maybe afraid to confront him, at least in front of me, and she played nervously with her hair where it stuck out under her hat, twisting it back and forth with her crooked fingers.

I tried to lighten the atmosphere of domestic strife. "You Strikers're going to have to hold down the celebration," I teased. "People been calling up about you two disturbing the peace."

"He don't want credit, Dillon," Issabell said in guilty exasperation. "A cloud's passed over the man's golden moment in the sun."

Here was a change of heart for which I was not prepared. "Willie," I began, but stopped. You have to allow a man's differences and I was about to tell him he was acting backwards. He cocked his chin to look up at me from under his cap, had his sunglasses off and the skin around his eyes was branded with a raccoon's mask of whiteness, and I'm telling you there was such a blast of ardent if not furious pride in his expression right then, and the chill of so much bitterness trapped in his mouth, it was something new and profound for me, to be in the presence of a fellow so deeply filled with hate for his life, and I saw there was no truth guiding his nature, I saw there was only will.

His face contorted and hardened with pitiless humor; he understood my revelation and mocked my concern, made an ogreish laugh in his throat and nodded like, *All right, my friend, so now you are in the presence of my secret, but since you're dumb as a jar of dirt, what does it matter,* and he passed his bottle of bohunk lightning to me. Say I was confused. Then he mooned over at Issabell and eased off, he took back the pint, rinsed the taste of undeserved years of hardship from his mouth with peppermint, and jerked his thumb aft.

"Where I come from," Willie said, rubbing the silvery stubble on his cheek, "we let them go when they are like that one." His face cracked into a net of shallow lines; he let a smile rise just so far and then refused it. "Too small." (*Smull* is how he said it.) "Not worth so much troubles."

I thought what the hell, let him be what he is, reached over and clapped him on the back, feeling the spareness of his frame underneath my palm. "Step on out of here now, Captain," I said. "Time for that beast to be strung up and made official."

"Willie," coaxed Issabell with a surge of hope, "folks want to shake your hand." He was unmoved by this thought. "It might mean nothing to you," she said, "but it makes a difference to me."

Striker didn't budge except to relight his meerschaum pipe and bite down stubbornly on its stem between packed front teeth. On the insides of his hands were welts and fresh slices where nylon line had cut, scars and streaks of old burns, calluses like globs of old varnish, boil-like infections from slime poison.

"What's the matter, honey?" Issabell persisted. "Tell me, Willie, because it hurts to know you can't look your own happiness in the face. We've both been like that far too long." She tried to smile but only made herself look desperate. "I wish," she said, "I wish . . ." Issabell faltered but then went on. "You know what I wish, Willie, I wish I knew you when you were young."

Issabell jumped up, brushed by me, and out back into the sunshine and the crowd. Willie just said he was staying put for a while, that he had a cramp in his leg and an old man's backache. He had let the fish exhilarate and transform him out alone on the water, and for that one brief moment when J. B. poured the victor's juice on his head, but the pleasure was gone, killed, in my opinion, by distaste for society, such as we were.

"Now she will despise me," Willie said suddenly, and I turned to leave.

J. B., me, and Brainless rigged the block and tackle and hoisted the beast to the scales. The crowd saw first the mouth rising over the gunnel like upturned jaws on a steam shovel, fixed to sink into sky. People roared when they saw the grisly, bulging eyeball, dead as glass but still gleaming with black wild mysteries. Its gill plates, the size of trash-can lids, were gashed with white scars, its pectoral fins like elephant ears, its back protected by a hedge of wicked spikes, and it smelled to me in my imagination like the inside of a castle in a cold and rainy land. You could hear all the camera shutters clicking, like a bushel of live crabs. When I started fidgeting with the counterweights, the whole place hushed, and out of the corner of my eye I could see Striker come to stand in his wheelhouse window looking on, the lines in his face all turned to the clenched pipe. He was in there percolating with vinegar and stubbornness and desire, you know, and I thought, What is it, you old bastard, is it the fish, or have you decided Issabell is worth the gamble? The grouper balanced. I wiped sweat from my brow and double-checked the numbers. Squirrelly had it all right, broke the state mark by more than two hundred pounds, the world by twenty-six pounds seven ounces. I looked over at him there in the wheelhouse, and brother he knew.

I made the announcement, people covered their ears while the fleet blasted air horns. A group of college boys mistook J. B. for the angler and attempted to raise him to their shoulders. A tape recorder was poked in his face; I saw Issabell push it away. Willie stepped out of the wheelhouse then and came ashore to assume command.

You might reasonably suspect that it was a matter of honor, that Willie was obliged to make us acknowledge that after twenty-five years on the Outer Banks his dues were paid, and furthermore obliged to let his wife, Issabell, share the blessing of public affections so the poor woman might for once experience the joy of popularity, just as she was quick to jump at the misery of leading a hidden life, so ready to identify with the isolation of the unwanted that night of Old Christmas all those years ago. Willie knew who he was but maybe he didn't know Issabell so well after all, didn't see she was still not at home in her life the way he was, and now she was asking him to take a step forward into the light, then one step over so she could squeeze next to him. You just can't figure bottom dwellers.

Anyway, I swear no man I am familiar with has ever been more vain about achievement, or mishandled the trickier rewards of success, than Willie after he climbed off the *Sea Eagle*. The crowd and the sun and the glamor went straight to his head and resulted in a boom of self-importance until we were all fed up with him. He came without a word to stand beside the fish as if it were a private place. As first he was wary and grave, then annoyingly humble as more and more glory fell his way, then a bit coy I'd say, and then Bull Newman plowed through the crowd, stooped down as if to tackle Willie but instead wrapped his arms around Willie's knees and lifted him up above our heads so that together like that they matched the length of the fish. The applause rallied from dockside to highway.

"I make all you no-goodniks famous today," Willie proclaimed, crooking his wiry arms like a body builder, showing off. Bull lowered him back down.

"Looks like you ran into some luck there, Squirrelly," Bull conceded.

"You will call me Mister Squirrel."

"Purty fish, Mister Squirrel."

"You are jealous."

"Naw," Bull drawled, "I've had my share of the big ones."

"So tell me, how many world records you have."

Bull's nostrils flared. "Records are made to be broken, *Mister* Squirrel," he said, grinding molars.

"Yah, yah." Willie's accent became heavier and clipped as he spoke. "Und so is noses."

Bull's wife pulled him out of there by the back of his pants. Willie strutted on bow legs and posed for picture takers. His old adversaries came forward to offer praise—Ootsie Pickering, Dave Johnson, Milford Lee, all the old alcoholic captains who in years gone by had worked Willie like a slave. They proposed to buy him a beer, come aboard their vessels for a toast of whiskey, come round the house for a game of cards, and Willie had his most fun yet acting like he couldn't quite recall their names, asking if they were from around here or Johnny-come-latelys, and I changed by mind about Willie hating himself so much since it was clear it was us he hated more. Leonard Purse, the owner of the fishhouse, was unable to approach closer than three-deep to Willie; he waved and yessirred until he caught Squirrelly's eye and an impossible negotiation ensued. Both spoke merrily enough but with an icy twinkle in their eyes.

"Purty fish, Willie. How much that monster weigh?"

"Eight dollars," Willie said, a forthright suggestion of an outrageous price per pound.

"Money like that would ruin your white-trash life. Give you a dollar ten as she hangs."

"Nine dollars," Willie said, crazy, elated.

"Dollar fifteen."

"You are a schwine."

"Meat's likely to be veined with gristle on a beast that size."

"I will kill you in your schleep."

"Heh-heh-heh. Must have made you sick to ask J. B. for help."

"Ha-ha! Too bad you are chicken of der wadder, or maybe I could ask you."

Vickilee fought her way out of the store to inform me that the phone had been ringing off the hook. TV people from New Bern and Raleigh, Greenville and Norfolk were scheduled by her one after the other for the morning. Newspaper people had already arrived from up the coast; she and Emory had talked to them and they were waiting for the crowd to loosen up before they tried to push through to us, and one of them had phoned a syndicate, so the news had gone out on the wire, which meant big-city coverage from up north, and of course all the sport magazines said they'd try to send somebody down, and make sure the fish stayed intact. Also, scientists were coming from the marine research center in

Wilmington, and professors from Duke hoped they could drive out tomorrow if we would promise to keep the fish in one piece until they got here. The beer trucks were going to make special deliveries in the morning, the snack man too. Charters were filling up for weeks in advance.

So you see Squirrelly and his grouper were instant industry. The event took on a dimension of its own and Willie embraced his role, knew he was at last scot-free to say what he pleased without limit and play the admiral without making us complain. He sponged up energy off the crowd and let it make him boastful and abrupt, a real nautical character, and the folks not from around here loved his arrogance and thought we were all little squirrelly devils. Issabell seemed anxious too, this was not quite how she had envisioned Willie behaving, him telling reporters he was the only man on Hatteras who knew where the big fish were, but she beamed naively and chattered with the other wives and seemed to enjoy herself, even her goofed eye shined with excitement. It was a thrill, maybe her first one of magnitude, and she wasn't going to darken it for herself by being embarrassed.

Willie left the fish suspended until after the sun went down, when I finally got him to agree to put it back on the boat and layer it with ice. Its scales had stiffened and dried, its brown- and brownish-green-marbled colors turned flat and chalky. Both he and Issabell remained on the boat that night, receiving a stream of visitors until well past midnight, whooping it up and having a grand time, playing country music on the radio so loud I could hear it word for word in my apartment above the store. I looked out the window once and saw Willie waltzing his wife under one of the security lightpoles, a dog and some kids standing there watching as they carefully spun in circles. I said to myself, That's the ticket, old Squirrel.

Life in Hatteras is generally calm, but Tuesday was carnival day from start to finish. Willie was up at his customary time before dawn, fiddling around the *Sea Eagle* as if it were his intention to go to work. When the fleet started out the harbor though, he and Issabell promenaded across the road for breakfast at the café, and when he got back I helped him winch the fish into the air and like magic we had ourselves a crowd again, families driving down from Nags Head, families who took the ferry from Ocracoke, Willie signing autographs for children, full of coastal authority and lore for the adults, cocky as hell to any fisherman who wandered over. A camera crew pulled up in a van around ten, the rest arrived soon after. What's it feel like to catch a fish so big? they asked. For a second he was hostile, glaring at the microphone, the camera lens, the interviewer with his necktie loosened in the heat. Then he grinned impishly and said, I won't tell you. You broke the world's record, is that right? Maybe, he allowed indifferently and winked over the TV person's shoulder at me and Issabell. When the next crew set up, he more or less hinted he was God Almighty and predicted his record would never be broken. After two more crews finished with him the sun was high; I made him take the fish down, throw a blanket of ice on it. Every few minutes Emory was on the P.A., informing Squirrelly he had a phone call. Vickilee came out and handed Willie a telegram from the governor, commending him for the "catch of the century." I guess the biggest treat for most of us was when the seaplane landed outside the cut, though nobody around here particularly cared for the fellows crammed in there, Fish and Game boys over to authenticate the grouper, so we pulled the fish back out of the boat and secured it to the scales. Hour later Willie took it down again to stick in ice, but not ten minutes after that a truck came by with a load of National Park Rangers wanting to have individual pictures taken with Squirrelly and the grouper, so he hung it back up, then a new wave of sightseers came by at midafternoon, another wave when the fleet came in at five, so he just let it dangle there on the arm of the hoist, beginning to sag from the amount of euphoric handling and heat, until it was too dark for cameras and that's when he relented to lower it down and we muscled it back to the boat, he took her down past the slips to the fishhouse, to finally sell the beast to Leonard I thought, but no, he collected a fresh half ton of ice. Willie wanted to play with the grouper for still another day.

That's almost all there is to tell if it wasn't for Squirrelly's unsolved past, the youth that Issabell regretted she had missed. On Wednesday he strung the fish up and dropped it down I'd say about a dozen times, the flow of onlookers and congratulators and hangarounds had decreased, Issabell was as animated as a real-estate agent and as girlish as we'd ever seen, but by midday the glow was off. She had been accidentally bumped into the harbor by a fan, was pulled out muddy and slicked with diesel oil, yet still she had discovered the uninhibiting powers of fame and swore that she had been endowed by the presence of the fish with clearer social vision.

By the time Squirrelly did get his grouper over to the fishhouse and they knifed it open, it was all mush inside, not worth a penny. He shipped the skin, the head, and the fins away to a taxidermist in Florida, and I suppose the pieces are all still there, sitting in a box like junk.

Now if you didn't already know, this story winds up with a punch from so far out in left field there's just no way you could see it coming, but I can't apologize for that, no more than I could take responsibility for a hurricane. About a week after everything got back to normal down here, and Squirrelly seemed content with memories and retreated back to his habits of seclusion, Brainless came crashing through the screen door, arms and legs flapping, his tongue too twisted with what he was dying to say for us to make any sense of his message.

Emory looked up from his books. I was on the phone to a man wanting a half-day charter to the Stream, arguing with him that there was no such thing as a half-day charter that went out that far. "When's that boy gonna grow up," Emory clucked. He told Brainless to slow down and concentrate on speaking right.

"They'se takin' Squirrelly away," Brainless said. He pointed back out the door.

I told the fellow on the line I might call him back if I had something and hung up, went around the counter and outside on the porch, Emory too, everybody came in fact, Vickilee and Buddy and Junior and Albert and two customers in the store. It was a foggy, drizzly morning, the security lamps casting soupy yellow columns of light down to the dock; most of the boats hadn't left yet but their engines were warming up. I don't think the sun had come up yet but you couldn't be sure. The boy was right, a group of men in mackintoshes were putting handcuffs on

Squirrelly and taking him off the *Sea Eagle*. The other captains and crews stood around in the mist, watching it happen. The men had on street shoes and looked official, you know, as you'd expect, and they led Willie to a dark sedan with government license plates. One of them opened the rear door for Willie, who kept his head bowed, and sort of helped him, pushed him, into the car. None of us tried to stop it, not one of us spoke up and said, Hey, what's going on? He was still an outsider to us and his life was none of our business. None of us said or even thought of saying, Willie, good-bye. We all just thought: There goes Willie, not in high style. The sedan pulled out of the lot and turned north.

"He's a goddamn natsy!" squealed Brainless, shaking us out of our spell.

"I told you not to cuss around here," Emory said. That was all anybody said.

Squirrelly's true name, the papers told us, was Wilhelm Strechenberger, and they took him back somewhere to Europe or Russia, I believe it was, to stand trial for things he supposedly did during the war. The TV said Squirrelly had been a young guard for the Germans in one of their camps. He had been "long sought" by "authorities," who thought he was living in Ohio. One of his victims who survived said something like Squirrelly was the cruelest individual he had ever met in his entire life.

Boy, oh boy—that's all we could say. Did we believe it? Hell no. Then, little by little, yes, though it seemed far beyond our abilities to know and to understand.

Issabell says it's a case of mistaken identity, although she won't mention Willie when she comes out in public, and if you ask me I'd say she blames us for her loss of him, as if what he had been all those years ago as well as what he became when he caught the fish—as if that behavior were somehow our fault.

Mitty Terbill was convinced it was Willie who grabbed her Prince Ed for some unspeakable purpose. She's entitled to her opinion, of course, but she shouldn't have expressed it in front of Issabell, who forfeited her reputation as the last and only docile Preddy by stamping the widow Terbill on her foot and breaking one of the old lady's toes. She filed assault charges against Issabell, saying Issabell and Willie were two of a kind.

Like Mitty, you might think that Willie Striker being a war criminal explains a lot, you might even think it explains everything, but I have to tell you I don't.

Now that we know the story, or at least think we do, of Willie's past, we still differ about why Willie came off the boat that day to expose himself, to be electronically reproduced all over the land—was it for Issabell or the fish?—and I say I don't know if Willie actually liked fishing, I expect he didn't unless he craved punishing work, and I don't know what he felt about Issabell besides safe, but I do know this: Like many people around here, Willie liked being envied. The Willie we knew was a lot like us, that's why he lasted here when others from the outside didn't, and that's what we saw for ourselves from the time he conked Bull Newman on the nose to the way he abused what he gained when he brought in that beast from the deep and hung it up for all to admire. He was, in his manner, much like us.

We still talk about the grouper all right, but when we do we automatically disconnect that prize fish from Willie—whether that's right or wrong is not for me to say—and we talk about it hanging in the air off the scale reeking a powerful smell of creation, Day One, so to speak, and it sounds like it appeared among us like . . . well, like an immaculate moment in sport. We've been outside things for a long time here on the very edge of the continent, so what I'm saying, maybe, is that we, like Issabell, we're only just discovering what it's like to be part of the world.

The setting for this story is much celebrated for its fine fly-fishing: the Escanaba River in Michigan's Upper Peninsula. The reader will find another surprise ending, one of the hallmarks of a good short story. The author, Robert Traver, was himself an avid fisherman of the Escanaba. His bestselling novel Anatomy of a Murder *(1958) was made into a great movie.*

Robert Traver

THE INTRUDER (1960)

IT WAS ABOUT NOON WHEN I put down my fly rod and sculled the little cedar boat with one hand and ate a sandwich and drank a can of beer with the other, just floating and enjoying the ride down the beautiful broad main Escanaba River. Between times I watched the merest speck of an eagle tacking and endlessly wheeling far up in the cloudless sky. Perhaps he was stalking my sandwich or even, dark thought, stalking me. . . . The fishing so far had been poor; the good trout simply weren't rising. I rounded a slow double bend, with high gravel banks on either side, and there stood a lone fisherman—the first person I had seen in hours. He was standing astride a little feeder creek on a gravel point on the left downstream side, fast to a good fish, his glistening rod hooped and straining, the line taut, the leader vibrating and sawing the water, the fish itself boring far down out of sight.

Since I was curious to watch a good battle and anxious not to interfere, I eased the claw anchor over the stern—*plop*—and the little boat hung there, gurgling and swaying from side to side in the slow deep current. The young fisherman either did not hear me or, hearing, and being a good one, kept his mind on his work. As I sat watching he shifted the rod to his left hand, shaking out his right wrist as though it were asleep, so I knew then that the fight had been a long one and that this fish was no midget. The young fisherman fumbled in his shirt and produced a cigarette and lighter and lit up, a real cool character. The fish made a sudden long downstream run and the fisherman raced after him, prancing through the water like a yearling buck, gradually coaxing and working him back up to the deeper slow water across from the gravel bar. It was a nice job of handling and I wanted to cheer. Instead I coughed discreetly and he glanced quickly upstream and saw me.

"Hi," he said pleasantly, turning his attention back to his fish.

"Hi," I answered.

"How's luck?" he said, still concentrating.

"Fairish," I said. "But I haven't anything quite like you seem to be on to. How you been doin'—otherwise, I mean?"

"Fairish," he said. "This is the third good trout in this same stretch—all about the same size."

"My, my," I murmured, thinking ruefully of the half-dozen-odd barely legal brook trout frying away in my sun-baked creel. "Guess I've just been out floating over the good spots."

"Pleasant day for a ride, though," he said, frowning intently at his fish.

"Delightful," I said wryly, taking a slow swallow of beer.

"Yep," the assured young fisherman went on, expertly feeding out line as his fish made another downstream sashay. "Yep," he repeated, nicely taking up slack on the retrieve, "that's why I gave up floating this lovely river. Nearly ten years ago, just a kid. Decided then 'twas a hell of a lot more fun fishing a hundred yards of her carefully than taking off on these all-day floating picnics."

I was silent for a while. Then: "I think you've got something there," I said, and I meant it. Of course he was right, and I was simply out joy-riding past the good fishing. I should have brought along a girl or a camera. On this beautiful river if there was no rise a float was simply an enforced if lovely scenic tour. If there was a rise, no decent fisherman ever needed to float. Presto, I now had it all figured out. . . .

"Wanna get by?" the poised young fisherman said, flipping his cigarette into the water.

"I'll wait," I said. "I got all day. My pal isn't meeting me till dark—'way down at the old burned logging bridge."

"Hm . . . trust you brought your passport—you really are out on a voyage," he said. "Perhaps you'd better slip by, fella—by the feel of this customer it'll be at least ten-twenty minutes more. Like a smart woman in the mood for play, these big trout don't like to be rushed. C'mon, just bear in sort of close to me, over here, right under London Bridge. It won't bother us at all."

My easy young philosopher evidently didn't want me to see how really big his fish was. But being a fisherman myself I knew, I knew. "All right," I said, lifting the anchor and sculling down over his way and under his throbbing line. "Thanks and good luck."

"Thanks, chum," he said, grinning at me. "Have a nice ride and good luck to you."

"Looks like I'll need it," I said, looking enviously back over my shoulder at his trembling rod tip. "Hey," I said, belatedly remembering my company manners, "want a nice warm can of beer?"

Smiling: "Despite your glowing testimonial, no thanks."

"You're welcome," I said realizing we were carrying on like a pair of strange diplomats.

"And one more thing, please," he said, raising his voice a little to be heard over the burbling water, still smiling intently at his straining fish. "If you don't mind, please keep this little stretch under your hat—it's been all mine for nearly ten years. It's really something special. No use kidding you—I see you've spotted my bulging creel and I guess by now you've got a fair idea of what I'm on to. And anyway I've got to take a little trip. But I'll be back—soon I hope. In the meantime try to be good to the place. I know it will be good to you."

"Right!" I shouted, for by then I had floated nearly around the downstream bend. "Mum's the word." He waved his free hand and then was blotted from view by a tall doomed spruce leaning far down out across the river from a crumbling water-blasted bank. The last thing I saw was the gleaming flash of his rod, the long taut line, the strumming leader. It made a picture I've never forgotten.

That was the last time ever that I floated the Big Escanaba River. I had learned my lesson well. Always after that when I visited this fabled new spot I hiked in, packing my gear, threading my way down river through a pungent needled maze of ancient deer trails, like a fleeing felon keeping always slyly away from the broad winding river itself. My strategy was twofold: to prevent other sly fishermen from finding and deflowering the place, and to save myself an extra mile of walking.

Despite the grand fishing I discovered there, I did not go back too often. It was a place to hoard and save, being indeed most good to me, as advertised. And always I fished it alone, for a fisherman's pact had been made, a pact that became increasingly hard to keep as the weeks rolled into months, the seasons into years, during which I never again encountered my poised young fisherman. In the morbid pathology of trout fishermen such a phenomenon is mightily disturbing. What had become of my fisherman? Hadn't he ever got back from his trip? Was he sick or had he moved away? Worse yet, had he died? How could such a consummate young artist have possibly given up fishing such an enchanted spot? Was he one of that entirely mad race of eccentric fishermen who cannot abide the thought of sharing a place, however fabulous, with even *one* other fisherman?

By and by, with the innocent selfishness possessed by all fishermen, I dwelt less and less upon the probable fate of my young fisherman and instead came smugly to think it was I who had craftily discovered the place. Nearly twenty fishing seasons slipped by on golden wings, as fishing seasons do, during which time I, fast getting no sprightlier, at last found it expedient to locate and hack out a series of abandoned old logging roads to let me drive within easier walking distance of my secret spot. The low cunning of middle age was replacing the hot stamina of youth. . . . As a road my new trail was strictly a springbreaking broncobuster, but at least I was able to sit and ride, after a fashion, thus saving my aging legs for the real labor of love to follow.

Another fishing season was nearly done when, one afternoon, brooding over that gloomy fact, I suddenly tore off my lawyer-mask and fled my office, heading for the Big Escanaba, bouncing and bucking my way in, finally hitting the Glide—as I had come to call the place—about sundown. For a long time I just stood there on the high bank, drinking in the sights and pungent river smells. No fish were rising, and slowly, lovingly, I went through the familiar ritual of rigging up; scrubbing out a fine new leader, dressing the tapered line, jointing the rod and threading the line, pulling on the tall patched waders, anointing myself with fly dope. No woman dressing for a ball was more fussy. . . . Then I composed myself on my favorite fallen log and waited. I smoked a slow pipe and sipped a can of beer, cold this time, thanks to the marvels of dry ice and my new road. My watching spot overlooked a wide bend and commanded a grand double view: above, the deep slow velvet glide with its little feeder stream where I first met my young fisherman; below a sporty and productive broken run of white water stretching nearly a half-mile. The old leaning spruce that used to be there below me had long since bowed in surrender and been swept away by some forgotten spring torrent. As I sat waiting the wind had died, the shadowing waters had taken on the brooding blue hush of evening, the dying embers of sundown suddenly lit a great blazing forest fire in the tops of the tall spruces across river from me, and an unknown bird that I have always called simply the "lonely" bird sang timidly its ancient haunting plaintive song. I arose and took a deep breath like a soldier advancing upon the enemy.

The fisherman's mystic hour was at hand.

First I heard and then saw a young buck in late velvet slowly, tentatively splashing his way across to my side, above me and beyond the feeder creek, ears twitching and tall tail nervously wigwagging. Then he winded me, freezing in midstream, giving me a still and liquid stare for a poised instant; then came charging on across in great pawing incredibly graceful leaps, lacquered flanks quivering, white flag up and waving, bounding up the bank and into the anonymous woods, the sounds of his excited blowing fading and growing fainter and then dying away.

In the meantime four fair trout had begun rising in the smooth tail of the glide just below me. I selected and tied on a favorite small dry fly and got down below the lowest riser and managed to take him on the first cast, a short dainty float. Without moving I stood and lengthened line and took all four risers, all nice firm brook trout upwards of a foot, all the time purring and smirking with increasing complacency. The omens were good. As I relit my pipe and waited for new worlds to conquer I heard a mighty splash above me and wheeled gaping at the spreading magic ring of a really good trout, carefully marking the spot. Oddly enough he had risen just above where the young buck had just crossed, a little above the feeder creek. Perhaps, I thought extravagantly, perhaps he was after the deer. . . . I waited, tense and watchful, but he did not rise again.

I left the river and scrambled up the steep gravelly bank and made my way through the tall dense spruces up to the little feeder creek. I slipped down the bank like a footpad, stealthily inching my way out to the river in the silted creek itself, so as not to scare the big one, *my* big one. I could feel the familiar shock of icy cold water suddenly clutching at my ankles as I stood waiting at the spot where I had first run across my lost fisherman. I quickly changed to a fresh fly in the same pattern, carefully snubbing the knot. Then the fish obediently rose again, a savage easy engulfing roll, again the undulant outgoing ring, just where I had marked him, not more than thirty feet from me and a little beyond the middle and obliquely upstream. Here was, I saw, a cagey selective riser, lord of his pool, and one who would not suffer fools gladly. So I commanded myself to rest him before casting. "Twenty-one, twenty-two, twenty-three . . ." I counted.

The cast itself was indecently easy and, finally releasing it, the little Adams sped out on its quest, hung poised in midair for an instant, and then settled sleepily upon the water like a thistle, uncurling before the leader like the languid outward folding of a ballerina's arm. The fly circled a moment, uncertainly, then was caught by the current. Down, down it rode, closer, closer, then—*clap!*—the fish rose and kissed it, I flicked my wrist and he was on, and then away he went roaring off downstream, past feeder creek and happy fisherman, the latter hot after him.

During the next mad half-hour I fought this explosive creature up and down the broad stream, up and down, ranging at least a hundred feet each way, or so it seemed, without ever once seeing him. This meant, I figured, that he was either a big brown or a brook. A rainbow would surely have leapt a dozen times by now. Finally I worked him into the deep safe water off the feeder creek where he sulked nicely while I panted and rested my benumbed rod arm. As twilight receded into dusk with no sign of his tiring I began vaguely to wonder just who had latched on to whom. For the fifth or sixth time I rested my aching arm by transferring the rod to my left hand, professionally shaking out my tired wrist just as I had once seen a young fisherman do.

Nonchalantly I reached in my jacket and got out and tried to light one of my rigidly abominable Italian cigars. My fish, unimpressed by my show of aplomb, shot suddenly away on a powerful zigzag exploratory tour upstream, the fisherman nearly swallowing his unlit cigar as he scrambled up after him. It was then that I saw a lone man sitting quietly in a canoe, anchored in midstream above me. The tip of his fly rod showed over the stern. My heart sank: after all these years my hallowed spot was at last discovered.

"Hi," I said, trying to convert a grimace of pain into an amiable grin, all the while keeping my eye on my sulking fish. The show must go on.

"Hi," he said.

"How you doin'?" I said, trying to make a brave show of casual fish talk.

"Fairish," he said, "but nothing like you seem to be on to."

"Oh, he isn't so much," I said, lying automatically if not too well. "I'm working a fine leader and don't dare to bull him." At least that was the truth.

The stranger laughed briefly and glanced at his wrist watch. "You've been on to him that I know of for over forty minutes—and I didn't see you make the strike. Let's not try to kid the Marines. I just moved down a bit closer to be in on the finish. I'll shove away if you think I'm too close."

"Nope," I answered generously, delicately snubbing my fish away from a partly submerged windfall. "But about floating this lovely river," I pontificated, "there's nothing in it, my friend. Absolutely nothing. Gave it up myself eighteen-twenty years ago. Figured out it was better working one stretch carefully than shoving off on those floating picnics. Recommend it to you, comrade."

The man in the canoe was silent. I could see the little red moon of his cigarette glowing and fading in the gathering gloom. Perhaps my gratuitous pedagogical ruminations had offended him; after all, trout fishermen are a queer proud race. Perhaps I should try diversionary tactics. "Wanna get by?" I inquired silkily. Maybe I could get him to go away before I tried landing this unwilling porpoise. He still remained silent. "Wanna get by?" I repeated. "It's perfectly O.K. by me. As you see—it's a big roomy river."

"No," he said dryly. "No thanks." There was another long pause. Then: "If you wouldn't mind too much I think I'll put in here for the night. It's getting pretty late—and somehow I've come to like the looks of this spot."

"Oh," I said in a small voice—just "Oh"—as I disconsolately watched him lift his anchor and expertly push his canoe in to the near gravelly shore, above me, where it grated halfway in and scraped to rest. He sat there quietly, his little neon cigarette moon glowing, and I felt I just had to say something more. After all I didn't *own* the river. "Why sure, of course, it's a beautiful place to camp, plenty of pine knots for fuel, a spring-fed creek for drinking water and cooling your beer," I ran on gaily, rattling away like an hysterical realtor trying to sell the place. Then I began wondering how I would ever spirit my noisy fish car out of the woods without the whole greedy world of fishermen learning about my new secret road to this old secret spot. Maybe I'd even have to abandon it for the night and hike out. . . . Then I remembered there was an uncooperative fish to be landed, so I turned my full attention to the unfinished and uncertain business at hand. "Make yourself at home," I lied softly.

"Thanks," the voice again answered dryly, and again I heard the soft chuckle in the semidarkness.

My fish had stopped his mad rushes now and was busily boring the bottom, the long leader vibrating like the plucked string of a harp. For the first time I found I was able gently to pump him up for a cautious look. And again I almost swallowed my still unlit stump of cigar as I beheld his dorsal fin cleaving the water nearly a foot back from the fly. He wallowed and shook like a dog and then rolled on his side, then recovered and fought his way back down and away on another run, but shorter this time. With a little pang I knew then that my fish was a done, but the pang quickly passed—it always did—and again I gently, relentlessly pumped him up, shortening line, drawing him in to the familiar daisy hoop of landing range, kneeling and stretching and straining out my opposing aching arms like those of an extravagant archer. The net slipped fairly under him on the first try and, clenching my cigar, I made my pass and lo! lifted him free and dripping from the water. "Ah-h-h . . ." He was a glowing superb spaniel-sized brown. I staggered drunkenly away from the water and sank anywhere to the ground, panting like a winded miler.

"Beautiful, *beautiful*," I heard my forgotten and unwelcome visitor saying like a prayer. "I've dreamed all this—over a thousand times I've dreamed it."

I tore my feasting eyes away from my fish and glowered up at the intruder. He was half standing in the beached canoe now, one hand on the side, trying vainly to wrest the cap from a bottle, of all things, seeming in the dusk to smile uncertainly. I felt a sudden chill sense of concern, of vague nameless alarm.

"Look, chum," I said, speaking lightly, very casually, "is everything all O.K.?"

"Yes, yes, of course," he said shortly, still plucking away at his bottle. "There . . . I—I'm coming now."

Bottle in hand he stood up and took a resolute broad step out of the canoe, then suddenly, clumsily he lurched and pitched forward, falling heavily, cruelly, half in the beached canoe and half out upon the rocky wet shore. For a moment I sat staring ruefully, then I scrambled up and started running toward him, still holding my rod and the netted fish, thinking this fisherman was indubitably potted. "No, no, no!" he shouted at me, struggling and scrambling to his feet in a kind of wild urgent frenzy. I halted, frozen, holding my sagging dead fish as the intruder limped toward me, in a curious sort of creaking stiffly mechanical limp, the uncorked but still intact bottle held triumphantly aloft in one muddy wet hand, the other hand reaching gladly toward me.

"Guess I'll never get properly used to this particular battle stripe," he said, slapping his thudding and unyielding right leg. "But how are you, stranger?" he went on, his wet eyes glistening, his bruised face smiling. "How about our having a drink to your glorious trout—and still another to reunion at our old secret fishing spot?"

In a tongue-in-cheek yarn, the narrator of this story shoots verbal darts at his friend as they angle for weakfish in Atlantic coast waters. It may not seem fair that the friend, who does everything wrong, catches more fish. But that's part of the fun. Elmer Ransom's books include The Last Trumpeters and Other Stories *(1941),* The Woodland Book *(1945), and* Fishing's Just Luck and Other Stories *(1945).*

Elmer Ransom

FISHING'S JUST LUCK (1945)

SAM IS NATURALLY ORNERY AND contentious. Anybody who knows about winter trout will tell you that a sinking plug, most times, has got it all over a floater—that is, over a so-called crippled minnow. But you can't argue with Sam—the perfect fisherman. He harbors some fool notion that if you catch a fish with an under-water lure, you've done something low and indecent; slipping up on the blind side, so to speak. Take brook trout for instance. Sam will loosen his belt in contemplation of the fish you've cooked, thankful that he limited his breakfast to twelve battercakes, three eggs, four slices of bacon, and two cups of coffee—not to mention a goodly bait of that universal southern dish, hominy grits.

Then, while he folds himself around pound after pound of your fish, he'll revile you for using a wet fly. One time, in Canada, he even refused to eat more than four fish because he claimed that I'd used worms. As if worms would hurt the flavor of a fish. Pfff!

He reminds me of a vegetarian who wears a fur coat and leather shoes. Consistency, that's what he lacks—consistency.

He helped me with the canoe, lifting the light end, of course, the bum, and he fussed over the tackle and cushions while I got the motor and the gasoline. He blew on his hands to warm them and muttered something about winter being the time for hunting, and about Framp needing a work-out. Framp is his pointer dog, and he suits Sam to a T. Framp's got ants in his breeches, too, and snoots all winter fishermen.

The Perfect Fisherman appropriated the two cushions and made himself comfortable. We drifted with the tide while I cranked the motor.

"Let's get going," he shouted, after I'd yanked the rope a fourth time. I looked at him bitterly and went back to cranking. The motor *would* cut up with Sam along, and after I'd bragged that it always started on the first turn.

He let me crank for five minutes—deliberately before he said: "And why not turn on the gas? It does use gas, doesn't it?"

I didn't answer him. I acted dignified and turned on the gas, and we roared up Broad River with the tide behind us and the wind in our faces. Which meant a rough trip.

Sam fumbled in the bottom of the boat for something and, seeing my chance, I quartered the canoe into a curling whitecap, and ducked my head. The spray drummed into my rain shirt. Looking up, I saw Sam wiping behind his ears, and read his lips.

"Damn it," he was saying. "You did that on purpose." He had no proof. I pretended not to understand. Wasn't I astern, taking spray all the time, while he was dry and comfortable forward?

He reached for my parka—my gorgeous red parka, intended, on other occasions, as colorful proof that I was a man and not a moose—and pulled it over his head, leaving the hood around his shoulders. He knew darned well I wouldn't wet him if he had that parka on.

We were after winter trout, which are your old friends the sea trout, spotted squeateague, spotted weakfish, or, if you are a college professor, *Cynoscion nebulosus.*

And the guy who named them weakfish had a distorted sense of humor. Like calling Jack Dempsey a sissy.

The immortal Jordan, who ought to know, says of them: "As a game fish the squeateague is the greatest of the family. No saltwater fish of our Atlantic coast affords more sport to the angler than this species."

The winter trout has other points in his favor. No man can forbid your fishing the waters in which he abounds and no state legislature can require a license for his taking. Poor man, rich man, beggar man, thief—he's there for all who have the love of the salt in their bones, and the skill to take him. He may strike gently or with a reckless, hilarious abandon. Always, he puts up a grand battle.

He moves from place to place so that many fellows of the angle may have their chance, but he does admit a healthy partiality to more southern waters. Who wouldn't? Over much of his range he may be taken every month in the year. In the waters of Georgia and South Carolina the months from October through January are best.

He hankers after artificial lures. I know because I am a doodle-bug fisherman when the occasion demands, never knowingly denying a hungry fish the morsel of his choice. Time and again I've seen experienced plug fisherman, using black-bass casting tackle, with the right sort of artificial minnow, wallop a bait fisherman operating from the same boat.

Take it or leave it, two of us, using sinking plugs, caught 157 on one tide. Oh, we didn't keep them all. But there was no ethical reason why we shouldn't had we been so inclined, for commercial fishermen take thousands of pounds daily in their nets, offering them in most markets serving the Atlantic seaboard. There is no possible chance for the rod-and-reel fishermen to deplete the species; the blue fish and the netters kill more in one day than the rod-and-reel fishermen do in a season—not to mention the professionals who go "striking" at night with a brilliant light and a three-pronged gig. So ease your conscience, if you have a good catch, and take a few to your friends. The situation is different from that prevailing with freshwater fish.

Sure, I love the winter trout. He has put the salt spray in my nostrils when my mind was lower than the belly of a snake and every damn thing gone wrong. He has fought me, fed me, rejuvenated me, brought me back believing there was some sense to this twisted warp called life.

There are, perhaps, a few fish of his size that fight better. Certainly, the striped bass, royalty incarnate, and possibly that grand old aristocrat the channel bass (known as school bass in the smaller weights). But the stripers are most often hard to find, and the channel bass more temperamental.

Locate a shell bank at low tide and fish it as the tide covers it, or stop at almost any bridge or trestle over southern salt water, and at the right season and tide you will be likely to strike winter trout. And always, peel your eye for the terns and gulls. Where they congregate, diving to the surface for small morsels, you'll find that a school is working, and the minnows on which they feed are leaping to escape them. Work your lure slowly through this water, and you may have a strike on every cast until the school moves away or ceases to feed.

Avoid fishing in the full or the new moon. Don't ask me why. Possibly it is because the higher tides permit the fish to gorge themselves in the covered marshes, or maybe it is just as Uncle Jake says: "Dey mouth is sore, suh. Dey yenty gwine strike much."

This day Sam and I were going to fish near the Seaboard trestle on Broad River, a wide estuary of the sea that cuts away from Port Royal Sound, behind Parris Island, in the South Carolina Low Country. We rode a sponson-equipped canoe—a good, safe boat for rough water—powered by a light twin outboard.

We took four casting rods. And why four rods? Because, in fishing the salt, you can never be quite sure what is going to strike. One time I hooked a monster cabio. No, I didn't land him. Another day a small tarpon took my lure in waters where tarpon were almost unknown.

Our reels were regular quadruple multiplying casting reels, carrying a hundred yards of eighteen-pound-test silk line, hard braided. Cuttyhunk lasts longer, and in the six thread is fairly satisfactory, but it is definitely more difficult to cast, most likely to backlash.

Of lures there is no end, from the home-made clothespin plug or the imitation mud minnow, both of which are given their elusive motion by the manipulation of the rod tip, to gaudy creations warranted to out-wiggle a strip-tease dancer. It was this matter of lures that was to start our next argument, but then something had to start any argument if Sam were to remain happy. Me? I don't argue unless Sam goads me into it by one of his absurd contentions with which I don't agree.

After fighting the chop for four miles, I cut the motor near the trestle and yelled for Sam to let the anchor go.

It wasn't my fault that he snubbed the rope too close and the anchor dragged in the swift tide, throwing us out of position, but he bellyached no end about pulling it in again. As though handling the anchor in twenty feet of water was any job at all compared to skippering the canoe four miles against a head wind.

Six or eight people were fishing from the trestle. While we maneuvered to position two fish were caught. I shouted "What luck?" The hopeful cry of all fishermen.

"Plenty," exulted a big guy on the trestle.

He took a long swig from a flask (drat him), and then held up a string of fish that would make any man's eyes bug out. I could see that we were late.

Sam snapped his floater close to the trestle, gave it an expert flip. It was just too bad but I had to break the news sometime.

"In this wind," I told him as gently as I could, "they won't be striking on top."

He turned a stony eye my way, and averred that I'd misled him. I merely shrugged my shoulders. What are you ever going to do with a stubborn man?

I dropped my sinking plug close to the trestle, let it ride down, and slowly, almost bumping the bottom, I retrieved with a jerking motion. At the third flip, I had a smashing strike. The fish ran to starboard, and Sam let his line get in the way.

I lost the fish and, naturally, very firmly told Sam what I thought of a guy who was so jealous that he would do a thing of this kind. He paid me no attention, whatever, for the trestle fraternity was doing business right along, and Sam gets excited when fish are being caught. Disregarding my appropriate remarks, he hissed. "If these fish won't hit a surface lure I'm going to drown you." His reputation was at stake.

And would you believe it? Sam threw that floater close to the trestle, and for a second I thought the bridge was falling down. The whole school must have ganged up on that one plug. Sam said, "Ha!" snapped his wrist, and set the hook.

"Don't press him, you dumbbell," I urged. "Your hook will pull out."

He eyed me coldly, out of one corner, and replied: "Are *you* advising *me*!" That's just the way he said it. He didn't ask it either.

The fish swept under the anchor rope, and Sam did a Houdini, passing the rod after the fish while I grabbed his leg to keep him inboard. I didn't mind about Sam, but he had my parka on.

Some guys have all the luck. I'm telling you, Sam did everything wrong. Everything! And still he landed the fish. Then he smoothed his hair, set his hat on straight and told me to take his picture.

Sam's not much to look at in my opinion, but one of these iridescent beauties, spotted and gleaming in the winter sunshine, is a model fit for the camera of a king. With a long, able body, pointed head, fighting mouth, and one or two keen canine teeth in the projecting lower jaw, he has all the swift and savage beauty of the under-water, with its age-long, immutable law that only the fit survive. And keep your hands out of that mouth and away from the sharp gillrakes.

"Well," Sam said, giving me the evil eye, "what is it to be?"

My conscience didn't hurt me at all. Not one bit. He was asking for it. This surface strike was sheer accident, and science was bound to triumph.

"Low man pays for shells, transportation, and grub next Saturday," I suggested.

He wet his lips in greedy contemplation. "And some raw meat for Framp," he added, sticking his neck out.

The tide began to slacken. The fishing is always more furious at the turn, either low or high tide.

I bumped the plug on the bottom, and a fish struck and ran toward the boat. He was a bit smaller than the fish Sam had landed. Then I hooked a fish on each of six successive casts and landed five of them.

Sam's temper was about to get the best of him. But then it was his own fault. It always is. I advised that he change to an under-water plug, being far enough ahead to be generous with advice. Next Saturday we might drive down to the Florida line where I had a long overdue date with some coveys of quail. We would spend the night at a good little hotel I knew about. What did I care for Sam's expense? Between strikes I mouthed the plan over.

"All right," he bellowed, "all right." Sounding like he meant anything but all right. "You hooked me but just wait, I'll get you." Just like Sam holding a grudge when all he had to do was to listen to what a fisherman told him.

Being mad, he wasn't ready for the next strike. I don't knew what he snagged, but it broke his line on the first long rush, and the fish and Sam's floater disappeared toward Port Royal Sound.

He grunted. That fish might mean the pot. Oh yeah! And suppose I'd landed the one he tangled in his line. He had a lot to grouch over, now didn't he? He scrambled around the bottom looking for his box of floaters. He came up, solemn eyed and accusing, asking where I'd put them. Yes, where I'd put them! Ain't that just like Sam? They were on the mantel at the shack.

"You did it on purpose," he complained bitterly. "You knew they'd strike on top."

It was this unwarranted bickering that caused my backlash. I had worked the lure close to the boat when the granddaddy of them all hit my plug. He jerked the reel handle out of my hand, slapped the rod on the side of the boat, smashing the tip, thumbed his fins at me in disgust and swam away.

"Look what you've done," I bellowed. Sam actually grinned. The camera clicked as I worked to untangle the snarl. When I looked up Sam was casting a sinking plug.

I heard him grunt. His rod arched, and there was something lively on the far end of his line. I looked away. I couldn't bear to see it. The man had hooked two fish on a single cast, one on each gang of hooks. No telling what he'd catch if he really put some hooks on a plug.

"Take your time," he called as I fought the backlash. He brought in another fish and added: "Time out for a picture." I looked at him witheringly but he didn't wither.

"Dry fly fisherman," I said with appropriate sarcasm. "Floating plug! I knew you'd crook me if you got a chance."

"Now, now," he answered comfortably. "Just take your time with that snarl while papa brings home the bacon."

He snapped up the rod tip again, and set the hook with a satisfying "Ugh!" and then as the fish began to cut up he added: "I'm thinking of the grub, the meat for Framp, the shells and the gas and oil that you are going to buy next Saturday. Would you like to make a small wager that your potlicker pup finds one covey to Framp's two?"

I told him where he could go.

My rod was rigged when a fish struck Sam close to the boat. Now a winter trout does his fighting mostly under the water, but this one surprised Sam; I'd say the fish even scared him. He yanked that fish hard enough to loosen the tonsils of a tarpon. But do you think the fish got away? He did not. Instead he gave one frenzied leap and flopped in the boat.

"Count 'em, my lad," Sam exulted, "or even weigh 'em if you wish. They have scales." Which was an old and rotten pun. "We are now even and all your shenanigans have gained you nothing. Honesty is the best policy. You ought to try it sometime."

I didn't say what I was thinking. Instead I cast close to the bridge, and very expertly began to retrieve with that sure, slow wiggle of mine which, if I do say it as shouldn't, is known among the winter trout themselves as "the great irresistible."

Of course Sam had no chance. He had never fished the salt before. He fished too fast. He wouldn't let his lure sink far enough. He didn't hoochie-koochie his plug to give it fish appeal. Anybody could tell that. I would have felt sorry for him if he hadn't been so ornery.

Even when he caught the next fish I grinned at him encouragingly. For a novice he hadn't done too bad. I was one down but I even the count in less than five minutes.

Then the fish stopped striking as completely as though someone had rung a dinner bell downriver. The tide was running out swiftly by now. I hung up on an oyster shell and lost my plug. Sam accused me of getting excited. We cast for forty minutes more without a strike. The lucky stiff. The fish *would* move off just in time to save his hide.

The sun dropped low and the biting chill crept into my bones. A *rum chaud* was to be had at the shack, steaming and savory.

"Oh, hum," Sam yawned. "You're a lucky guy."

He pulled on the anchor, blaming me that the water was cold and wet. I put my rod in its rack on the side of the canoe, pushed the motor down, turned on the gas—please note that—primed her. As I was about to twist her tail, Sam made one last, lazy, indifferent cast.

He started the lure in when suddenly his rod tip slapped the water. The reel handle banged against his knuckles. He gasped as the line ran out and out.

"After him, you big stiff," he shouted, "he's taking all my line."

I saw a swirl, the flip of a tail as the fish "nodded," and I groaned.

A channel bass, at the wrong place, on the wrong plug, at the wrong tide and time, but, above all else, by the wrong fisherman.

When the fish was in the boat, six pounds of it, Sam muttered something about next Saturday, pulled up the hood of my parka, curled himself comfortably into a ball under the bow and out of the wind, and went to sleep while I drove the boat home.

Science? Fishing is just luck.

What follows are literary tricks and treats from the master of the macabre, Stephen King. The youthful fisherman in the story finds himself in a hellish situation when he meets a devil of a fellow who has the nerve to eat his fish and tell lies about his mother. Ghoulishly funny, the story is vintage King, set in his home state of Maine. One of America's bestselling novelists, King's blockbuster hits include Carrie *(1974),* Firestarter *(1980),* Cujo *(1981),* Pet Sematary *(1983), and* Hearts in Atlantis *(1999).*

THE MAN IN THE
BLACK SUIT (1994)

I AM NOW A VERY OLD MAN and this is something that happened to me when I was very young—only nine years old. It was 1914, the summer after my brother, Dan, died in the west field and not long before America got into the First World War. I've never told anyone about what happened at the fork in the stream that day, and I never will. I've decided to write it down, though, in this book, which I will leave on the table beside my bed. I can't write long, because my hands shake so these days and I have next to no strength, but I don't think it will take long.

Later, someone may find what I have written. That seems likely to me, as it is pretty much human nature to look in a book marked "Diary" after its owner has passed along. So, yes—my words will probably be read. A better question is whether anyone will believe them. Almost certainly not, but that doesn't matter. It's not belief I'm interested in but freedom. Writing can give that, I've found. For twenty years I wrote a column called "Long Ago and Far Away" for the Castle Rock *Call,* and I know that sometimes it works that way—what you write down sometimes leaves you forever, like old photographs left in the bright sun, fading to nothing but white.

I pray for that sort of release.

A man in his eighties should be well past the terrors of childhood, but as my infirmities slowly creep up on me, like waves licking closer and closer to some indifferently built castle of sand, that terrible face grows clearer and clearer in my mind's eye. It glows like a dark star in the constellations of my childhood. What I might have done yesterday, who I might have seen here in my room at the nursing home, what I might have said to them or they to me—those things are gone, but the face of the man in the black suit grows ever clearer, ever closer, and I remember every word he said. I don't want to think of him but I can't help it, and sometimes at night my old heart beats so hard and so fast I think it will tear itself right clear of my chest. So I uncap my fountain pen and force my trembling old hand to write this pointless anecdote in the diary one of my great-grandchildren—I can't remember her name for sure, at least not right now, but I know it starts with an "S"—gave to me last Christmas, and which I have never written in until now. Now I will write in it. I will write the story of how I met the man in the black suit on the bank of Castle Stream one afternoon in the summer of 1914.

The town of Motton was a different world in those days—more different than I could ever tell you. That was a world without airplanes droning overhead, a world almost without cars and trucks, a world where the skies were not cut into lanes and slices by overhead power lines. There was not a single paved road in the whole town, and the business district consisted of nothing but Corson's General Store, Thut's Livery & Hardware, the

Methodist church at Christ's Corner, the school, the town hall, and half a mile down from there, Harry's Restaurant, which my mother called, with unfailing disdain, "the liquor house."

Mostly, though, the difference was in how people lived—how *apart* they were. I'm not sure people born after the middle of the century could quite credit that, although they might say they could, to be polite to old folks like me. There were no phones in western Maine back then, for one thing. The first one wouldn't be installed for another five years, and by the time there was a phone in our house, I was nineteen and going to college at the University of Maine in Orono.

But that is only the roof of the thing. There was no doctor closer than Casco, and there were no more than a dozen houses in what you would call town. There were no neighborhoods (I'm not even sure we knew the word, although we had a verb—"neighboring"—that described church functions and barn dances), and open fields were the exception rather than the rule. Out of town the houses were farms that stood far apart from each other, and from December until the middle of March we mostly hunkered down in the little pockets of stove warmth we called families. We hunkered and listened to the wind in the chimney and hoped no one would get sick or break a leg or get a headful of bad ideas, like the farmer over in Castle Rock who had chopped up his wife and kids three winters before and then said in court that the ghosts made him do it. In those days before the Great War, most of Motton was woods and bog—dark long places full of moose and mosquitoes, snakes and secrets. In those days there were ghosts everywhere.

This thing I'm telling about happened on a Saturday. My father gave me a whole list of chores to do, including some that would have been Dan's, if he'd still been alive. He was my only brother, and he'd died of a bee sting. A year had gone by, and still my mother wouldn't hear that. She said it was something else, *had* to have been, that no one ever died of being stung by a bee. When Mama Sweet, the oldest lady in the Methodist Ladies' Aid, tried to tell her—at the church supper the previous winter, this was—that the same thing had happened to her favorite uncle back in '73, my mother clapped her hands over her ears, got up, and walked out of the church basement. She'd never been back since and nothing my father could say to her would change her mind. She claimed she was done with church, and that if she ever had to see Helen Robichaud again (that was Mama Sweet's real name) she would slap her eyes out. She wouldn't be able to help herself, she said.

That day Dad wanted me to lug wood for the cookstove, weed the beans and the cukes, pitch hay out of the loft, get two jugs of water to put in the cold pantry, and scrape as much old paint off the cellar bulkhead as I could. Then, he said I could go fishing, if I didn't mind going by myself—he had to go over and see Bill Eversham about some cows. I said I sure didn't mind going by myself, and my dad smiled as if that didn't surprise him so very much. He'd given me a bamboo pole the week before—not because it was my birthday or anything but just because he liked to give me things sometimes—and I was wild to try it in Castle Stream, which was by far the troutiest brook I'd ever fished.

"But don't you go too far in the woods," he told me. "Not beyond where the water splits."

"No, sir."

"Promise me."

"Yessir, I promise."

"Now promise your mother."

We were standing on the back stoop; I had been bound for the springhouse with the water jugs when my dad stopped me. Now he turned me around to face my mother, who was standing at the marble counter in a flood of strong morning sunshine falling through the double windows over the sink. There was a curl of hair lying across the side of her forehead and touching her eyebrow—you see how well I remember it all? The bright light turned that little curl to filaments of gold and made me want to run to her and put my arms around her. In that instant I saw her as a woman, saw her as my father must have seen her. She was wearing a housedress with little red roses all over it, I remember, and she was kneading bread. Candy Bill, our little black Scottie dog, was standing alertly beside her feet, looking up, waiting for anything that might drop. My mother was looking at me.

"I promise," I said.

She smiled, but it was the worried kind of smile she always seemed to make since my father brought Dan back from the west field in his arms. My father had come sobbing and bare-chested. He had taken off his shirt and draped it over Dan's face, which had swelled and turned color. *My boy!* he had been crying. *Oh, look at my boy! Jesus, look at my boy!* I remember that as if it were yesterday. It was the only time I ever heard my dad take the Saviour's name in vain.

"What do you promise, Gary?" she asked.

"Promise not to go no further than where the stream forks, Ma'am."

"Any further."

"Any."

She gave me a patient look, saying nothing as her hands went on working in the dough, which now had a smooth, silky look.

"I promise not to go any further than where the stream forks, Ma'am."

"Thank you, Gary," she said. "And try to remember that grammar is for the world as well as for school."

"Yes, Ma'am."

Candy Bill followed me as I did my chores, and sat between my feet as I bolted my lunch, looking up at me with the same attentiveness he had shown my mother while she was kneading her bread, but when I got my new bamboo pole and my old, splintery creel and started out of the dooryard, he stopped and only stood in the dust by an old roll of snow fence, watching. I called him but he wouldn't come. He yapped a time or two, as if telling me to come back, but that was all.

"Stay, then," I said, trying to sound as if I didn't care. I did, though, at least a little. Candy Bill *always* went fishing with me.

My mother came to the door and looked out at me with her left hand held up to shade her eyes. I can see her that way still, and it's like looking at a photograph of someone who later became unhappy, or died suddenly. "You mind your dad now, Gary!"

"Yes, Ma'am, I will."

She waved. I waved, too. Then I turned my back on her and walked away.

The sun beat down on my neck, hard and hot, for the first quarter-mile or so, but then I entered the woods, where double shadow fell over the road and it was cool and fir-smelling and you could hear the wind hissing through the deep, needled groves. I walked with my pole on my shoulder the way boys did back then, holding my creel in my other hand like a valise or a salesman's sample case. About two miles into the woods along a road that was really nothing but a double rut with a grassy strip growing up the center hump, I began to hear the hurried, eager gossip of Castle Stream. I thought of trout with bright speckled backs and pure-white bellies, and my heart went up in my chest.

The stream flowed under a little wooden bridge, and the banks leading down to the water were steep and brushy. I worked my way down carefully, holding on where I could and digging my heels in. I went down out of summer and back into mid-spring, or so it felt. The cool rose gently off the water, and there was a green smell like moss. When I got to the edge of the water I only stood there for a little while, breathing deep of that mossy smell and watching the dragonflies circle and the skitterbugs skate. Then, further down, I saw a trout leap at a butterfly—a good big brookie, maybe fourteen inches long—and remembered I hadn't come here just to sightsee.

I walked along the bank, following the current, and wet my line for the first time, with the bridge still in sight upstream. Something jerked the tip of my pole down once or twice and ate half my worm, but whatever it was was too sly for my nine-year-old hands—or maybe just not hungry enough to be careless—so I quit that place.

I stopped at two or three other places before I got to the place where Castle Stream forks, going southwest into Castle Rock and southeast into Kashwakamak Township, and at one of them I caught the biggest trout I have ever caught in my life, a beauty that measured nineteen inches from tip to tail on the little ruler I kept in my creel. That was a monster of a brook trout, even for those days.

If I had accepted this as gift enough for one day and gone back, I would not be writing now (and this is going to turn out longer than I thought it would, I see that already), but I didn't. Instead I saw to my catch right then and there as my father had shown me—cleaning it, placing it on dry grass at the bottom of the creel, then laying damp grass on top of it—and went on. I did not, at age nine, think that catching a nineteen-inch brook trout was particularly remarkable, although I do remember being amazed that my line had not broken when I, netless as well as artless, had hauled it out and swung it toward me in a clumsy tail-flapping arc.

Ten minutes later, I came to the place where the stream split in those days (it is long gone now; there is a settlement of duplex homes where Castle Stream once went its course, and a district grammar school as well, and if there is a stream it goes in darkness), dividing around a huge gray rock nearly the size of our outhouse. There was a pleasant flat space here, grassy and soft, overlooking what my dad and I called South Branch. I squatted on my heels, dropped my line into the water, and almost immediately snagged a fine rainbow trout. He wasn't the size of my brookie—only a foot or so—but a good fish, just the same. I had it cleaned out before the gills had stopped flexing, stored it in my creel, and dropped my line back into the water.

This time there was no immediate bite, so I leaned back, looking up at the blue stripe of sky I could see along the stream's course. Clouds floated by, west to east, and I tried to think what they looked like. I saw a unicorn, then a rooster, then a dog that looked like Candy Bill. I was looking for the next one when I drowsed off.

Or maybe slept. I don't know for sure. All I know is that a tug on my line so strong it almost pulled the bamboo pole out of my hand was what brought me back into the afternoon. I sat up, clutched the pole, and suddenly became aware that something was sitting on the tip of my nose. I crossed my eyes and saw a bee. My heart seemed to fall dead in my chest, and for a horrible second I was sure I was going to wet my pants.

The tug on my line came again, stronger this time, but although I maintained my grip on the end of the pole so it wouldn't be pulled into the stream and perhaps carried away (I think I even had the presence of mind to snub the line with my forefinger), I made no effort to pull in my catch. All my horrified attention was fixed on the fat black-and-yellow thing that was using my nose as a rest stop.

I slowly poked out my lower lip and blew upward. The bee ruffled a little but kept its place. I blew again and it ruffled again—but this time it also seemed to shift impatiently, and I didn't dare blow anymore, for fear it would lose its temper completely and give me a shot. It was too close for me to focus on what it was doing, but it was easy to imagine it ramming its stinger into one of my nostrils and shooting its poison up toward my eyes. And my brain.

A terrible idea came to me; that this was the very bee that had killed my brother. I knew it wasn't true, and not only because honeybees probably didn't live longer than a single year (except maybe for the queens; about them I was not so sure). It couldn't be true, because honeybees died when they stung, and even at nine I knew it. Their stingers were barbed, and when they tried to fly away after doing the deed, they tore themselves apart. Still, the idea stayed. This was a special bee, a devil-bee, and it had come back to finish the other of Albion and Loretta's two boys.

And here is something else: I had been stung by bees before, and although the stings had swelled more than is perhaps usual (I can't really say for sure), I had never died of them. That was only for my brother, a terrible trap that had been laid for him in his very making—a trap that I had somehow escaped. But as I crossed my eyes until they hurt, in an effort to focus on the bee, logic did not exist. It was the *bee* that existed, only that—the bee that had killed my brother, killed him so cruelly that my father had slipped down the straps of his overalls so he could take off his shirt and cover Dan's swollen, engorged face. Even in the depths of his grief he had done that, because he didn't want his wife to see what had become of her firstborn. Now the bee had returned, and now it would kill me. I would die in convulsions on the bank, flopping just as a brookie flops after you take the hook out of its mouth.

As I sat there trembling on the edge of panic—ready to bolt to my feet and then bolt anywhere—there came a report from behind me. It was as sharp and peremptory as a pistol shot, but I knew it wasn't a pistol shot; it was someone clapping his hands. One single clap. At that moment, the bee tumbled off my nose and fell into my lap. It lay there on my pants with its legs sticking up and its stinger a threatless black thread against the old scuffed brown of the corduroy. It was dead as a doornail, I saw that at once. At the same moment, the pole gave another tug—the hardest yet—and I almost lost it again.

I grabbed it with both hands and gave it a big stupid yank that would have made my father clutch his head with both hands, if he had been there to see. A rainbow trout, a good bit larger than either of the ones I had already caught, rose out of the water in a wet flash, spraying fine drops of water from its tail—it looked like one of those fishing pictures they used to put on the covers of men's magazines like *True* and *Man's Adventure* back in the forties and fifties. At that moment hauling in a big one was about the last thing on my mind, however, and when the line snapped and the fish fell back into the stream, I barely noticed. I looked over my shoulder to see who had clapped. A man was standing above me, on the edge of the trees. His face was very long and pale. His black hair was combed tight against his skull and parted with rigorous care on the left side of his narrow head. He was very tall. He was wearing a black three-piece suit, and I knew right away that he was not a human being, because his eyes were the orangey red of flames in a woodstove. I don't mean just the irises, because he *had* no irises, and no pupils, and certainly no whites. His eyes were completely orange—an orange that shifted and flickered. And it's really too late not to say exactly what I mean, isn't it? He was on fire inside, and his eyes were like the little isinglass portholes you sometimes see in stove doors.

My bladder let go, and the scuffed brown the dead bee was lying on went a darker brown. I was hardly aware of what had happened, and I couldn't take my eyes off the man standing on top of the bank and looking down at me—the man who had apparently walked out of thirty miles of trackless western Maine woods in a fine black suit and narrow shoes of gleaming leather. I could see the watch chain looped across his vest glittering in the summer sunshine. There was not so much as a single pine needle on him. And he was smiling at me.

"Why, it's a fisherboy!" he cried in a mellow, pleasing voice. "Imagine that! Are we well met, fisherboy?"

"Hello, sir," I said. The voice that came out of me did not tremble, but it didn't sound like my voice, either. It sounded older. Like Dan's voice, maybe. Or my father's, even. And all I could think was that maybe he would let me go if I pretended not to see what he was. If I pretended I didn't see there were flames glowing and dancing where his eyes should have been.

"I've saved you a nasty sting, perhaps," he said, and then, to my horror, he came down the bank to where I sat with a dead bee in my wet lap and a bamboo fishing pole in my nerveless hands. His slick-soled city shoes should have slipped on the low, grassy weeds dressing the steep bank, but they didn't; nor did they leave tracks, I saw. Where his feet had touched—or seemed to touch—there was not a single broken twig, crushed leaf, or trampled shoe-shape.

Even before he reached me, I recognized the aroma baking up from the skin under the suit—the smell of burned matches. The smell of sulfur. The man in the black suit was the Devil. He had walked out of the deep woods between Motton and Kashwakamak, and now he was standing here beside me. From the corner of one eye I could see a hand as pale as the hand of a store-window dummy. The fingers were hideously long.

He hunkered beside me on his hams, his knees popping just as the knees of any normal man might, but when he moved his hands so they dangled between his knees, I saw that each of those long fingers ended in not a fingernail but a long yellow claw.

"You didn't answer my question, fisherboy," he said in his mellow voice. It was, now that I think of it, like the voice of one of those radio announcers on the big-band shows years later, the ones that would sell Geritol and Serutan and Ovaltine and Dr. Grabow pipes. "Are we well met?"

"Please don't hurt me," I whispered, in a voice so low I could barely hear it. I was more afraid than I could ever write down, more afraid than I want to remember. But I do. I do. It never crossed my mind to hope I was having a dream, although it might have, I suppose, if I had been older. But I was nine, and I knew the truth when it squatted down beside me. I knew a hawk from a handsaw, as my father would have said. The man who had come out of the woods on that Saturday afternoon in mid-summer was the Devil, and inside the empty holes of his eyes his brains were burning.

"Oh, do I smell something?" he asked, as if he hadn't heard me, although I knew he had. "Do I smell something . . . wet?"

He leaned toward me with his nose stuck out, like someone who means to smell a flower. And I noticed an awful thing; as the shadow of his head travelled over the bank, the grass beneath it turned yellow and died. He lowered his head toward my pants and sniffed. His glaring eyes half closed, as if he had inhaled some sublime aroma and wanted to concentrate on nothing but that.

"Oh, bad!" he cried. "Lovely-bad!" And then he chanted: "Opal! Diamond! Sapphire! Jade! I smell Gary's lemonade!" He threw himself on his back in the little flat place and laughed.

I thought about running, but my legs seemed two counties away from my brain. I wasn't crying, though; I had wet my pants, but I wasn't crying. I was too scared to cry. I suddenly knew that I was going to die, and probably painfully, but the worst of it was that that might not be the worst of it. The worst might come later. *After* I was dead.

He sat up suddenly, the smell of burnt matches fluffing out from his suit and making me feel gaggy in my throat. He looked at me solemnly from his narrow white face and burning eyes, but there was a sense of laughter about him, too. There was always that sense of laughter about him.

"Sad news, fisherboy," he said. "I've come with sad news."

I could only look at him—the black suit, the fine black shoes, the long white fingers that ended not in nails but in talons.

"Your mother is dead."

"No!" I cried. I thought of her making bread, of the curl lying across her forehead and just touching her eyebrow, of her standing there in the strong morning sunlight, and the terror swept over me again, but not for myself this time. Then I thought of how she'd looked when I set off with my fishing pole, standing in the kitchen doorway with her hand shading her eyes, and how she had looked to me in that moment like a photograph of someone you expected to see again but never did. "No, you lie!" I screamed.

He smiled—the sadly patient smile of a man who has often been accused falsely. "I'm afraid not," he said. "It was the same thing that happened to your brother, Gary. It was a bee."

"No, that's not true," I said, and now I *did* begin to cry. "She's old, she's thirty-five—if a bee sting could kill her the way it did Danny she would have died a long time ago, and you're a lying bastard!"

I had called the Devil a lying bastard. I was aware of this but the entire front of my mind was taken up by the enormity of what he'd said. My mother dead? He might as well have told me that the moon had fallen on Vermont. But I believed him. On some level I believed him completely, as we always believe, on some level, the worst thing our hearts can imagine.

"I understand your grief, little fisherboy, but that particular argument just doesn't hold water, I'm afraid." He spoke in a tone of bogus comfort that was horrible, maddening, without remorse or pity. "A man can go his whole life without seeing a mockingbird, you know, but does that mean mockingbirds don't exist? Your mother—"

A fish jumped below us. The man in the black suit frowned, then pointed a finger at it. The trout convulsed in the air, its body bending so strenuously that for a split second it appeared to be snapping at its own tail, and when it fell back into Castle Stream it was floating lifelessly. It struck the big gray rock where the waters divided, spun around twice in the whirlpool eddy that formed there and then floated away in the direction of Castle Rock. Meanwhile, the terrible stranger turned his burning eyes on me again, his thin lips pulled back from tiny rows of sharp teeth in a cannibal smile.

"Your mother simply went through her entire life without being stung by a bee," he said. "But then—less than an hour ago, actually—one flew in through the kitchen window while she was taking the bread out of the oven and putting it on the counter to cool."

I raised my hands and clapped them over my ears. He pursed his lips as if to whistle and blew at me gently. It was only a little breath, but the stench was foul beyond belief–clogged sewers, outhouses that have never known a single sprinkle of lime, dead chickens after a flood.

My hands fell away from the sides of my face.

"Good," he said. "You need to hear this, Gary; you need to hear this, my little fisherboy. It was your mother who passed that fatal weakness on to your brother. You got some of it, but you also got a protection from your father that poor Dan somehow missed." He pursed his lips again, only this time he made a cruelly comic little *tsk-tsk* sound instead of blowing his nasty breath at me. "So although I don't like to speak ill of the dead, it's almost a case of poetic justice, isn't it? After all, she killed your brother Dan as surely as if she had put a gun to his head and pulled the trigger."

"No," I whispered. "No, it isn't true."

"I assure you it is," he said. "The bee flew in the window and lit on her neck. She slapped at it before she even knew what she was doing–*you* were wiser than that, weren't you, Gary?–and the bee stung her. She felt her throat start to close up at once. That's what happens, you know, to people who can't tolerate bee venom. Their throats close and they drown in the open air. That's why Dan's face was so swollen and purple. That's why your father covered it with his shirt."

I stared at him, now incapable of speech. Tears streamed down my cheeks. I didn't want to believe him, and knew from my church schooling that the Devil is the father of lies, but I *did* believe him just the same.

"She made the most wonderfully awful noises," the man in the black suit said reflectively, "and she scratched her face quite badly, I'm afraid. Her eyes bulged out like a frog's eyes. She wept." He paused, then added: "She wept as she died, isn't that sweet? And here's the most beautiful thing of all. After she was dead, after she had been lying on the floor for fifteen minutes or so with no sound but the stove ticking and with that little thread of a bee stinger still poking out of the side of her neck–so small, so small–do you know what Candy Bill did? That little rascal licked away her tears. First on one side, and then on the other."

He looked out at the stream for a moment, his face sad and thoughtful. Then he turned back to me and his expression of bereavement disappeared like a dream. His face was as slack and as avid as the face of a corpse that has died hungry. His eyes blazed. I could see his sharp little teeth between his pale lips.

"I'm starving," he said abruptly. "I'm going to kill you and eat your guts, little fisherboy. What do you think about that?"

No, I tried to say, *please no*, but no sound came out. He meant to do it, I saw. He really meant to do it.

"I'm just so *hungry*," he said, both petulant and teasing. "And you won't want to live without your precious mommy, anyhow, take my word for it. Because your father's the sort of man who'll have to have some warm hole to stick it in, believe me, and if you're the only one available, you're the one who'll have to serve. I'll save you all the discomfort and unpleasantness. Also, you'll go to Heaven, think of that. Murdered souls *always* go to Heaven. So we'll both be serving God this afternoon, Gary. Isn't that nice?"

He reached for me again with his long, pale hands, and without thinking what I was doing, I flipped open the top of my creel, pawed all the way down to the bottom, and brought out the monster brookie I'd caught earlier—the one I should have been satisfied with. I held it out to him blindly, my fingers in the red slit of its belly, from which I had removed its insides as the man in the black suit had threatened to remove mine. The fish's glazed eye stared dreamily at me, the gold ring around the black center reminding me of my mother's wedding ring. And in that moment I saw her lying in her coffin with the sun shining off the wedding band and knew it was true—she had been stung by a bee, she had drowned in the warm, bread-smelling kitchen air, and Candy Bill had licked her dying tears from her swollen cheeks.

"Big fish!" the man in the black suit cried in a guttural, greedy voice. "Oh, *biiig fiiish!*"

He snatched it away from me and crammed it into a mouth that opened wider than any human mouth ever could. Many years later, when I was sixty-five (I know it was sixty-five, because that was the summer I retired from teaching) I went to the aquarium in Boston and finally saw a shark. The mouth of the man in the black suit was like that shark's mouth when it opened, only his gullet was blazing orange, the same color of his eyes, and I felt heat bake out of it and into my face, the way you feel a sudden wave of heat come pushing out of a fireplace when a dry piece of wood catches alight. And I didn't imagine that heat, either—I know I didn't—because just before he slid the head of my nineteen-inch brook trout between his gaping jaws, I saw the scales along the sides of the fish rise up and begin to curl like bits of paper floating over an open incinerator.

He slid the fish in like a man in a travelling show swallowing a sword. He didn't chew, and his blazing eyes bulged out, as if in effort. The fish went in and went in, his throat bulged as it slid down his gullet, and now he began to cry tears of his own—except his tears were blood, scarlet and thick.

I think it was the sight of those bloody tears that gave me my body back. I don't know why that should have been, but I think it was. I bolted to my feet like a Jack released from its box, turned with my bamboo pole still in one hand, and fled up the bank, bending over and tearing tough bunches of weeds out with my free hand in an effort to get up the slope more quickly.

He made a strangled, furious noise—the sound of any man with his mouth too full—and I looked back just as I got to the top. He was coming after me, the back of his suit coat flapping and his thin gold watch chain flashing and winking in the sun. The tail of the fish was still protruding from his mouth and I could smell the rest of it, roasting in the oven of his throat.

He reached for me, groping with his talons, and I fled along the top of the bank. After a hundred yards or so I found my voice and went to screaming—screaming in fear, of course, but also screaming in grief for my beautiful dead mother.

He was coming after me. I could hear snapping branches and whipping bushes, but I didn't look back again. I lowered my head, slitted my eyes against the bushes and low-hanging branches along the stream's bank, and ran as fast as I could. And at every step I expected to feel his hands descending on my shoulders, pulling me back into a final burning hug.

That didn't happen. Some unknown length of time later—it couldn't have been longer than five or ten minutes, I suppose, but it seemed like forever—I saw the bridge through layerings of leaves and firs. Still screaming, but breathlessly now, sounding like a teakettle that has almost boiled dry, I reached this second, steeper bank and charged up.

Halfway to the top, I slipped to my knees, looked over my shoulder, and saw the man in the black suit almost at my heels, his white face pulled into a convulsion of fury and greed. His cheeks were splattered with his bloody tears and his shark's mouth hung open like a hinge.

"*Fisherboy!*" he snarled, and started up the bank after me, grasping at my foot with one long hand. I tore free, turned, and threw my fishing pole at him. He batted it down easily, but it tangled his feet up somehow and he went to his knees. I didn't wait to see any more; I turned and bolted to the top of the slope. I almost slipped at the very top, but managed to grab one of the support struts running beneath the bridge and save myself.

"You can't get away, fisherboy!" he cried from behind. He sounded furious, but he also sounded as if he were laughing. "It takes more than a mouthful of trout to fill *me* up!"

"Leave me alone!" I screamed back at him. I grabbed the bridge's railing and threw myself over it in a clumsy somersault, filling my hands with splinters and bumping my head so hard on the boards when I came down that I saw stars. I rolled over on my belly and began crawling. I lurched to my feet just before I got to the end of the bridge, stumbled once, found my rhythm, and then began to run. I ran as only nine-year-old boys can run, which is like the wind. It felt as if my feet only touched the ground with every third or fourth stride, and, for all I know, that may be true. I ran straight up the right-hand wheel rut in the road, ran until my temples pounded and my eyes pulsed in their sockets, ran until I had a hot stitch in my left side from the bottom of my ribs to my armpit, ran until I could taste blood and something like metal shavings in the back of my throat. When I couldn't run anymore I stumbled to a stop and looked back over my shoulder, puffing and blowing like a wind-broken horse. I was convinced I would see him standing right there behind me in his natty black suit, the watch chain a glittering loop across his vest and not a hair out of place.

But he was gone. The road stretching back toward Castle Stream between the darkly massed pines and spruces was empty. And yet I sensed him somewhere near in those woods, watching me with his grassfire eyes, smelling of burned matches and roasted fish.

I turned and began walking as fast as I could, limping a little—I'd pulled muscles in both legs, and when I got out of bed the next morning I was so sore I could barely walk. I kept looking over my shoulder, needing again and again to verify that the road behind me was still empty. It was each time I looked, but those backward glances seemed to increase my fear rather than lessen it. The firs looked darker, massier, and I kept imagining what lay behind the trees that marched beside the road—long, tangled corridors of forest, leg-breaking deadfalls, ravines where anything might live. Until that Saturday in 1914, I had thought that bears were the worst thing the forest could hold.

A mile or so farther up the road, just beyond the place where it came out of the woods and joined the Geegan Flat Road, I saw my father walking toward me and whistling "The Old Oaken Bucket." He was carrying his own rod, the one with the fancy spinning reel from Monkey Ward. In his other hand he had his creel, the one with the ribbon my mother had woven through the handle back when Dan was still alive. "Dedicated to Jesus" that ribbon said. I had been walking, but when I saw him I started to run again, screaming *Dad! Dad! Dad!* at the top of my lungs and staggering from side to side on my tired, sprung legs like a drunken sailor. The expression of surprise on his face when he recognized me might have been comical under other circumstances. He dropped his rod and creel into the road without so much as a downward glance at them and ran to me. It was the fastest I ever saw my dad run in his life; when we came together it was a wonder the impact didn't knock us both senseless, and I struck my face on his belt buckle hard enough to start a little nosebleed. I didn't notice that until later, though. Right then I only reached out my arms and clutched him as hard as I could. I held on and rubbed my hot face back and forth against his belly, covering his old blue workshirt with blood and tears and snot.

"Gary, what is it? What happened? Are you all right?"

"Ma's dead!" I sobbed. "I met a man in the woods and he told me! Ma's dead! She got stung by a bee and it swelled her all up just like what happened to Dan, and she's dead! She's on the kitchen floor and Candy Bill . . . licked the t-t-tears . . . off her . . . off her . . ."

Face was the last word I had to say, but by then my chest was hitching so bad I couldn't get it out. My own tears were flowing again, and my dad's startled, frightened face had blurred into three overlapping images. I began to howl—not like a little kid who's skinned his knee but like a dog that's seen something bad by moonlight—and my father pressed my head against his hard flat stomach again. I slipped out from under his hand, though, and looked back over my shoulder. I wanted to make sure the man in the black suit wasn't coming. There was no sign of him; the road winding back into the woods was completely empty. I promised myself I would never go back down that road again, not ever, no matter what, and I suppose now that God's greatest blessing to His creatures below is that they can't see the future. It might have broken my mind if I had known I *would* be going back down that road, and not two hours later. For that moment, though, I was only relieved to see we were still alone. Then I thought of my mother—my beautiful dead mother—and laid my face back against my father's stomach and bawled some more.

"Gary, listen to me," he said a moment or two later. I went on bawling. He gave me a little longer to do that, then reached down and lifted my chin so he could look down into my face and I could look up into his. "Your mom's fine," he said.

I could only look at him with tears streaming down my cheeks. I didn't believe him.

"I don't know who told you different or what kind of dirty dog would want to cut a scare like that into a little boy, but I swear to God your mother's fine."

"But . . . but he said . . ."

"I don't care *what* he said. I got back from Eversham's earlier than I expected—he doesn't want to sell any cows, it's all just talk—and decided I had time to catch up with you. I got my pole and my creel and your mother made us a couple of jelly fold-overs. Her new bread. Still warm. So she was fine half an hour ago, Gary, and there's nobody knows any different that's come from this direction, I guarantee you. Not in just half an hour's time." He looked over my shoulder. "Who was this man? And where was he? I'm going to find him and thrash him within an inch of his life."

I thought a thousand things in just two seconds—that's what it seemed like, anyway—but the last thing I thought was the most powerful: if my Dad met up with the man in the black suit, I didn't think my Dad would be the one to do the thrashing. Or the walking away.

I kept remembering those long white fingers, and the talons at the ends of them.

"Gary?"

"I don't know that I remember," I said.

"Were you where the stream splits? The big rock?"

I could never lie to my father when he asked a direct question—not to save his life or mine. "Yes, but don't go down there." I seized his arm with both hands and tugged it hard. "Please don't. He was a scary man." Inspiration struck like an illuminating lightning bolt. "I think he had a gun."

He looked at me thoughtfully. "Maybe there wasn't a man," he said, lifting his voice a little on the last word and turning it into something that was almost but not a quite a question. "Maybe you fell asleep while you were fishing, son, and had a bad dream. Like the ones you had about Danny last winter."

I *had* had a lot of bad dreams about Dan last winter, dreams where I would open the door to our closet or to the dark, fruity interior of the cider shed and see him standing there and looking at me out of his purple strangulated face; from many of these dreams I had awakened screaming, and awakened my parents as well. I had fallen asleep on the bank of the stream for a little while, too—dozed off, anyway—but I hadn't dreamed, and I was sure I had awakened just before the man in the black suit clapped the bee dead, sending it tumbling off my nose and into my lap. I hadn't dreamed him the way I had dreamed Dan, I was quite sure of that, although my meeting with him had already attained a dreamlike quality in my mind, as I suppose supernatural occurrences always must. But if my Dad thought that the man had only existed in my own head, that might be better. Better for him.

"It might have been, I guess," I said.

"Well, we ought to go back and find your rod and your creel."

He actually started in that direction, and I had to tug frantically at his arm to stop him again and turn him back toward me.

"Later," I said. "Please, Dad? I want to see Mother. I've got to see her with my own eyes."

He thought that over, then nodded. "Yes, I suppose you do. We'll go home first, and get your rod and creel later."

So we walked back to the farm together, my father with his fish pole propped on his shoulder just like one of my friends, me carrying his creel, both of us eating folded-over slices of my mother's bread smeared with black-currant jam.

"Did you catch anything?" he asked as we came in sight of the barn.

"Yes, sir," I said. "A rainbow. Pretty good-sized." *And a brookie that was a lot bigger,* I thought but didn't say.

"That's all? Nothing else?"

"After I caught it I fell asleep." This was not really an answer but not really a lie, either.

"Lucky you didn't lose your pole. You didn't, did you, Gary?"

"No, sir," I said, very reluctantly. Lying about that would do no good even if I'd been able to think up a whopper—not if he was set on going back to get my creel anyway, and I could see by his face that he was.

Up ahead, Candy Bill came racing out of the back door, barking his shrill bark and wagging his whole rear end back and forth the way Scotties do when they're excited. I couldn't wait any longer. I broke away from my father and ran to the house, still lugging his creel and still convinced, in my heart of hearts, that I was going to find my mother dead on the kitchen floor with her face swollen and purple, as Dan's had been when my father carried him in from the west field, crying and calling the name of Jesus.

But she was standing at the counter, just as well and fine as when I had left her, humming a song as she shelled peas into a bowl. She looked around at me, first in surprise and then in fright as she took in my wide eyes and pale cheeks.

"Gary, what is it? What's the matter?"

I didn't answer, only ran to her and covered her with kisses. At some point my father came in and said, "Don't worry, Lo—he's all right. He just had one of his bad dreams, down there by the brook."

"Pray God it's the last of them," she said, and hugged me tighter while Candy Bill danced around our feet, barking his shrill bark.

"You don't have to come with me if you don't want to, Gary," my father said, although he had already made it clear that he thought I should— that I should go back, that I should face my fear, as I suppose folks would say nowadays. That's very well for fearful things that are make-believe, but two hours hadn't done much to change my conviction that the man in the black suit had been real. I wouldn't be able to convince my father of that, though. I don't think there was a nine-year-old who ever lived would have been able to convince his father he'd seen the Devil walking out of the woods in a black suit.

"I'll come," I said. I had come out of the house to join him before he left, mustering all my courage to get my feet moving, and now we were standing by the chopping block in the side yard, not far from the wood- pile.

"What you got behind your back?" he asked.

I brought it out slowly. I would go with him, and I would hope the man in the black suit with the arrow-straight part down the left side of his head was gone. But if he wasn't, I wanted to be prepared. As prepared as I could be, anyway. I had the family Bible in the hand I had brought out from behind my back. I'd set out just to bring my New Testament, which I had won for memorizing the most psalms in the Thursday-night Youth Fellowship competition (I managed eight, although most of them except the Twenty-third had floated out of my mind in a week's time), but the little red Testament didn't seem like enough when you were maybe going to face the Devil himself, not even when the words of Jesus were marked out in red ink.

My father looked at the old Bible, swollen with family documents and pictures, and I thought he'd tell me to put it back, but he didn't. A look of mixed grief and sympathy crossed his face, and he nodded. "All right," he said. "Does your mother know you took that?"

"No, sir."

He nodded again. "Then we'll hope she doesn't spot it gone before we get back. Come on. And don't drop it."

Half an hour or so later, the two of us stood on the bank at the place where Castle Stream forked, and at the flat place where I'd had my encounter with the man with the red-orange eyes. I had my bamboo rod in my hand—I'd picked it up below the bridge—and my creel lay down below, on the flat place. Its wicker top was flipped back. We stood looking down, my father and I, for a long time, and neither of us said anything.

Opal! Diamond! Sapphire! Jade! I smell Gary's lemonade! That had been his unpleasant little poem, and once he had recited it, he had thrown himself on his back, laughing like a child who has just discovered he has enough courage to say bathroom words like shit or piss. The flat place down there was as green and lush as any place in Maine that the sun can get to in early July. Except where the stranger had lain. There the grass was dead and yellow in the shape of a man.

I was holding our lumpy old family Bible straight out in front of me with both thumbs pressing so hard on the cover that they were white. It was the way Mama Sweet's husband, Norville, held a willow fork when he was trying to dowse somebody a well.

"Stay here," my father said at last, and skidded sideways down the bank, digging his shoes into the rich soft soil and holding his arms out for balance. I stood where I was, holding the Bible stiffly out at the ends of my arms, my heart thumping. I don't know if I had a sense of being watched that time or not; I was too scared to have a sense of anything, except for a sense of wanting to be far away from that place and those woods.

My dad bent down, sniffed at where the grass was dead, and grimaced. I knew what he was smelling; something like burnt matches. Then he grabbed my creel and came on back up the bank, hurrying. He snagged one fast look over his shoulder to make sure nothing was coming along behind. Nothing was. When he handed me the creel, the lid was still hanging back on its cunning little leather hinges. I looked inside and saw nothing but two handfuls of grass.

"Thought you said you caught a rainbow," my father said, "but maybe you dreamed that, too."

Something in his voice stung me. "No, sir," I said. "I caught one."

"Well, it sure as hell didn't flop out, not if it was gutted and cleaned. And you wouldn't put a catch into your fisherbox without doing that, would you, Gary? I taught you better than that."

"Yes, sir, you did, but—"

"So if you didn't dream catching it and if it was dead in the box, something must have come along and eaten it," my father said, and then he grabbed another quick glance over his shoulder, eyes wide, as if he had heard something move in the woods. I wasn't exactly surprised to see crops of sweat standing out on his forehead like big clear jewels. "Come on," he said. "Let's get the hell out of here."

I was for that, and we went back along the bank to the bridge, walking quick without speaking. When we got there, my dad dropped to one knee and examined the place where we'd found my rod. There was another patch of dead grass here, and the lady's slipper was all brown and curled in on itself, as if a blast of heat had charred it. I looked in my empty creel again. "He must have gone back and eaten my other fish, too," I said.

My father looked up at me. "*Other* fish!"

"Yes, sir. I didn't tell you, but I caught a brookie, too. A big one. He was awful angry, that fella." I wanted to say more, and the words trembled just behind my lips but in the end I didn't.

We climbed up the bridge and helped each other over the railing. My father took my creel, looked into it, then went to the railing and threw it over. I came up beside him in time to see it splash down and float away like a boat, riding lower and lower in the stream as the water poured in between the wicker weavings. . . .

"It smelled bad," my father said, but he didn't look at me when he said it, and his voice sounded oddly defensive. It was the only time I ever heard him speak just that way.

"Yes, sir."

"We'll tell your mother we couldn't find it. If she asks. If she doesn't ask, we won't tell her anything."

"No, sir, we won't."

And she didn't and we didn't, and that's the way it was.

That day in the woods is eighty years gone, and for many of the years in between I have never even thought of it—not awake, at least. Like any other man or woman who ever lived, I can't say about my dreams, not for sure. But now I'm old, and I dream awake, it seems. My infirmities have crept up like waves that will soon take a child's abandoned sand castle, and my memories have also crept up, making me think of some old rhyme that went, in part, "Just leave them alone / And they'll come home / Wagging their tails behind them." I remember meals I ate, games I played, girls I kissed in the school cloakroom when we played post-office, boys I chummed with, the first drink I ever took, the first cigarette I ever smoked (cornshuck behind Dicky Hamner's pig shed, and I threw up). Yet of all the memories the one of the man in the black suit is the strongest, and glows with its own spectral, haunted light. He was real, he was the Devil, and that day I was either his errand or his luck. I feel more and more strongly that escaping him was my luck—*just* luck, and not the intercession of the God I have worshiped and sung hymns to all my life.

As I lie here in my nursing-home room, and in the ruined sand castle that is my body, I tell myself that I need not fear the Devil—that I have lived a good, kindly life, and I need not fear the Devil. Sometimes I remind myself that it was I, not my father, who finally coaxed my mother back to church later on that summer. In the dark, however, these thoughts have no power to ease or comfort. In the dark comes a voice that whispers that the nine-year-old fisherboy I was had done nothing for which he might legitimately fear the Devil, either, and yet the Devil came—to him. And in the dark I sometimes hear that voice drop even lower, into ranges that are inhuman. *Big fish!* it whispers in tones of hushed greed, and all the truths of the moral world fall to ruin before its hunger.

We journey next to a fishing village in Russia. The protagonists are commercial fishermen, and the plot centers on trying to save a dolphin trapped in a net in the icy waters of the Black Sea. Author Joyce Renwick was a student of literature at the University of Virginia and Lincoln College, Oxford, but her profession was registered nurse. She was working as a nurse at Middlebury College when this story, her first, was written. Initially published in Choice, *a former literary magazine from the State University of New York at Binghamton, it also appeared in* The Best American Short Stories 1982.

Joyce Renwick

THE DOLPHIN STORY (1980)

DICRAN STOOD ON THE PORCH, the mug of hot, strong tea in his hands, and watched the choppy black water before him. The stars were still out. A cold March land wind, carrying the familiar smells of garlic and sweet tea, whipped through the ancient town at his back. The smells seeped from the kitchens, the samovars of Kobuleti, this Black Sea fishing town that had been the home of his family for centuries. A bell clanged, but the call to the boats had not yet sounded. This morning, as he watched the rising tide, he knew the fishing would not be good. He knew they should already be moving out to the fishing grounds, and he was angry again at the fools of the Fishing Collective who knew nothing of the sea. They knew politics, that was all—not the tides, the seasons, the directions of the wind.

The samovar was still boiling in the house behind him. Someone would find it. He had passed through the dark house, hitting a chair leg with his boot, stopping only long enough in the kitchen to open the small paper sack, spoon the dry, black tea into a pot and wait until it was drinkable. When he had entered the room he'd noticed a flicker from the charcoal fire under the samovar, still warm from the night before. Mr. Noblakoff had been up late playing his balalaika, and Dicran had not slept well, hearing the laughing and singing rising from below. While he waited impatiently for the tea to steep, he'd felt around on the dark shelf for a mug. He'd poured the black tea carefully before coming out on the porch, trying to be quiet to avoid meeting anyone in the kitchen, though it would be unusual for any of the others to be up before the sun.

Although the house had once been his, he didn't associate with the other roomers. Now only a few things were left of the old life. Perhaps he still had Lizaveta's nest of dolls, he wasn't sure. The dim lantern hung on a post outside the house, and in his room under the bed he kept the handmade chessboard that had been his father's.

At last the call to the boat—a horn blared from the pier below him—and then a half-dozen progressively fainter sounds came out of the darkness down the coast. No doubt Captain Yorkovitya enjoyed sounding the call with the other captains of the Fishing Collective. Once, with a wave of his arm, he'd told Dicran that each morning he imagined he was an ancient seaman, blowing a conch shell horn, calling to the argonauts to sail over these same waters.

Fool, Dicran had thought, and he had turned away and looked down at his feet, wondering if the line was from one of the Captain's speeches. It had the ring of preparation, repetition. It was probably part of one of his speeches for the Collective—no, not serious enough for that—for the café late at night, then, when everyone was drunk after a long dinner. He had heard that the Captain never ate at the café—he ate at home with his fat wife and all their children—but he would come in later when the fishermen were drunk, stand on a chair and test his speeches, bowing and smiling to their applause. Dicran was sure it was the speeches that had won him his position. The Captain was a small man, extremely careful of his clothes and mustache, unlike most of the men. Dicran supposed he had sea experience, though it seemed that without warning he was suddenly Captain. Although Dicran rarely went to the meetings, he'd always thought his friend Ivan would be appointed. He had taught Ivan all he knew.

The horn sounded again and voices rose from the dock below. Dicran spilled his cold tea over the railing, flung open the door to the kitchen, and tossed the mug into the house. It landed on something soft. No matter. He pulled on his knitted cap, yanked his collar up around his ears, and swung down the yielding steps to the pier.

Ivan was pulling the nets down from the pilings where they had been hung last night to dry. His light hair curled up around his cap and his nose made a shadow across his cheek in the lantern light.

"Hey, Dicran, smile," he said in greeting.

Dicran nodded but didn't smile. "Too early. Mr. Noblakoff played his damn balalaika again half the night."

"Ah." Ivan, still smiling, looked down at the net. He pulled at the cork floats, and then stooped to pick up a suspicious-looking one. It crumbled in his hand.

Dicran took his place beside Ivan. Pulling the net section by section between his extended arms, he spread the jute, testing for weak spots, looking for tears. They had used the same nets for as long as he could remember, repairing, renewing them until they were not the original nets at all but a patchwork, from the sweet-smelling new rope to the musty gray of the oldest sections. He pulled a fold open before him and turned it toward the lantern light. Was this a portion his father had mended or a section his grandfather had made? He couldn't tell.

Ivan was bent over the net. He replaced the float and then rose to help Dicran, as the rest of the men dragged the last of the nets on board. Ivan cast off the lines. He threw them to Dicran, who caught the lines in midair and coiled them like fat snakes on the deck. After the first few coughs of the engine, the fishing boat rattled in idle.

The tide was rising rapidly. Pulled on board by one of the crew, Ivan turned to talk to the man as Captain Yorkovitya came running down the pier. No one offered the Captain a hand—he didn't seem to need one—and he leaped into the boat just as it cleared the dock. The small man nodded and saluted one and then another of the men. He stroked down his mustache and muttered, "Morning, comrades, morning," as he stepped over feet and sprawled legs on the way to the pilothouse.

One of the younger crewmen, sitting with his friends at the stern, shouted to Dicran, asking why he had missed last night's meeting. As the young man waited for a reply, some of the others stopped to listen.

"The nets needed mending," Dicran shouted above the drone of the engines. He turned so the man would not question him further.

Ivan had been sitting with the group of younger men. He rose to his feet and joined Dicran at the bow. "Will the weather break today?" he asked, wiping his hands on his slicker.

Dicran looked at the gray clouds hugging the early morning moon and shook his head. The wind seemed to sit heavily on his shoulders. After circling the Red Sea, sweeping over Iran and the yellow hills of Turkey, it now blew its stale breath at their backs. Dicran knew these winds as he knew the sturgeon and herring. He could point out the winds and weather as he could point to the slick of the fishes' feeding spots even in murky water, not needing to rely on the gulls to signal their presence.

"Overcast and cold. The fishing won't be good," he said.

Ivan studied the sky for a moment, then rejoined the small group of men at the stern. The young men were lively, passing a flask, laughing at a skinny boy doing a jig on the deck, hands in pockets, boot laces flying. The older men sat apart, against the gunnel on overturned boxes and bait pails. They'd be telling the old stories again. The few oldest men sat quietly, leather-skinned and red-cheeked, bundled against the cold, their ropy brown hands clasping their knees.

He remembered how his father had looked—mornings going out to the fishing grounds, and evenings in the flickering light of the lantern. Each night after mending the nets, they had played chess in the old house. When his father died, Dicran had abandoned the nets for long walks. One night he'd discovered the chess games in the park.

He supposed the old man had taught him, almost wordlessly, about the winds, the fish. He never mentioned his father to the others. The prejudice against the man had been maintained—like the nets—in additions and repairs until there was nothing more of the original than a remembered grudge. Years ago the old man had spoken strongly against the Revolution; he had wanted no more killing. Dicran did not remember standing on the shore as a child watching the dock burn, although his father had told him he had been there and both of them had escaped unharmed before the flames blocked their exit. Someone had told him his father had shouted over and over to Lizaveta to jump. Dicran's sister had been playing at the end of the dock as they mended nets, unaware of the person with a torch in the skiff below her. She had cried, then screamed, but wouldn't jump off the high dock into the water. Dicran didn't remember any of it. He had watched the old man become quiet, mending nets in the evening, weaving his convictions into a web of silence floating noiseless as nets in the sea.

He moved further forward in the bow and watched pink caps form on the water as the moon disappeared and the sun crept over the horizon. Ivan left the stern, slapping one of the crewmen on the back as he rose, and joined Dicran.

"Smile, Dicran, the nets are almost out." Ivan leaned against the gunnel. His yellow slicker contrasted with the damp, dark wood behind him.

"Smile?" Dicran looked at him. "I know your smiles, Ivan. You think the whole world's been drinking with Yolana." He took a tobacco pouch from his pocket and offered it. Ivan shook his head.

It was getting light, the rising sun making a path in front of them. Dicran knew soon it would be his turn to work, to find the school, pull the purse line, haul in the encircling net over and over again until the hull, full of fish, settled low in the water. In front of them gulls swooped at the debris on the water—a tree branch, strange out so far, and a few weathered boards, half submerged. Looking at the debris as they steered around it, he remembered something he had once seen in a book, a sketch showing the feeding cycle of the oceans, and he imagined, deep below the green limb and the rotting wood they had passed, small particles of life being carried in poorly filtered light toward the jellyfish that would engulf them. He saw oysters closing their ruffled shells, except for one, a pearly eye open to innumerable species of fish swimming into the dark caves of larger and larger mouths, moving in his mind, from small to large, large to small, like the legless wooden dolls of his sister's childhood, arms and smiles painted on, one within the other, enameled, bright-colored, smaller and smaller until he remembered she had picked out a doll smaller than her thumb, and she had squealed with pleasure at the toy he had given her.

Years later, Moira had squealed too with pleasure at this doll, or perhaps in pleasure with him when she had seen the child's things the day she visited him in the old house by the pier. They had had tea that day, and she had insisted on making it. He had complained about the leaves she never seemed to be able to strain completely from the tea. He had wanted it pure, clear yellow, and she had been unable after three pots to please him, or keep her patience. Although she was the only woman he had allowed himself to love, he had demanded perfection and it had been too much for her. Memories can be perfect, she had told him, never people. He did not remember it clearly. Moira—had she too been lost in the fire? No, that fire had been of a different kind, but she was gone and just as well extinguished from him now as if she had been on that flaming dock with his sister.

"Dicran."

Ivan was beside him. He had forgotten.

"Dicran." Ivan was smiling, his eyes slits on his large face. "You should have heard the Captain's speech at the meeting last night." Ivan wiped the back of his hand across his mouth to cover his smile.

Dicran watched him.

Ivan laughed. "Coming out we were talking about it. The speech was the funniest in a long time, one of the Captain's best. You should have seen his face, his gestures." The winch screeched behind them, peeling out the net.

"In the middle of the meeting he stood up on his chair and everyone—"

"I've heard enough of them," Dicran interrupted.

The nets out, conversations died away and it was quiet except for the screeching gulls and the water slapping at the hull. Dicran pulled on his pipe. The sturgeon were there, let the nets do their work. He would wait. He knew this was a lie, the nets didn't work at all, it was the action of men, the laying out and pulling in that produced the catch. Without the lines, the winches, the sweat, the nets would do nothing more than float away with the tide, imprisoning, entangling without purpose.

He sat back against the dark bulkhead, the chill wind still pressing against his cheeks. Even though the sun had risen, it had not gotten much warmer. He brought out his worn pouch and worked cold fingers into the tobacco, pushing the dry apple slice aside and filling the bowl with the black pungent shreds. He looked over the water. At some distance he thought he saw the silver back of a dolphin.

He strained to see, thinking it might be one of the group they usually saw playing in the evening as they were coming in with the catch. Ever since he was a boy he had imagined they called to him, a high, soft sound through their blowholes. He leaned forward, seeing one dorsal fin and then another coming up fast. He moved closer to the rail and then called to Ivan, who looked up drowsily and then made his way through the men to the ladder.

"At least twenty of them," Dicran said as Ivan pulled himself up beside him.

Ivan looked over the water. "Maybe thirty."

Dicran heard the rest of the crew moving and talking behind them. They too were leaning over the side to watch the school of dolphins approaching the boat. They all knew dolphins meant good luck and fair weather. Perhaps their fishing would be good today after all.

Ivan was shaking his head and smiling. He clapped Dicran on the shoulder. "The crew's making more noise than the women who wait at night for the boats to come in."

Dicran looked at him. "Women, that's all you think about."

"Not women now. Listen to the crew, the dolphins," Ivan said, smiling and leaning over the gunnel.

Dicran grunted.

The dolphins seemed to be coming at them from all directions, crowding around the boat, jumping and calling, squealing and clicking, grunting and sculling, moving to the north and back again. Their sounds were high-pitched, hysterical. They seemed to have forgotten those manlike sounds, those smiles and hellos the men knew so well.

Some of the crewmen moved to the bow with Dicran and Ivan. They laughed and shouted above the sounds of the dolphins swimming below them in sleek-bodied frenzy, the water splashing in the men's faces as the dolphins jumped high above the surface and plunged deep again. Dicran had never seen a school of dolphins this close before, never before felt from them this urgency. Seeing other fishing boats in the distance, he wondered why the dolphins were circling their boat, jumping, splashing, inundating them with bursting, pulsating sound. There was no doubt they were begging the men to follow.

Dicran put down his pipe as he noticed one of the dolphins backwatering and looking directly at him. It was larger than the others, almost completely out of the water, resting on its churning tail. The dolphin looked at him directly, the eyes wide and circled in black, the gaze not the dead stare of a blind man but the look of something seeing and perceiving. Dicran felt momentarily frightened.

Shaking his head, he patted at his jacket until he found the breast pocket, where he deposited his cold pipe. He backed up against the bulkhead, not looking at the dolphin, trying not to listen to his whistle, a piercing falsetto, unlike the others. He watched Ivan go down to the aft deck, watched him pointing to the water and turning his head this way and that as he talked to the rest of the men.

Captain Yorkovitya burst out of the pilothouse, pulling on his windbreaker. The shrill sounds of the dolphins, overriding the men's excited talk, was confusing, deafening. Dicran couldn't hear what Ivan was saying. He watched his friend talk seriously to the Captain. He shook his head and pointed alternately at the water, the net, the dolphins. Soon the Captain, too, was shaking his head affirmatively. The Captain, Dicran thought, is a man easily persuaded. He must think he is going to benefit from this, although Dicran could not imagine at the moment what the benefit would be.

He slid down the ladder and joined the group around Ivan and the Captain. As soon as he arrived he was sorry; he recognized a look on the Captain's face that always preceded a speech.

"Comrades," the Captain began, surveying the crewmen, who were gathered around him, talking among themselves. He dumped a bait pail over, then stood on it. "Comrades," he shouted. He raised an arm to gain their attention.

Dicran groaned. Ivan smiled and put a finger to his lips.

"Often," the Captain exclaimed, "we find we must deviate from the line of duty to answer the call of a greater duty."

The men were standing in small groups with their arms folded, solemn looks on their faces. When the Captain looked away they rolled their eyes at their companions.

The Captain swung his arm toward the dolphins who were circling the boat. "Today this greater duty is upon us." His face was somber as he lowered his arm and then raised his hand over his heart. Dicran looked at his boots.

The Captain pointed to the dolphins and then panned the group for their reactions. Satisfied with their serious expressions, he continued. "You might ask, can we take time to follow the call of these intelligent beings? Can we waste the Collective's time to pursue an unknown mission we are being so persuasively called to accomplish? I say this—" he turned to look at Dicran—"this is our universal duty: to repay these dolphins, who through the ages have been the friends of men." He took a deep breath. "They are not harnessed by man, nor are they beaten down nor domesticated, no, they roam free in the great sea, playing and loving; it is their life."

"Playing and loving," Dicran heard Ivan whisper to the squint-eyed man at his right, "I like that." The man burst into a laugh, then quickly shielded his face with his hand. They composed themselves and looked back at the Captain, who was still speaking and swinging his arms in grandiose gestures, to the concealed amusement of the men. Dicran stepped back from the group.

"But sometimes," the Captain was saying, "the dolphins find they have need of us. They do not ask often; they do not expect gratitude for the numerous friendly acts of the past." The Captain looked at Ivan and smiled. "Remember the dolphin who carried the boy to school over the Bosphorus. The dolphin died when he discovered the boy drowned."

A tall man at the front leaned over to say something to his shorter companion. The Captain continued, "Remember the dolphins who guided to shore the horses pushed overboard from sinking ships; dolphins who supported unconscious sailors to the safety of other islands; dolphins who herd mullets to shore as Mauritian fishermen beat the water with clubs . . ."

"Of course they aren't dumb," Dicran mumbled as he moved up beside Ivan. "We all know this."

Ivan, still watching the Captain, put a hand on Dicran's arm and whispered, "He's enjoying himself, watch."

The Captain was swaying as he spoke. "There are times when we must put business aside and lift the standard of universality." He lifted an imaginary standard high above his head. "Life is dull enough without ignoring dolphins."

There was silence, and then someone or something whistled from the back of the crowd. Another whistle rose here, and then there, until the whole crew was whistling and stomping their boots on the deck, cheering the Captain, who smiled broadly at his men. One man began a Georgian dance. He fell over almost before he began—pushed by his laughing companions. The Captain watched from atop his bait pail. Dicran, parallel to the Captain, leaned against the side of the boat. He cleared his throat and looked at the Captain's shoe for a long time before he turned and spat in the water.

Dicran tried to speak over the noisy crew. He wondered why he was the only one who was concerned about their fishing. As he watched the Captain move the bait pail out of the way, he thought of dolphin fish. Not these large intelligent mammals who were circling their boat now, but the blunt-nosed fish that hide under floating debris and, when caught, flash rainbows of yellow, purple, and blue. After a few minutes in the air they become gray and soft, and if the cook's silver spoon turns black in the pan, they're quickly thrown back to sea. "We should leave them to their own lives," Dicran shouted over the noise of the crew and the squealing dolphins. "The fishing hasn't been good. There's sturgeon out there. We'll never meet our quota." No one seemed to hear him.

Some of the men were leaning over the side, trying to touch the dolphins for good luck; someone was passing a flask, and one man—really no more than a boy—was doing back flips, landing with a thud each time on the deck. Two of the men were clumsily pulling Captain Yorkovitya with them to the stern.

Ivan remained behind. He put his hand on Dicran's back and spoke softly. "Dicran, join us—here, have a drink." He offered him his flask.

Dicran shook his head. "No."

"All right, all right." Ivan moved closer. "For the women who loved you." Ivan smiled.

"What women?" Dicran pulled his collar up around his neck.

"Moira did once." Ivan smiled again.

"You're never serious." Dicran scowled and slapped his leg, then pulled out his pipe. He watched the water churning with dolphins.

"The largest dolphin," Ivan continued, "listen to his whistle—can you ignore that?"

"Yes." Dicran dug into his pocket for his pouch.

Ivan pounded his fist on the gunnel. "We should follow them. Where's your sense of adventure?"

"Where's your sense of duty? We have a quota."

"Quota—" Ivan laughed. "You heard the Captain."

Dicran looked over the water. He saw a dolphin flipping like a silver coin on the horizon. The son of Poseidon, he thought. As he looked, more dolphins were appearing, coming over the horizon like a silver horde. He saw not porpoises, not the wheel-like rolls of the puffing pigs, but the high-jumping movements of dolphins. Their slender bodies flashing, their flukes twisting above the surface, they cavorted, calling to him. Once he had heard that, years ago, a hundred thousand dolphins had gathered at one time around a ship, their numbers increasing, their pulsing sonar calling more and more of their kind. A hundred thousand dolphins–their sounds deafening the men on the ship who wandered lost at sea until the dolphins realized they had confounded them. The dolphins had gathered and, pressing their smiling beaks against the ship, pushed it to shore. He didn't believe it. Yet now, seeing the hordes coming, he wanted to believe. But perhaps it was not hordes, perhaps it was only one more dolphin he saw, and then another and another, and he imagined hordes.

Ivan clapped Dicran on the arm, slid down the ladder and joined the others at the stern who were busy pulling in the net.

The crewmen quickly sorted the catch and, and leaving the trash fish to the gulls, followed the dolphins northward. The sun was high now, but the air was cool. The engines sputtered. Dicran took off his jacket and opened his collar. There was little wind, surprising on a March day, no more breeze than that made by the movement of the boat, and no sounds except for the entreaties of the dolphins who swam ahead, criss-crossing their bow. Above them, stillness, as if a portion of the wind was holding its breath until they passed. There were no turbulent winds from Siberia, not the cold anticyclone common this time of year, only an almost imperceptible breeze from the west. To Dicran it smelled of the foehn wind, warm from the mountains of the Crimea. Moira had been born there. "No matter," he said aloud. She had not stayed.

Dicran was still standing at the gunnel when Ivan came back. "We'll follow the dolphins," he said breathlessly, his face flushed. "The men agreed–if there's anything to be done"–he took a breath–"Dicran, you and I will do it."

"Anything to be done," Dicran repeated, shaking his head. "Ivan, what's this foolishness?"

"Foolishness." Ivan grinned as he sat down against the pilot house and dug his hands deep into the pockets of his slicker.

The dolphins led them steadily northward, along the coast. Ivan scanned the shoreline. "Look, we must be nearing Sochi. Haven't you ever gone to one of the sanitariums for vacation, Dicran? A twenty-eight-day cure–."

Dicran quickly broke in. "I don't need a cure," he said, "I'm never ill." He looked down at his dark hands resting on the gunnel and watched the water parting easily before their bow.

They followed the dolphins. Dicran watched them rub against each other as they swam, seeming to touch shoulders, to comfort each other as they called back and forth. Each seemed to have a characteristic sound, a signature whistle. It was something he had never noticed before. He remembered his father had always spoken of dolphins with respect; he had never completely understood why. One summer when a boy, while aimlessly combing the beach, he had found a dolphin—eyes filmed over—purple and stinking in the sun. He wanted to touch it but hadn't dared. He had wondered at this dolphin lying so close to the pier, so close to the leaning porch of his father's house. He had told his father of the discovery, hoping for an explanation, but the old man only looked out to sea, his mouth moving as if speaking to himself. He remembered at the time thinking about his mother, who had died a long time before—he remembered now only the printed kerchief she wore—but his father had acted as if he had forgotten Dicran was there. After a few minutes of silence Dicran left, deciding to walk up the hill to the old town. At the square he watched the village boys play lapta on the cobblestones.

They were in the shallows now. The shore was rocky at the base of the mountains that rose in front of them. The sun was high overhead. The wind had picked up and it was cool and biting now at midday. In the creaking vessel Dicran was grateful for the channel markers, grateful for the bell buoy he could hear clanging ahead. As they neared it, the dolphins began to swim faster before them, whistling to each other. Although the buoy was still at some distance, Dicran could see it swaying, the sunlight reflecting off its surface. The dolphins were circling the buoy, circling and calling back to them on the fishing boat. Someone passed Dicran a pair of battered binoculars. Now he could see why they had been called. A dolphin calf was tangled in a net, caught in the arms of the bell buoy. The other dolphins were anxiously churning a path from the buoy to the boat.

"Ivan, look at this," Dicran shouted over the dolphins' whistles, and he waved the binoculars. "We'll use the lifeboat."

Ivan looked at him strangely, took the binoculars, and then lurched ahead to grab the oars from the overhead in the pilot house. As Dicran followed, he heard a loud discussion coming from the stern. One of the new crewmen was saying he, not Dicran, should go out in the lifeboat. Dicran didn't even go to the Collective meetings. When the voices got loud, Captain Yorkovitya demanded silence. He listened quietly, smoothing his mustache, as Ivan reminded the crew that they had earlier agreed that Dicran was not only his partner but also the best seaman.

Dicran unlashed one of the lifeboats, ignoring the discussion, and set the boat swinging on the davits. Somewhat grudgingly, the others pushed the lifeboat outside the hull and, after Dicran and Ivan climbed in, lowered it into the choppy water. Dicran and Ivan watched from the rocking boat as the engines were reversed and the fishing boat noisily backed off to deeper water. The dolphins began to circle the lifeboat.

Dicran settled himself in the bow. "Row, Ivan," he told his friend. "I'm the water man." He looked at the bleak sky and could not say whether it was gray or blue. The clouds were huddled on the horizon like dirty sheep from the steppes.

Ivan fit the oars into the locks and moved his feet to the sides of the boat to avoid the water in the bottom. He pulled on the oars, his back to the buoy. He pulled with all of his body, and Dicran noted that he seemed to be smiling at the effort, enjoying the strain on his muscles.

The jumping dolphins were swamping their boat. The wind seemed colder, stronger, close to the water, and a fine spray blew in their faces. Dicran found a rusty can under his seat and began bailing, all the while talking to the large dolphin swimming beside the boat. He watched the creature's eye, circled in black, appearing, disappearing, as he rode the water beside them. "Easy now, old man, easy now," Dicran said as he watched the dolphin swim close and then plunge beneath the boat. Two other dolphins circled them, grunting and chirping. Ivan rowed steadily toward the buoy. When they were clearly out of hearing distance of the fishing boat Ivan stopped.

"I thought you were going to spit on the Captain's shoe after that speech." He looked at Dicran with a half smile on his wide face.

Dicran laughed. "I thought of it," he said as he dumped the water from the bailing can over the side.

Ivan looked at him steadily. "I know you did."

"He was so busy swinging his arms and jumping up and down he never would have noticed." Dicran scraped the can along the bottom of the boat.

Ivan leaned toward him. "The men wouldn't have said a word"—he leaned back—"though the new man might." He pulled a flask from his hip pocket.

"They're sheep in a fishing boat," Dicran said as he continued to bail. Ivan took a drink from the flask and then offered it to Dicran. Dicran shook his head.

"Why don't you relax sometime?" Ivan asked as he put the flask back in his pocket and then pulled on the oars. He leaned so far back he almost hit the seat behind him.

"Why?" Dicran asked. "We're following the dolphins. You wanted this. We're soaked from their splashing." He dipped the rusty can into the water at his feet.

Ivan shook his head and pulled on the oars. Dicran turned and stared at something behind them, the bailing can still in his hand.

Another lifeboat was zigzagging toward them through the school of dolphins, and in it, rowing furiously, was Captain Yorkovitya. Dicran turned away.

Ivan waved and looked back at Dicran. "Ah ho—he must be sweating even in this cold. Didn't think he could miss this." Ivan laughed. "Just watch, it'll soon be his story. He needs a new speech." Ivan pulled on the oars, not waiting for the Captain.

The sky was brighter now, the water slate-colored. As they reached the buoy the dolphins stopped their high-pitched whistling and became ominously mute. Looking closely, Dicran could see the small dolphin was caught in a purse seine that was wedged between the rusted arms of the buoy. The calf looked uneasy; he probably had never seen a man before. Dicran watched the circling dorsal fins and realized that he, too, had an uncomfortable feeling in his stomach. The sun was hot, the air cold. The wind was blowing stronger from the northeast, and their boat rocked as Ivan tried to steady it with the oars. He looked at Dicran.

"Are you going in?"

"No other way." Dicran struggled with his boots, watching the rocking bell buoy. "He's wedged in tight."

At that moment the other lifeboat pulled alongside. The Captain started to speak. Dicran ignored him and eased himself over the side. In the rocky shoals the water was dark gray and choppy. Dicran had forgotten the shock of seawater in March. He treaded water for a few minutes and then began to swim toward the buoy. Thrashing, fighting the water and his clothes, he made his way between the gliding dolphins. His wool shirt tugged at him, pulling him down. He should have taken it off with his boots. Treading water, he unbuttoned it, shuddering as he wrung it above his head and then threw it to Ivan. Just short of Ivan's grasp, it sunk below the surface. Ivan sat down again, shaking his head, and pulled an oar to keep the boat turned so he could see the buoy. In the other lifeboat the Captain struggled with the oars. He was saying something Dicran couldn't hear.

Swimming was somewhat easier without his shirt. Dicran reached the buoy and held on with one hand. The small dolphin's eyes were half hidden by the net. It was twisted over his head, wrapping him tightly against the buoy, his blowhole barely above the lapping water; the dolphin was lucky he hadn't drowned. Seeing the dented buoy, Dicran knew the dolphins had spent a long time pushing it, butting it, trying to free the calf, before they had called on them.

He examined the net, pulling at it to test its strength. It was newly mended, the firm new rope spliced and tied carefully. Whoever had mended it knew what he was doing.

Suddenly two of the dolphins raised themselves to their full height, backwatering and whistling shrilly. Ivan pulled his boat closer. "The dolphins are impatient," he called.

Dicran looked in all directions to see if there was something else that might be alarming the dolphins. The cold water splashed at his chest. He saw and heard nothing but the men in the lifeboats, the dolphins themselves and, beyond that, the faintly squalling cloud of gulls gliding and dipping over the fishing boat rocking in the distance. He turned back to the buoy and pulled violently at the net, holding on with one hand and working with the other.

"Use your knife," Captain Yorkovitya shouted from his lifeboat.

What, no speech? Dicran thought as he struggled with the net a few minutes longer. "I will untangle it," he yelled back.

Dicran's hands were red from the frigid water, the knuckles raw from repeated scraping against the rough jute. His efforts, the wind, the choppy sea, all kept the buoy rocking. The calf was making soft, frightened noises, and one dolphin, perhaps the mother, kept coming over to nudge at him. She'd circle, look at Dicran and then pass close to the calf, making a shrill sound like crying. Another dolphin, maybe a nursemaid, clicked loudly and rubbed against her each time she left the baby. Dicran decided the small dolphin was a newborn; there were no marks on his smooth gray skin.

"Use your knife," the Captain shouted again.

Dicran looked at Ivan, who was pulling impatiently at the oars, not looking at the man in the boat beside his.

"No," Dicran replied breathlessly, "a good net." He noticed an outer ring of dolphins circling beyond the lifeboats. A shark screen, he thought.

As he worked, Dicran tried to be gentle, although his large hands were numb and clumsy with cold. The calf was quiet, the frigid water sharp as a scythe cutting his legs at the thighs. He couldn't feel his legs below mid-thigh, and he began to wonder if they had dropped off his body like icicles off a roof.

The Captain's voice, despite all his speech making, wasn't strong, and he had difficulty projecting it over the insistent cries of the dolphins.

"Watch the baby," Ivan shouted over the Captain. "What's a net?"

Dicran didn't look up as he continued to tug at the purse seine, moving aside the white marker floats and pulling at the wet knots that seemed to get tighter the longer he worked at them. A dolphin swam close, looking at Dicran quizzically. It circled nearer and nearer, finally rubbing its smooth side against him. Dicran pulled away in surprise.

The Captain put down his oars and gingerly stood up in his rocking boat. The sun was bright behind his back; the cool wind flapped his large windbreaker at his sides. "Gods harness dolphins to chariots, not buoys," the Captain yelled.

He's acting again, Dicran thought. "Ivan." Dicran motioned to his friend and ignored the Captain. "Ivan," he shouted, "I can't do it. The cold."

As he spoke he hung onto the buoy, moving his legs to keep the circulation going even though he could not feel them anymore. It seemed to get suddenly colder. Dicran looked up to see a cloud had momentarily covered the sun. The sky was chalky gray with clouds, now dark gray, massing in the east. He hung on the buoy by his elbow and lowered his head to blow into his hands. He rubbed them together as best he could while the rusted bell clanged rhythmically in his ear. He had not noticed the bell before, hanging above his head.

"Try again," shouted the Captain, who was leaning down, holding on to the side of Ivan's boat to stabilize his own. He stood up again and shouted, "Dolphins are reincarnations of the Pharaoh's men, lost when the Red Sea parted."

Dicran was hanging on the buoy and moving an arm in large fanning motions, trying to keep warm. In the bottom of a swell, he couldn't see the fishing boat, and for a moment wondered if the crew had drunkenly mutinied and left them behind. He stretched his neck trying to see the cloud of gulls above the boat, feeling he had to at least keep them in sight. He moved his dead legs to be sure they had not fallen off frozen into the net, and spread his fingers, seeing for the first time they were bleeding, but unable to feel the sting of the abrasions.

He turned back to the small dolphin and saw it was looking at him, an eye visible through the net. As he watched, he thought he saw one eye slowly close and then open again.

"Ivan," Dicran shouted to his friend, "he winked."

"Foolishness," Ivan shouted back. "Dolphins can't wink."

"Use your teeth," yelled the Captain. "He will drown. He will starve. Dolphins nurse under water."

Dicran tried again, pulling at the net with all his strength, though the tingling and then the numbness that had begun at his fingertips had now gone up his fingers and palms to his wrists. His hands seemed no longer connected to his arms. Breaking a few strands of the jute with his teeth, he heard a tearing sound from below, but he soon realized this method would be too slow. The small dolphin was showing signs of exhaustion. His chirps were weaker, and, Dicran thought, a film was beginning to form over his eye. Dicran tried again to untangle the net, his fingers stiff as if they belonged to someone else, the water slapping his face.

"Use your knife," the Captain shouted, leaning toward him over the hull of Ivan's rocking boat. The sky turned dark again as the mass of gray clouds obscured the sun.

Hoarsely, Dicran called back as he yanked at the net, "A net lasts for years."

"A dolphin lives thirty," the Captain shouted through the wind.

The bell clanged over Dicran's head. "The net is—" Dicran began, and then stopped in midsentence. He thought of plankton floating toward the clear danger of jellyfish, and other mouths opening and eating, chewing and spewing out into the sea. He thought of his sister playing with the nest of dolls and finding the smallest one, of the pot of camomile tea, the yellow debris floating on top in the hands of the woman who would not stay, his father meticulously mending nets beside him in the flickering lantern light, the old man's mouth moving in the darkness, saying nothing. And then he heard again the cries of the dolphins and felt the sleek bodies gliding around him, appealing with blunt noses, fins without usable fingers, all emotion without the capability to act skillfully, decisively, finally.

Dicran tore at the knife case at his belt. "You're right, you're right," he shouted.

At this the dolphins, who had been keeping back from the buoy, moved in close and began swimming around and around him, noisily grunting and squealing, whistling to each other and churning up a wake that washed over his head and tore him off the buoy. He surfaced, sputtering. He wiped an arm across his face and then dove beneath the water. Two of the dolphins followed him, and although he could see nothing in the darkness, he felt their presence. They called to each other; he had forgotten the creatures could make as much noise below the surface as above it. One swam closely by him. He was overwhelmed by its size. It was as long as he was tall. He felt its power, yet it glided by him without ruffling the water. Breathless, he surfaced. There was no sound from the calf. He felt something wet on his face. He pulled the seaweed away, the knife still in his hand.

"The baby's not moving," Ivan shouted over the choppy water.

Frantically, Dicran sawed through the net and cut the baby free. "He's all right," Dicran called hoarsely. The young dolphin didn't move. "You're free." He slapped the dolphin calf on the side and gently pushed him clear of the net.

An explosion of activity seized the dolphins. Two swam on either side of the calf and carried him along with the raw energy of their thrust. The others charged around Dicran, smiling and squealing and churning up the water. He locked his elbow around the arm of the buoy as the water sloshed over his head. His teeth chattering, he no longer felt his forearms or legs. The air was filled with grunts and chirps, barks and whistles. Finally, the dolphins quieted and Ivan rowed in close to the buoy to pull Dicran on board. "It was a fine rescue," Ivan said, grinning as he leaned over, grabbed Dicran's belt and pulled him into the boat.

Captain Yorkovitya rowed up beside them. The oars floated in their locks as he struggled to take off his windbreaker. "Here—take my jacket," he said as he handed it to Dicran, who accepted it without comment, pulling it around his naked chest. Ivan tossed him his flask and Dicran took a long swig, his hands shaking so violently he could hardly keep the flask at his mouth.

The Captain watched them for a minute. Then, saluting Dicran, he pushed off against the side of their boat and rowed his own in a zigzagged course toward the fishing boat. Not far from them, the dolphins were gathered around the calf.

Ivan let the Captain outdistance them as he rowed toward the waiting boat. He looked at Dicran somberly as the other man shivered and held the Captain's jacket close around him. As Ivan rowed, Dicran sat at the bow, hunched over, his legs and hands still numb, unfeeling. The wind blew colder. Soon they reached the fishing boat, and from the way the men were noisily celebrating, it was obvious the Captain had already given his speech.

The men clasped Ivan's arm and pumped Dicran's hand as they helped them on board. Dicran was surprised when the Captain appeared and offered him a mug of brandy. The raw liquid tore at his throat. Numb, he thought of changing his clothes, thought of moving below, as the Captain came around again, cradling the bottle of brandy to his chest, the label facing outward. The oily, gold Serbian Plum Brandy was supposed to be the best. Perhaps he should sip it. Ah, yes, he accepted some more. It tingled on his tongue and burned his throat.

"A fine brandy, Captain," he said.

He went below to put on dry clothes. When he got back on deck, he was feeling warmer, the brandy mug empty in his hand, the Captain's windbreaker again around his shoulders. He went forward and found to his surprise the dolphins massed at their bow. Watching the calf, he remembered the net they had left tangled in the buoy. They should have retrieved it, he thought, he could have mended it.

Dicran went up by the pilothouse to smoke, and Ivan sprung up the ladder to join him.

"Hey, Dicran—" Ivan seemed restless. "A vodka tonight, for the dolphins?" Dicran didn't answer. "Have supper with us in the café," Ivan urged him. "Tell the story, Yolana will enjoy it."

Dicran said no, looking over the water. "Not tonight." He puffed on his pipe and looked at the sky washed pink with late afternoon.

"What are you doing tonight?" Ivan moved against the bulkhead. The dolphins had broken formation and were crisscrossing their bow.

"You forget," Dicran said impatiently, "the tournament at the park." He moved his pipe to the other side of his mouth. "Tonight I'll watch."

"Ah, yes," Ivan said as he turned toward shore, "the chess match."

Dicran looked at his pipe and then knocked it against the side of the boat. He stood silent for a few minutes. He could hear the dolphins playing in their wake, their high, soft sounds above the squall of the gulls and the wash of the water against the hull.

Dicran grabbed Ivan and turned him by the shoulders. Roughly, he kissed one blond, bristly cheek and then the other.

Ivan was wide-eyed. "You're crazy, Dicran."

"Not so crazy. We'll drink tonight."

The dolphins' sleek bodies cut through the wake. When they reached a certain spot on the water they stopped and rose on their tails. Seeing this, Ivan swung into the pilot house. The engines stopped. The dolphins were backwatering, emitting a chorus of sound. Further out, dolphins in a ring were flipping like coins on the horizon.

The crewmen were suddenly stretching, awake, looking up, asking what was going on, talking among themselves.

Ivan called from the pilot house. "We're there."

Dicran turned toward his voice. "Where?"

"Where the dolphins first met us. We're at the same latitude, the same longitude," Ivan shouted. "Dicran, look." He learned out the window of the pilot house and alternately beckoned to Dicran and pointed to shore. "Look at the coastline. Look how the sun dips over the mountains." He pointed to the sky. "Look at the gulls, they're the same."

Dicran looked at the sky, the coastline. "You're right," he said smiling. "Everything–even the gulls–the same."

This is an old story with a modern ring. A man wants his wife to take up an avocation he enjoys—in this case fishing—so they can enjoy more recreation together. The outcome of the story is felicitous, but not in the way the fellow planned. Henry Van Dyke (1852–1933) wrote several books on fishing, in-cluding Fisherman's Luck *(1899), where this story is from. His other books in-clude* The Blue Flower *(1902) and* The Poetry of Tennyson *(1920).*

Henry Van Dyke

THE FATAL SUCCESS (1899)

BEEKMAN DE PEYSTER WAS PROBABLY the most passionate and tri-umphant fisherman in the Petrine Club. He angled with the same dash and confidence that he threw into his operations in the stock-market. He was sure to be the first man to get his flies on the water at the opening of the season. And when we came together for our fall meeting, to com-pare notes of our wanderings on various streams and make up the fish-stories for the year, Beekman was almost always "high hook." We expected, as a matter of course, to hear that he had taken the most and the largest fish.

It was so with everything that he undertook. He was a masterful man. If there was an unusually large trout in a river, Beekman knew about it before any one else, and got there first, and came home with the fish. It did not make him unduly proud, because there was nothing uncommon about it. It was his habit to succeed, and all the rest of us were hardened to it.

When he married Cornelia Cochrane, we were consoled for our partial loss by the apparent fitness and brilliancy of the match. If Beekman was a masterful man, Cornelia was certainly what you might call a mistressful woman. She had been the head of her house since she was eighteen years old. She carried her good looks like the family plate; and when she came into the breakfast-room and said good-morning, it was with an air as if she presented every one with a check for a thousand dollars. Her tastes were accepted as judgments, and her preferences had the force of laws. Wherever she wanted to go in the summer-time, there the finger of household destiny pointed. At Newport, at Bar Harbour, at Lenox, at Southampton, she made a record. When she was joined in holy wedlock to Beekman De Peyster, her father and mother heaved a sigh of satisfaction, and settled down for a quiet vacation in Cherry Valley.

It was in the second summer after the wedding that Beekman admitted to a few of his ancient Petrine cronies, in moments of confidence (unjustifiable, but natural), that his wife had one fault.

"It is not exactly a fault," he said, "not a positive fault, you know. It is just a kind of a defect, due to her education, of course. In everything else she's magnificent. But she doesn't care for fishing. She says it's stupid,— can't see why one should like the woods,—calls camping out the lunatic's diversion. It's rather awkward for a man with my habits to have his wife take such a view. But it can be changed by training. I intend to educate her and convert her. I shall make an angler of her yet."

And so he did.

The new education was begun in the Adirondacks, and the first lesson was given at Paul Smith's. It was a complete failure.

Beekman persuaded her to come out with him for a day on Meacham River, and promised to convince her of the charm of angling. She wore a new gown, fawn-colour and violet, with a picture-hat, very taking. But the Meacham River trout was shy that day; not even Beekman could induce him to rise to the fly. What the trout lacked in confidence the mosquitoes more than made up. Mrs. De Peyster came home much sunburned, and expressed a highly unfavourable opinion of fishing as an amusement and of Meacham River as a resort.

"The nice people don't come to the Adirondacks to fish," said she; "they come to talk about the fishing twenty years ago. Besides, what do you want to catch that trout for? If you do, the other men will say you bought it, and the hotel will have to put in another for the rest of the season."

The following year Beekman tried Moosehead Lake. Here he found an atmosphere more favourable to his plan of education. There were a good many people who really fished, and short expeditions in the woods were quite fashionable. Cornelia had a camping-costume of the most approved style made by Dewlap on Fifth Avenue,—pearl-gray with linings of rose-silk,—and consented to go with her husband on a trip up Moose River. They pitched their tent the first evening at the mouth of Misery Stream, and a storm came on. The rain sifted through the canvas in a fine spray, and Mrs. De Peyster sat up all night in a waterproof cloak, holding an umbrella. The next day they were back at the hotel in time for lunch.

"It was horrid," she told her most intimate friend, "perfectly horrid. The idea of sleeping in a shower-bath, and eating your breakfast from a tin plate, just for sake of catching a few silly fish! Why not send your guides out to get them for you?"

But, in spite of this profession of obstinate heresy, Beekman observed with secret joy that there were signs, before the end of the season, that Cornelia was drifting a little, a very little but still perceptibly, in the direction of a change of heart. She began to take an interest, as the big trout came along in September, in the reports of the catches made by the different anglers. She would saunter out with the other people to the corner of the porch to see the fish weighed and spread out on the grass. Several times she went with Beekman in the canoe to Hardscrabble

Point, and showed distinct evidences of pleasure when he caught large trout. The last day of the season, when he returned from a successful expedition to Roach River and Lily Bay, she inquired with some particularity about the results of his sport; and in the evening, as the company sat before the great open fire in the hall of the hotel, she was heard to use this information with considerable skill in putting down Mrs. Minot Peabody of Boston, who was recounting the details of her husband's catch at Spencer Pond. Cornelia was not a person to be contented with the back seat, even in fish-stories.

When Beekman observed these indications he was much encouraged, and resolved to push his educational experiment briskly forward to his customary goal of success.

"Some things can be done, as well as others," he said in his masterful way, as three of us were walking home together after the autumnal dinner of the Petrine Club, which he always attended as a graduate member. "A real fisherman never gives up. I told you I'd make an angler out of my wife; and so I will. It has been rather difficult. She is 'dour' in rising. But she's beginning to take notice of the fly now. Give me another season, and I'll have her landed."

Good old Beekman! Little did he think—But I must not interrupt the story with moral reflections.

The preparations that he made for his final effort at conversion were thorough and prudent. He had a private interview with Dewlap in regard to the construction of a practical fishing-costume for a lady, which resulted in something more reasonable and workmanlike than had ever been turned out by that famous artist. He ordered from Hook & Catchett a lady's angling-outfit of the most enticing description,—a split-bamboo rod, light as a girl's wish, and strong as a matron's will; an oxidized silver reel, with a monogram on one side, and a sapphire set in the handle for good luck; a book of flies, of all sizes and colours, with the correct names inscribed in gilt letters on each page. He surrounded his favourite sport with an aureole of elegance and beauty. And then he took Cornelia in September to the Upper Dam at Rangeley.

She went reluctant. She arrived disgusted. She stayed incredulous. She returned—Wait a bit, and you shall hear how she returned.

The Upper Dam at Rangely is the place, of all others in the world, where the lunacy of angling may be seen in its incurable stage. There is a cosy little inn, called a camp, at the foot of a big lake. In front of the inn is a huge dam of gray stone, over which the river plunges into a great oval pool, where the trout assemble in the early fall to perpetuate their race. From the tenth of September to the thirtieth, there is not an hour of the day or night when there are no boats floating on that pool, and no anglers trailing the fly across its waters. Before the late fishermen are ready to come in at midnight, the early fishermen may be seen creeping down to the shore with lanterns in order to begin before cock-crow. The number of fish taken is not large,—perhaps five or six for the whole company on an average day,—but the size is sometimes enormous,—nothing under three pounds is counted,—and they pervade thought and conversation at the Upper Dam to the exclusion of every other subject. There is no driving, no dancing, no golf, no tennis. There is nothing to do but fish or die.

At first, Cornelia thought she would choose the latter alternative. But a remark of that skilful and morose old angler, McTurk, which she overheard on the verandah after supper, changed her mind.

"Women have no sporting instinct," said he. "They only fish because they see men doing it. They are imitative animals."

That same night she told Beekman, in the subdued tone which the architectural construction of the house imposes upon all confidential communications in the bedrooms, but with resolution in every accent, that she proposed to go fishing with him on the morrow.

"But not on that pool, right in front of the house, you understand. There must be some other place, out on the lake, where we can fish for three or four days, until I get the trick of this wobbly rod. Then I'll show that old bear, McTurk, what kind of an animal woman is."

Beekman was simply delighted. Five days of diligent practice at the mouth of Mill Brook brought his pupil to the point where he pronounced her safe.

"Of course," he said patronizingly, "you haven't learned all about it yet. That will take years. But you can get your fly out thirty feet, and you can keep the tip of your rod up. If you do that, the trout will hook himself, in rapid water, eight times out of ten. For playing him, if you follow my directions, you'll be all right. We will try the pool to-night, and hope for a medium-sized fish."

Cornelia said nothing, but smiled and nodded. She had her own thoughts.

At about nine o'clock Saturday night, they anchored their boat on the edge of the shoal where the big eddy swings around, put out the lantern and began to fish. Beekman sat in the bow of the boat, with his rod over the left side; Cornelia in the stern, with her rod over the right side. The night was cloudy and very black. Each of them had put on the largest possible fly, one a "Bee-Pond" and the other a "Dragon;" but even these were invisible. They measured out the right length of line, and let the flies drift back until they hung over the shoal, in the curly water where the two currents meet.

There were three other boats to the left of them. McTurk was their only neighbour in the darkness on the right. Once they heard him swearing softly to himself, and knew that he had hooked and lost a fish.

Away down at the tail of the pool, dimly visible through the gloom, the furtive fisherman, Parsons, had anchored his boat. No noise ever came from that craft. If he wished to change his position, he did not pull up the anchor and let it down again with a bump. He simply lengthened or shortened his anchor rope. There was no click of the reel when he played a fish. He drew in and paid out the line through the rings by hand, without a sound. What he thought when a fish got away, no one knew, for he never said it. He concealed his angling as if it had been a conspiracy. Twice that night they heard a faint splash in the water near his boat, and twice they saw him put his arm over the side in the darkness and bring it back again very quietly.

"That's the second fish for Parsons," whispered Beekman, "what a secretive old Fortunatus he is! He knows more about fishing than any man on the pool, and talks less."

Cornelia did not answer. Her thoughts were all on the tip of her own rod. About eleven o'clock a fine, drizzling rain set in. The fishing was very slack. All the other boats gave it up in despair; but Cornelia said she wanted to stay out a little longer, they might as well finish up the week.

At precisely fifty minutes past eleven, Beekman reeled up his line, and remarked with firmness that the holy Sabbath day was almost at hand and they ought to go in.

"Not till I've landed this trout," said Cornelia.

"What? A trout! Have you got one?"

"Certainly; I've had him on for at least fifteen minutes. I'm playing him Mr. Parsons' way. You might as well light the lantern and get the net ready; he's coming in towards the boat now."

Beekman broke three matches before he made the lantern burn; and when he held it up over the gunwale, there was the trout sure enough, gleaming ghostly pale in the dark water, close to the boat, and quite tired out. He slipped the net over the fish and drew it in,—a monster.

"I'll carry that trout, if you please," said Cornelia, as they stepped out of the boat; and she walked into the camp, on the last stroke of midnight, with the fish in her hand, and quietly asked for the steelyard.

Eight pounds and fourteen ounces,—that was the weight. Everybody was amazed. It was the "best fish" of the year. Cornelia showed no sign of exultation, until just as John was carrying the trout to the ice-house. Then she flashed out:—

"Quite a fair imitation, Mr. McTurk,—isn't it?"

Now McTurk's best record for the last fifteen years was seven pounds and twelve ounces.

So far as McTurk is concerned, this is the end of the story. But not for the De Peysters. I wish it were. Beekman went to sleep that night with a contented spirit. He felt that his experiment in education had been a success. He had made his wife an angler.

He had indeed, and to an extent which he little suspected. That Upper Dam trout was to her like the first taste of blood to the tiger. It seemed to change, at once, not so much her character as the direction of her vital energy. She yielded to the lunacy of angling, not by slow degrees, (as first a transient delusion, then a fixed idea, then a chronic infirmity, finally a mild insanity,) but by a sudden plunge into the most violent mania. So far from being ready to die at Upper Dam, her desire now was to live there—and to live solely for the sake of fishing—as long as the season was open.

There were two hundred and forty hours left to midnight on the thirtieth of September. At least two hundred of these she spent on the pool; and when Beekman was too exhausted to manage the boat and the net and the lantern for her, she engaged a trustworthy guide to take Beekman's place while he slept. At the end of the last day her score was twenty-three, with an average of five pounds and a quarter. His score was nine, with an average of four pounds. He had succeeded far beyond his wildest hopes.

The next year his success became even more astonishing. They went to the Titan Club in Canada. The ugliest and most inaccessible sheet of water in that territory is Lake Pharaoh. But it is famous for the extraordinary fishing at a certain spot near the outlet, where there is just room enough for one canoe. They camped on Lake Pharaoh for six weeks, by Mrs. De Peyster's command; and her canoe was always the first to reach the fishing-ground in the morning, and the last to leave it in the evening.

Some one asked him, when he returned to the city, whether he had good luck.

"Quite fair," he tossed off in a careless way; "we took over three hundred pounds."

"To your own rod?" asked the inquirer, in admiration.

"No-o-o," said Beekman, "there were two of us."

There were two of them, also, the following year, when they joined the Natasheebo Salmon Club and fished that celebrated river in Labrador. The custom of drawing lots every night for the water that each member was to angle over the next day, seemed to be especially designed to fit the situation. Mrs. De Peyster could fish her own pool and her husband's too. The result of that year's fishing was something phenomenal. She had a score that made a paragraph in the newspapers and called out editorial comment. One editor was so inadequate to the situation as to entitle the article in which he described her triumph "The Equivalence of Woman." It was well-meant, but she was not at all pleased with it.

She was now not merely an angler, but a "record" angler of the most virulent type. Wherever they went, she wanted, and she got, the pick of the water. She seemed to be equally at home on all kinds of streams, large and small. She would pursue the little mountain-brook trout in the early spring, and the Labrador salmon in July, and the huge speckled trout of the northern lakes in September, with the same avidity and resolution. All that she cared for was to get the best and the most of the fishing at each place where she angled. This she always did.

And Beekman,—well, for him there were no more long separations from the partner of his life while he went off to fish some favourite stream. There were no more home-comings after a good day's sport to find her clad in cool and dainty raiment on the verandah, ready to welcome him with friendly badinage. There was not even any casting of the fly around Hardscrabble Point while she sat in the canoe reading a novel, looking up with mild and pleasant interest when he caught a larger fish than usual, as an older and wiser person looks at a child playing some innocent game. Those days of a divided interest between man and wife were gone. She was now fully converted, and more. Beekman and Cornelia were one; and she was the one.

The last time I saw the De Peysters he was following her along the Beaverkill, carrying a landing-net and a basket, but no rod. She paused for a moment to exchange greetings, and then strode on down the stream. He lingered for a few minutes longer to light a pipe.

"Well, old man," I said, "you certainly have succeeded in making an angler of Mrs. De Peyster."

"Yes, indeed," he answered,—"haven't I?" Then he continued, after a few thoughtful puffs of smoke, "Do you know, I'm not quite so sure as I used to be that fishing is the best of all sports. I sometimes think of giving it up and going in for croquet."

Old friends, one from the country, one from the city, get together to fish. Of greater interest in the story, however, is what the city guy has been up to in his personal life. What is behind his poor health and what, if anything, is he trying to escape? The camaraderie in the story is nicely depicted and the air of mystery sustains the reader's interest. Geoffrey Norman has written top-drawer stories and novels such as Midnight Water *(1983) and* Deep End *(1995).*

Geoffrey Norman

COWBOYS
(1988)

JOHNSON CALLED TO SAY HE WANTED to go fishing and was I available. I said yes . . . automatically, the way a society woman does when the clerk asks her if she'd like to charge it.

I assumed he meant to come down from the city for a day or two. He was big in arbitrage and never took much time off. I'd seen him get sweaty palms from spending a couple of hours away from the telephone.

But this time Johnson said he wanted to take a week. And he wanted to go back to the cabin that belonged to the club and stay there the whole time. I said it sounded like a fine idea to me; but since there was no telephone in that cabin, I wondered what was up.

I had a day to get ready, so I bought groceries and some beer. I inventoried my tackle and put what I thought I'd need into my four-wheel-drive wagon, which I gassed up and then checked out to make sure there was oil in the crankcase, water in the radiator, and air in the tires. I felt pretty well prepared when I went to the small local airport to meet Johnson's plane.

But I wasn't ready for the way he looked. Nothing could have prepared me for that. He'd lost a lot of weight and looked gaunt and weak. His clothes hung limply on him, and his face was the chalky gray color of cooling ash. I'd always figured him as a heart attack waiting to happen, but now I thought that maybe one of those fast-breeding cancers was just eating him up. I felt something growing in my throat, choking me, and I wasn't sure I'd be able to speak.

When we met, we gave each other the usual fractional embrace, shook hands, and said how glad we were to see each other. Johnson said I looked good and, without thinking, I said he did, too.

"Kind of you to say so," he said dryly, but he didn't elaborate.

We went to the baggage claim to wait for his gear. I was expecting a lot of it, since he'd come for the week. I'd seen him arrive with three big bags and a rod case just for an in-and-out trip. Johnson was on everyone's mailing list, and if the people at Orvis and Eddie Bauer didn't hear from him for a week or two, they'd probably assume he was dead.

"That's it," he said, and nodded at an olive-green bag coming our way on the conveyor. He lifted it without much effort and followed me out into the parking lot.

"Beautiful day," he said. "Just beautiful. You know, I wouldn't mind if October were a year long."

"I know what you mean."

He pitched his duffel in the back with the rest of the stuff, then took off his suit coat and threw it back there, too. He pulled the knot out of his tie and flung it in on top of the coat.

146

"All right," he said. "Let's get there."

"On the way."

"How far away am I from my first bass?"

"One hour," I said. "Hour and ten minutes, tops. It's faster since they finished the Interstate."

"I can remember when it took four hours to get to that camp," Johnson said. "Longer, if there was rain."

"You remember that time we got stuck so bad?" I said. "We'd been in that slough shooting wood ducks."

"Missed the homecoming dance."

"My love life has never been the same."

"Got a limit, though."

"Matter of fact."

"They call that 'having your priorities in order,' I believe," Johnson said and sighed. "Man, but I've had a lot of good times back in that swamp."

I nodded.

"Shot my first deer in there. Thanksgiving Day. I was twelve years old."

"I remember."

"Deer herd still in good shape?"

"From what I hear." I'd never been much of a deer hunter. They were just too big for me to feel good about killing them. That was the part Johnson liked, though. He'd been that kind of boy, and he'd grown up to be that kind of man.

"I haven't been deer hunting in . . . I'll bet it's been ten years."

"Season starts in another month. You could hunt the club as my guest."

"Kind of you to offer," he said. "But I think I'd better pass." Then he put his head back and closed his eyes. I couldn't remember seeing him sleep in a car. It was as shocking, in a way, as his appearance.

He woke when I turned onto the dirt road that led from browned-over farm country, through plantation pines, and into the big, dense cathedral of hardwoods that grew in the bottom land. It was cool and dim under the big trees.

"I believe this is the best-looking stand of trees in the state," Johnson said. "How much you figure the timber is worth?"

"Somebody offered eight million a couple of years ago."

"Don't take it," Johnson said firmly. "No matter how much they offer, don't ever let 'em cut these trees."

I parked in front of the cabin, and we took a few minutes to unload and change. Johnson's khakis hung loosely, like prison clothes, on his thin frame. He looked so bad that I couldn't help staring. When he caught me, I looked away.

"Let's get out on the water," Johnson said abruptly. "I need to be fishing."

We took an old juniper skiff that was beached at the head of a slough. I sculled from the stern, because I was so much better at it than Johnson. He always wanted to catch fish so bad that he couldn't remember to keep the boat under control. Me, I was lazier. I'd take a lick or two on the sculling oar, and when I saw the boat was lined up right, I'd make a cast. Johnson would have made a half-dozen by then.

We eased down the slough into a wide, shallow lake that had been formed by water backed up behind a matrix of beaver ponds. There were cyprus and gum trees growing up out of the shallow water and Spanish moss hung from the branches like crepe. Even though the day was hot, it felt cool under the trees. Johnson sat very still in the bow and didn't seem in any hurry to start fishing.

"There's more water in here than I remember," he said over his shoulder.

"More beaver. They're about to flood us out."

"You need to shoot a few."

"We try."

"You and I could have kept them under control," he said, without turning around. "With our Marlin .22s, remember? We were a couple of hard-shooting cowboys."

All this nostalgia was getting to me, or maybe I just didn't like where it was leading. Whatever, I changed the subject. "We're over an old creek bed here," I said. "Anywhere along that line of snags ought to be good."

"Right." Johnson worked his fly rod a few times, and when the loop was pushing forty feet, he dropped his deerhair Bug precisely at the base of a dead, bleached hickory tree. I'd never known a better caster. He'd saved and saved when we were kids so that he could buy a fly rod. Then he'd practiced endlessly in his back yard. It was the way true sportsmen fished, he said.

In later years, I was always getting letters from places like Islamorada and Pez Maya with pictures of Johnson smiling and holding a big bone-fish in one hand and his fly rod in the other. He went to tournaments and won trophies.

We worked down the old creek bed, casting to the snags that marked its flanks. True to form, Johnson made six casts for each of mine. But I kept the distance and enjoyed the feel of the blade of the oar as it sliced through the water. I had tried one of those trolling motors once–Johnson bought it–but I went back to sculling. I missed the feel of the oar and the delicacy of control I had with it.

Johnson caught the first bass. It hit the deerhair Bug in an oily surge of water, and Johnson shouted, "All *right*," when he set the hook.

The fish jumped three or four times and tried to go around a stump to break the leader, but Johnson controlled him with a firm hand and in five minutes he had him at the boat. He reached over the side and took the fish by its pugnacious lower lip.

"I believe he'll do for supper," Johnson said.

"Absolutely."

So he put the fish on a stringer and trailed it over the side. He rinsed his hand in the water, dried it on the leg of his khakis, and started casting again. I gave the oar a stroke to straighten us out and looked or a target to cast to. Except for all the questions, it felt like old times.

We fished through the afternoon, on into evening, when it started to get a little cool. We caught a good number of fish. Johnson caught three to each of mine, which was the normal ratio. We kept two fish for supper and threw the rest back. We cleaned the unlucky two at the bank where we beached the skiff. Johnson had a little folding filleting knife, and he took the slabs from the backbone with clean, efficient strokes and then took the pad of bronzed skin the same way. He carried our gear and the four white fillets back to the cabin.

I fried a slab of bacon for grease and then dusted the fillets with corn meal and black pepper and dropped them in the skillet. I boiled some greens, and Johnson fried potatoes in another skillet. When the fillets were pecan brown, I drained them on paper and put them on two old chipped white plates with the greens and potatoes. We opened two bottles of beer and went out to the porch of the cabin to eat. It was cool, and the mosquitoes were down.

"Good," Johnson said when he took his first bite of fish. "Real damned good."

"Glad you like it."

We ate, and the sun set, and Johnson went inside the cabin with the dishes and came back with two coffee cups full of bourbon. I figured the time had come. Johnson was going to tell me he was dying.

He was entitled to it, no question about that. We went back that far and had shared that much, anyway. But I didn't know what I could say to him, so I wished, in a way, that we were back in that cowboy world of ours with our Marlin .22s. In that world, you didn't complain when it came time to die. You didn't even mention it. I wanted to be wise enough, profound enough, to say something that would comfort him, and at that moment, when I realized there wasn't a chance in hell of that, I felt all my inadequacies more keenly than ever before. So much easier to be a cowboy and let the silence pass for meaning.

But Johnson didn't say a thing about dying. He sipped his whisky and identified it as Black Jack and then told a long story about how he and a bunch of the boys in his fraternity had gone to Lynchburg in an open Army-surplus jeep one December to visit the Jack Daniel's shrine. It was a good story and it didn't make any difference that I'd heard it before.

When he'd finished telling it, and our cups were empty, Johnson said, "What's on for tomorrow?"

"More of the same, I suppose."

"You know what I'd like to do?"

"What's that?"

"I'd like to catch some crickets and dig some worms. Then rig up a couple of cane poles and go sit on a brim bed somewhere."

"Little early for that."

"Seems like we found 'em this time of year before," Johnson said. "Anyway, let's give it a try."

"Sure," I said. I hadn't ever expected to see Johnson using a cane pole again. It would be like seeing Jackie Kennedy with her hair in pigtails.

But in the morning, after we'd eaten eggs and bacon and brewed a pot of sawmill coffee on the old wood-burning stove, we went out in back of a crumbling stable where the camp mules had been kept years ago and dug worms from a mound of old manure and leaves. It was alive with night crawlers, and in half an hour we'd filled a coffee can. We pulled a loose board from the floor of another crumbling building and uncovered hundreds of crickets. We put three dozen in an old mayonnaise jar.

There were some old cane poles stored under the camp house. We pulled two out and dusted off the spider webs, then rerigged them and put them in the skiff. We didn't even take our fly rods.

I sculled us down past the beaver pond to the main lake. We jumped a few teal along the way, and I said something about how it was a shame duck season hadn't opened.

"Didn't come to hunt ducks," Johnson said, as though duck season was too far in the future even to contemplate. Actually, it was only a month off.

So we did what he apparently had come to do, which was fish for bluegills with crickets and worms.

We found a bank where the water dropped off to eight or ten feet very rapidly, and when we could see small, gleaming white patches on the bottom, we dropped anchor. The white places were stone and shell that had been exposed when the fish fanned away bottom silt for spawning. When you were over a bed, you could smell it. It smelled like the mound of leaves and old manure out behind the mule barn.

"God," Johnson said when we'd anchored, "what a beautiful smell."

He caught the first fish, as usual. "Look at this little sumbitch *pull*, would you," he said happily, as the fat bluegill ran in strong tight circles, bending the limber cane pole and making the monofilament sing. When he got that fish in, he baited his hook again, quickly, and went back for another.

"Believe we have found us the spot," he said. "Come on and help me catch some."

The sun was warm and high by the time we started back for the landing below the cabin. We'd caught at least fifty bluegills, but, even so, Johnson was plainly sorry to be quitting.

"What a great morning," he said, stretching and looking up at the sky. "What an absolutely great goddamned morning."

I thought there was a tone of regret in his words, as you would get from a man who didn't expect to see many more mornings. But then, maybe it was my imagination.

We had kept six of the little fish and we had them for lunch, fried, with cornbread and beer. After lunch, we went to different rooms in the old cabin and took naps.

I dreamed hectic dreams, as I always do when I sleep in the afternoon. One of the dreams ended in metallic sounds, which woke me. After a minute, I realized the noise came from inside the house. I put my feet on the floor and walked until I reached the room where Johnson was working.

"Sorry," he said. "I didn't mean to wake you up."

"I'd slept too long, anyway," I said. "What are you doing?" He was up to his knees in old coffeepots, campstools, riding tack, and other such junk that had accumulated over the fifty-year life of the camp. It all looked forlorn and worthless.

"Looking for a gig."

"A gig?"

"Thought it might be a good night to paddle around and look for some bullfrogs. We'll need some kind of light, too."

It was a little late for bullfrogs, but I didn't say anything, since it had been a little early for bedding bluegill, too. Instead, I helped him go through that locker and two others. In the end, we had one rusty old gig and an old miner's hat with a battery-powered lamp. The battery, miraculously, was not dead.

When the sun had set, we took the skiff out into the swamp. It wasn't as good as it would have been in July, but we did find seven or eight big bull-frogs by the hot glow of their eyes. I eased in close, and Johnson speared them neatly with his needle-sharp gig. On the way back, we saw a small gater. Its eyes were six inches apart and shone like chunks of charcoal.

We had frog legs for dinner.

Johnson had found an old bolt-action .22 in one of the lockers, so the next morning nothing would do but to go out in the swamp and kill some of the beavers that were damming the creeks and flooding the timber. We did it just the way we did when we were kids, except we didn't have our old imitation saddle rifles.

We also skinned out the few beavers we shot, even though the pelts were worthless at that time of year. But Johnson seemed to think it had been a day well spent. We ate fried ham steaks that night and went to bed early. Johnson had an appetite and he didn't seem to tire quickly, the way you would if you were sick. I couldn't make sense of his behavior as I lay in the dark listening to a nearby owl and wondering what had brought me here, to the camp, with my old friend.

Johnson hadn't told me anything. He hadn't even tried to sell me on any of the investments he handled, the way he usually did. I had told him, once, that I didn't trust New York paper—news or commercial. That hadn't stopped him from trying, except this time. He hadn't talked about anything this trip except the old days.

The next morning, he wanted to go dove shooting. There were a couple of old rusted Fox doubles in one of the lockers and a few boxes of bird loads. We cleaned the guns and in the afternoon hid around a small patch of browntop that would have taken ten men to stand properly. Even so, we shot birds. Johnson got a limit—twelve birds—and I got half that many.

"Did you bring some onions?" he asked me on the way back to the cabin.

"Sure."

"Potatoes?"

"Yes."

"Well, let's make that hash we used to eat. You wouldn't believe the number of times I've dreamed about that hash. And the places where I've had those dreams."

We plucked birds for an hour and a half. I made the hash in a cast-iron stewpot, and we ate at the kitchen table.

"Delicious, as always," Johnson said. It was probably my imagination, but he looked like he'd gained weight and taken on some color. He sure didn't have the appetite or the disposition of a dying man.

"Glad you like it."

"One thing I'm sorry about," he said in an offhand fashion, "is that my son never got to see any of this." Johnson had been married long enough to have one child before a mean divorce. His wife got custody and promptly took off for California. She had remarried, and the boy had been adopted by her new husband. Johnson never saw him or mentioned him . . . until now.

I didn't say anything.

"He'll grow up short on memories," Johnson said. "He won't have anything like this dove hash to fall back on when everyone is raving about the latest poached fish in kumquat sauce. You know what I mean?"

"Sure."

"I thought about kidnapping him once. I really did. I was going to bring him right here. They'd find us, eventually. When they did, he'd go back to California and I'd go to jail. But we'd both have something to carry us."

"What happened?"

"Lost my nerve."

I nodded again. Stupidly.

"My great regret," Johnson said with a lean smile, "is that my boy never got to eat your dove hash."

We shot squirrels and snapping turtles the next day, and ate squirrel and dumplings for supper. I decided that Johnson was definitely dying but that he wanted to spare me any talk about it. He was still a good cowboy that way. And I made up my mind to follow his lead. So, if he wanted to shoot squirrels, the way we had when we were still too young to shave, then I would shoot squirrels and do it with enthusiasm just like I had back in those days.

Without the phone and without any other men around, it was easy to slip back into the mood of those days. Once, while I was waiting for a fat, copper-colored fox squirrel to come in range, I found my hands trembling.

We made soup from a big, surly snapping turtle that had been sunning itself on an old snag when Johnson shot it squarely in the head. The turtle was rank, but the soup was delicious. "Better than the Four Seasons'," Johnson said.

We rigged a trotline and baited it with scraps from the turtle. In the morning, we had nine shiny channel cats and one blue. We skinned them and fried the fillets with hush puppies.

That was the last night of our week at the camp. Johnson hadn't said anything about leaving, and I figured that was up to him. So I waited while we sat out on the porch and watched the sun go down over the river bottom. Waited for him to say something.

It took a while.

"Well, I've enjoyed it," he said. "And I feel better than I've felt in a long, long time."

"That's good."

"I wasn't in the best shape when I got here."

"No."

"This has been great for me. I appreciate all you've done." His voice was husky and final.

"I haven't done anything," I said. "I've enjoyed it myself."

"Hard to believe, sometimes, the way things happen," Johnson said, and paused. I had the nervous feeling that he was about to say something profound. What could I answer? That I'd miss him? That the river bottom would be here after he was gone? That I'd be along after a while? If there was a suitable thing to say, it was beyond my knowing it. I waited.

"Well, I guess we ought to leave early," he said. "I don't want to miss my plane and get stuck in that airport."

"No."

"I'll see you in the morning."

"Right."

With that Johnson went inside to his room.

I waited, feeling relieved and a little cowardly, and then I went inside, too.

We packed up and got out early, and neither of us said much on the drive back. Johnson looked far better than he had when I'd picked him up, and his silence seemed content and satisfied. I didn't want to break in on it.

After he'd checked his bag and been assigned his seat, we walked down to the security checkpoint. Before he went through the detector, Johnson shook my hand in a way that indicated this wasn't just one more temporary parting.

"Take care of yourself," he said.

"You too."

"And thanks for not asking. If I'd told you, it would have put you in a box. You'll know what I mean in a couple of days."

I didn't get it, but he didn't give me a chance to ask any questions. He turned and went to his gate. I waited until the plane took off.

Two days later, the FBI called. It seems Johnson was involved in some kind of big insider scheme. I told the agent that I'd been fishing with Johnson and that I'd put him on a plane. He got the date and the flight number, thanked me, and said he'd be in touch.

He never called again. But I heard a lot about Johnson from people who called. Some were old mutual friends. Some were his own new enemies. I also heard from a lot of reporters. One of them tried to get me to show him where Johnson and I had spent our week fishing together. I refused. Politely, I think. I wanted to tell him I wouldn't take him back there unless I planned on using him for gater bait.

I read the stories that came out until they all started repeating each other. They all had one or two little things wrong, the way all of those "in-depth" stories do. In one of them, we had gone into the swamps to hunt for deer and in another we were "bait-casting for bass."

I didn't recognize the Johnson they wrote about. The five-million-dollar apartment. Place in the country with horses. The women.

It seemed like he had gotten hooked on the money the way other addicts get hooked on their drugs. Having it wasn't all that great, but not having it was unendurable. So he kept raising the stakes until he got caught.

He was in Costa Rica, according to some sources. Other people had him in Chile. I didn't know and didn't expect I ever would, but both were plausible. There was good tarpon fishing in Costa Rica and excellent trout fishing in Chile. Either way, Johnson would be all right. In some ways I felt bad for him. From now on, he could give up even hoping he'd ever see his son again.

But every time I thought about Johnson, I had to smile. He'd actually made it back to his hideaway one last time. And when he went down, he didn't take his sidekick with him. The way I saw it, that meant he was still a good cowboy.

Here is another old story, written during the Prohibition era, dealing with conflicting interests between husband and wife. Few stories surpass this one in matrimonial humor or its caricature of the bemused spouse. George Baldwin Potter is a fanatical fly-fisherman whose wife doesn't care a fig about the sport. Isabelle, on the other hand, has her own idiosyncrasies that are driving poor George over the edge. Will love win out? John Taintor Foote is renowned for his humorous fishing tales, and this is his best.

John Taintor Foote

A WEDDING GIFT
(1923)

GEORGE BALDWIN POTTER IS A PURIST. That is to say, he either takes trout on a dry fly or he does not take them at all. He belongs to a number of fishing clubs, any member of which might acquire his neighbor's wife, beat his children or poison a dog and still cast a fly, in all serenity, upon club waters; but should he impale on a hook a lowly though succulent worm and immerse the creature in those same waters it would be better that he send in his resignation at once, sooner than face the shaken committee that would presently wait upon him.

George had become fixed in my mind as a bachelor. This, of course, was a mistake. I am continually forgetting that purists rush into marriage when approaching or having just passed the age of forty. The psychology of this is clear.

For twenty years, let us say, a purist's life is completely filled by his efforts to convert all reasonable men to his own particular method of taking trout. He thinks, for example, that a man should not concern himself with more than a dozen types of standard flies. The manner of presenting them is the main consideration. Take any one of these flies, then, and place it, by means of an eight-foot rod, a light, tapered line and a mist-colored leader of reasonable length, on fast water—if you want trout. Of course, if you want to listen to the birds and look at the scenery, fish the pools with a long line and a twelve-foot leader. Why, it stands to reason that—

The years go by as he explains these vital facts patiently, again and again, to Smith and Brown and Jones. One wet, cold spring, after fighting a muddy stream all day, he re-explains for the better part of an evening and takes himself, somewhat wearily, upstairs. The damp and chill of the room at whatever club he may be fishing is positively tomb-like. He can hear the rain drumming on the roof and swishing against the windows. The water will be higher than ever tomorrow, he reflects, as he puts out the lights and slides between the icy sheets. Steeped to the soul in cheerless dark, he recalls numbly that when he first met Smith and Brown and Jones they were fishing the pools with a long line. That was, let's see—fifteen—eighteen—twenty years ago. Then he must be forty. It isn't possible! Yes, it is a fact. It is also a fact that Smith and Brown and Jones are still fishing the pools with a long line.

In the first faint light of dawn he falls into an uneasy, muttering slumber. The dark hours between have been devoted to intense thought and a variety of wiggles which have not succeeded in keeping the bedclothes against his shoulder blades.

Sometime within the next six months you will remember that you have forgotten to send him a wedding present.

George, therefore, having arrived at his fortieth birthday, announced his engagement shortly thereafter. Quite by chance I ran across his bride-to-be and himself a few days before the ceremony and joined them at lunch. She was a blonde in the early twenties, with wide blue eyes and a typical rose-and-white complexion. A rushing, almost breathless account of herself, which she began the moment we were seated, was curious, I thought. It was as though she feared an interruption at any moment. I learned that she was an only child, born and reared in Greater New York; that her family had recently moved to New Rochelle; that she had been shopping madly for the past two weeks; that she was nearly dead, but that she had some adorable things.

At this point George informed me that they would spend their honeymoon at a certain fishing club in Maine. He then proceeded to describe the streams and lakes in that section at some length—during the rest of the luncheon, as a matter of fact. His fiancée, who had fallen into a wordless abstraction, only broke her silence with a vague murmur as we parted.

Owing to this meeting I did not forget to send a wedding present. I determined that my choice should please both George and his wife through the happy years to come.

If I had had George only to consider, I could have settled the business in two minutes at a sporting-goods store. Barred from these for obvious reasons, I spent a long day in a thoroughly exhausting search. Late in the afternoon I decided to abandon my hopeless task. I had made a tremendous effort and failed. I would simply buy a silver doodad and let it go at that.

As I staggered into a store with the above purpose in view, I passed a showcase devoted to fine china and halted as my eyes fell on a row of fish plates backed by artfully rumpled blue velvet. The plates proved to be hand painted. On each plate was one of the different varieties of trout, curving up through green depths to an artificial fly just dropping on the surface of the water.

In an automatic fashion I indicated the plates to a clerk, paid for them, gave him my card and the address and fled from the store. Sometime during the next twenty-four hours it came to me that George Potter was not among my nearest and dearest. Yet the unbelievable sum I had left with that clerk in exchange for those fish plates could be justified in no other way.

I thought this fact accounted for the sort of frenzy with which George flung himself upon me when next we met, some two months later. I had been weekending in the country and encountered him in the Grand Central Station as I emerged from the lower level. For a long moment he wrung my hand in silence, gazing almost feverishly into my face. At last he spoke:

"Have you got an hour to spare?"

It occurred to me that it would take George an hour at least to describe his amazed delight at the splendor of my gift. The clock above Information showed that it was 12:45. I therefore suggested that we lunch together.

He, too, glanced at the clock, verified its correctness by his watch and seized me by the arm.

"All right," he agreed, and was urging me toward the well-filled and somewhat noisy station café before I grasped his intention and tried to suggest that we go elsewhere. His hand only tightened on my arm.

"It's all right," he said; "good food, quick service—you'll like it."

He all but dragged me into the café and steered me to a table in the corner. I lifted my voice above an earnest clatter of gastronomical utensils and made a last effort.

"The Biltmore's just across the street."

George pressed me into my chair, shoved a menu card at me and addressed the waiter.

"Take his order." Here he jerked out his watch and consulted it again. "We have forty-eight minutes. Service for one. I shan't eat anything; or, no—bring me some coffee—large cup—black."

Having ordered mechanically, I frankly stared at George. He was dressed, I now observed, with unusual care. He wore a rather dashing gray suit. His tie, which was an exquisite shade of gray-blue, was embellished by a handsome pearl. The handkerchief, appearing above his breast pocket, was of the same delicate gray-blue shade as the tie. His face had been recently and closely shaven, also powdered; but above that smooth whiteness of jowl was a pair of curiously glittering eyes and a damp, a beaded brow. This he now mopped with his napkin.

"Good God," said I, "what is it, George?"

His reply was to extract a letter from his inside coat pocket and pass it across the table, his haunted eyes on mine. I took in its few lines at a glance:

Father has persuaded me to listen to what you call your explanation. I arrive Grand Central 2:45, daylight saving, Monday.

ISABELLE

Poor old George, I thought; some bachelor indiscretion; and now, with his honeymoon scarcely over, blackmail, a lawsuit, heaven only knew what.

"Who," I asked, returning the letter, "is Isabelle?"

To my distress, George again resorted to his napkin. Then, "My wife," he said.

"Your wife!"

George nodded.

"Been living with her people for the last month. Wish he'd bring that coffee. You don't happen to have a flask with you?"

"Yes, I have a flask." George brightened. "But it's empty. Do you want to tell me about your trouble? Is that why you brought me here?"

"Well, yes," George admitted. "But the point is—will you stand by me? That's the main thing. She gets in"—here he consulted his watch—"in forty-five minutes, if the train's on time." A sudden panic seemed to seize him. His hand shot across the table and grasped my wrist. "You've got to stand by me, old man—until the ice is broken. That's all I ask. Just stick until the train gets in. Then act as if you knew nothing. Say you ran into me here and stayed to meet her. I'll tell you what—say I didn't seem to want you to stay. Kid me about wanting her all to myself, or something like that. Get the point? It'll give me a chance to sort of—well, you understand."

"I see what you mean, of course," I admitted. "Here's your coffee. Suppose you have some and then tell me what this is all about—if you care to, that is."

"No sugar, no cream," said George to the waiter; "just pour it. Don't stand there waving it about—pour it, pour it!" He attempted to swallow a mouthful of steaming coffee, gurgled frightfully and grabbed his water glass. "Great jumping Jehoshaphat!" he gasped, when he could speak, and glared at the waiter, who promptly moved out into the sea of diners and disappeared among a dozen of his kind.

"Steady, George," I advised as I transferred a small lump of ice from my glass to his coffee cup.

George watched the ice dissolve, murmured, "Idiot," several times and presently swallowed the contents of the cup in two gulps.

"I had told her," he said suddenly, "exactly where we were going. She mentioned Narragansett several times—I'll admit that. Imagine—Narragansett! Of course I bought her fishing things myself. I didn't buy knickers or woolens or flannel shirts—naturally. You don't go around buying a girl breeches and underwear before you're married. It wouldn't be—well, it isn't done, that's all. I got her the sweetest three-ounce rod you ever held in your hand. I'll bet I could put out sixty feet of line with it against the wind. I got her a pair of English waders that didn't weigh a pound. They cost me forty-five dollars. The rest of the outfit was just as good. Why, her fly box was a Truxton. I could have bought an American imitation for eight dollars. I know a lot of men who'll buy leaders for themselves at two dollars apiece and let their wives fish with any kind of tackle. I'll give you my word I'd have used anything I got her myself. I sent it all out to be packed with her things. I wanted her to feel that it was her own—not mine. I know a lot of men who give their wives a high-class rod or an imported reel and then fish with it themselves. What time is it?"

"Clock right up there," I said. But George consulted his watch and used his napkin distressingly again.

"Where was I?"

"You were telling me why you sent her fishing things out to her."

"Oh, yes! That's all of that. I simply wanted to show you that from the first I did all any man could do. Ever been in the Cuddiwink district?"

I said that I had not.

"You go in from Buck's Landing. A lumber tug takes you up to the head of Lake Owonga. Club guides meet you there and put you through in one day—twenty miles by canoe and portage up the west branch of the Penobscot; then nine miles by trail to Lost Pond. The club's on Lost Pond. Separate cabins, with a main dining and loafing camp, and the best squaretail fishing on earth—both lake and stream. Of course, I don't fish the lakes. A dry fly belongs on a stream and nowhere else. Let me make it perfectly clear."

George's manner suddenly changed. He hunched himself closer to the table, dropped an elbow upon it and lifted an expository finger.

"The dry fly," he stated, with a new almost combative ring in his voice, "is designed primarily to simulate not only the appearance of the natural insect but its action as well. This action is arrived at through the flow of the current. The moment you move a fly by means of a leader you destroy the—"

I saw that an interruption was imperative.

"Yes, of course," I said; "but your wife will be here in . . ."

It was pitiful to observe George. His new-found assurance did not flee—flee suggests a withdrawal, however swift—it was immediately and totally annihilated. He attempted to pour himself some coffee, take out his watch, look at the clock and mop his brow with his napkin at one and the same instant.

"You were telling me how to get to Lost Pond," I suggested.

"Yes, to be sure," said George. "Naturally you go in light. The things you absolutely have to have—rods, tackle, waders, wading shoes, and so forth, are about all a guide can manage at the portages in addition to the canoe. You pack in extras yourself—change of underclothes, a couple of pairs of socks and a few toilet articles. You leave a bag or trunk at Buck's Landing. I explained this to her. I explained it carefully. I told her either a weekend bag or one small trunk. Herb Trescott was my best man. I left everything to him. He saw us on the train and handed me tickets and reservations just before we pulled out. I didn't notice in the excitement of getting away that he'd given me three trunk checks all stamped 'Excess.' I didn't notice it till the conductor showed up, as a matter of fact. Then I said, 'Darling, what in heaven's name have you brought three trunks for?' She said—I can remember her exact words—'Then you're not going to Narragansett?'

"I simply looked at her. I was too dumfounded to speak. At last I pulled myself together and told her that in three days we'd be whipping the best squaretail water in the world. I took her hand, I remember, and said, 'You and I together, sweetheart,' or something like that."

George sighed and lapsed into a silence which remained unbroken until his eye happened to encounter the face of the clock. He started and went on:

"We got to Buck's Landing, by way of Bangor, at six in the evening of the following day. Buck's Landing is a railroad station with grass growing between the ties, a general store and hotel combined, and a lumber wharf. The store keeps canned peas, pink-and-white-candy and felt boots. The hotel part is—well, it doesn't matter except that I don't think I ever saw so many deer heads; a few stuffed trout, but mostly deer heads. After supper the proprietor and I got the three trunks up to the largest room. We just got them in and that was all. The tug left for the head of the lake at seven next morning. I explained this to Isabelle. I said we'd leave the trunks there until we came out, and offered to help her unpack the one her fishing things were in. She said, 'Please go away!' So I went. I got out a rod and went down to the wharf. No trout there, I knew; but I thought I'd limber up my wrist. I put on a Cahill Number Fourteen— or was it Sixteen—"

George knitted his brows and stared intently but unseeingly at me for some little time.

"Call it a Sixteen," I suggested.

George shook his head impatiently and remained concentrated in thought.

"I'm inclined to think it was a Fourteen," he said at last. "But let it go; it'll come to me later. At any rate, the place was alive with big chub—a foot long, some of 'em. I'll bet I took fifty—threw 'em back, of course. They kept on rising after it got dark. I'd tell myself I'd go after one more cast. Each time I'd hook a big chub, and—well, you know how the time slips away.

"When I got back to the hotel all the lights were out. I lit matches until I got upstairs and found the door to the room. I'll never forget what I saw when I opened that door—never! Do you happen to know how many of the kind of things they wear a woman can get into one trunk? Well, she had three and she'd unpacked them all. She had used the bed for the gowns alone. It was piled with them—literally piled; but that wasn't a starter. Everywhere you looked was a stack of things with ribbons in 'em. There were enough shoes and stockings for a girls' school; silk stockings, mind you, and high-heeled shoes and slippers." Here George consulted clock and watch. "I wonder if that train's on time," he wanted to know.

"You have thirty-five minutes, even if it is," I told him; "go right ahead."

"Well, I could see something was wrong from her face. I didn't know what, but I started right in to cheer her up. I told her all about the chub fishing I'd been having. At last she burst into tears. I won't go into the scene that followed. I'd ask her what was the matter and she'd say, 'Nothing,' and cry frightfully. I know a lot of men who would have lost their tempers under the circumstances, but I didn't; I give you my word. I simply said, 'There, there,' until she quieted down. And that isn't all. After a while she began to show me her gowns. Imagine—at eleven o'clock at night, at Buck's Landing! She'd hold up a dress and look over the top of it at me and ask me how I liked it, and I'd say it was all right. I know a lot of men who wouldn't have sat there two minutes.

"At last I said, 'They're all all right, darling,' and yawned. She was holding up a pink dress covered with shiny dingle-dangles, and she threw the dress on the bed and all but had hysterics. It was terrible. In trying to think of some way to quiet her it occurred to me that I'd put her rod together and let her feel the balance of it with the reel I'd bought her—a genuine Fleetwood, mind you—attached. I looked around for her fishing things and couldn't find them. I'll tell you why I couldn't find them." George paused for an impressive instant to give his next words the full significance due them. "They weren't there!"

"No?" I murmured weakly.

"No," said George. "And what do you suppose she said when I questioned her? I can give you her exact words—I'll never forget them. She said, 'There wasn't any room for them.'" Again George paused. "I ask you," he inquired at last, "I ask you as man to man: what do you think of that?"

I found no adequate reply to this question and George, now thoroughly warmed up, rushed on.

"You'd swear I lost my temper then, wouldn't you? Well, I didn't. I did say something to her later, but I'll let you be the judge when we come to that. I'll ask you to consider the circumstances. I'll ask you to get Old Faithful in your mind's eye."

"Old Faithful?" I repeated. "Then you went to the Yellowstone later?"

"Yellowstone! Of course not! Haven't I told you we were already at the best trout water in America? Old Faithful was a squaretail. He'd been in the pool below Horseshoe Falls for twenty years, as a matter of record. We'll come to that presently. How are we off for time?"

"Thirty-one minutes," I told him. "I'm watching the clock—go ahead."

"Well, there she was, on a fishing trip with nothing to fish with. There was only one answer to that—she couldn't fish. But I went over everything she'd brought in three trunks and I'll give you my word she didn't have a garment of any sort you couldn't see through.

"Something had to be done and done quick, that was sure. I fitted her out from my own things with a sweater, a flannel shirt and a pair of knickerbockers. Then I got the proprietor up and explained the situation. He got me some heavy underwear and two pairs of woolen stockings that belonged to his wife. When it came to shoes it looked hopeless, but the proprietor's wife, who had got up, too, by this time, thought of a pair of boy's moccasins that were in the store and they turned out to be about the right size. I made arrangements to rent the room we had until we came out again to keep her stuff in, and took another room for the night—what was left of it after she'd repacked what could stay in the trunks and arranged what couldn't so it wouldn't be wrinkled.

"I got up early, dressed and took my duffel down to the landing. I wakened her when I left the room. When breakfast was ready I went to see why she hadn't come down. She was all dressed, sitting on the edge of the bed. I said, 'Breakfast is ready, darling,' but I saw by her face that something was wrong again. It turned out to be my knickers. They fitted her perfectly—a little tight in spots—except in the waist. They would simply have fallen off if she hadn't held them up.

"Well, I was going in so light that I only had one belt. The proprietor didn't have any—he used suspenders. Neither did his wife—she used—well, whatever they use. He got me a piece of clothesline and I knotted it at each end and ran it through the what-you-may-call-'ems of the knickers and tied it in front. The knickers sort of puckered all the way round, but they couldn't come down—that was the main thing. I said, 'There you are, darling.' She walked over and tilted the mirror of the bureau so that she could see herself from head to foot. She said, 'Who are going to be at this place where we are going?' I said, 'Some of the very best dry-fly men in the country.' She said, 'I don't mean them; I mean the women. Will there be any women there?'

"I told her, certainly there would be women. I asked her if she thought I would take her into a camp with nothing but men. I named some of the women: Mrs. Fred Beal and Mrs. Brooks Carter and Talcott Ranning's sister and several more.

"She turned around slowly in front of the mirror, staring into it for a minute. Then she said, 'Please go out and close the door.' I said, 'All right, darling; but come right down. The tug will be here in fifteen minutes.'

"I went downstairs and waited ten minutes, then I heard the tug whistle for the landing and ran upstairs again. I knocked at the door. When she didn't answer I went in. Where do you suppose she was?"

I gave it up.

"In bed!" said George in an awe-struck voice. "In bed with her face turned to the wall; and listen, I didn't lose my temper as God is my judge. I rushed down to the wharf and told the tug captain I'd give him twenty-five dollars extra if he'd hold the boat till we came. He said all right and I went back to the room.

"The breeches had done it. She simply wouldn't wear them. I told her that at a fishing camp in Maine clothes were never thought of. I said, 'No one thinks of anything but trout, darling.' She said, I wouldn't let a fish see me looking like that.'" George's brow beaded suddenly. His hands dived searchingly into various pockets. "Got a cigarette? I left my case in my other suit."

He took a cigarette from me, lighted it with shaking fingers and inhaled deeply.

"It went on like that for thirty minutes. She was crying all the time, of course. I had started down to tell the tug captain it was all off, and I saw a woman's raincoat hanging in the hall. It belonged to someone up in one of the camps, the proprietor told me. I gave him seventy-five dollars to give to whoever owned it when he came out and took it upstairs. In about ten minutes I persuaded her to wear it over the rest of her outfit until we got to camp. I told her one of the women would be able to fix her up all right when we got there. I didn't believe it, of course. The women at camp were all old-timers; they'd gone in as light as the men; but I had to say something.

"We had quite a trip going in. The guides were at the head of the lake all right—Indian Joe and a new man I'd never seen, called Charlie. I told Joe to take Isabelle—he's one of the best canoemen I ever saw. I was going to paddle bow for my man, but I'd have bet a cooky Indian Joe could stay with us on any kind of water. We had to beat it right through to make camp by night. It's a good stiff trip, but it can be done. I looked back at the other canoe now and then until we struck about a mile of white water that took all I had. When we were through the other canoe wasn't in sight. The river made a bend there, and I thought it was just behind and would show up any minute.

"Well, it didn't show up and I began to wonder. We hit our first portage about ten o'clock and landed. I watched downstream for twenty minutes, expecting to sight the other canoe every instant. Then Charlie, who hadn't opened his head, said, 'Better go back,' and put the canoe in again. We paddled downstream for all that was in it. I was stiff with fright. We saw 'em coming about three miles lower down and back-paddled till they came up. Isabelle was more cheerful-looking than she'd been since we left New York, but Joe had that stony face an Indian gets when he's sore.

"I said, 'Anything wrong?' Joe just grunted and drove the canoe past us. Then I saw it was filled with wild flowers. Isabelle said she'd been picking them right off the banks all the way along. She said she'd only had to get out of the boat once, for the blue ones. Now, you can't beat that—not in a thousand years. I leave it to you if you can. Twenty miles of stiff current, with five portages ahead of us and a nine-mile hike at the end of that. I gave that Indian the devil for letting her do such a thing, and tipped the flowers into the Penobscot when we unloaded for the first portage. She didn't speak to me on the portage, and she got into her canoe without a word.

"Nothing more happened going in, except this flower business had lost two hours, and it was so dark when we struck the swamp at Loon Lake that we couldn't follow the trail well and kept stumbling over down timber and stepping into bog holes. She was about fagged out by then, and the mosquitoes were pretty thick through there. Without any warning she sat down in the trail. She did it so suddenly I nearly fell over her. I asked her what was the matter and she said, 'This is the end'—just like that—'this is the end!' I said, 'The end of what, darling?' She said, 'Of everything!' I told her if she sat there all wet and muddy she'd catch her death. She said she hoped so. I said, 'It's only two miles more, darling. Just think, tomorrow we'll be on the best trout water in the world!' With that she said, 'I want my mother, my darling mother,' and bowed her head in her hands. Think it over, please; and remember, I didn't lose my temper. You're sure there's nothing left in your flask?"

"Not a drop, George," I assured him. "Go ahead; we've only twenty-five minutes."

George looked wildly at the clock, then at his watch.

"A man never has it when he wants it most. Have you noticed that? Where was I?"

"You were in the swamp."

"Oh, yes! Well, she didn't speak after that, and nothing I could say would budge her. The mosquitoes had got wind of us when we stopped and were coming in swarms. We'd be eaten alive in another ten minutes. So I told Joe to give his pack to Charlie and help me pick her up and carry her. Joe said, 'No, by damn!' and folded his arms. When an Indian gets sore he stays sore, and when he's sore he's stubborn. The mosquitoes were working on him good and plenty, though, and at last he said, 'Me carry packs. Charlie help carry—that.' He flipped his hand over in the direction of Isabelle and took the pack from Charlie.

"It was black as your hat by now, and the trail through there was only about a foot wide with swamp on each side. It was going to be some job getting her out of there. I thought Charlie and I would make a chair of our arms and stumble along with her some way; but when I started to lift her up she said, 'Don't touch me!' and got up and went on. A blessing if there ever was one. We got to camp at ten that night.

"She was stiff and sore next morning—you expect it after a trip like that—besides, she'd caught a little cold. I asked her how she felt, and she said she was going to die and asked me to send for a doctor and her mother. The nearest doctor was at Bangor and her mother was in New Rochelle. I carried her breakfast over from the dining camp to our cabin. She said she couldn't eat any breakfast, but she did drink a cup of coffee, telling me between sips how awful it was to die alone in a place like that.

"After she'd had the coffee she seemed to feel better. I went to the camp library and got *The Dry Fly on American Waters,* by Charles Darty. I consider him the soundest man in the country. He's better than Pell or Fawcett. My chief criticism of him is that in his chapter on Streams East of the Alleghenies—east of the Alleghenies, mind you—he recommends the Royal Coachman. I consider the Lead-Wing Coachman a serviceable fly on clear, hard-fished water; but the Royal—never! I wouldn't give it a shade over the Professor or the Montreal. Just consider the body alone of the Royal Coachman—never mind the wings and hackle—the body of the Royal is—"

"Yes. I know, George," I said; "but—"

I glanced significantly at the clock. George started, sighed, and resumed his narrative.

"I went back to the cabin and said, 'Darling, here is one of the most intensely interesting books ever written. I'm going to read it aloud to you. I think I can finish it today. Would you like to sit up in bed while I read?' She said she hadn't strength enough to sit up in bed, so I sat down beside her and started reading. I had read about an hour, I suppose, when she did sit up in bed quite suddenly. I saw she was staring at me in a queer, wild way that was really startling. I said, 'What is it, darling?' She said, 'I'm going to get up. I'm going to get up this instant.'

"Well, I was delighted, naturally. I thought the book would get her by the time I'd read it through. But there she was, as keen as mustard before I'd got well into it. I'll tell you what I made up my mind to do, right there. I made up my mind to let her use my rod that day. Yes, sir—my three-ounce Spinoza, and what's more, I did it."

George looked at me triumphantly, then lapsed into reflection for a moment.

"If ever a man did everything possible to—well, let it go. The main thing is, I have nothing to reproach myself with—nothing. Except—but we'll come to that presently. Of course, she wasn't ready for dry flies yet. I borrowed some wet flies from the club steward, got some cushions for the canoe and put my rod together. She had no waders, so a stream was out of the question. The lake was better, anyway, that first day; she'd have all the room she wanted for her back cast.

"I stood on the landing with her before we got into the canoe and showed her just how to put out a fly and recover it. Then she tried it." A sort of horror came into George's face. "You wouldn't believe any one could handle a rod like that," he said huskily. "You couldn't believe it unless you'd seen it. Gimme a cigarette.

"I worked with her a half-hour or so and saw no improvement—none whatever. At last she said, 'The string is too long. I can't do anything with such a long string on the pole.' I told her gently—gently, mind you—that the string was an eighteen-dollar double-tapered Hurdman line, attached to a Gebhardt reel on a three-ounce Spinoza rod. I said, 'We'll go out on the lake now. If you can manage to get a rise, perhaps it will come to you instinctively.'

"I paddled her out on the lake and she went at it. She'd spat the flies down and yank them up and spat them down again. She hooked me several times with her back cast and got tangled up in the line herself again and again. All this time I was speaking quietly to her, telling her what to do. I give you my word I never raised my voice—not once—and I thought she'd break the tip every moment.

"Finally she said her arm was tired and lowered the rod. She'd got everything messed up with her last cast and the flies were trailing just over the side of the canoe. I said, 'Recover your cast and reel in, darling.' Instead of using her rod, she took hold of the leader close to the flies and started to pull them into the canoe. At that instant a little trout—couldn't have been over six inches—took the tail fly. I don't know exactly what happened, it was all over so quickly. I think she just screamed and let go of everything. At any rate, I saw my Spinoza bounce off the gunwale of the canoe and disappear. There was fifty feet of water just there. And now listen carefully: not one word did I utter—not one. I simply turned the canoe and paddled to the landing in absolute silence. No reproaches of any sort. Think that over!"

I did. My thoughts left me speechless. George proceeded:

"I took out a guide and tried dragging for the rod with a gang hook and heavy sinker all the rest of the day. But the gangs would only foul on the bottom. I gave up at dusk and paddled in. I said to the guide—it was Charlie—I said, 'Well, it's all over, Charlie.' Charlie said, 'I brought Mr. Carter in and he had an extra rod. Maybe you could borrow it. It's a four-ounce Meecham.' I smiled. I actually smiled. I turned and looked at the lake. 'Charlie,' I said, 'somewhere out there in that dark water, where the eye of man will never behold it again, is a three-ounce Spinoza—and you speak of a Meecham.' Charlie said, 'Well, I just thought I'd tell you.' I said, 'That's all right, Charlie. That's all right.' I went to the main camp, saw Jean, the head guide, and made arrangements to leave the next day. Then I went to our cabin and sat down before the fire. I heard Isabelle say something about being sorry. I said, 'I'd rather not talk about it, darling. If you don't mind, we'll never mention it again.' We sat there in silence, then, until dinner.

"As we got up from dinner, Nate Griswold and his wife asked us to play bridge with them that evening. I'd told no one what had happened, and Nate didn't know, of course. I simply thanked him and said we were tired, and we went back to our cabin. I sat down before the fire again. Isabelle seemed restless. At last she said, 'George.' I said, 'What is it, darling?' She said, 'Would you like to read to me from that book?' I said, 'I'm sorry darling; if you don't mind I'll just sit here quietly by the fire.'

"Somebody knocked at the door after a while. I said, 'Come in.' It was Charlie, I said, 'What is it, Charlie?' Then he told me that Bob Frazer had been called back to New York and was going out next morning. I said, 'Well, what of it?' Charlie said, 'I just thought you could maybe borrow his rod.' I said, 'I thought you understood about that, Charlie.' Charlie said, 'Well, that's it. Mr Frazer's rod is a three-ounce Spinoza.'

"I got up and shook hands with Charlie and gave him five dollars. But when he'd gone I began to realize what was before me. I'd brought in a pint flask of prewar Scotch. Prewar—get that! I put this in my pocket and went over to Bob's cabin. Just as I was going to knock I lost my nerve. I sneaked away from the door and went down to the lake and sat on the steps of the canoe landing. I sat there for quite a while and took several nips. At last I thought I'd just go and tell Bob of my loss and see what he said. I went back to his cabin and this time I knocked. Bob was putting a few odds and ends in a shoulder pack. His rod was in its case, standing against the wall.

"I said, 'I hear you're going out in the morning.' He said, 'Yes, curse it, my wife's mother has to have some sort of a damned operation or other.' I said, 'How would a little drink strike you, Bob?' He said, 'Strike me! Wait a minute! What kind of a drink?' I took out the flask and handed it to him. He unscrewed the cap and held the flask to his nose. He said, 'Great heavens above, it smells like–' I said, 'It is.' He said, 'It can't be!' I said, 'Yes, it is.' He said, 'There's a trick in it somewhere.' I said, 'No, there isn't–I give you my word.' He tasted what was in the flask carefully. Then he said, 'I call this white of you, George,' and took a good stiff snort. When he was handing back the flask he said, 'I'll do as much for you some day, if I ever get the chance.' I took a snifter myself.

"Then I said, 'Bob, something awful has happened to me. I came here to tell you about it.' He said, 'Is that so? Sit down.' I sat down and told him. He said, 'What kind of a rod was it?' I said, 'A three-ounce Spinoza.' He came over and gripped my hand without a word. I said, 'Of course, I can't use anything else.' He nodded, and I saw his eyes flicker toward the corner of the room where his own rod was standing. I said, 'Have another drink, Bob.' But he just sat down and stared at me. I took a good stiff drink myself. Then I said. 'Under ordinary circumstances, nothing on earth could hire me to ask a man to–' I stopped right there.

"Bob got up suddenly and began to walk up and down the room. I said, 'Bob, I'm not considering myself–not for a minute. If it was last season, I'd simply have gone back tomorrow without a word. But I'm not alone any more. I've got the little girl to consider. She's never seen a trout taken in her life–think of it, Bob! And here she is, on her honeymoon, at the best water I know of. On her honeymoon, Bob!' I waited for him to say something, but he went to the window and stared out, with his back to me. I got up and said good night and started for the door. Just as I reached it he turned from the window and rushed over and picked up his rod. He said, 'Here, take it,' and put the rod case in my hands. I started to try to thank him, but he said, 'Just go ahead with it,' and pushed me out the door."

The waiter was suddenly hovering above us with his eyes on the dishes.

"Now what do you want?" said George.

"Never mind clearing here," I said. "Just bring me the check. Go ahead, George."

"Well, of course, I can't any more than skim what happened finally, but you'll understand. It turned out that Ernie Payton's wife had an extra pair of knickers and she loaned them to Isabelle. I was waiting outside the cabin while she dressed next morning, and she called out to me, 'Oh, George, they fit!' Then I heard her begin to sing. She was a different girl when she came out to go to breakfast. She was almost smiling. She'd done nothing but slink about the day before. Isn't it extraordinary what will seem important to a woman? Gimme a cigarette."

"Fifteen minutes, George," I said as I supplied him.

"Yes, yes, I know. I fished the Cuddiwink that day. Grand stream, grand. I used a Pink Lady–first day on a stream with Isabelle–little touch of sentiment–and it's a darn good fly. I fished it steadily all day. Or did I try a Seth Green about noon? It seems to me I did, now that I recall it. It seems to me that where the Katahdin brook comes in I–"

"It doesn't really matter, does it, George?" I ventured.

"Of course, it matters!" said George decisively. "A man wants to be exact about such things. The precise details of what happens in a day's work on a stream are of real value to yourself and others. Except in the case of a record fish, it isn't important that you took a trout; it's exactly how you took him that's important."

"But the time, George," I protested.

He glanced at the clock, swore softly, mopped his brow–this time with the blue-gray handkerchief–and proceeded.

"Isabelle couldn't get into the stream without waders, so I told her to work along the bank a little behind me. It was pretty thick along there, second growth and vines mostly; but I was putting that Pink Lady on every foot of good water and she kept up with me easily enough. She didn't see me take many trout, though. I'd look for her, after landing one, to see what she thought of the way I'd handled the fish, and almost invariably she was picking ferns or blueberries, or getting herself untangled from something. Curious things, women. Like children, when you stop to think of it."

George stared at me unseeingly for a moment.

"And you never heard of Old Faithful?" he asked suddenly. "Evidently not, from what you said a while ago. Well, a lot of people have, believe me. Men have gone to the Cuddiwink district just to see him. As I've already told you, he lay beside a ledge in the pool below Horseshoe Falls. Almost nothing else in the pool. He kept it cleaned out. Worst sort of cannibal, of course–all big trout are. That was the trouble–he wanted something that would stick to his ribs. No flies for him. Did his feeding at night.

"You could see him dimly if you crawled out on a rock that jutted above the pool and looked over. He lay in about ten feet of water, right by his ledge. If he saw you he'd back under the ledge, slowly, like a sub-

marine going into dock. Think of the biggest thing you've ever seen, and that's the way Old Faithful looked, just lying there as still as the ledge. He never seemed to move anything, not even his gills. When he backed in out of sight he seemed to be drawn under the ledge by some invisible force.

"Ridgway—R. Campbell Ridgway—you may have read his stuff, *Brethren of the Wild,* that sort of thing—claimed to have seen him move. He told me about it one night. He said he was lying with just his eyes over the edge of the rock, watching the trout. Said he'd been there an hour, when down over the falls came a young red squirrel. It had fallen in above and been carried over. The squirrel was half drowned, but struck out feebly for shore. Well, so Ridgway said—Old Faithful came up and took Mister Squirrel into camp. No hurry; just came drifting up, sort of inhaled the squirrel and sank down to the ledge again. Never made a ripple, Ridgway said; just business.

"I'm telling you all this because it's necessary that you get an idea of that trout in your mind. You'll see why in a minute. No one ever had hold of him. But it was customary, if you fished the Cuddiwink, to make a few casts over him before you left the stream. Not that you ever expected him to rise. It was just a sort of gesture. Everybody did it.

"Knowing that Isabelle had never seen trout taken before, I made a day of it—naturally. The trail to camp leaves the stream just at the falls. It was pretty late when we got to it. Isabelle had her arms full of—heaven knows what—flowers and grass and ferns and fir branches and colored leaves. She'd lugged the stuff for hours. I remember once that day I was fighting a fourteen-inch fish in swift water and she came to the bank and wanted me to look at a ripe blackberry—I think it was—she'd found. How does that strike you? And listen! I said, 'It's a beauty, darling.' That's what I said—or something like that. . . . Here, don't you pay that check! Bring it here, waiter!"

"Go on, George!" I said. "We haven't time to argue about the check. You'd come to the trail for camp at the falls."

"I told Isabelle to wait at the trail for a few minutes, while I went below the falls and did the customary thing for the edification of Old Faith-

ful. I only intended to make three or four casts with the Number Twelve
Fly and the hair-fine leader I had on, but in getting down to the pool I
hooked the fly in a bush. In trying to loosen it I stumbled over something and fell. I snapped the leader like a thread, and since I had to put
on another, I tied on a fairly heavy one as matter of form.

"I had reached for my box for a regulation fly of some sort when I remembered a fool thing that Billy Roach had given me up on the Beaverkill
the season before. It was fully two inches long; I forget what he called it.
He said you fished it dry for bass or large trout. He said you worked the
tip of your rod and made it wiggle like a dying minnow. I didn't want the
contraption, but he'd borrowed some fly oil from me and insisted on my
taking it. I'd stuck it in the breast pocket of my fishing jacket and forgotten it until then.

"Well, I felt in the pocket and there it was. I tied it on and went down
to the pool. Now let me show you the exact situation." George seized a
fork. "This is the pool." The fork traced an oblong figure on the table-
cloth. "Here is Old Faithful's ledge." The fork deeply marked this impressive spot. "Here are the falls, with white water running to here. You
can only wade to this point here, and then you have an abrupt six-foot
depth. 'But you can put a fly from here to here with a long line,' you say.
No, you can't. You've forgotten to allow for your back cast. Notice this
bend here? That tells the story. You're not more than twenty feet from a
lot of birch and what not, when you can no longer wade. 'Well then, it's
impossible to put a decent fly on the water above the sunken ledge,' you
say. It looks like it, but this is how it's done: right here is a narrow point
running to here, where it dwindles off to a single flat rock. If you work
out on the point you can jump across to this rock—situated right there—
and there you are, with about a thirty-foot cast to the sunken ledge. Deep
water all around you, of course, and the rock is slippery; but—there you
are. Now notice this small cove, right here. The water from the falls
rushes past it in a froth, but in the cove it forms a deep eddy, with the
current moving round and round, like this." George made a slow circular motion with the fork. "You know what I mean?"

I nodded.

"I got out on the point and jumped to the rock; got myself balanced, worked out the right amount of line and cast the dingaree Bill had forced on me, just above the sunken ledge. I didn't take the water lightly and I cast again, but I couldn't put it down decently. It would just flop in—too much weight and too many feathers. I suppose I cast it a dozen times, trying to make it settle like a fly. I wasn't thinking of trout—there would be nothing in there except Old Faithful—I was just monkeying with this doodlebug thing, now that I had it on.

"I gave up at last and let it lie out where I had cast it. I was standing there looking at the falls roaring down, not thinking about anything in particular, when I remembered Isabelle, waiting up on the trail. I raised my rod preparatory to reeling in and the what-you-may-call-'em made a kind of a dive and wiggle out there on the surface. I reached for my reel handle. Then I realized that the thingamajig wasn't on the water. I didn't see it disappear, exactly; I was just looking at it, and then it wasn't there. 'That's funny,' I thought, and struck instinctively. Well, I was fast—so it seemed—and no snags in there. I gave it the butt three or four times, but the rod only bowed and nothing budged. I tried to figure it out. I thought perhaps a water-logged timber had come diving over the falls and up-ended right there. Then I noticed the rod take more of a bend and the line began to move through the water. It moved out slowly, very slowly, into the middle of the pool. It was exactly as though I was hooked onto a freight train just getting under way.

"I knew what I had hold of then, and yet I didn't believe it. I couldn't believe it. I kept thinking it was a dream, I remember. Of course, he could have gone away with everything I had any minute if he'd wanted to, but he didn't. He just kept moving slowly, round and round the pool. I gave him what pressure the tackle would stand, but he never noticed a little thing like that, just kept moving around the pool for hours, it seemed to me. I'd forgotten Isabelle; I admit that. I'd forgotten everything on earth. There didn't seem to be anything else on earth, as a matter of fact, except the falls and the pool and Old Faithful and me. At last Isabelle showed up on the bank above me, still lugging her ferns and what not.

She called down to me above the noise of the falls. She asked me how long I expected her to wait alone in the woods, with night coming on.

"I hadn't had the faintest idea how I was going to try to land the fish until then. The water was boiling past the rock I was standing on, and I couldn't jump back to the point without giving him slack and perhaps falling in. I began to look around and figure. Isabelle said, 'What on earth are you doing?' I took off my landing net and tossed it to the bank. I yelled, 'Drop that junk quick and pick up that net!' She said, 'What for, George?' I said, 'Do as I tell you and don't ask questions!' She laid down what she had and picked up the net and I told her to go to the cove and stand ready.

"She said, 'Ready for what?' I said, 'You'll see presently. Just stand there.' I'll admit I wasn't talking quietly. There was the noise of the falls to begin with, and—well, naturally I wasn't.

"I went to work on the fish again. I began to educate him to lead. I thought if I could lead him into the cove he would swing right past Isabelle and she could net him. It was slow work—a three-ounce rod—imagine! Isabelle called, 'Do you know what time it is?' I told her to keep still and stand where she was. She didn't say anything more after that.

"At last the fish began to come. He wasn't tired—he'd never done any fighting, as a matter of fact—but he'd take a suggestion as to where to go from the rod. I kept swinging him nearer and nearer the cove each time he came around. When I saw he was about ready to come I yelled to Isabelle. I said, 'I'm going to bring him right past you, close to the top. All you have to do is to net him.'

"When the fish came round again I steered him into the cove. Just as he was swinging past Isabelle the stuff she'd been lugging began to roll down the bank. She dropped the landing net on top of the fish and made a dive for those leaves and grasses and things. Fortunately the net handle lodged against the bank, and after she'd put her stuff in a nice safe place she came back and picked up the net again. I never uttered a syllable. I deserve no credit for that. The trout had made a surge and shot out into the pool and I was to busy just then to give her any idea of what I thought.

"I had a harder job getting him to swing in again. He was a little leery of the cove, but at last he came. I steered him toward Isabelle and lifted him all I dared. He came up nicely, clear to the top. I yelled, 'Here he comes! For God's sake, don't miss him!' I put everything on the tackle it would stand and managed to check the fish for an instant right in front of Isabelle.

"And this is what she did: it doesn't seem credible—it doesn't seem humanly possible; but it's a fact that you'll have to take my word for. She lifted the landing net above her head with both hands and brought it down on top of the fish with all her might!"

George ceased speaking. Despite its coating of talcum powder, I was able to detect an additional pallor in his countenance.

"Will I ever forget it as long as I live?" he inquired at last.

"No, George," I said, "but we've just exactly eleven minutes left."

George made a noticeable effort and went on:

"By some miracle the fish stayed on the hook; but I got a faint idea of what would have happened if he'd taken a real notion to fight. He went around that pool so fast it must have made him dizzy. I heard Isabelle say, 'I didn't miss him, George'; and then—well, I didn't lose my temper; you wouldn't call it that exactly. I hardly knew what I said. I'll admit I shouldn't have said it. But I did say it; no doubt of that; no doubt of that whatever."

"What was it you said?" I asked.

George looked at me uneasily.

"Oh, the sort of thing a man would say impulsively—under the circumstances."

"Was it something disparaging about her?" I inquired.

"Oh, no," said George, "nothing about her. I simply intimated—in a somewhat brutal way, I suppose—that she'd better get away from the pool—er—not bother me any more is what I meant to imply."

For the first time since George had chosen me for a confidant I felt a lack of frankness on his part.

"Just what did you say, George?" I insisted.

"Well, it wasn't altogether my words," he evaded. "It was the tone I

used, as much as anything. Of course, the circumstances would excuse—
Still, I regret it. I admit that. I've told you so plainly."

There was no time in which to press him further.

"Well, what happened then?" I asked.

"Isabelle just disappeared. She went up the bank, of course, but I didn't
see her go. Old Faithful was still nervous and I had to keep my eye on
the line. He quieted down in a little while and continued to promenade
slowly around the pool. I suppose this kept up for half an hour more.
Then I made up my mind that something had to be done. I turned very
carefully on the rock, lowered the tip until it was on a line with the fish,
turned the rod under my arm until it was pointing behind me and
jumped.

"Of course, I had to give him slack; but I kept my balance on the point
by the skin of my teeth, and when I raised the rod he was still on. I
worked to the bank, giving out line, and crawled under some bushes and
things and got around to the cove at last. Then I started to work again to
swing him into the cove, but absolutely nothing doing. I could lead him
anywhere except into the cover. He'd had enough of that; I didn't blame
him, either.

"To make a long story short, I stayed with him for two hours. For a
while it was pretty dark; but there was a good-sized moon that night, and
when it rose it shone right down on the pool through a gap in the trees
fortunately. My wrist was gone completely, but I managed to keep some
pressure on him all the time, and at last he forgot about what had happened to him in the cove. I swung him in and the current brought him
past me. He was on his side by now. I don't think he was tired even then—
just discouraged. I let him drift over the net, heaved him out on the bank
and sank down beside him, absolutely all in. I couldn't have got to my
feet on a bet. I just sat there in a sort of daze and looked at Old Faithful,
gleaming in the moonlight.

"After a half-hour's rest I was able to get up and go to camp. I planned
what I was going to do on the way. There was always a crowd in the main
camp living room after dinner. I simply walked into the living room without a word and laid Old Faithful on the center table.

"Well, you can imagine faintly what happened. I never got any dinner—couldn't have eaten any, as a matter of fact. I didn't even get a chance to take off my waders. By the time I'd told just how I'd done it to one crowd, more would come in and look at Old Faithful; and then stand and look at me for a while; and then make me tell it all over again. At last everybody began to dig up anything they had with a kick in it. Almost every one had a bottle he'd been hoarding. There was Scotch and gin and brandy and rye and a lot of experimental stuff. Art Bascom got a tin dishpan from the kitchen and put it on the table beside Old Faithful. He said 'Pour your contributions right in here, men.' So each man dumped whatever he had into the dishpan and everybody helped himself.

"It was great, of course. The biggest night of my life, but I hope I'll never be so dog-tired again. I felt as though I'd taken a beating. After they'd weighed Old Faithful—nine pounds five and half ounces; and he'd been out of water two hours—I said I had to go to bed, and went.

"Isabelle wasn't in the cabin. I thought, in a hazy way, that she was with some of the women, somewhere. Don't get the idea I was stewed. But I hadn't had anything to eat, and the mixture in that dishpan was plain TNT.

"I fell asleep as soon as I hit the bed; slept like a log till daylight. Then I half woke up, feeling that something terrific had happened. For a minute I didn't know what; then I remembered what it was. I had landed Old Faithful on a three-ounce rod!

"I lay there and went over the whole thing from the beginning, until I came to Isabelle with the landing net. That made me look at where her head should have been on the pillow. It wasn't there. She wasn't in the cabin. I thought perhaps she'd got up early and gone out to look at the lake or the sunrise or something. But I got up in a hurry and dressed.

"Well, I could see no signs of Isabelle about camp. I ran into Jean just coming from the head guide's cabin and he said, 'Too bad about your wife's mother.' I said, 'What's that?' He repeated what he'd said, and added, 'She must be an awful sick woman.' Well, I got out of him finally that Isabelle had come straight up from the stream the evening before, taken two guides and started for Buck's Landing. Jean had urged her to wait until morning, naturally; but she'd told him she must get to her mother at once, and took on so, as Jean put it, that he had to let her go.

"I said, 'Let me have Indian Joe, stern, and a good man, bow. Have 'em ready in ten minutes.' I rushed to the kitchen, drank two cups of coffee and started for Buck's Landing. We made the trip down in seven hours, but Isabelle had left with her trunks on the 10:40 train.

"I haven't seen her since. Went to her home once. She wouldn't see me; neither would her mother. Her father advised not forcing things—just waiting. He said he'd do what he could. Well, he's done it—you read the letter. Now you know the whole business. You'll stick, of course, and see me through just the first of it, old man. Of course, you'll do that, won't you? We'd better get down to the train now. Track Nineteen."

George rose from the table. I followed him from the café, across the blue-domed rotunda to a restraining rope stretched before the gloomy entrance to track Nineteen.

"George," I said, "one thing more: just what did you say to her when she—"

"Oh, I don't know," George began vaguely.

"George," I interrupted, "no more beating about the bush. What did you say?"

I saw his face grow even more haggard, if possible. Then it mottled into a shade resembling the brick on an old colonial mansion.

"I told her—" he began in a low voice.

"Yes?" I encouraged.

"I told her to get the hell out of there."

And now a vision was presented to my mind's eye; a vision of twelve fish plates, each depicting a trout curving up through green waters to an artificial fly. The vision extended on through the years. I saw Mrs. George Baldwin Potter ever gazing upon those rising trout and recalling the name on the card which had accompanied them to her door.

I turned and made rapidly for the main entrance of the Grand Central Station. In doing so I passed the clock above Information and saw that

I still had two minutes in which to be conveyed by a taxicab far, far from the entrance to Track Nineteen.

I remember hearing the word "quitter" hurled after me by a hoarse, despairing voice.

Wily Ozark mountain folk are featured in this story of a giant bass that has been eluding would-be captors for a long time. The game warden is lurking about in case of foul play, and there is a nice angle of a man helping a boy in pursuit of the big fish. The conclusion is unpredictable and cleverly orches-trated. This story first appeared in Field and Stream.

Weldon Stone

THE BIG BUFFALO BASS (1938)

ACCORDING TO THE OLD SAYING, "Where there is smoke there is fire"; and likewise, where there are tales of big fish there is bound to be one. That's what I say now, but a week ago I wouldn't have believed it.

My third consecutive summer in the Arkansas Ozarks was about to end, and I was still hearing stories of a big bass that had never been caught. I had first heard of him two years before, when I had only begun to fall in love with the Big Buffalo River, particularly that part of it just above the forks in Newton County, Arkansas. That day I had been work-ing slowly downstream, doing more exploring than fishing, when I came to a spring shaded by a giant chinquapin. I drank my fill, rolled a cigarette, and lay down in the shade to rest.

While I was wondering how many bushels of chinquapins such a tree would bear I heard a squirrel scolding something on the rocky bluff across the river. I spotted the squirrel in a scrubby pine, and then, lower down, I saw a man sitting in a niche of rock. He had a gun held ready, and he was still as the cliff itself.

The only sure sign that the fellow was not dead or sleeping was the peering attitude of his head. He was leaning forward and staring into the river below him. Apparently he had not heard the squirrel, though it was only about ten steps above and behind him.

I whistled. The man looked at me, and I pointed to the squirrel. He turned his head toward where I pointed; then he casually lifted the gun and shot the squirrel. The report of the gun, rebounding from the bluff, was deafening. The squirrel came tumbling down so near the man that he had only to get to his feet to pick it up.

Then he climbed easily up the bluff and entered the thick, scrubby growth of cedar and pine on the top. A few minutes later he appeared on the spring path and dropped the squirrel at my feet.

"Hit's yourn," he said and, leaning his rifle against the chinquapin, kneeled down and drank from the spring.

"But you shot it," I protested, "so it's really yours."

"I don't hanker after squirrel meat," he replied, wiping his mouth with the back of a lean brown hand. His face was like his hand—lean and hard, unsmiling, but not unfriendly.

"But why—?"

Then I stopped. I had already learned not to ask too many questions of these mountain folk; and besides, I had noticed that the squirrel's head was completely missing. Glancing at the man's rifle, I saw that it was a .30–30, old but well-kept.

I pulled out my sack of tobacco and offered it. He rolled a cigarette and handed it back to me without a word. He stood and smoked in a silence that was embarrassing to me but not, apparently, to him. I couldn't think of anything to say.

"Well, he said finally, "I reckon I jest as well to git on home," and, picking up his rifle, he was gone before I could thank him for the squirrel.

He had scarcely disappeared when I heard a rustling of leaves behind me and a man stepped out of the undergrowth in back of the spring. He was the same man I had met as a fly fisherman a few days before, but now there were two revolvers strapped to his hips. Intuitively I knew he was the game warden. I glanced at the squirrel involuntarily; I knew the season was closed. But the man was grinning.

"Thet's all right. I seen it all," he said.

"That's lucky for me," I said, "but I really caused him to shoot it. I thought he was hunting squirrels for food."

"No, he wa'n't huntin' nothin' thet lives in trees or wears fur. He was huntin' ol' King Solomon."

"I see," I said, though I didn't at all. A triangle affair possibly, or a mountain feud. I waited while the warden cut a chew from his plug.

"Ol' King Solomon is a bass," he said. "We call him thet because he's so smart nobody can't catch him. Thet feller with the gun hooked 'im once, but couldn't hold 'im. Ever since, he's been tryin' off an' on to shoot 'im. Well, thet's agin' the law; an' besides, I'm acquainted with King Solomon myself, an' they ain't nobody a-goin' to shoot 'im if I can help it. I had my hand on 'im once."

"How big was he?" I couldn't keep from asking that one.

"I don't choose fer strangers to think I'm a-lyin'," he said, "even when I'm a-tellin' the truth."

And that was all I could get out of him about the size of King Solomon, but that was enough. I determined then and there to keep a sharp lookout for this monarch of Big Buffalo bass.

"Where does King Solomon hold court most of the time?" I asked with a studied effort to be casual.

"Up an' down," he replied; "first one hole, then t'other."

"It seems that our friend with the gun expects to find him in this hole. Has he ever been seen here?"

"Once. 'Bout a year ago. Might be a mile or two up or down by now.

Bass is like folks: they travel some when the vittles is scarce. Well, I reckon I jest as well to get on back to town. See ya agin."

"I'll look out for you," I said. And I would look out for him, especially when he had his fly rod along. King Solomon would likely be not far away.

All of this took place two years ago, during my first summer in the Ozarks. I did see the warden several times after that; and when I saw him, I usually saw the man with the gun. The game they played is a popular one with boys and girls; it's called tag. The man with the gun was trying to tag King Solomon; the warden was bent on tagging the man with the gun. I liked to see them at their game, for as long as they played it I knew the big bass had not been caught.

The rest of that summer and all during the next two summers I looked for King Solomon and mentioned his name to all the natives I chanced to meet. They all knew of him, and most of them had stories to tell about the time they had seen him or hooked him; but no one was able or willing to tell me just where and when he might be found. So I never met King Solomon till quite recently, and then it was through Dee Thompson, a boy of twelve.

The few times I tried to talk with Dee it seemed that he was a little different from the many lean and taciturn boys of all ages whom I came across on Big Buffalo River. All were hard to talk to; few seemed to have any interest in fishing. I probably never would have got to know Dee any better than the others if I had not mentioned King Solomon. He was a different boy then.

"Hev ye seen 'im?" he asked.

"No, I haven't seen him—just heard about him. But I guess you have," I suggested.

"I seen a big bass one day," he answered, and that was as far as I got with him then.

Another time, however, when Dee saw me with a good day's catch, he opened up and told me about the time King Solomon had broken his line after he had lifted him out of the water by the line. Dee is a tough, hickory-fibered boy, pure mountain stock, a natural stoic; yet it seemed to me that his voice quavered a bit just there, and I remember that his head was turned away.

"But I'm a-goin' to git 'im some day," he added. "It won't be with one o' them fine pretty-things like yourn, but I'm a-goin' to ketch 'im. I know somethin' thet'll git 'im."

I knew it would be futile as well as ill-mannered to ask Dee just what bait he intended to use to bring about King Solomon's downfall, but I thought he might tell me when he hoped to accomplish it.

"Hit won't be long," he told me. "When the signs is right agin."

"When do you reckon that will be?" I asked and then wished I hadn't. Dee was looking me too steadily in the eye.

"Do ye want to go with me?" he asked.

"I sure do. You know I've spent a lot of time looking for King Solomon, and even if I can't catch him I'd like to see him—just so I can tell the folks back in Texas how big these Ozark bass really get to be."

"I'll let ye know when I'm a-goin' atter 'im agin," Dee promised and left me to wonder when that would be.

Three or four days later, while I was having a second cup of coffee and trying to decide whether to go upstream or downstream that day or to try Little Buffalo for a change, Dee walked into my camp.

"I'm a goin'," he announced.

"And may I trail along?" I asked, too hopefully, I feared.

"Thet's whut I said t'other day," he replied.

In five minutes we were on our way, downstream. I hurried after the tough bare feet ahead of me, over sharp rocks that made me cringe in spite of my thick rubber soles. Dee led me straight to the hole by the chinquapin spring, where just two years before I had first heard of King Solomon from the game warden. We had a good drink of water, and I rolled a cigarette.

Dee took from his pocket a ball of stout cotton cord and tied the free end to the middle of the 12-foot cane pole he had brought with him. He measured off twice the length of his pole and cut the cord. Then he bent to the line a three-foot piece of copper wire and to that a new bronzed "catfish hook" of a murderous size.

"I'm about ready," he said.

"Go to it, boy," I said. "I hope you get him."

"Ain't ye a-goin to fish any?" he asked.

"No," I answered, but not very firmly, "King Solomon is your fish. I'll watch. I just want to see him."

"I can show 'im to ye if ye'll climb the bluff."

He looked across the river. The sun was just topping the ridge.

"Hit's the right time," he said.

With Dee leading, we crossed below the spring and followed a goat trail up to a ledge of the bluff. There we sat down. The river was about ten feet below us. It was still and shaded by the ridge behind us—all but a narrow strip along the opposite bank.

"Do ye see thet there sycamore log, catty-cornered down the crick?" Dee asked, pointing toward the sunny strip of water.

"Yes, I caught a good one there last summer," I replied. I had tried it many times since without a single strike.

"Thet's where King Solomon lives," Dee said. "He stays under thet old log, an' he won't let no other bass come around it. I seen 'im drive 'em away. Watch."

Dee broke off a piece of limestone the size of a dime and thumbed it into the middle of the narrow stream. I wasn't prepared for what happened. An underlying limb detached itself from the log and shot like a torpedo to the spot where the piece of rock had struck the water. There it stopped dead-still a couple of feet beneath the surface. I saw fins parrying, a bulldog jaw champing, and two bulging eyes glaring upward at the widening ripples above them. At last I was looking upon King Solomon in all of his glory!

"Thet's him," Dee said quietly—and that's the only time I ever knew Dee to waste a word.

"I believe you, Dee," I said reverently.

Then he looked at me with the same expression that I had seen on his face when he asked me if I wanted to come with him to meet King Solomon.

"Do ye want to try fer 'im with one o' yer fine pretty-things?" he asked.

"Do I?" I almost shouted. "No, Dee. No. Of course not. I'd rather just watch. You go ahead. Go ahead, Dee. But where's your bait? What are you going to use for bait?"

"Hit's in a good place. But you go ahead and try 'im. I ain't in no hurry."

I did try him. But I was in a hurry. Afraid of casting over him, I thumbed the reel, and the plug fell short by several feet of my intended mark. King Solomon rose slowly till he was only a few inches below the surface. There he stood, champing his jaws like a bulldog waiting in the pit for somebody's pet poodle.

I retrieved in a sweat. Then, shaking with bass-ague, I tried again, this time miraculously placing the lure where I aimed it—three feet to the rear of King Solomon. Action exploded. King Solomon turned and struck with a fury and speed that made him invisible, but I saw my plug. It shot upward out of the water and then dropped back with a listless splash and a slack line.

Then, as the froth cleared from the water, I saw King Solomon. He was slowly heading for his sycamore log. I sat on the ledge as limp as my line and looked at the spot where I had seen his broad tail wave me farewell.

Just then I heard Dee walking away, down the trail to the crossing. I felt pretty sick. I reeled in and stood up to go back to camp, back home, back to Texas where a bungler like me belonged, where there was more room to bungle in and fewer folks per square mile to know about it.

As I started down I met Dee coming up the trail. He had something dangling from his hook—something so monstrous that I failed, at the first glance, to recognize it. The thing was a crawfish—a rough, gnarled, clawing, red crawfish with pincers that might have dared a lobster to a pinch-as-pinch-can combat.

Dee had run the hook through the third joint of the crawfish's tail. I looked at it incredulously and then at Dee.

"Thet's a craw-dad," he stated. "I got five more in a live-box at the end of the hole. Watch."

Between the thumb and middle finger of his left hand, which also held the pole, Dee coiled a part of his line; then, whirling in his right hand the lobster-sized crawfish, he let it fly. The crawfish dropped like a horse-shoe beside the sunken sycamore log, at the particular spot where King Solomon had given me the Shanghai gesture.

Upon striking the water, the crawfish began gyrating in crazy downward spirals, instinctively tailing for dark water, a hiding place under a rock, a ledge, a log—any sanctuary away from deep, open water. He disappeared in the dark shadow under the log.

Dee jerked his line sharply twice, and then let it go slack again. Suddenly there was a jerk from the other end of the line and several feet of it were snaked under the log as he lowered the tip of his pole.

"Hook 'im! Hook 'im!" I yelled.

But Dee waited. The line twitched, and Dee struck. The long cane pole bent; and though Dee had both hands on it, with the butt of it braced in his groin, the tip jerked down and pointed to the darkness under the log. There were three savage lunges that I thought would tear the pole from the boy's hands or strip the line from it; then King Solomon came out to fight in the open.

He broke water first midway of the stream, and as he did so he shot the crawfish out of his jaws so savagely that it was forced up the copper wire to the line. But the hook held, and King Solomon felt it as he burrowed deep to the bed of the river; up he came again, shaking his head and shooting his jaw. We could see that the hook had gone through the toughest part of his lower lip.

Giving up his surface tactics, he went down again to stay, not under the log this time, but under the ledge directly beneath us. Dee tried to pull him out. The stout cane pole bent perilously, cracked, then splintered and broke a third of its length below the tip. But the line was tied below the break; so King Solomon was still fast, though far from landed. I didn't believe he could be landed from where we were—on a ledge ten feet above the water. But Dee had his own idea about it.

"You jest hold this yere pole a spell," he said.

Slipping off his overalls and shirt, he dived in. He came up, caught hold of the line, and dived again. I could tell by the jerking of the line that he was following it under the ledge. He was gone a long time, so long that I caught myself holding my breath; then the line went slack, and he popped up. He was paddling with his right hand and holding on the line with his left. I knew by the way his left arm was darting about that he still had King Solomon.

"Jest drop the pole in," he spluttered. "I'm a-goin' to swim across with 'im."

Dubiously I obeyed. The boy swam on his side with a strong scissors kick. Occasionally I could see a flash of white beside him. That was King Solomon showing his belly—all tired out.

Barring a last-minute accident, I knew that Dee had won—and he did win. I watched him scramble up the shallow bank, with his fingers through King Solomon's gill-flap, and go to the spring, where he deposited his catch and threw himself down for a well-earned rest. I picked up my rod and Dee's clothes, followed the trail down from the ledge to the rocky riffle, and crossed over to him.

This took several minutes, but he was still breathing hard when I came up. He was lying on his side, with his head propped up on one hand, while he stared in the spring pool. There was King Solomon, also lying on his side and breathing hard but regularly. He was beaten so far as the score was concerned, but not by any means in spirit. He glared at us out of one amber-rimmed defiant eye.

"Well," I remarked inanely, "You caught him."

"I reckin I did," Dee said, "but I wouldn't hev if you hadn't made 'im hungry with thet there fine pretty-thing o' yourn."

I looked at the boy closely, but could detect not the slightest hint of a smile on his face. He was watching King Solomon again. The big fish was now upright, fanning water and champing his jaw.

Just then I heard a rustling sound behind me. Turning, I saw the warden with his two guns strapped to his hips.

"Thet fine pretty-thing didn't have nary a thing to do with it," he stated definitely. "I seen it all," and the warden went down on his hands and knees to inspect King Solomon closely.

"Thet's him," he said. "There's the scar on his upper lip where I hooked 'im. Thet's him, all right. How much do ye reckin he'll weigh?"

"I wouldn't want an old friend to think I was lying," I told him, "even if I was telling the truth."

He looked at me sharply, and then grinned.

"No," he said, pulling out his plug of chewing, "I don't reckin ye would, no more 'n me."

"He's got another scar, too," Dee said. "Look at his shoulder."

I leaned over the spring pool. There was a deep livid furrow down the side of King Solomon's right shoulder. I looked at the warden.

"What do you think might have caused that?" I asked.

"I wouldn't want an old friend to think I was lyin'," he said, and looked across the river to the bluff.

I followed the direction of his glance. There, in the niche of rock below the scrubby pine where I had seen the squirrel, and just one ledge above that one from which Dee had hooked King Solomon, sat the man with the gun.

"I wouldn't," I said.

"Well," said the warden, "I reckin I jest as well to git on back to town. Better watch ol' Solomon, boy. Ye may lose him yet."

With that parting advice the warden went back the way he had come.

"I'm ready to call it a day, too," I said.

"I'm willin'," Dee said. "You can go on ahead. I'll ketch ye."

Presuming that he wanted to salvage his line and the remains of his pole, I followed his suggestion and started back to camp. A few minutes later I heard him running along the trail behind me. Turning to wait for him, I saw that his hands were empty. So—the warden had spoken a prophecy. King Solomon, wily King Solomon, had, after all, got away.

But the boy's face was serene—not the face of a boy who had just lost the biggest fish he ever saw. If Dee had ever smiled, he would have been smiling then. I supposed I would have to resort to cross-examination to get the truth—and I might fail to get it all then. But I got far more than I expected.

"Where's King Solomon?"

"Back yanner under thet ol' sycamore log," he answered.

"You staked him out? Won't somebody find him?" I wondered.

"Twouldn't do 'em no good. I turned 'im loose."

Here was something I had hardly dared to hope for. Here was a boy of twelve–a mountain boy–who had done the thing I had wished I might have the courage to do if I ever caught King Solomon. Then I thought of the man on the ledge with the gun. He must have seen the boy put the fish back. I remembered his deadly aim, how casually he had blown off the head of that squirrel.

"But he'll get killed. That man on the bluff will shoot him," I groaned.

"Won't neither," Dee said. "Since I worked on the sights o' thet gun t'other day Pa couldn't hit a hawg with it."

If a werewolf is a man who takes the form of a wolf, then a wer-trout is a man who takes the form of a fish. This eerie tale was first published in Esquire *and later came out in* Heart Songs and Other Stories *(1988). E. Annie Proulx won the 1994 Pulitzer Prize for Fiction, the 1993 National Book Award, and the 1993 PEN/Faulkner Award. Her stories often appear in the* New Yorker. *Proulx's best-known book is* The Shipping News *(1993), and her latest is* Close Range: Wyoming Stories *(1999).*

E. Annie Proulx

THE WER-TROUT
(1979)

SAUVAGE AND RIVERS ARE NEIGHBORS for a year before they meet. Sauvage and his wife live in a trailer a mile beyond the Riverses' house. Rivers has noticed the wife driving the Jeep up from the mailbox at the base of the mountain, her animal-brown hair long and tangled, shooting away from her head like dark, charged wires, her beaked nose, bloodless lips, black eyes like wet stones. The invisible husband, Sauvage, is away at work early and late, the soft purling of his truck's descent half-heard an hour before dawn, the nocturnal return a fiery wink of taillights from the kitchen window before he turns the curve and vanishes into the tunnel of trees above. Rivers often waves at the woman, thinking of country neighbors, of a little mountain gossip, and maybe of something more. She never waves back; her black eyes are locked on distant sights.

It is the same this May morning. Rivers is driving down to his shop, The March Brown. She is driving up from the mailbox. As he lifts his hand, she turns her head away. He makes a certain gesture, an angry bunch of fingers from the days when his father's name was Riverso—Misfortune, Reverse, Wrong Side. He smooths his thick, white hair, looking into the rearview mirror. He is not an old fool yet. Calm, calm, he thinks, and recites an ancient Chinese poem:

On the southern slopes flocks of crows make their home,
On the northern slopes people set nets to catch them.
But when they fly, inaccessible on the winds,
Of what use then are nets and bird traps?

Bitch, he thinks, Mrs. Crow Bitch dressed in black wool and living on the south slope of the mountain, evading the traps of neighbors' pleasantries. Has she seen that gesture? His wife calls her bitch, too. His wife's hands are serious, with tapered fingers as smooth as white jade. She embroiders birds on linen. A museum has published a book of her designs with lists of matching silk colors. *The American Bittern*—celadon, pearl, medium dove, *tête de Nègre*, fawn, faded meadow grass. She calls herself a needlecrafter and poses by the window in a brocade slipper chair. Her spare needles lie on the mahogany sewing table like a school of minnows. In her fingers a metallic shiver trails thread as fine as child's hair, but there is a curious sense of dreary labor in the finished work.

She phones him at the shop later that morning. He leaves a Blue Dun poised in the vise. Outside the south wind cracks the glossy end branches of the trees like whips.

"That goddamn woman—" He knows who she means. "That crazy, rat-haired bitch, she drove right across the yard, smashed the little apple tree, went through the garden, then back onto the road and up the mountain."

This is the first year of bloom for the Golden Russet. White blossoms are loosely scattered in its crown like a drifting cloud of mayflies. His wife says the top half of the tree now hangs upside down nearly touching the lawn, held to the main trunk only by a strip of bark. She can see the bull's-eye center of its heartwood. There are four great curved furrows in the earth from the Jeep's tires.

"A great little couple," she says, her voice twanging hard as a knotted linen cord. "Her and that husband that's never around. Got your eye on her too, haven't you? Our neighbors. A great place you picked to live, here. A fishing alky who can't make a living and crazy neighbors, that's what *I* end up with." She slams down the receiver. He can hear finality. She has had enough for a long time and says so, often.

At noon she calls again. There is a sound like lightening in the wire. Here it comes, he thinks. She says she is going back to the city, taking her bird designs, her sewing box, her watercolors of wild mushrooms, and the bottles of vitamin pills. He can have the rest. He knows this speech, has heard it before, how he lured her away from her city friends to live on a back road where tongue-tied, hostile natives squat in claptrap trailers. She names his faults and bad habits, then says she is not getting any younger. He has what *he* wants, but she has nothing. Her voice rings plangent with self-pity. He feels angry, but what she says is true. He has his own plea-sure in The March Brown, with its custom-tied flies, antique rods, im-ported English creels and old fishing prints, his books of Chinese poetry. He likes the snugness of the shop in winter with the stove kicking out breakers of heat, the glint of a fallen piece of peacock herl, the stacked boxes of moose mane, wild-turkey wing, hare masks, and grizzly necks. The March Brown, steadily losing the retirement money, silently eating up his golden-age coin, and the sad, subtle poems about autumn mist, fallen leaves, and flowing water putting out his last sparks of ambition. He doesn't know if this is contentment or deadly inertia. Let her go embroi-der her goddamn birds. One can live cheaper than two.

He comes home at dusk. Her car is gone, and already the house has as-sumed a different aspect, an angular flatness. The lawn is plowed and scored not with four, but with hundreds of deep grooves. The apple tree is a flattened knot of broken branches. Is this his wife's goodbye, or Sauvage's wife's hello? Will he find, inside his door, Mrs. Bitch, her black skirts bunched and pulled up behind, wagging them at him like the quivering tail display of a lustful female crow? He notices that the sky fits like a dove's breast between the bud-swollen branches of maple. There is no one inside the house, nor a letter of goodbye. The vitamin pills and Dr. Bronner's Breakfast Tonic are gone. The living room seems to have arched its ceiling higher, the chair legs are more graceful, the window glass brilliantly clear, holding the dulling light for long minutes before the dark. Red taillights go up the mountain—Sauvage homeward bound. The familiar fragrance of his wife is still in the room, will be for a long time. Li Bo, he thinks.

. . . though the scent remains
In person she'll not come again
A love that is something, something *falling*
Or white dew wet on the something *moss*

He tries a stiff sob, but it is for Li Bo, not his gone wife. Sauvage's headlights are coming back down the mountain, yellow torches flaring through the hardwoods, first to east, then to west on the switchbacks, then along the straight and into the driveway. He will apologize for the multiple tire trenches in the lawn or perhaps bear a last message from the vanished embroiderer.

Sauvage has a French-Canadian face, long and narrow with skin the color of neutral shoe polish, a nose made for the nasalities of *joual*. There are circles around his eyes like bruises. He is twenty years younger than Rivers. He folds a card in his small fingers and folds again.

"I got trouble up home. Hey, I got to use your phone?" He has on a black-and-red checked wool cap of the type favored by old deer hunters, brown cotton twill work pants, and felt-lined pac-boots. There is a draggled Dark Cahill in his hat. "I got to use your phone," he says again. "I come home, my wife's eating a mouse. She don't talk, just eating it there with the skin on—" He gags, recovers.

Rivers thinks of that pale mouth reddened. A piece of wet gravel falls from the edge of Sauvage's boot onto the floor with an infinitesimal tick.

"She put the phone in the sink, it's full of hot water. I got to call her doctor. She has these troubles." There is an upward rock to the rhythm of his sentences.

Rivers points to his wall phone and goes into the living room out of courtesy, closing the door behind him. He hears a murmur, coughing, then the outside kitchen door closing. The red tail-lights go steadily back up the mountain.

Later the ambulance rushes up, a bonfire flying through the trees. Rivers leans against the cold window, his breath clouding the glass and obscuring the reflection of his aging face. It has begun to rain, spring rain, good for young apple trees, good for young trout. The ambulance descends, its headlights shining on the curved lakes that fill the wheel ruts in his ruined lawn. Sauvage trails behind in his truck, solitary mourner in a cortege.

Rivers has a sense of narrow escape from disaster, like the victim of an earthquake who sees the houses on each side in dust-plumed rubble while his own is untouched. He feels that some powerful divine force has summoned away the two women who lived on the south side of the mountain. Well, they had to take their turns at misery; he has had his, he thinks, years before, the drinker stuttering into the glass caverns of bottles, so wounded by the circumstances of his wretched life that it seemed the knots of his heart could never be unpicked, even with an awl. He has found a way to cure himself of all suffering and worry by memorizing ancient Chinese poems and casting artificial flies in moving water. He is solaced by the faint parallels between his own perception of events and those of the stringy-bearded scholars of the Tang, enjoying, as he does, a sad peace at the sight of feathered ephemera balanced on the dark-flowing river.

In bed he reads the paper. A woman has found god through a car accident, saying, "What happened to me brought out my religion like crazy." Below this is a one-line filler: "Some say to dream of doves means happiness." Rivers has heard his wife say this differently– "Bird dreams mean sunbeams." But in fact how many people do dream of doves? Ornithologists? Hawkish politicians who wake in hot sweats of resentment rather than happiness? "Dream of trout," says Rivers in his bed.

He dreams of a crow. A malignant crow with a red eye like rock bass. Human fat glistens on its beak, as cruelly curved as secateurs. A glint of light burns on the steely edge and becomes a flashing needle, the crow itself an embroidered bird worked by the erratic electric impulses of his sleeping brain. He wakes, his heart flailing like a netted trout. The window is a grey rectangle in the blackness of the wall. He hears an engine laboring up the mountain. Sauvage going back to his trailer.

It is still raining in the morning when he goes to The March Brown. The black locust trees lean against the stained sky, the water on the road hisses. There are no customers all morning.

In the afternoon he is reading how Yuan Mei's cook falls ill with hallucinations and thinks sunlight is snow, when Sauvage comes in. He is bigger than he was in the kitchen. He says he has stopped by to thank Rivers for the use of his phone last night. He looks around the shop. The rain still beats against the window, but inside it is warm, scented with fine oils and dry feathers, with burning beech, seasoned bamboo, and the thin, intoxicating odor of head cement. Certain emanations come from the shelf of Chinese poets—the returning boat, moon water, and river weeds. Sauvage seems calm, as calm as Rivers. He looks beyond the streaming window, deciding some private matter.

"You know the Yellow Bogs?" Sauvage asks, leaning on the counter and cocking his right leg comfortably. Neither wants to talk about vanished needlecrafters or mad rodent appetites. "Yellow Bogs is up in the north." There are stoic folds at the corners of his mouth. He knows of the place because of his grandfather's stories. The old man worked up in the northcountry swamps in the early twenties, cutting timber and pulp. Sauvage has never been there himself, but he knows the fables of the country and can salt his sentences with Quebecois expletives.

The Logger Brook, the Yellow Branch, and the Black Branch come thrashing down the steep mountains through a tangle of deadfalls and slash, in company with fifty nameless streams and brooks. All this water flattens out in the Bogs in random sloughs and ponds. Black fountains well up like the fuming outlets of an underground river flowing in secret torrents through cavities under the mountains. Sauvage murmurs, drawing invisible lines across the counter with his yellow fingers. Rivers feels the floor of The March Brown shift under his feet like flooding sand.

Yes, says Sauvage, that Yellow Bogs is bad country. Bear hunters lose their dogs in there. Once a team of horses went down in a bottomless pool, dragging the driver with them below the stinking black mud. It is cold in the Bogs, shrouded in thick mists and rain, and August snow stings the swamp maples. The drops of moisture on the tips of the spruce branches never dry before rain falls again. Rivers can hear the northern rain stored in the empty woods, hear it falling on the humped boulders at the water's edge.

Sauvage leans closer, his finger taps, and he says that in the cold, rain-stippled rivers, in the deep sinkholes of Yellow Bogs, there are native brook trout. Old trout. Giants of the water. Some of them, says Sauvage, go over eight pounds. In his inner eye Rivers sees the Yellow Bogs shaped like a huge black bottle, and himself, smaller than a mote of dust, drawn into the neck by an invisible current of desire.

Sauvage and Rivers jounce on the front seat of the truck. The logging road marked on the topographical map has fallen back to wilderness in the decades since the last survey. Twice they prize the truck out of mudholes with a cut popular for a lever, Sauvage lunging, Rivers rocking the wallowing vehicle as the wheels spin out gouts of cold mud. Thick snow still lies in the northern hollows. The road vanishes before they reach the Bogs.

"Shank's mare!" cries Rivers in a new, high-pitched voice. It is late afternoon, the air chilly and raw after the snug truck cab. Sauvage takes up the small canoe like a cross.

Rivers walks in front with a heavy pack, an adversary that tries to pull him to the ground. Sauvage's right to go first is stronger because of his grandfather's presence sixty years earlier on this same trail, but Rivers burns with hotter lust to penetrate the Bogs. He has brought his old Garrison bamboo rod, his favorite when he was a young man, a rod with memories. Sauvage's rod is a cheap, discount-store bargain.

After half a mile they rest. Sauvage smokes a cigarette. Rivers sucks the smell of leaf mold and wet ferns into his nose. There is a burning spot between his shoulder blades coming from the whiskey bottles carefully wrapped and buried in the depths of the pack. They send out a feeling like a hot-water bottle and he feels safe in their company, although he has not had a drink for six years and has taught himself to think of alcohol as a corrosive lye that will burn out his liver and lights. The embroiderer made him take an oath never to drink again. He remembers the fluttering candle, himself naked on his knees on the pine floor, his right hand held high, his fervent swearing never, never to take another drink of alcohol, not sherry, not rum, not beer, and certainly never whiskey, while the woman in the ice-blue satin nightgown embroidered all around the hem with stooping falcons smiled down on him with wet and gleaming teeth.

The light seeps from the sky as they go along the faint trail. Swamp chill comes up from the ground and mosquitoes whine. A pale strip of water glimmers through the trees, and Rivers has a sense of pleasant loneliness, of being at the edge of a cliff. It is Yellow Bogs. The light bleeds away and a dark angle of shadow spreads over the water. The waterweeds go a deep, sinking black.

Rivers struggles to put up the tent. In the west a heavy roll of clouds holds a deep bronze patina. A mosquito hawk rows through the lake of sky like a feathered boat, his wings trailing a stuttering sound. The yellow flames of Sauvage's fire leap, and Rivers frames words with his lips: "How about a drink?" He does not say them. It is all for himself, and he can still wait a little longer.

Sauvage cries, "Tomorrow, big trout watch out! I hope I brought a frying pan big enough to hold one of them big ones. Hey, Rivers, how you like this place?"

"Feels like home," says Rivers.

"Gives me the creeps in the dark," answers Sauvage. A few drops of rain fall, each a spit in the fire. The silence has a heavy weight. Rivers thinks a little of the Five-bottle Scholar, Wang Chi, who died from overindulgence in wine. There are worse ways.

This habit of his of sinking backward into the past sets him outside the events of the present. Everything has happened before: the deaths of children, the house burning in the night, the barred shadows of poplars lying across the road in late autumn, sharp-toothed illness biting into soft bones, loneliness, the village scourged by bearded invaders, the people cruelly tortured, a drunken reveler singing a half-forgotten verse in the dusk, the scent of bruised grass, the emptied cup, the slow wingbeat of a dying crow. He recognizes himself as a struggling spentwing floating briefly on time's river. Before he falls asleep in the faintly musty tent, he touches some of his shining bottles. The rain comes across the Bogs and onto the tent like an iron threshing machine in a prairie wheat field.

His watch says 5:20. Fine cold points of mist touch his face, then dissolve in the heat from his body. He crawls out into the dim morning. Larch branches like severed arms writhe and float in the fog. Yellow Bogs is hidden behind opaque layers of mist, and the drenched earth runs in streams and rivulets.

There is Sauvage, kneeling in front of a neat pyramid of shaved dead spruce branches, their dry hearts exposed, curls of birch bark bunched underneath. In a second the flames catch. A wavering globe of orange light hangs in the mist around him, his long face still creased with the lines of sleep. Rivers is contrary this morning; he does not want fire and breakfast, he wants to find the secret pools in Yellow Bogs where the giant trout lie waiting, their fins gently strumming the water.

But Sauvage wants to stay on the margin, fishing the edge of the Bogs. "How about keep this camp until the fog burns off?" he says. "I seen this thick stuff hang in most of the day. Look at it, you don't see thirty feet."

"This is only the edge. We get any trout in here, they'll be fleas," mutters Rivers. The *lunkers*—he says—will be deep in the coiled entrail of the Bogs, maybe a two-day journey in. "We got to make some time," he says. "No point in coming two hundred miles up here to catch midget trout."

They paddle in silence, the wet tent bunched between them. The water narrows, broadens, narrows again. Sauvage looks left and right, over each shoulder. Spruce, larch and cedar, monotonously similar, loom from unsuspected shores, then fell away.

"Islands," says Sauvage. Then, mournfully, "Jesus, in here less than a day and I bet we're lost."

"Not lost," lies Rivers. "I got the direction all lined out. Been following the main current. Got my compass." He has the reckless feeling that nothing matters except going forward. A willow leaf curves away from them and they can hear the muffled rushing of stream water into the Bogs away to their right. They drag the canoe over barriers of wedged and woven sticks and branches in stout beaver dams. Channels twist and curve, dozens of tiny streams and rivulets tinkle and splash into the grass-choked marshy perimeter of the Bogs. The water is brown and deep. Once Rivers sees a submerged log move, a trick of the cloudy water or the ponderous drift of a big fish. Trout are here. He can smell them. Nymphs, he thinks, maybe where the streams run in, maybe go up some of the bigger brooks a little way. Wet flies, black gnats, spentwings, everything drowning, wet, underwater, and lost in tail-churned mud or shroud-like fog. But there is enmity in Sauvage's paddling, and Rivers thinks it is too early for that. Rivers guides them to a small sandbar under the cracked arm of a cedar.

There is a snug sense of shelter under the trees. Rivers sets up the tent, a silent apology to Sauvage for pushing ahead in bad weather. "We can stay here a few days if the fishing's good, wait for the weather to break," he says. "We're in pretty deep now, anyway."

Sauvage quickly makes a solid fireplace with a double ring of stones. "Think we're on an island?"

"Don't know. Dumb to go any farther in this fog. It's got to lift sometime, and while we wait we can try the water."

Sauvage looks into his cheap plastic fly case while Rivers looks over the characterless spread of water, flattened and smoothed by the heavy mist like a bolt of satin by a warm iron. Then they hear it. Somewhere out on the flat water behind the cape of muffling fog a ponderous weight plunges down, a vast splash like a granite monument falling into the Bogs.

"What the hell was that?" says Sauvage.

"One of the big ones." It is only what Rivers has expected.

"No, no," says Sauvage, "they don't come *that* big. Had to be a beaver. A big buck beaver telling us to get the hell out of his territory. Slap his tail, you know?" Then another crashing plunge, nearer in the mist. Not the sharp crack of a flat beaver tail on the smooth water, but the rushing collapse of a wall of water into a monstrous cavity. Rivers can easily imagine a tremendous trout the size of a gun case, but the splash is followed by a thick, coughing cry that dies away in the reeds.

"Sweet Jesus," says Sauvage.

"What the hell, let's fish," says Rivers.

"Maybe stick together, though," says Sauvage.

In a flash of intuition Rivers knows Sauvage is afraid of what he cannot see, maybe haunted by the mysterious behavior of his wife, or by the French-Canadian grandfather stories of loupgarou, of windigo, evil forests, and swamp demons, of all the dark riddles of superstition.

He looks at the water. Strange water, not the dead onyx mirror of a bog pond, but the swollen overflow of a dammed river. The main current pulses faintly eastward. He has felt it against his paddle all morning. Before him lies a deep, eddying pool out of the current's main thrust. He thinks he sees moving shadows near the bottom. Onshore the blackflies are bad. Rivers takes a tiny number twenty-two black midge nymph from his case irresolutely; the grey mist and bad light—maybe something flashier. But he ties it on anyway. Sauvage, seventy feet above him, gives a cry and Rivers turns to see his arm curved in a familiar arch, the rod tip down and an orange-bellied brookie the size of a young bass boring into the water. Sauvage is deft but not delicate. He tends to haul in the trout, cutting short the sweet struggle.

"Nice one!" he congratulates himself, giving Rivers a triumphant smirk. Rivers sees that Sauvage is a competitor; an aggressive, posturing contest winner, not someone who can understand self-made solitude.

Rivers turns away and thinks himself deep for the trout, casts the tiny weighted midge and watches the line, waiting for the halt or the trembling leap forward. Nothing. He starts it back to him in tiny jerks, lets it rest, again the miniature, tender twitch and a trout takes it just under the surface, smashing the water, tail walking, rearing up like a sea serpent, and writhing is muscular body in the fluid river like a corkscrew. Then it is over. The fish comes down on the fine tippet and breaks it, running for the bottom with Rivers's little black nymph. Sauvage, who has been watching, whinnies.

"You smart-ass bastard," says Rivers to the spreading ring on the water, "I'm going to get you."

At two o'clock Rivers starts the first bottle. He sits on a stump, taking good swallows from it and watching Sauvage cook his trout. He has skewered the thick, limp bodies on peeled willow sticks and set them over a circle of coals. The delicate membrane of ash is disturbed by smoking drops that fall from the fish. The trout twist in a semicircle as though they are trying to bite their own flanks, like dogs after fleas. Sauvage peels the cooked flesh from the laddered backbones in steaming orange chucks. Rivers refuses to eat.

"I didn't catch any yet. I'll wait."

"That's funny, you didn't catch *anything?* I thought you was the Great Fisherman. Me. I caught what, five, six? Big ones, too. By god, they taste good. What you using?"

"Dry flies," lies Rivers.

"Look, you oughta try wets or try some of them nymphs. Here, sometimes the real little ones are good. I used this one to get these here." Patronizingly he stretches out his hand to Rivers.

"Where'd you get this?" says Rivers, sure that he recognizes the too-big head and the off-kilter wings of the number twenty-two black midge nymph he lost a few hours earlier.

"Had it a long time," answers Sauvage, eating a trout as he would a slice of watermelon.

In an hour Rivers is halfway down the bottle and sets off through the woods looking for private water. His steps seem cushioned on thick, matted grass, but there is only spruce duff and an occasional etiolated fern clump underfoot. It is the whiskey that makes the ground so yielding. The trees seem to shift way from him slyly on both sides, but he marches in a straight line through the swampy hummocks and wet, slapping branches until he finds the water again, hung with opaque shawls of wooly grey, a solitary place, pungent with decay, and far away from Sauvage. The bottle is his companion.

His waders and hat are in the tent. He takes his clothes off except for his boots and walks into the water to escape the knotted alders, pulling the Yellow Bogs around him like a cold sheet. His shirt is wound about his head against the blackflies. For the next hours he makes a superb series of casts, running through everything in his repertoire and his monogrammed leather fly case, for the water is changeable, shaping itself before his eyes, first into glassy pools, then frothy falls, rapid snaking currents, yellow ribbons of crumpled silk over sandbars, deep onyx mines of still water bent under sunless vaults of alder, milky absinthe cloud runs of chalk stream, and the stump-pocked moon face of a beaver pond. The trout torment him with their wavering outlines. He sees the elliptical underwater silver of trout rooting in the gravel, big browns lying like corpses on their own shadows, nymph-feeding rainbows bulging the water into hilly landscapes, fly takers sucking holes in the fragile tissue of the surface film, leaping brookies trying for flying morsels on the wing like cats after sparrows. He catches nothing, a white-haired, shivering fool with a tired arm and an empty whiskey bottle. He dresses again and wanders back through light evening rain to the wet tent and Sauvage.

Sauvage has an enormous fire burning and sits within the circle of light peering out at the crawling shadows under the black spruce. "Jesus, where the hell you been! I been waiting here for a couple of hours. I thought you mighta fell in and drowned." Sauvage fussily unwraps a silver cigar of aluminum foil, disclosing the baked bodies of two large brook trout.

One of them, a good fifteen inches long, wounds Rivers's heart that someone other than he should have caught it. He goes into the tent and gets the second bottle. "I don't want any fish. You eat them," he says.

Sauvage pouts like a spurned bride while the rain falls on the hot trout, diluting the juices. Sauvage begins to eat mournfully, with every mouthful looking up at Rivers on the stump, the rain dripping off the underside of his upraised bottle.

"There's somebody else here in the Bogs," Sauvage says suddenly. "I seen him."

"Yeah? Who is it, the fish cop?"

"No. I don't think so. He looks like he's crazy, a crazy fisherman. He's fishing over there across the channel. First I see only this shape, this human shape, casting and casting. Then the fog lifts a little and I can see the guy pretty good. He's buck naked, standing there in that cold water up to his knees, no waders, no vest, and over his head he's got some kind of cloth so I don't see his face. Casts—roll casts, S-casts, bow-and-arrow, double-hauls—everything, just like at an exhibition. So I yell at him, 'Any luck?' but he don't answer. Then the mist comes down heavy again, and the way it comes in, see, it makes it look like the guy starts walking out into the deep water, looks like he goes right down under the water."

"Sauvage, we got real trouble now," says Rivers from behind his bottle. "What you saw was the Wer-Trout, the Wer-Trout of Yellow Bogs."

"Hey, come on, Rivers, don't make jokes about that kind of stuff."

"No joke, Sauvage, that's what you saw. The body of a man, the head of a trout. That's why he covered up his face, so you couldn't see those big, flat eyes and no chin and ugly teeth. Don't worry, though, he only goes for you if you kill his women. You didn't catch any girl trouts, did you?"

Sauvage's grease-dappled chin shines at Rivers in the firelight. "I think you're drunk, Rivers," he says.

Rivers laughs stagily. He feels his words falling as precise as snowflakes, as luminous as sunlight. "Yeah? Remember that big splash we heard? That you said was a beaver? That was the Wer-Trout. Thank god *I* didn't catch any of his pals. And what was that you said to him? 'Any luck?'! Christ, he'll really be after you now. Also, Sauvage, that's how come our wives are gone. In the daytime when we weren't there the Wer-Trout came around, showed his face in the window, and scared them away. That's why the little ladies always go."

"Knock it off, Rivers. We come out here to do some fishing, get away from our troubles, and you go off half the day, get drunk, start this kind of talk. I think we head back in the morning."

"Caw, caw, caw," says Rivers, showing his teeth and winking both eyes. Sauvage, insulted, crawls into the tent. Rivers stays up, blowing across the neck of his bottle, making a sound like a coyote in a cider barrel. After a while he notices a tiny scurrying shape at the morsels of fish Sauvage has let drop on the ground. He stalks the mouse with his bottle for a weapon, his thumb thrust into the neck against spillage, and mashes it dead with temporary dexterity. He places it in the center of Sauvage's frying pan, where it sticks in the congealing grease, then goes back to his stump.

He comes to, lying in the pricking rain near the stump, his body convulsed with shivers, his teeth clacking. He feels wizened and cold to the heart. The fire is a stinging black circle of muddy ash as he crawls over it toward the tent, hoping he won't throw up in the sleeping bag. It hurts to breathe, to move, to live. Just beyond the stump his knee comes down on something like a slender twig. The sound is only a small, dry crack, but Rivers knows at once what it is. He has been dreading that inevitable sound for more than twenty years, and it is as sharp as an embroidery needle thrust into his eardrum. He has broken his Garrison bamboo. He picks it up in the dark, the upper half dangling uselessly like his snapped apple tree. He thinks he can feel its spirit dribbling out of the crushed hexogonal heart like a string of hardening wax. His apple tree is dead, his lawn ruined, his wife gone, his Garrison broken, and he has caught no fish nor will catch any now. Yet he tells himself these transitory ills are like duckweed on the water. There is no mouse on his plate.

Inside the tent he lights a candle and unwraps the last bottle, from his wife's blue satin nightgown. In the shining curve of glass he sees his reflection: the chinless throat, the pale snout, the vacant rusted eyes of the Wer-Trout.

This endearing story is told from the perspective of the fish. "Old Croc" is a big old northern pike. Northerns are game fish that fight with wriggling fury, providing a culinary reward for the lucky angler. A pair of callow youths are out to hook this titan of the weedy lake. The story was written for Sports Afield. *Jason Lucas was a mainstay of* Sports Afield's *regular staff for many years, and wrote the authoritative* Lucas on Bass Fishing *(1949).*

Jason Lucas

OLD CROC
(1947)

LONG, LONG YEARS AGO OLD CROC was hatched. There was a shallow, weedy spot near the shore of Tamarack Lake, and to it came a huge northern pike laden with eggs and escorted by three or four much smaller males. She had spawned there, she had laid more than half a million eggs at one time! Three days later she had chanced to meet one of her mates. There had been a streaking dart through the water, a swirl that barely showed on the surface, and where there had been two fish there now was only one, a huge female who looked much bulkier than a moment before, and who sank slowly to the bottom, lazily opening and closing her great gills in contentment. Such was the heritage of Old Croc.

At first Croc was only a tiny barred needle which seemed to shoot through the water without the slightest movement of tail or fin. Now she would be motionless; now she would be streaking off like an arrow from the bow. Straight as an arrow was her aim; many was the tiny water creature which entered those diminutive but rapacious jaws.

The needle grew. Larger insects were engulfed in those ever-hungry jaws . . . bugs, larvae, everything that moved. Larger grew the needle. There were thousands of other needles among the weeds, but this one grew fastest of all. At last came the day when this large needle swallowed one of the smallest needles—one of her brothers. This was much more nourishing food than the bugs and spiders, so her size increased in leaps and bounds while the other needles vanished.

There were little minnows; there were tiny fry of other species; but to this little cannibal nothing seemed so tasty and desirable as one of her own kind. On this one thing the larger pike of earlier hatches thoroughly and whole-heartedly agreed with her . . . they agreed among themselves that young Croc would provide a most delightful lunch if she could be caught. Of course, two pike had to be of practically the same size to agree on anything; if they were not, the larger swallowed the smaller as the quickest way of settling all arguments.

Croc took very good care not to be swallowed. Not that she resented the attitude of the larger pike; well she knew the one great moral code of her tribe, "Swallow that which moves and is smaller than thou." Had a bigger fish failed to try to live up to this rule, she would have wondered . . . but her brain was far too tiny for such abstruse things as wonder. In that little brain was room for nothing but the overpowering desire to chase, to kill, to swallow.

It was not long until the time came when she was over a foot in length, although she was still endowed with the shape of a huge needle. Now she had her adult coloration, a sort of greenish-gray, thickly speckled with yellowish-white spots. Toward the back she grew darker, almost black, and her belly was silvery-white. Her tail and fins were a beautiful transparent bright red with black blotches. Already she had become a little terror to the smaller species of the lake, so much so that she fancied herself mature and made her first jaunt to the deep water. This over-confidence almost ended her history there and then.

Out from the shallow weeds near the shore she swam with wonderful grace. Her tail seemed stiff behind her; not a fin seemed to move; still she glided along like some diminutive, noiseless submarine bent on death and destruction. She was almost invisible from any side. Seen from the bottom, the white of her belly blended with the sky and the shimmering surface of Tamarack Lake. From above, her dark back merged with the muddy bottom perfectly. From either side the gray-green ground color and dapplings of yellowish could hardly be seen.

Three feet of water—four—five—ten. Nothing had happened . . . nothing but little fish flying in panic to the weeds at her stealthy approach. She rose higher, and drifted like a slender shadow above the tops of the weeds. Now she had come to the edge of this particular stretch of weedy forest, but far ahead she could see another. Of course there was a long distance of open bottom between; but was she not a pike, whom all things feared?

She hesitated a moment, scanning the water with her fierce eyes. Nothing could look more peaceful. In fact, there was but one thing in sight, some great fluffy thing that floated quietly on the surface of the water halfway across, with two broad paddles very slowly waving in the water beneath it.

Croc started forward slowly, watching those slowly-moving paddles cautiously. Of course it was some creature of the other world, the world where there was no water, but it was well to keep an eye on it. Instinct made Croc sink deeper and deeper as she approached the air-creature above. Presently she was almost beneath it, and here she paused, her cold, evil eyes fixed on the paddles. They were moving, therefore they might be good to eat.

Then there was a slight splash beside the floating thing; a long, snake-like neck was thrust far under the surface; jetty, expressionless eyes swept the bottom. But Croc had hung motionless, so the loon had not seen her. The great bird raised his head, opened his bill, and sent a wild, laughing call to his mate at the other end of the lake. With head on one side he waited for the answer, and having heard it his neck went under again.

This time Croc was not so cautious; she was becoming accustomed to that air-thing floating innocently above. So it was that she permitted a slight waving motion of her tail. Immediately, where the loon had been, a silvery explosion of light broke the surface of the water, a great burst of light that dazzled Croc when she looked that way. Then the blinding light was traveling outward in ever-growing circles, and in the middle of it appeared a dusky shape that came downward like a bolt . . . the loon, strong wings and webbed feet sending him through the water at a terrific rate, sharp bill straight ahead to cleave a way.

Across the barren bottom shot Croc—never before had she looked so like a well-sped arrow as now—straight toward the nearest point of the weed-bed. She heard a snap like a closing steel-trap just behind her, and the tip of her tail seemed to burn. Instinctively she knew that it would be only an instant until the next snap came. The weeds were now only ten feet off, but she could not reach them.

Croc doubled her body and shot straight toward the surface. After her sped the loon, agile as herself. Next a wild letter S, and then a broken circle. Around and around in wild gyrations went the two—two indistinct, whirling blurs, so fast they doubled and maneuvered. Again and again Croc felt the quick tremor of the water as the strong beak of the loon snapped, barely missing its mark by a fraction of an inch.

There came a snap that was duller than the others. Croc felt her movements suddenly arrested, felt a great weight hanging to her tail—a dull pain in that tail. The loon had seized her!

Then against Croc's side came the scraping of strong weeds—bare inches to safety! The pike's body doubled like a snake's, seeking purchase among the weeds; her tail thrashed wildly. There was the vibration of something tearing dully, and the pike was flashing into the weed-bed, a tiny stream of red behind where skin and flesh had been torn loose close to her tail . . . lucky that the loon had not had a better hold! Into the weeds, too, shot the great bird, only to soon have its wings hopelessly entangled. For a few seconds it struggled to go forward, little black pupils expanded to see in the half-light and seeking the fish that had barely escaped. Then it rose slowly, angrily, to the surface, where it shook its bill and sent a wild, baffled call to its mate.

For perhaps an hour Croc lay there invisible in the weeds. Her tail hurt—slightly—nothing could hurt her dull nerves very much. At first she was very cautious, but this caution did not last long; soon it was drowned in her one great passion—to kill, to eat! She had almost forgotten the loon, but when next she would see one the memory would come back, dimly, just enough to make her careful.

She was hungry—rarely was she otherwise. She worked slowly out to the very edge of the weed-bed, sank close to the bottom, and waited, motionless as a water-logged stick. Presently she saw a brownish shape approaching; a young dogfish. That would be her meat! Dogfish, she had decided, was just as good to eat as another pike. A blue-gill passed, a small bass. These she ignored—she ate such occasionally, but that ridge of terrible spines on their backs made the bass and his relatives undesirable as a rule.

Apparently without her willing it, she sank lower and lower into the level bed of weeds under her, until nothing showed but her eyes—cold, motionless eyes that saw everything but were themselves unseen. Now the unsuspecting dogfish was almost over her. Then, somehow, Croc was no longer in the weeds. She had not seemed to move, but now she hung in the water above and down her capacious throat was traveling a flopping tail. Slowly she sank back, gill-covers working lazily. That had been a good meal! Nor did she know that it had been also a good deed, for the scavenger dogfish is one of the greatest destroyers of the spawn of pike, bass, and other game fish. Perhaps if she had known it was a good deed she would not have eaten him, for her dull little brain held nothing but evil and voracity.

Evening came, and she stirred lazily. She was already hungry again—it was one of the days when fish, for some unknown reason, are always ravenous no matter what they have eaten. Again she worked close to the edge of the weed-bed, and again her cold eyes searched the water for prey.

Soon she saw it—some strange little fish that she did not recognize. It was long and thin and round, and kept curling and uncurling its pinkish body as though in pain. There was some slender thing running from it to the surface of the water where what appeared to be a great log floated harmlessly. Croc did not know what the little fish was, but it had life and therefore should be eaten.

She drifted toward it slowly, ready to make a dash if it tried to escape. She smelled it—it had the odor of earth. Slowly, she took it in her mouth.

Immediately something seemed to almost tear her head from her body. She whirled in consternation and headed back toward the weeds, but something brought her around in a half-circle. Again she tried to turn, but before she knew what was happening she felt herself shooting out of the water, to land flopping in the bottom of a boat.

There was a whoop of joy as two tattered, freckle-faced boys bent over her. She shook the hook from her lips, but that helped none at all, for the sides of the boat were high and she did not know that beyond them lay the open water. One of the boys—his skin was much lighter colored than the other's, although his nose was very red—reached quickly for a short club that lay under a seat.

"Let's kill him!" he yelled, and he sounded fearfully blood-thirsty for so small a boy.

But the other boy, no larger, kicked the club back out of the way. His freckled nose—what there was of a nose—wrinkled up superciliously.

"Huh!" he grunted, and his tone showed how very superior he knew himself to be; "My father says I should let all the little fish go without hurting them, and other kids should do the same . . . and even grown men. My father always lets 'em go. He says then there'll be lots of big fish for all of us when we get to be men, but if we don't turn 'em loose, why, we won't have any big fish later on."

"We–we won't?" the other little boy had wrinkled up his face . . . he had never heard of such a thing.

"No, we won't–that's what my dad says, an' he knows all about fish. Gosh!" his mouth opened. "Wouldn't it be turrible if there was no big fish to catch?" He was actually gasping at the thought of such an awful calamity.

"Well, yes–but–Well, this ain't such a very little fish; mebbe we'd better–"

"No, *sir*! My dad says anyone who kills a little fish ain't a sportsman, an' he says if a man ain't a sportsman he'll bear watchin' in everything because he's likely to be just no-'count every way. You just ain't been livin' near the lake as long as I have, an' you don't know things like I do." Evidently he was trying hard to make allowances for the other's terrible ignorance, but was having a hard time of it.

"Well–uh–all right, let him go. Gosh, I hope we ketch a big one–a great big whopper! 'Spose we will, Hank?"

"Sure! If we're good sportsmen we'll have good luck, but if we ain't– well, what could you expect?"

All of which conversation was not at all edifying to the pike who lay in the hot air with rapidly-drying gills. But presently the amateur lecture on sportsmanship was finished. Croc was seized by the gills, and gently placed back in the water. There she lay on her side apparently dead, the boys watching her anxiously. They had now firmly decided that the pike's death would ruin their chances of getting a "whopper" for that day at least. To complicate matters, it occurred to Harry Weaver–"Hank," his chums generally called him–that this pike by dying would automatically shut him, Hank, out of the ranks of true sportsmen.

It was a painful moment for all three. At length the second boy reached out a cautious hand to touch the apparently dead Croc. Immediately the water boiled, the boy got a sound slap from a strong tail, and the pike was gone. They could see it swim toward the weeds slowly, apparently dazed. But anyway it was alive, and they were sportsmen–which fact was a huge relief after all the suspense.

Years went by, years that would have been monotonous to anyone but Croc. Still she grew and grew. At last came the blissful time when she need fear no creature of the lake, not even the loon himself. Her bright colors had dimmed somewhat now, until she looked more than ever like the muddy, weedy bottom. Her head had grown to an immense thing more than a quarter the length of her body, and a terrible mouth split it its full length—a grisly mouth armed with hundreds of needle-sharp teeth slanting backward, so that what entered that awful cavern must go down, never back up.

Thousands were the fish that had entered there. Dogfish mostly, and other pike, but nothing was quite safe from her. Even the smaller water-birds swimming on the surface, even an occasional muskrat, had a way of suddenly disappearing in a swirl, never to rise again. Once she had swallowed a young loon and when its father dived and pursued her into her weed-bed she had felt more annoyance than fright, for what could he do more than break her skin slightly? She did not know it, but this was the same old male loon who had once almost proved her end.

More years passed and still she grew, though not so rapidly now, until she was truly a monster of her kind. Guides began to talk of her, and sportsmen. At one time she had so many as two spoon-hooks and one red-headed plug hanging from her wicked lips at the same time, but one after another they had dropped away or been caught on some snag and torn loose. Half a dozen hooks had been corroded and eaten away by the sides of her always-hungry stomach.

Only once had she been brought close to a boat . . . the guide, indeed, was reaching his sharp gaff toward her. She had been exposed, exhausted on the surface, but still back up. Only her wicked flat head and murderous devilish eyes were clearly to be seen by the three in the boat, and they were the head and eyes of the Congo crocodile, features which have been rare since the bloody Mesozoic age when huge reptiles held the earth. Those men had seen that awful head in the water, but no closer. One of the sportsmen in his eagerness had leaned too far over the side of the boat, so that Croc's last spasmodic swirl had upset the men into the water. That evening in camp they had all nodded solemn agreement when one recalled how like a crocodile she had looked. They swore to come back and get her again. They began by calling her the old crocodile, but that name was too long so they shortened it to Old Croc, and thus she became known for many miles around.

They did come back next year, and many years thereafter. They hooked her again, for she never learned to control her voracious appetite when something went wriggling and flashing past. But hooking her and landing her were two different things. She had learned to keep close to beds of strong and tangled weeds, and to dart into these weeds the instant she felt that she was on the end of a line.

Once or twice she failed to reach the weeds immediately but she had always succeeded in circling back to them to foul the line. The tale was told of how once in whirling back she had spun a canoe half around as though a cyclone had struck it. So her reputation grew, and sportsmen jokingly asked each other, "Well, going to catch Old Croc today?" But they said it in very much the spirit that the Bible asks, "Wouldst take leviathan with a hook?"

Resorts were built around the lake, and their logs weathered and grew old, for Tamarack Lake had become famous for many great fish, and especially famous for Old Croc, the monster with the evil face and the knack of breaking all tackle with which it connected. Many a sportsman had felt the great wrench of Old Croc's strike, and many a sportsman had been rowed to shore, swearing or groaning as the case might be, and ruefully looking at the remains of what had once been a beautiful split bamboo rod.

Even now she was still growing, though very slowly. She did not eat quite so often now, but when she did eat the meal was generally of gargantuan proportions. Hour after hour she would lie on top of the weeds, all hidden but her two evil eyes that never moved but saw everything that came near, waiting for prey.

Now she subsisted almost entirely on dogfish; they were big and fat and satisfying, and easier to catch than other pike. She would just lie there, murder in her eyes, until some big dogfish who was himself a scourge of the lake happened to swim over her on a scavenging expedition. She waited motionless until he reached a certain point, and then, effortlessly but not too fast, she just reached up and seized him. To an onlooker it would seem that her comparatively slow movements gave him time to get away, but he never did. Perhaps sheer terror of that fierce, reptilian face paralyzed him for the moment it took her to reach him. Now she swallowed very slowly, when her prey was large . . . it might take a long time for the tip of the still weakly-flapping tail to disappear down her throat.

Now she rarely troubled to catch smaller fish; it would take almost a bushel of them to appease her appetite, and she had grown too lazy to bother to catch them. It was much easier to allow what would be called large fish to eat those smaller ones, and then she would eat the large ones. But even now she could rarely resist some little thing that went flashing and wiggling through the water, some little thing of silver, gold, or gaudy colors. And so the record of smashed tackle grew.

One day she was lying in her favorite place on the top of the weeds, when a boat came over, very, very slowly. For more than two hours it hung there, now moving forward, now back, now in slow, lazy circles. Over the edge of the boat hung two faces framed in slightly graying hair, one a pink, jolly face, the other lean, weather-lined and tanned a dark brown. The pink-faced man looked puzzled, and spent more time staring around than looking into the water, and sometimes he yawned. But the brown-faced man did not yawn; his eyes scanned the bottom as would a loon, his brow knitted as he tried to fix every solitary weed-stem in his memory.

The next day was windy, with the waves high, and so was the third. But the fourth was fairly calm, with bright sunshine. This day the boat returned again, and now it dropped an anchor not far from where Old Croc lay. She sank slowly into the weeds until even her eyes were covered.

Now a black, tubular thing came over the side of the boat. One end of it went slightly under the surface of the water, and on the other was the face of the bronzed man, his head covered by a coat that he could see the better. The pink-faced man yawned, grumbled, took a nap, woke up again, yawned again. At last the end of his patience seemed to be reached, and he growled:

"Excuse me for interrupting your fun, but I just want to ask if you died a couple of hours ago—it's that long since you moved. How about trying a few casts?"

The bronzed face came very slowly and cautiously out of the improvised water-telescope, and there was a tolerant grin on it:

"Doc, you're a great specialist now. *Of course* you just start and cut a customer up without taking time to study the case?"

"Well," sighed the specialist, "thank Heavens I'm not a great fishing authority like you. What a heck of a profession you chose! As I was saying—about casting—?"

He reached tentatively for his rod.

"Wait a minute, Doc; there seems to be—"

The rest of what he said was muffled as the face disappeared under the coat again. A moment later a dull bellow came out of it, and in another moment the face came out, with the mouth wide open.

"Oh, my gosh, Doc! Old Croc—! He's as big as they say he is—he just reached up and grabbed some fish passing over him. *Whew-w-w!*" The great fishing authority blinked and gasped.

"No doubt—no doubt!" The doctor was too weary from sitting still to become enthusiastic. "Hank, maybe it's that little fellow we turned loose here that time—you remember it was somewhere about this hole." His voice sounded sarcastic. Hank laughed tolerantly— of course he knew the Doctor was only joking.

Croc saw the boat row slowly away without a single cast having been made. But the next day it came back. It anchored quietly a very long way off—so far off that Old Croc did not even trouble to sink into the weeds, although she did keep motionless, even when a good-sized juicy fish swam overhead. There was no movement from the boat, not the slightest sound of a scraping foot to send little tremors through the water. So presently, she forgot it entirely.

It was fully an hour after the boat had anchored that Old Croc heard a slight splash in toward the shore—some little fish jumping. Then straight over her came a wiggling, darting thing of silver. It hung in the water, dived down, shot up again, fluttered, and performed the thousand evolutions a wobbling spoon can perform when handled by an expert. Straight over her it went, and toward the boat—the boat she had forgotten. Her tail twitched slightly, and her great gill-covers worked a little faster, but she let it pass. She was not feeding well that day.

Again the little silvery thing came over, and this time she rose halfway out of the weeds—only to sink back. A third time it came. Now it was traveling very slowly, with a new motion to it—a tantalizing, rocking, crippled movement. Not three feet above her eyes it passed. It was too great a temptation!

A wave of her tail, and she was following it, her nose not six inches from the single trailing hook. Once or twice she opened her mouth, but she did not quite take the bait. Still, she could not help following lazily.

Then, halfway to the boat, the little silvery thing seemed suddenly to see her. It darted forward like a streak, paused, shot side-wise, darted forward again. Her wicked, cold eyes glared suddenly, and seemed to bulge. Oh! It would try to get away from her, would it! With a rush she lunged forward and snapped—only to miss . . . it had darted straight down.

Fury swept over her, a fury that was almost madness. It could not get away! She *had* to catch it! Her terrible armed mouth opened to its widest and her great tail-muscles sent her ahead with a great lunge. It tried to dodge, but could not. There came a snap that broke many teeth and left deep scars on the metal of the spoon.

"Got 'er!" A whoop went up in the boat. Harry Caton Weaver, the great fishing authority, had decided that the taking of Old Croc was to be the crowning achievement of his career—that one glimpse he had got of her told him that she was easily a breaker of all records.

Old Croc turned back toward the weeds. Gone now was her voracity. She had a feeling of being swindled, tricked. It made her furious. She shook her head like a bulldog, and drove straight ahead. Not quite straight—somehow she found herself turned aside from the point of the weeds, although the pressure was not strong. Still she did not worry—she had broken too many lines in her long life to have real fear of them.

She doubled and twisted, not with the dash and fire of her youth, but with a terrible strength and slowness. The weeds—somehow she always just missed reaching them. Oh, well—she knew a better way! She allowed herself to be led easily almost to the boat, so close, indeed, that the florid-faced Doctor saw her, sat down suddenly, gasping, and mopped his face . . . he was beyond all words after seeing such a monster.

Then she doubled her body, whipped her tail, and was shooting back toward the weeds again. *That* would take them off their guard, break something! But it did not! Even in the midst of her whirl the pressure of the line did not seem to vary an ounce, and not once did it grow slack so that she could throw the hook by a shake of her great head.

She sulked on the bottom and refused to budge, but finally the taunting jerks stirred her up again. She would try swimming off somewhere else—surely nothing could stop her! Swim she did, but not straight—that slight, steady pull always brought her in a circle, and nearer and nearer the boat.

Then, suddenly an awful realization came to her. Where were the weeds? Somehow, she had gotten far from them, away out into deep, clear water where there was nothing to foul the line. How had she got there?

Now the pressure was even lighter than before; the great fishing expert was using all his skill. Her rushes grew more and more futile, though still sometimes punctuated by a mad drive toward the now far distant weeds. Panic came to her. What a little, thin line! . . . the lightest she had ever seen—but she could not break it. She sawed her vicious teeth, but evil though they were they could not cut the slender strand of piano wire.

At last she was within six feet of the boat, her huge, wicked head partly out of the water, her eyes glaring as though she were indeed a crocodile. She opened her mouth, and the sun flashed on a multitude of reptilian teeth, on a shiny spoon far down, near her gills.

"Gaff 'er, Doc!"

"Gosh, I—I'm afraid of losing her. You do it."

Hank Weaver grinned, but without once taking his eyes from the monster floating closer and closer, he reached back and took the gaff the other handed him. Very quietly he thrust the hook under the water and led the great pike over it. His wrist muscles tensed for the stroke.

Then, almost in the same instant, he was standing there, consternation on his face, a smashed rod in his hand, and a foot or two of line dangling gently in the air. Hazily he remembered seeing a dark streak shoot under the boat. What had happened? Had the line backlashed from the jerk and a loop gone over the reel-handle? Or had it caught on a splinter on the bottom of the boat?

But one thing was certain. Old Croc had escaped again, broken another rod. The great fisherman sat down weakly . . . he could hardly believe his senses. He could not believe that a fish could break his rod in open water. The Doctor sank his head in his hands and groaned. There was a silence, and the great fisherman looked up. He was not groaning; he looked almost pleased:

"The she-devil! But there's one consolation, Doc—if I'd caught her—well, I'd have her. Now, whenever I find time to come back here I'll have something to look forward to. What a brute—and still to be caught!"

Back in the weed-bed, Old Croc lay shaking her huge head savagely. There was something in the great cavern of her mouth—something that tickled—something that would neither go down nor up. Sometimes she would rest, and sometimes she would shake her head again. But it seemed hopeless to try to dislodge it.

It was almost dark when she saw a great dogfish approaching, and she sank out of sight. Tickle or no tickle, she was hungry and that dogfish looked fat. Toward her he came, unsuspectingly, until he was almost directly over her. Quietly she reached up and engulfed him. He was small enough to enter her capacious maw at one swallow, big though he was in actual size.

She sank back into the weeds contentedly, her stomach full. Something was trying to force itself into her tiny, fierce brain, some thought trying to crowd in where there was no room for thought. What was it?

Oh, yes—something that had been tickling her mouth inside, but it was gone. Maybe the dogfish had swept it down her throat.

Oh, well, such things were too trifling to worry about. Chasing those little shiny things made her fierce spirit feel good. When would the next be along? But at that she felt tired—she must be getting old. And so, thinking her vague, dull thoughts, she sank farther and farther down into the weeds and fell asleep.

Fishing flies are of two types. Dry flies float on the surface, while wet flies submerge. Purists usually prefer the dry variety. Both types are colorful works of art designed to attract the eye of trout, salmon, and other species that feed close to the surface. The best are fashioned by hand, out of feathers, fur, fishing line, yarn, wax, glue, hooks, and whatever. There is wonder in their exotic names, like the venerable Royal Coachman. The Parmachene Belle is a dry fly fraught in this story with nostalgic significance. The story is from Esquire.

Edwin L. Peterson

THE PARMACHENE BELLE (1940)

Nevertheless, here I must part with you; here in this now sad place, where I was so happy as first to meet you; but I shall long for the ninth of May; for then I hope again to enjoy your beloved company, at the appointed time and place.   —Izaak Walton

OLD SOLOMON WAS A FISHERMAN and a fly tier. He was a gunsmith, too, and had traveled with Buffalo Bill on the Keith Circuit. To the boys, he was a romantic figure, dim and heroic as Robin Hood and Jesse James. Our fathers used to say that no one in the country could tie artificial flies better than Solomon. Sometimes when you looked at them, it seemed as though they would take wing and flutter into the dusty air of Solomon's shop.

My mother did not quite approve of Solomon. Few mothers did. They said he was "given to drink." One afternoon, though, when my mother and I were downtown, I coaxed her until she promised to stop at Solomon's shop. I was seven then, and I wanted her to see Solomon in all his glory.

A bell above the door tinkled as we went in. The air smelled of Hoppe's Number Nine and varnish and dust. There were old chairs and tables covered with revolvers, shotguns, and fishing rods, and there were four or five bicycles, too, for Solomon repaired our bikes, as well as our fathers' guns.

We stayed at the door awhile. Solomon pretended he did not know we were there. He sat hunched over a bench, an electric bulb above him throwing a pyramid of dusty light down on his long, white hair. I went over and watched him. He was tying flies. My mother stayed close to the door.

"What you doin', Sol?" Of course I knew, but it seemed proper to ask.

"I'm liken to make a Yellow Sally," he said, without looking up from his vise.

"Gee, she's a pretty one," I said.

"Sure she's pretty, but she ain't no good," said Sol.

I heard my mother cough, but I did not know why. The cough meant that I should come to her.

"What's that one?" I asked, pointing to a fly on the table. It was best, I thought, to ignore my mother's cough.

"Thaten?" said Sol. "That's the Parmachene Belle." His voice stopped, then went on. "She ain't no good either."

The name stuck in my mind. It was mysterious and significant, like the Rocky Mountains and Queen Aliquippa and Lief the Lucky.

"Why you like to make 'em, Sol, if they ain't any good?" I asked.

Then he looked up at me. His pale blue eyes looked through my head, looked back through the years. "They're fer old-timers," he said slowly, "old-timers like me an' yer dad. Someday, mebbe you, too."

"Huh?" I said.

"Folks buy 'em," he said, looking back at his vise, "jest 'cause they're purty."

Once again I heard my mother cough.

I pointed quickly and asked, "What's that one, Sol?"

"Her? Next to that Lord Baltimore? She's jest a Flight's Fancy."

Then I heard my mother's voice. "Son!" it said. It said other things, too, by implication.

"Guess I gotta be goin', Sol," I said, but he did not look up.

The bell tinkled again and we were outside.

"I never did think much of that man," my mother said. Her voice was grim.

I felt unhappy and started to tell her what a nice man Solomon was, but she only said, "Humph!"

When we got down near the hardware store, she said, "Who was he talking about?"

"Talkin' about? No one, Mother. Honest."

"No one honest, is right," she said contemptuously. "Where'd he get those names if he wasn't talking about anyone?"

"What names, Mother?"

"Humph!" she said.

"What names?" I persisted.

"Lord Baltimore!" she said.

II

But that was not the end. By the fifteenth of April, I was eight years old. In the cold before dawn, we were speeding along the highway towards Shade Creek. I was in the back seat. Between me and the misty blur from the headlights were the blackness of Solomon's big hat and the red glow of my father's cigarette.

The car swerved from the highway, and we bumped over the rocks and ruts of another road. Soupy Campbell had caught a trout once, but it was just an accident. They had been on a picnic and he had used ham for bait. That was not right. That was something I should never do. My father had explained it all.

When we got out of the car, it was still dark. We put our rods together and threaded them. I leaned mine against the car. This was important.

What if I should put the reel on backwards? Solomon would laugh, and my father would be ashamed.

"All ready, boy?" my father asked.

"Yes, sir," I said, and we started down the logging road.

They walked ahead of me: Solomon six feet two; my father six feet one, heroes against the vague horizon. The stream roared and whispered to our left. Solomon, Buffalo Bill, Indians, my father's face when he gave me my rod at Christmas, my mother's doubtful enthusiasm, Queen Aliquippa, stones rattling from our feet down the stream. Everything was cold and big. Sometimes my father would say something to Solomon. If I had been closer I could have heard, for I was old enough now. I could even have spoken. We walked a long way.

When we stopped it was almost dawn. "I'll liken to go in here," Solomon said. "I'll be awaitin' fer you at the bridge."

We watched him crawl down the bank. He walked out into the stream and I saw the water pull at his trouser legs. It was wonderful. Then my father started on.

"Do you want to use worms, boy?" he said.

"I'd liken to use a Parmachene Belle," I answered.

"Parmachene Belle isn't much good," he said. He wiped his reel with the palm of his hand. "She's better for old-timers like Sol and me. Maybe for you, afterwhile."

"The dull flies are the best," he said. "Anyway, I think a worm would be better."

"I'll use a worm," I said.

As we walked, he took a gob of worms from the bait box at his belt and reached over and stuffed them into my box. Mine was new and green, with holes in the top.

After while he said, "This is a good place for you to start. Fish down, slowly. I'll go down a bit and fish up to you."

"Yes, sir," I said. "Should I use a split-shot, do you think?"

"Yes, a split-shot would be good," he said. He hesitated, and I knew he wanted to say more.

"Son," he said.

"Yes, sir."

"You be careful. The water's fast and deep."

He said it so that I did not feel hurt. "Yes, sir," I said. "I'll be careful."

He looked at me a long time. "Good luck, boy," he said.

"Good luck to you, too," I said.

He kept on looking at me even after that. Then he turned and clumped down the road. For a minute I felt queer and I wanted to cry, but I crawled down the bank instead.

Beside the stream, I did not thread the worm on the hook as I had done before for sunfish. I remembered what he had said. "Not for trout. For trout, you loop it."

All day, after that, the water swirled against my legs. It was hardly a day at all. It was something else. It was cold like a wet branch against your face. It was the pale sunlight of April. It was manhood, muscles, and the sudden rush of a trout upstream. It was the desperate feel of a trout in my hand and the cruel jaw with teeth and rainbow colors in the creel and being alone all day to dark, except at lunch when my father came from nowhere to eat with me. It was real fishing—and for trout—with Solomon and my father and Buffalo Bill. It was water singing, first in the stream, then in my blood, then everywhere, singing and singing. And then coolness, and the sun going down, and shadows, and growing loneliness, except that sometimes I thought I could see my father at the bend behind me.

In the darkness on the bridge, Solomon said to my father, "Any luck?"

"Six," said my father.

"Nine purty ones," said Solomon.

Then my father turned to me. "Any luck, boy?"

"One," I said.

"You caught a trout?" He lifted the lid of my new creel. "It's a beauty," he said, but his voice was unnatural. "Sol," he said, "the boy just caught a trout."

"I'm liken to be proud of you, kid," said Solomon. My father put his hand on my shoulder.

III

I am going to Shade Creek again on the fifteenth of April. I shall go alone, for the two tall men who first took me there are fishing other waters now, and have been for many years. Perhaps I shall be lonely, with no one to show my trout to, and I shall eat my lunch alone on a flat stone in the sunlight, but there will be reunion, too. The stream will say familiar things, its whispers and its roars will be echoed from the rocks, and there will be singing everywhere.

The water will pull at my boots, and the air will smell of hemlock. The tips of the hemlocks will be bright green, and a chickadee will scold.

All day, I shall fish against the current, sending an Iron Blue Dun or a Quill Gordon through the air ahead of me. The dull fly, I have learned, is the best. It will wing its way forward, like a living fly, and will curve to left or to right. It will drop like willow fuzz upon the water, and the leader will fall like a strand of spider web. Once in a while there will be an olive swirl and a splatter of rainbow spray, and a king of the mountain waters will sweep towards the rocks and roots. The rod will vibrate, the line will rise from the water, and he will take to the air again in an arc of liquid sunset. After a time, he will come to net and to creel. There will be sadness, but the sunlight will seem warmer, the air sweeter.

Then, when evening comes and the creel hangs heavy from the shoulder and the bridge is only a few yards away, I shall snip the dull fly from the leader. In its place I shall tie a creature of gold and white and scarlet. I shall whip her dryly through the air and then send her forward, the Parmachene Belle, into the dusk. She is a creature of fancy and of evening. She settles on the water with quivering lightness and glides through the shadows like a luminous moth. Timeless and not of this earth, she drifts through the darkness and rides upon the water like the reflection of a star.

At the bridge I shall make the last cast. The Parmachene Belle is for old-timers. "Like me and yer dad. Someday, mebbe fer you."

She will sail through the night and fall softly as a dream and sweep back towards me. I shall not stop her. She will sail on past me into the water that has been fished, and I shall turn around to watch her go back into currents and time that are no longer near.

Later, when the moon comes up, I shall stand on the bridge, looking downstream. Through the darkness below will come the tinkle of a bell, the smell of Hoppe's Number Nine, two men walking in the dawn, loneliness, the feel of a hand on my shoulder. Standing on the bridge, I shall hear a voice from the moonlit riffles, saying, "Good luck, boy," and again, "Good luck." It will be the same voice that once talked of stars and trout and trees.

Then I shall hear another voice. It will sound like mine, only older. In the bigness of the night it will say, "Good luck to you, too. Here in this now sad place, where our Parmachene Belle floats high, I send you greetings—wherever you are—greetings and good luck, too."

Tom Skelton is a shrewd and cynical captain of a party boat. He charters out to well-heeled clients seeking saltwater gamefish on the Atlantic coast. Skelton, like other autocratic captains, does things his way, as the struggle with a permit fish in this story illustrates. The story is a selection from a novel called Ninety-Two in the Shade *(1973). Thomas McGuane is a prominent writer with many stories and novels to his credit, including* The Sporting Club *(1969),* Nobody's Angel *(1981),* Keep the Change *(1989), and* Nothing but Blue Skies *(1992).*

Thomas McGuane

SKELTON'S PARTY (1973)

"**M**A'AM, YOU WANT TO HAND ME that lunch so I can stow it?" Skelton took the wicker basket from Mrs. Rudleigh; and then the thermos she handed him. "I've got plenty of water," he said.

"That's not water."

"What is it?"

"Gibsons."

"Let me put them in the cooler for you then—"

"We put them in the thermos," said Rudleigh, "so we don't have to put them in the cooler. We like them where we can get at them. In case we need them, you know, real snappy."

Tom Skelton looked up at him. Most people when they smile expose a section of their upper teeth; when Rudleigh smiled, he exposed his lower teeth.

"Hold the thermos in your lap," Skelton said. "If that starts rolling around the skiff while I'm running these banks, I'll throw it overboard."

"An ecologist," said Mrs. Rudleigh.

"Are you sure Nichol cannot appeal his sentence, Captain?" asked Rudleigh.

"I'm sure," said Skelton.

Mrs. Rudleigh reached out one hand and bent it backward so her fingernails were all in display; she was thinking of a killer line but it wouldn't come; so she didn't speak.

Skelton knew from other guides he could not let the clients run the boat for him; but he had never expected this; now all three of them were glancing past one another with metallic eyes.

Mrs. Rudleigh came and Skelton put her in the forward chair. Rudleigh followed in squeaking bright deck shoes and sat aft, swiveling about in the chair with an executive's preoccupation.

"Captain," Rudleigh began. Men like Rudleigh believed in giving credit to the qualified. If an eight-year-old were running the skiff, Rudleigh would call him "Captain" without irony; it was a credit to his class. "Captain, are we going to bonefish?" Mrs. Rudleigh was putting zinc oxide on her thin nose and on the actual edges of her precise cheekbones. She was a thin pretty woman of forty who you could see had a proclivity for hysterics, slow burns, and slapping.

"We have a good tide for bonefish."

"Well, Missus Rudleigh and I have had a good deal of bonefishing in Yucatán and we were wondering if it mightn't be an awfully long shot to fish for permit . . ."

Skelton knew it was being put to him; finding permit—big pompano—was a guide's hallmark and he didn't particularly have a permit tide. "I can find permit," he said though, finishing a sequence Rudleigh started with the word "Captain."

Carter strolled up. He knew the Rudleighs and they greeted each other. "You're in good hands," he said to them, tilting his head toward Skelton. "Boy's a regular fish hawk." He returned his head to the perpendicular.

"Where are your people, Cart?" Skelton asked to change the subject.

"They been partying, I guess. Man said he'd be late. Shortens my day."

Skelton choked the engine and started it. He let it idle for a few minutes and then freed up his lines. The canal leading away from the dock wandered around lazily, a lead-green gloss like pavement.

"Ought to find some bonefish in the Snipes on this incoming water," Carter said. Skelton looked at him a moment.

"We're permit fishing, Cart."

"Oh, really. Why, permit huh."

"What do you think? Boca Chica beach?"

"Your guess is as good as mine. But yeah okay, Boca Chica."

Skelton idled on the green tidal gloss of the canal until he cleared the entrance, then ran it up to 5,000 rpm and slacked off to an easy plane in the light chop. He leaned back over his shoulder to talk to Rudleigh. "We're going to Boca Chica beach. I think it's our best bet for permit on this tide."

"Fine, fine."

"I hate to take you there, a little bit, because it's in the landing pattern.

"I don't mind if the fish don't mind."

Skelton swung in around by Cow Key channel, past the navy hospital, under the bridge where boys were getting in some snapper fishing before it would be time for the military hospitals; then out the channel along the mangroves with the great white wing of the drive-in theater to their left, with an unattended meadow of loudspeaker stanchions; and abruptly around the corner to an expanse of blue Atlantic. Skelton ran tight to the beach, inside the boat-wrecking niggerheads; he watched for sunken ice cans and made the run to Boca Chica, stopping short.

The day was clear and bright except for one squall to the west, black with etched rain lines connecting it to sea; the great reciprocating engine of earth, thought Skelton, looks like a jellyfish.

"Go ahead and get ready, Mr. Rudleigh, I'm going to pole us along the rocky edge and see what we can see." Skelton pulled the pushpole out of its chocks and got up in the bow; Rudleigh was ready in the stern behind the tilted engine. It took two or three leaning thrusts to get the skiff underway; and then they were gliding over the sand, coral, sea fans, staghorn, and lawns of turtle grass. Small cowfish, sprats, and fry of one description or another scattered before them and vanished in the glare. Stone crabs backed away in bellicose, Pentagonian idiocy in the face of the boat's progress. Skelton held the boat into the tide at the breaking edge of the flat and looked for moving fish.

A few small sharks came early on the flood and passed down light, yellow-eyed and sweeping back and forth schematically for something in trouble. The first military aircraft came in overhead, terrifyingly low; a great delta-winged machine with howling, vulvate exhausts and nervous quick-moving control flaps; so close were they that the bright hydraulic shafts behind the flaps glittered; small rockets were laid up thickly under the wings like insect eggs. The plane approached, banked subtly, and the pilot glanced out at the skiff; his head looking no larger than a cocktail onion. A moment after the plane passed, its shock wave swept toward them and the crystal, perfect world of the flat paled and vanished; not reappearing until some minutes later and slowly. The draconic roar of the engines diminished and twin blossoms of flame shrank away toward the airfield.

"It must take a smart cookie," said Mrs. Rudleigh, "to make one of those do what it is supposed to."

"It takes balls for brains," said Rudleigh.

"That's even better," she smiled.

"Only that's what any mule has," Rudleigh added.

Mrs. Rudleigh threw something at her husband, who remained in the stern, rigid as a gun carriage.

Skelton was so determined that this first day of his professional guiding be a success that he felt with some agony the ugliness of the aircraft that came in now at shorter and shorter intervals, thundering with their volatile mists drifting over the sea meadow.

The Rudleighs had opened the thermos and were consuming its contents exactly as the heat of the day began to spread. Skelton was now poling down light, flushing small fish; then two schools of bonefish, not tailing but pushing wakes in their hurry; Rudleigh saw them late and bungled the cast, looking significantly at Mrs. Rudleigh after each failure.

"You've got to bear down," she said.

"I'm bearing down."

"Bear down harder, honey."

"I said: I'm bearing down."

Now the wading birds that were on the flat in the early tide were flooded out and flew northwest to catch the Gulf of Mexico tide. Skelton knew they had about lost their water.

"It's kind of slow, Captain," said Rudleigh.

"I've been thinking the same thing," Skelton said, his heart chilling within him. "I'm going to pole this out and make a move."

A minute later, he was running to Saddlebunch and got there in time to catch the incoming water across the big sand spot; he hardly had a moment to stake the skiff when the bonefish started crossing the sand. Now Mrs. Rudleigh was casting, driving the fish away. Rudleigh snatched the rod from her after her second failure.

"*Sit down!*"

Rudleigh was rigidly prepared for the next fish. Skelton would have helped him but knew in advance it would make things worse. He felt all of his efforts pitted against the contents of the thermos.

"You hawse's oss," said Mrs. Rudleigh to her husband. He seemed not to have heard. He was in the vague crouch of lumbar distress.

"I can fish circles around you, queen bee," he said after a bit. "Always could."

"What about Peru? What about Cabo Blanco?"

"You're always throwing Cabo Blanco in my face without ever, repeat, ever a word about Tierra del Fuego."

"What about Piñas Bay, Panama."

"Shut up."

"Seems to me," she said, "that Raúl commented that the señora had a way of making the señor look real bum."

A small single bonefish passed the skiff. Rudleigh flushed it by casting right into its face. "*Cocksucker.*"

"That's just the way you handled striped marlin. Right there is about what you did with those stripes at Rancho Bueno Vista."

Rudleigh whirled around and held the point of his rod under Mrs. Rudleigh's throat. "*I'm warning you.*"

"He had a tantrum at the Pez Maya Club in Yucatán," Mrs. Rudleigh told Skelton.

"Yes, ma'am. I see."

"*Uh, Captain—*"

"I'm right here, Mr. Rudleigh."

"I thought this was a permit deal."

"I'm looking for permit on this tide. I told you they were a long shot."

"Captain, I know about permit. I have seen permit in the Bahamas, Yucatán, Costa Rica, and at the great Belize camps in British Honduras. I know they are a long shot."

Skelton said, "Maybe your terrific familiarity with places to fish will tell us where we ought to be right now."

"Captain, I wouldn't presume."

A skiff was running just off the reef, making sheets of bright water against the sun.

"Do you know what today's tides are?" Skelton asked.

"No."

"Which way is the Gulf of Mexico?"

Rudleigh pointed all wrong. Skelton wanted to be home reading Proudhon, studying the winos, or copulating.

"Is that a permit?" Mrs. Rudleigh asked. The black fork of a large permit surfaced just out of casting range: beyond belief. Rudleigh stampeded back into position. Skelton slipped the pole out of the sand and began to ghost quietly toward the fish and stopped. Nothing visible. A long moment passed. Again, the black fork appeared.

"Cast."

Rudleigh threw forty feet beyond the permit. There was no hope of retrieving and casting again. Then out of totally undeserved luck, the fish began to change course toward Rudleigh's bait. Rudleigh and Mrs. Rudleigh exchanged glances.

"Please keep your eye on the fish." Skelton was overwhelmed by the entirely undeserved nature of what was transpiring. In a moment, the big fish was tailing again.

"Strike him."

Rudleigh lifted the rod and the fish was on. Skelton poled hard, following the fish, now streaking against the drag for deep water. The same skiff that passed earlier appeared, running the other direction; and Skelton wondered who it could be.

"God, Captain, will I be able to cope with this at all? I mean, I knew the fish was strong! But honest to God, this is a nigger with a hotfoot!"

"I'm still admiring your cast, darling."

Skelton followed watching the drawn bow the rod had become, the line shearing water with precision.

"What a marvelously smooth drag this reel has! A hundred smackers seemed steep at the time; but when you're in the breach, as I am now, a drag like this is the last nickel bargain in America!"

Skelton was poling after the fish with precisely everything he had. And it was difficult on the packed bottom with the pole inclining to slip out from under him.

His feeling of hope for a successful first-day guiding was considerably modified by Rudleigh's largely undeserved hooking of the fish. And now the nobility of the fish's fight was further eroding Skelton's pleasure.

When they crossed the edge of the flat, the permit raced down the reef line in sharp powerful curves, dragging the line across the coral. "Gawd, gawd, gawd," Rudleigh said. "This cookie is stronger than I am!" Skelton poled harder and at one point overtook the fish as it desperately rubbed the hook on the coral bottom; seeing the boat, it flushed once more in terror, making a single long howl pour from the reel. A fish that was exactly noble, thought Skelton, who began to imagine the permit coming out of a deep-water wreck by the pull of moon and tide, riding the invisible crest of the incoming water, feeding and moving by force of blood; only to run afoul of an asshole from Connecticut.

The fight continued without much change for another hour, mainly outside the reef line in the green water over a sand bottom: a safe place to fight the fish. Rudleigh had soaked through his khaki safari clothes; and from time to time Mrs. Rudleigh advised him to "bear down." When Mrs. Rudleigh told him this, he would turn to look at her, his neck muscles standing out like cords and his eyes acquiring broad white perimeters. Skelton ached from pursuing the fish with the pole; he might have started the engine outside the reef line, but he feared Rudleigh getting his line in the propeller and he had found that a large fish was held away from the boat by the sound of a running engine.

As soon as the fish began to show signs of tiring, Skelton asked Mrs. Rudleigh to take a seat; then he brought the big net up on the deck beside him. He hoped he would be able to get Rudleigh to release this hugely undeserved fish, not only because it was undeserved but because the fish had fought so very bravely. No, he admitted to himself, Rudleigh would never let the fish go.

By now the fish should have been on its side. It began another long and accelerating run, the pale sheet of water traveling higher up the line, the fish swerving somewhat inshore again; and to his terror, Skelton found himself poling after the fish through the shallows, now and then leaning over to free the line from a sea fan. They glided among the little hammocks and mangrove keys of Saddlebunch in increasing vegetated congestion, in a narrowing tidal creek that closed around and over them with guano-covered mangroves and finally prevented the boat from following another foot. Nevertheless, line continued to pour off the reel.

"Captain, consider it absolutely necessary that I kill the fish. This one doubles the Honduran average."

Skelton did not reply, he watched the line slow its passage from the reel, winding out into the shadowy creek; then stop. He knew there was a good chance the desperate animal had reached a dead end.

"Stay here."

Skelton climbed out of the boat and, running the line through his fingers lightly, began to wade the tidal creek. The mosquitoes found him quickly and held in a pale globe around his head. He waded steadily, flushing herons out of the mangroves over his head. At one point, he passed a tiny side channel, blocking the exit of a heron that raised its stiff wings very slightly away from its body and glared at him. In the green shadows, the heron was a radiant, perfect white.

He stopped a moment to look at the bird. All he could hear was the slow musical passage of tide in the mangrove roots and the low pattern of bird sounds more liquid than the sea itself in these shallows. He moved away from the side channel, still following the line. Occasionally, he felt some small movement of life in it; but he was certain now the permit could go no farther. He had another thirty yards to go, if he had guessed right looking at Rudleigh's partially emptied spool.

Wading along, he felt he was descending into the permit's world; in knee-deep water, the small mangrove snappers, angelfish, and baby barracudas scattered before him, precise, contained creatures of perfect mobility. The brilliant blue sky was reduced to a narrow ragged band quite high overhead now and the light wavered more with the color of the sea and of estuarine shadow than that of vulgar sky. Skelton stopped and his eye followed the line back in the direction he had come. The Rudleighs were at its other end, infinitely far away.

Skelton was trying to keep his mind on the job he had set out to do. The problem was, he told himself, to go from Point A to Point B; but every breath of humid air, half sea, and the steady tidal drain through root and elliptical shadow in his ears and eyes diffused his attention. Each heron that leaped like an arrow out of his narrow slot, spiraling invisibly into the sky, separated him from the job. Shafts of light in the side channels illuminated columns of pristine, dancing insects.

Very close now. He released the line so that if his appearance at the dead end terrified the permit there would not be sufficient tension for the line to break. The sides of the mangrove slot began to yield. Skelton stopped.

An embowered, crystalline tidal pool: the fish lay exhausted in its still water, lolling slightly and unable to right itself. It cast a delicate circular shadow on the sand bottom. Skelton moved in and the permit made no effort to rescue itself; instead, it lay nearly on its side and watched Skelton approach with a steady, following eye that was, for Skelton, the last straw. Over its broad, virginal sides a lambent, moony light shimmered. The fish seemed like an oval section of sky—yet sentient and alert, intelligent as tide.

He took the permit firmly by the base of its tail and turned it gently upright in the water. He reached into its mouth and removed the hook from the cartilaginous operculum. He noticed that the suddenly loosened line was not retrieved: Rudleigh hadn't even the sense to keep tension on the line.

By holding one hand under the permit's pectoral fins and the other around the base of its tail, Skelton was able to move the fish back and forth in the water to revive it. When he first tentatively released it, it teetered over on its side, its wandering eye still fixed upon him. He righted the fish again and continued to move it gently back and forth in the water; and this time when he released the permit, it stayed upright, steadying itself in equipoise, mirror sides once again purely reflecting the bottom. Skelton watched a long while until some regularity returned to the movement of its gills.

Then he cautiously—for fear of startling the fish—backed once more into the green tidal slot and turned to head for the skiff. Rudleigh had lost his permit.

Some of the best fishing stories are about the relationship between kids and adults, with the experienced hand teaching the youthful novice. This story is a classic of the genre. It is told in the first person by a boy who worships an old fly fisherman who befriends and helps him. Their target is the aristocratic silver salmon. Roland Pertwee (1885–1963) was a revered storyteller in his day and, as this story demonstrates, has a lot to say to contemporary readers. Among his books are Men of Affairs *(1922),* The South Sea Bubble *(1924), and* Pursuit *(1930).*

Roland Pertwee

THE RIVER GOD (1928)

WHEN I WAS A LITTLE BOY I had a friend who was a colonel. He was not the kind of colonel you meet nowadays, who manages a motor showroom in the West End of London and wears crocodile shoes and a small mustache and who calls you 'old man' and slaps your back, independent of the fact that you may have been no more than a private in the war. My colonel was of the older order that takes a third of a century and a lot of Indian sun and Madras curry in the making. A veteran of the Mutiny he was, and wore side whiskers to prove it. Once he came upon a number of Sepoys conspiring mischief in a byre with a barrel of gunpowder. So he put the butt of his cheroot into the barrel and presently they all went to hell. That was the kind of man he was in the way of business.

In the way of pleasure he was very different. In the way of pleasure he wore an old Norfolk coat that smelt of heather and brine, and which had no elbows to speak of. And he wore a Sherlock Holmsey kind of cap with a swarm of salmon flies upon it, that to my boyish fancy was more splendid than a crown. I cannot remember his legs, because they were nearly always under water, hidden in great canvas waders. But once he sent me a photograph of himself riding on a tricycle, so I expect he had some knickerbockers, too, which would have been that tight kind, with box cloth under the knees. Boys don't take much stock of clothes. His head occupied my imagination. A big, brave, white-haired head with cherry-red rugose cheeks and honest, laughing, puckered eyes, with gunpowder marks in their corners.

People at the little Welsh fishing inn where we met said he was a bore; but I knew him to be a god and shall prove it.

I was ten years old and his best friend.

He was seventy something and my hero.

Properly I should not have mentioned my hero as soon in this narrative. He belongs to a latter epoch, but sometimes it is forgivable to start with a boast, and now that I have committed myself I lack the courage to call upon my colonel to fall back two paces to the rear, quick march, and wait until he is wanted.

The real beginning takes place, as I remember, somewhere in Hampshire on the Grayshott Road, among sandy banks, sentinel firs and plum-colored wastes of heather. Summer-holiday time it was, and I was among folks whose names have since vanished like lizards under the stones of forgetfulness. Perhaps it was a picnic walk; perhaps I carried a basket and was told not to swing it for fear of bursting its cargo of ginger beer. In those days ginger beer had big bulgy corks held down with a string. In a hot sun or under stress of too much agitation the string would break and the corks fly. Then there would be a merry foaming fountain and someone would get reproached.

250

One of our company had a fishing rod. He was a young man who, one day, was to be an uncle of mine. But that didn't concern me. What concerned me was the fishing rod and presently—perhaps because he felt he must keep in with the family—he let me carry it. To the fisherman born there is nothing so provoking of curiosity as a fishing rod in a case.

Surreptitiously I opened the flap, which contained a small grass spear in a wee pocket, and, pulling down the case a little, I admired the beauties of the cork butt, with its gun-metal ferrule and reel rings and the exquisite frail slenderness of the two top joints.

'It's got two top joints—two!' I exclaimed ecstatically.

'Of course,' said he. 'All good trout rods have two.'

I marveled in silence at what seemed to me then a combination of extravagance and excellent precaution.

There must have been something inherently understanding and noble about that young man who would one day be my uncle, for, taking me by the arm, he sat me down on a tuft of heather and took the pieces of rod from the case and fitted them together. The rest of the company moved on and left me in Paradise.

It is thirty-five years ago since that moment and not one detail of it is forgotten. There sounds in my ears today as clearly as then, the faint, clear pop made by the little cork stoppers with their boxwood tops as they were withdrawn. I remember how, before fitting the pieces together, he rubbed the ferrules against the side of his nose to prevent them sticking. I remember looking up the length of it through a tunnel of sneck rings to the eyelet at the end. Not until he had fixed a reel and passed a line through the rings did he put the lovely thing into my hand. So light it was, so firm, so persuasive; such a thing alive—a scepter. I could do no more than say 'Oo!' and again, 'Oo!'

'A thrill, ain't it?' said he.

I had no need to answer that. In my new-found rapture was only one sorrow—the knowledge that such happiness would not endure and that, all too soon, a blank and rodless future awaited me.

'They must be awfully—awfully 'spensive,' I said.

'Couple of guineas,' he replied offhandedly.

A couple of guineas! And we were poor folk and the future was more rodless than ever.

'Then I shall save and save and save,' I said.

And my imagination started to add up twopence a week into guineas. Two hundred and forty pennies to the pound, multiplied by two—four hundred and eighty—and then another twenty-four pennies—five hundred and four. Why, it would take a lifetime, and no sweets, no elastic for catapults, no penny novelty boxes or air-gun bullets or ices or anything. Tragedy must have been writ large upon my face, for he said suddenly, 'When's your birthday?'

I was almost ashamed to tell him how soon it was. Perhaps he, too, was a little taken aback by its proximity, for that future uncle of mine was not so rich as uncles should be.

'We must see about it.'

'But it wouldn't—it couldn't be one like that,' I said.

I must have touched his pride, for he answered loftily, 'Certainly it will.'

In the fortnight that followed I walked on air and told everybody I had as good as got a couple-of-guineas rod.

No one can deceive a child, save the child himself, and when my birthday came and with it a long brown paper parcel, I knew, even before I had removed the wrappers, that this two-guinea rod was not worth the money. There was a brown linen case, it is true, but it was not a case with a neat compartment for each joint, nor was there a spear in the flap. There was only one top instead of two, and there were no popping little stoppers to protect the ferrules from dust and injury. The lower joint boasted no elegant cork hand piece, but was a tapered affair coarsely made and rudely varnished. When I fitted the pieces together, what I balanced in my hand was tough and stodgy, rather than limber. The reel, which had come in a different parcel, was of wood. It had neither check nor brake, and the line overran and backwound itself with distressing frequency.

I had not read and reread Gamages' price list without knowing something of rods, and I did not need to look long at this rod before realizing that it was no match to the one I had handled on the Grayshott Road.

I believe at first a great sadness possessed me, but very presently imagination came to the rescue. For I told myself that I had only to think that this was the rod of all other rods that I desired most and it would be so. And it was so.

Furthermore, I told myself that, in this great wide ignorant world, but few people existed with such expert knowledge of rods as I possessed. That I had but to say, 'Here is the final word in good rods,' and they would accept it as such.

Very confidently I tried the experiment on my mother, with inevitable success. From the depths of her affection and her ignorance on all such matters, she produced:

'It's a magnificent rod.'

I went my way, knowing full well that she knew not what she said, but that she was kind.

With rather less confidence I approached my father, saying, 'Look, father! It costs two guineas. It's absolutely the best sort you can get.'

And he, after waggling it a few moments in silence, quoted cryptically:

'There is nothing either good or bad but thinking makes it so.'

Young as I was, I had some curiosity about words, and on any other occasion I would have called on him to explain. But this I did not do, but left hurriedly, for fear that he should explain.

In the two years that followed, I fished every day in the slip of a back garden of our tiny London house. And, having regard to the fact that this rod was never fashioned to throw a fly, I acquired a pretty knack in the fullness of time and performed some glib casting at the nasturtiums and marigolds that flourished by the back wall.

My parents' fortunes must have been in the ascendant, I suppose, for I call to mind an unforgettable breakfast when my mother told me that father had decided we should spend our summer holiday at a Welsh hotel on the river Lledr. The place was called Pont-y-pant, and she showed me a picture of the hotel with a great knock-me-down river creaming past the front of it.

Although in my dreams I had heard fast water often enough, I had never seen it, and the knowledge that in a month's time I should wake with the music of a cataract in my ears was almost more than patience could endure.

In that exquisite, intolerable period of suspense I suffered as only childish longing and enthusiasm can suffer. Even the hank of gut that I bought and bent into innumerable casts failed to alleviate that suffering. I would walk for miles for a moment's delight captured in gluing my nose to the windows of tackleists' shops in the West End. I learned from my grandmother—a wise and calm old lady—how to make nets and, having mastered the art, I made myself a landing net. This I set up on a frame fashioned from a penny schoolmaster's cane bound to an old walking stick. It would be pleasant to record that this was a good and serviceable net, but it was not. It flopped over in a very distressing fashion when called upon to lift the lightest weight. I had to confess to myself that I had more enthusiasm than skill in the manufacture of such articles.

At school there was a boy who had a fishing creel, which he swapped with me for a Swedish knife, a copy of Rogues of the Fiery Cross, and an Easter egg which I had kept on account of its rare beauty. He had forced a hard bargain and was sure he had the best of it, but I knew otherwise.

At last the great day dawned, and after infinite travel by train we reached our destination as the glow of sunset was graying into dark. The river was in spate, and as we crossed a tall stone bridge on our way to the hotel I heard it below me, barking and grumbling among great rocks. I was pretty far gone in tiredness, for I remember little else that night but a rod rack in the hall—a dozen rods of different sorts and sizes, with gaudy salmon flies, some nets, a gaff and an oak coffer upon which lay a freshly caught salmon on a blue ashet. Then supper by candlelight, bed, a glitter of stars through the open window, and the ceaseless drumming of water.

By six o'clock next morning I was on the river bank, fitting my rod together and watching in awe the great brown ribbon of water go fleetly by.

Among my most treasured possessions were half a dozen flies, and two of these I attached to the cast with exquisite care. While so engaged, a shadow fell on the grass beside me and, looking up, I beheld a lank, shabby individual with a walrus mustache and an unhealthy face, who, the night before, had helped with our luggage at the station.

'Water's too heavy for flies,' said he, with an uptilting inflection. 'This evening, yes; now, no—none whateffer. Better try with a worrum in the burrun.'

He pointed at a busy little brook which tumbled down the steep hillside and joined the main stream at the garden end.

'C-couldn't I fish with a fly in the—the burrun?' I asked, for although I wanted to catch a fish very badly, for honor's sake I would fain take it on a fly.

'Indeed, no,' he replied, slanting the tone of his voice skyward. 'You cootn't. Neffer. And that isn't a fly rot whateffer.'

'It is,' I replied hotly. 'Yes, it is.'

But he only shook his head and repeated, 'No,' and took the rod from my hand and illustrated its awkwardness and handed it back with a wretched laugh.

If he had pitched me into the river I should have been happier.

'It is a fly rod and it cost two guineas,' I said, and my lower lip trembled.

'Neffer,' he repeated. 'Five shillings would be too much.'

Even a small boy is entitled to some dignity.

Picking up my basket, I turned without another word and made for the hotel. Perhaps my eyes were blinked with tears, for I was about to plunge into the dark hall when a great, rough, kindly voice arrested me with:

'Easy does it.'

At the thick end of an immense salmon rod there stroke out into the sunlight the noblest figure I had ever seen.

There is no real need to describe my colonel again—I have done so already—but the temptation is too great. Standing in the doorway, the sixteen-foot rod in hand, the deer-stalker hat, besprent with flies, crowning his shaggy head, the waders, like seven-league boots, braced up to his armpits, the creel across his shoulder, a gaff across his back, he looked what he was—a god. His eyes met mine with that kind of smile one good man keeps for another.

'An early start,' he said. 'Any luck, old fellar?'

I told him I hadn't started—not yet.

'Wise chap,' said he. 'Water's a bit heavy for trouting. It'll soon run down, though. Let's vet those flies of yours.'

He took my rod and whipped it expertly.

'A nice piece—new, eh?'

'N-not quite,' I stammered; 'but I haven't used it yet, sir, in water.'

That god read men's minds.

'I know—garden practice; capital; nothing like it.'

Releasing my cast, he frowned critically over the flies—a Blue Dun and a March Brown.

'Think so?' he queried. 'You don't think it's a shade late in the season for these fancies?' I said I thought perhaps it was. 'Yes, I think you're right,' said he. 'I believe in this big water you'd do better with a livelier pattern. Teal and Red, Cock-y-bundy, Greenwell's Glory.'

I said nothing, but nodded gravely at these brave names.

Once more he read my thoughts and saw through the wicker sides of my creel a great emptiness.

'I expect you've fished most in southern rivers. These Welsh trout have a fancy for a spot of color.'

He rummaged in the pocket of his Norfolk jacket and produced a round tin which once had held saddle soap.

'Collar on to that,' said he; 'there's a proper pickle of flies and casts in that tin that, as a keen fisherman, you won't mind sorting out. Still, they may come in useful.'

'But, I say, you don't mean—' I began.

'Yes, go on; stick to it. All fishermen are members of the same club and I'm giving the trout a rest for a bit.' His eyes ranged the hills and trees opposite. 'I must be getting on with it before the sun's too high.'

Waving his free hand, he strode away and presently was lost to view at a bend in the road.

I think my mother was a little piqued by my abstraction during breakfast. My eyes never, for an instant, deserted the round tin box which lay open beside my plate. Within it were a paradise and a hundred miracles all tangled together in the pleasantest disorder. My mother said something about a lovely walk over the hills, but I had other plans, which included a very glorious hour which should be spent untangling and wrapping up in neat squares of paper my new treasures.

'I suppose he knows best what he wants to do,' she said.

So it came about that I was left alone and betook myself to a sheltered spot behind a rock where all the delicious disorder was remedied and I could take stock of what was mine.

I am sure there were at least six casts all set up with flies, and ever so many loose flies and one great stout, tapered cast, with a salmon fly upon it, that was so rich in splendor that I doubted if my benefactor could really have known that it was there.

I felt almost guilty at owning so much, and not until I had done full justice to everything did I fasten a new cast to my line and go a-fishing.

There is a lot said and written about beginner's luck, but none of it came my way. Indeed, I spent most of the morning extricating my line from the most fearsome tangles. I had no skill in throwing a cast with two droppers upon it and I found it was an art not to be learned in a minute. Then, from overeagerness, I was too snappy with my back cast, whereby, before many minutes had gone, I heard that warning crack behind me that betokens the loss of a tail fly. I must have spent half an hour searching the meadow for that lost fly and finding it not. Which is not strange, for I wonder has any fisherman ever found that lost fly. The reeds, the buttercups and the little people with many legs who run in the wet grass conspire together to keep the secret of its hiding place. I gave up at last, and with a feeling of shame that was only proper, I invested a new fly on the point of my cast and set to work again, but more warily.

In that hard racing water a good strain was put upon my rod, and before the morning was out it was creaking at the joints in a way that kept my heart continually in my mouth. It is the duty of a rod to work with a single smooth action and by no means to divide its performance into three sections of activity. It is a hard task for any angler to persuade his line austerely if his rod behaves thus.

When, at last, my father strolled up the river bank, walking, to his shame, much nearer the water than a good fisherman should, my nerves were jumpy from apprehension.

'Come along. Food's ready. Done any good?' said he.

Again it was to his discredit that he put food before sport, but I told him I had had a wonderful morning, and he was glad.

'What do you want to do this afternoon, old man?' he asked.

'Fish,' I said.

'But you can't always fish,' he said.

I told him I could, and I was right and have proved it for thirty years and more.

'Well, well,' he said, 'please yourself, but isn't it dull not catching anything?'

And I said, as I've said a thousand times since, 'As if it could be.'

So that afternoon I went downstream instead of up, and found myself in difficult country where the river boiled between the narrows of two hills. Stunted oaks overhung the water and great boulders opposed its flow. Presently I came to a sort of natural flight of steps—a pool and a cascade three times repeated—and there, watching the maniac fury of the waters in awe and wonderment, I saw the most stirring sight in my young life. I saw a silver salmon leap superbly from the caldron below into the pool above. And I saw another and another salmon do likewise. And I wonder the eyes of me did not fall out of my head.

I cannot say how long I stayed watching that gallant pageant of leaping fish—in ecstasy there is no measurement of time—but at last it came upon me that all the salmon in the sea were careering past me and that if I were to realize my soul's desire I must hasten to the pool below before the last of them had gone by.

It was a mad adventure, for until I had discovered that stout cast, with the gaudy fly attached in the tin box, I had given no thought to such noble quarry. My recent possessions had put ideas into my head above my station and beyond my powers. Failure, however, means little to the young, and, walking fast, yet gingerly, for fear of breaking my rod top against a tree, I followed the path downstream until I came to a great basin of water into which, through a narrow throat, the river thundered like a storm.

At the head of the pool was a plate of rock scored by the nails of fisherman's boots, and here I sat me down to wait while the salmon cast, removed from its wrapper, was allowed to soak and soften in a puddle left by the rain.

And while I waited a salmon rolled not ten yards from where I sat. Head and tail, up and down he went, a great monster of a fish, sporting and deriding me.

With that performance so near at hand, I have often wondered how I was able to control my fingers well enough to tie a figure-eight knot between the line and the cast. But I did, and I'm proud to be able to record it. Your true-born angler does not go blindly to work until he has first satisfied his conscience. There is a pride, in knots, of which the laity knows nothing, and if, through neglect to tie them rightly, failure and loss should result, pride may not be restored nor conscience salved by the plea of eagerness. With my trembling fingers I bent the knot and, with a pummeling heart, launched the line into the broken water at the throat of the pool.

At first the mere tug of the water against that large fly was so thrilling to me that it was hard to believe that I had not hooked a whale. The trembling line swung round in a wide arc into a calm eddy below where I stood. Before casting afresh I shot a glance over my shoulder to assure myself there was no limb of a tree behind me to foul the fly. And this was a gallant cast, true and straight, with a couple of yards more length than its predecessor, and a wider radius. Instinctively I knew, as if the surface had been marked with an X where the salmon had risen, that my fly must pass right over the spot. As it swung by, my nerves were strained like piano wires. I think I knew that something tremendous, impossible, terrifying, was going to happen. The sense, the certitude was so strong in me that I half opened my mouth to shout a warning to the monster, not to.

I must have felt very, very young in that moment. I, who that same day had been talked to as a man by a man among men. The years were stripped from me and I was what I was—ten years old and appalled. And then, with the suddenness of a rocket, it happened. The water was cut into a swathe. I remember a silver loop bearing downward—a bright, shining, vanishing thing like the bobbin of my mother's sewing machine—and a tug. I shall never forget the viciousness of that tug. I had my fingers tight upon the line, so I got the full force of it. To counteract a tendency to go headfirst into the spinning water below, I threw myself backward and sat down on the hard rock with a jar that shut my teeth on my tongue—like the jaws of a trap.

Luckily I had let the rod go out straight with the line, else it must have snapped in the first frenzy of the downstream rush. Little ass that I was, I tried to check the speeding line with my forefinger, with the result that it cut and burnt me to the bone. There wasn't above twenty yards of line in the reel, and the wretched contrivance was trying to be rid of the line even faster than the fish was wrenching it out. Heaven knows why it didn't snarl, for great loops and whorls were whirling, like Catherine wheels, under my wrist. An instant's glance revealed the terrifying fact that there were not more than half a dozen yards left on the reel and the fish showed no sign of abating his rush. With the realization of impending and inevitable catastrophe upon me, I launched a yell for help, which, rising above the roar of the waters, went echoing down the gorge.

And then, to add to my terrors, the salmon leaped—a winging leap like a silver arch appearing and instantly disappearing upon the broken surface. So mighty, so all-powerful he seemed in that sublime moment that I lost all sense of reason and raised the rod, with a sudden jerk, above my head.

I have often wondered, had the rod actually been the two-guinea rod my imagination claimed for it, whether it could have withstood the strain thus violently and unreasonably imposed upon it. The wretched thing that I held so grimly never even put up a fight. It snapped at the ferrule of the lower joint and plunged like a toboggan down the slanting line, to vanish into the black depths of the water.

My horror at this calamity was so profound that I was lost even to the consciousness that the last of my line had run out. A couple of vicious tugs advised me of this awful truth. Then, snap! The line parted at the reel, flickered out through the rings and was gone. I was left with nothing but the butt of a broken rod in my hand and an agony of mind that even now I cannot recall without emotion.

I am not ashamed to confess that I cried. I lay down on the rock, with my cheek in the puddle where I had soaked the cast, and plenished it with my tears. For what had the future left for me but a cut and burning finger, a badly bumped behind, the single joint of a broken rod and no faith in uncles? How long I lay there weeping I do not know. Ages, perhaps, or minutes, or seconds.

I was roused by a rough hand on my shoulder and a kindly voice demanding, 'Hurt yourself, Ike Walton?'

Blinking away my tears, I pointed at my broken rod with a bleeding forefinger.

'Come! This is bad luck,' said my colonel, his face grave as a stone. 'How did it happen?'

'I c-caught a s-salmon.'

'You what?' said he.

'I d-did,' I said.

He looked at me long and earnestly; then, taking my injured hand, he looked at that and nodded.

'The poor groundlings who can find no better use for a river than something to put a bridge over think all fishermen are liars,' said he. 'But we know better, eh? By the bumps and breaks and cuts I'd say you made a plucky fight against heavy odds. Let's hear all about it.'

So, with his arm round my shoulders and his great shaggy head near to mine, I told him all about it.

At the end he gave me a mighty and comforting squeeze, and he said, 'The loss of one's first big fish is the heaviest loss I know. One feels, whatever happens, one'll never–' He stopped and pointed dramatically. 'There it goes—see! Down there at the tail of the pool!'

In the broken water where the pool emptied itself into the shallows beyond, I saw the top joints of my rod dancing on the surface.

'Come on!' he shouted, and gripping my hand, jerked me to my feet. 'Scatter your legs! There's just a chance!'

Dragging me after him, we raced along by the river path to the end of the pool, where, on a narrow promontory of grass, his enormous salmon rod was lying.

'Now,' he said, picking it up and making the line whistle to and fro in the air with sublime authority, 'keep your eyes skinned on those shallows for another glimpse of it.'

A second later I was shouting, 'There! There!'

He must have seen the rod point at the same moment, for his line flowed out and the big fly hit the water with a plop not a couple of feet from the spot.

He let it ride on the current, playing it with a sensitive touch like the brushwork of an artist.

'Half a jiffy!' he exclaimed at last. 'Wait! Yes, I think so. Cut down to that rock and see if I haven't fished up the line.'

I needed no second invitation, and presently was yelling, 'Yes—yes, you have!'

'Stretch yourself out then and collar hold of it.'

With the most exquisite care he navigated the line to where I lay stretched upon the rock. Then:

'Right you are! Good lad! I'm coming down.'

Considering his age, he leaped the rocks like a chamois.

'Now,' he said, and took the wet line delicately between his forefinger and thumb. One end trailed limply downstream, but the other end seemed anchored in the big pool where I had had my unequal and disastrous contest.

Looking into his face, I saw a sudden light of excitement dancing in his eyes.

'Odd,' he muttered, 'but not impossible.'

'What isn't?' I asked breathlessly.

'Well, it looks to me as if the top joints of that rod of yours have gone downstream.'

Gingerly he pulled up the line, and presently an end with a broken knot appeared.

'The reel knot, eh?' I nodded gloomily. 'Then we lose the rod,' said he. That wasn't very heartening news. 'On the other hand, it's just possible the fish is still on—sulking.'

'Oo!' I exclaimed.

'Now, steady does it,' he warned, 'and give me my rod.'

Taking a pair of clippers from his pocket, he cut his own line just above the cast.

'Can you tie a knot?' he asked.

'Yes,' I nodded.

'Come on, then; bend your line onto mine. Quick as lightning.'

Under his critical eye, I joined the two lines with a blood knot. 'I guessed you were a fisherman,' he said, nodded approvingly and clipped off the ends. 'And now to know the best or the worst.'

I shall never forget the music of that check reel or the suspense with which I watched as, with the butt of the rod bearing against the hollow of his thigh, he steadily wound up the wet slack line. Every instant I expected it to come drifting downstream, but it didn't. Presently it rose in a tight slant form the pool above.

'Snagged, I'm afraid,' he said, and worked the rod with an easy straining motion to and fro. 'Yes, I'm afraid—no, by Lord Bobs, he's on!'

I think it was only right and proper that I should have launched a yell of triumph as, with the spoken word, the point at which the line cut the water shifted magically from the left side of the pool to the right.

'And a fish too,' said he.

In the fifteen minutes that followed, I must have experienced every known form of terror and delight.

'Youngster,' said he, 'you should be doing this, by rights, but I'm afraid the rod's a bit above your weight.'

'Oh, go on and catch him,' I pleaded.

'And so I will,' he promised; 'unship the gaff, young un, and stand by to use it, and if you break the cast we'll never speak to each other again, and that's a bet.'

But I didn't break the cast. The noble, courageous, indomitable example of my river god had lent me skill and precision beyond my years. When at long last a weary, beaten, silver monster rolled within reach of my arm into a shallow eddy, the steel gaff shot out fair and true, and sank home.

And then I was lying on the grass, with my arms around a salmon that weighed twenty-two pounds on the scale and contained every sort of happiness known to a boy.

And best of all, my river god shook hands with me and called me 'partner.'

That evening the salmon was placed upon the blue ashet in the hall, bearing a little card with its weight and my name upon it.

And I am afraid I sat on a chair facing it, for ever so long, so that I could hear what the other anglers had to say as they passed by. I was sitting there when my colonel put his head out of his private sitting room and beckoned me to come in.

'A true fisherman lives in the future, not the past, old man,' said he; 'though, for this once, it 'ud be a shame to reproach you.'

I suppose I colored guiltily—at any rate, I hope so.

'We got the fish,' said he, 'but we lost the rod, and the future without a rod doesn't bear thinking of. Now'—and he pointed at a long wooden box on the floor, that overflowed with rods of different sorts and sizes— 'rummage among those. Take your time and see if you can find anything to suit you.'

'But do you mean—can I—'

'We're partners, aren't we? And p'r'aps as such you'd rather we went through our stock together.'

'Oo, sir,' I said.

'Here, quit that,' he ordered gruffly. 'By Lord Bobs, if a show like this afternoon's don't deserve a medal, what does? Now, here's a handy piece by Hardy—a light and useful tool—or if you fancy greenheart in preference to split bamboo—'

I have the rod to this day, and I count it among my dearest treasures. And to this day I have a flick of the wrist that was his legacy. I have, too, some small skill in dressing flies, the elements of which were learned in his company by candlelight after the day's work was over. And I have countless memories of that month-long, month-short friendship—the closest and most perfect friendship, perhaps, of all my life.

He came to the station and saw me off. How I vividly remember his shaggy head at the window, with the whiskered cheeks and the gunpowder marks at the corners of his eyes! I didn't cry, although I wanted to awfully. We were partners and shook hands. I never saw him again, although on my birthdays I would have colored cards from him, with Irish,

Scotch, Norwegian postmarks. Very brief they were: 'Water very low.' 'Took a good fish last Thursday.' 'Been prawning, but don't like it.'

Sometimes at Christmas I had gifts—a reel, a tappered line, a fly book. But I never saw him again.

Came at last no more post cards or gifts, but in the Fishing Gazette, of which I was a religious reader, was an obituary telling how one of the last of the Mutiny veterans had joined the great majority. It seems he had been fishing half an hour before he died. He had taken his rod down and passed out. They had buried him at Totnes, overlooking the River Dart.

So he was no more—my river god—and what was left of him they had put into a box and buried it in the earth.

But that isn't true; nor is it true that I never saw him again. For I seldom go a-fishing but that I meet him on the river banks.

The banks of a river are frequented by a strange company and are full of mysterious and murmurous sounds—the cluck and laughter of water, the piping of birds, the hum of insects and the whispering of wind in the willows. What should prevent a man in such a place having a word and speech with another who is not there? So much of fishing lies in imagination, and mine needs little stretching to give my river god a living form.

'With this ripple,' says he, 'you should do well.'

'And what's it to be,' say I—'Blue Upright, Red Spinner? What's your fancy, sir?'

Spirits never grow old. He has begun to take an interest in dry-fly methods—that river god of mine, with his seven-league boots, his shaggy head and the gaff across his back.

Although this story is purely fantasy, Daniel Webster really was U.S. Secretary of State, a candidate for the presidency, and one of the great orators of all time. The tale of Webster's association with a monster of the deep is told with imagination and humor by one of America's great literary stylists. Stephen Vincent Benét (1898–1943) is well known for books such as The Devil and Daniel Webster *(1937) and* Thirteen O'Clock: Stories of Several Worlds *(1937). He was also an accomplished poet with several books of collections, including* John Brown's Body *(1928) and* Burning City *(1936).*

Stephen Vincent Benét

DANIEL WEBSTER AND THE SEA SERPENT (1937)

IT HAPPENED, ONE SUMMER'S DAY, that Dan'l Webster and some of his friends were out fishing. That was in the high days of his power and his fame, when the question wasn't if he was going to be President but when he was going to be President, and everybody at Kingston depot stood up when Dan'l Webster arrived to take the cars. But in spite of being Secretary of State and the biggest man in New England, he was just the same Dan'l Webster. He bought his Jamaica personal and in the jug at Colonel Sever's store in Kingston, right under a sign saying ENGLISH AND WEST INDIA GOODS, and he never was too busy to do a hand's turn for a friend. And, as for his big farm at Marshfield, that was just the apple of his eye. He buried his favorite horses with their shoes on, standing up, in a private graveyard, and wrote Latin epitaphs for them, and he often was heard to say that his big Hungarian bull, Saint Stephen, had more sense in his rear off hoof than most politicians. But, if there was one thing he loved better than Marshfield itself, it was the sea and the waters around it, for he was a fisherman born.

This time, he was salt-water fishing in the Comet, well out of sight of land. It was a good day for fishing, not too hazy, but not too clear, and Dan'l Webster enjoyed it, as he enjoyed everything in life, except maybe listening to the speeches of Henry Clay. He'd stolen a half-dozen days to come up to Marshfield, and well he needed the rest, for we'd nearly gone to war with England the year before, and now he was trying to fix up a real copper-riveted treaty that would iron out all the old differences that still kept the two countries unfriendly. And that was a job, even for Dan'l Webster. But as soon as he stepped aboard the Comet, he was carefree and heartwhole. He had his real friends around him and he wouldn't allow a word of politics talked on the boat—though that rule got broken this time, and for a good reason, as you'll see. And when he struck his first cod, and felt the fish take the hook, a kind of big slow smile went over his features, and he said, "Gentlemen, this is solid comfort." That was the kind of man he was.

I don't know how many there were of them aboard—half a dozen or so—just enough for good company. We'll say there were George Blake and Rufus Choate and young Peter Harvey and a boy named Jim Billings. And, of course, there was Seth Peterson, Dan'l's boat captain, in his red flannel shirt, New England as cod and beach plums, and Dan'l Webster's fast friend. Dan'l happened to be Secretary of State, and Seth Peterson happened to be a boat captain, but that didn't make any difference between them. And, once the Comet left dock, Seth Peterson ran the show, as it's right that a captain should.

Well, they'd fished all morning and knocked off for a bite of lunch, and some had had segars and snoozes afterward, and some hadn't, but in any case, it was around midafternoon, and everybody was kind of comfortable and contented. They still fished, and they fished well, but they knew in an hour or so they'd be heading back for home with a fine catch on board. So maybe there was more conversation than Seth Peterson would have approved of earlier, and maybe some jokes were passed and some stories told. I don't know, but you know how it is when men get together at the end of a good day. All the same, they were still paying attention to their business—and I guess it was George Blake that noticed it first.

"Dan'l," he said, breathing hard, "I've got something on my line that pulls like a Morgan horse."

"Well, yank him in!" sang out Dan'l, and then his face changed as his own line began to stiffen and twang. "George," he said, "I beat you! I got something on my line that pulls like a pair of steers!"

"Give 'em more line, Mr. Webster!" yells Seth Peterson, and Dan'l did. But at that, the line ran out so fast it smoked when it hit the water, and any hands but Dan'l Webster's would have been cut to the bone. Nor you couldn't see where it went to, except Something deep in the waters must be pulling it out as a cat pulls yarn from a ball. The veins in Dan'l Webster's arm stood out like cords. He played the fish and played the fish; he fought it with every trick he knew. And still the little waves danced and the other men gaped at the fight—and still he couldn't bring the Something to time.

"By the big elm at Marshfield!" he said at last, with his dark face glowing and a fisherman's pride in his eyes. "Have I hooked on to a frigate with all sails set? I've payed out a mile of my own particular line, and she still pulls like ten wild horses. Gentlemen, what's this?"

And even as he said it, the tough line broke in two with a crack like a musket-shot, and out of the deep of ocean, a mile away, the creature rose, majestic. Neighbors, that was a sight! Shaking the hook from its jaw, it rose, the sea serpent of the Scriptures, exact and to specifications as laid down in the Good Book, with its hairy face and its furlong on furlong of body, wallowing and thrashing in the troubled sea. As it rose, it gave a long low melancholy hoot, like a kind of forsaken steamboat; and when it gave out that hoot, young Jim Billings, the boy, fainted dead away on the deck. But nobody even noticed him—they were all staring at the sea serpent with bulging eyes.

Even Dan'l Webster was shaken. He passed his hand for a moment across his brow and gave a sort of inquiring look at the jug of Jamaica by the hatch.

"Gentlemen," he said in a low voice, "the evidence—the ocular evidence would seem to be conclusive. And yet, speaking as a lawyer—"

"Thar she blows! I never thought to see her again!" yells Seth Peterson, half driven out of his mind by the sight, as the sea serpent roiled the waters. "Thar she blows, by the Book of Genesis! Oh, why ain't I got a harpoon?"

"Quiet, Seth," said Dan'l Webster. "Let us rather give thanks for being permitted to witness this glorious and unbelievable sight." And then you could see the real majesty of the man., for no sooner were the words out of his mouth than the sea serpent started swimming straight toward the Comet. She came like a railway train and her wake boiled out behind her for an acre. And yet, there was something kind of skittish about her, too—you might say that she came kind of shaking her skirts and bridling. I don't know what there was about her that made you sure she was female, but they were all sure.

She came, direct as a bullet, till you could count the white teeth shining in her jaws. I don't know what the rest of them did—though doubtless some prayers were put up in a hasty way—but Dan'l Webster stood there and faced her, with his brow dark and his eyes like a sleepy lion's, giving her glance for glance. Yes, there was a minute, there, when she lifted her head high out of water and they looked at each other eye to eye. They say hers were reddish but handsome. And then, just as it seemed she'd crash plumb through the Comet, she made a wide wheel and turned. Three times she circled the boat, hooting lonesomely, while the Comet danced up and down like a cork on the waves. But Dan'l Webster kept his footing, one hand gripping the mast, and whenever he got a chance, he fixed her with his eye. Till finally, on the third circuit, she gave one last long hoot—like twenty foghorns at once, it was, and nearly deafened them all—and plunged back whence she'd come, to the bottomless depths of the sea.

But even after the waters were calm again, they didn't say anything for quite a while. Till, finally, Seth Peterson spoke.

"Well, Mr. Webster," he said, "that one got away"—and he grinned a dry grin.

"Leviathan of the Scriptures! Give me paper and pen," said Dan'l Webster. "We must write this down and attest it." And then they all began to talk.

Well, he wrote an account of just what they'd seen, very plain and honest. And everybody there signed his name to it. Then he read it over to them again aloud. And then there was another silence, while they looked at one another.

Finally, Seth Peterson shook his head, slow and thoughtful.

"It won't do, Dan'l," he said, in a deep voice.

"Won't do?" said Dan'l Webster, with his eyes blazing. "What do you mean, Seth?"

"I mean it just won't do, Dan'l," said Seth Peterson, perfectly respectful, but perfectly firm. "I put it up to you, gentlemen," he said, turning to the others. "I can go home and say I've seen the sea serpent. And everybody'll say, 'Oh, that's just that old liar, Seth Peterson.' But if it's Dan'l Webster says so—can't you see the difference?"

He paused for a minute, but nobody said a word.

"Well, I can," he said. He drawled out the words very slow. "Dan'l Webster—Secretary of State—sees and talks to a sea serpent—off Plymouth Bay. Why, it would plumb ruin him! And I don't mind being ruint, but it's different with Dan'l Webster. Would you vote for a man for President who claimed he'd saw the sea serpent? Well, would you? Would anybody?"

There was another little silence, and then George Blake spoke.

"He's right, Dan'l," he said, while the others nodded. "Give me that paper." He took it from Dan'l Webster's hand and threw it in the sea.

"And now," he said in a firm voice, "I saw cod. Nothing but cod. Except maybe a couple of halibut. Did any gentlemen here see anything else?"

Well, at that, it turned out, of course, that nobody aboard had seen anything but cod all day. And with that, they put back for shore. All the same, they all looked over their shoulders a good deal till they got back to harbor.

And yet Dan'l Webster wasn't too contented that evening, in spite of his fine catch. For, after all, he had seen the sea serpent, and not only seen her but played her on the line for twenty-seven minutes by his gold repeater, and being a fisherman, he'd like to have said so. And yet, if he did—Seth was right—folks would think him crazy or worse. It took his mind off Lord Ashburton and the treaty with England—till, finally, he pushed aside the papers on his desk.

"Oh, a plague on the beast!" he said, kind of crossly. "I'll leave it alone and hope it leaves me alone." So he took his candle and went up to bed. But just as he was dropping off to sleep, he thought he heard a long low hoot from the mouth of Green Harbor River, two miles away.

The next night the hooting continued, and the third day there was a piece in the Kingston paper about the new Government foghorn at Rocky Ledge. Well, the thing began to get on Dan'l Webster's nerves, and when his temper was roused he wasn't a patient man. Moreover, the noises seemed to disturb the stock—at least his overseer said so—and the third night his favorite gray kicked half the door out of her stall. "That sea serpent's getting to be an infernal nuisance," thought Dan'l Webster. "I've got to protect my property." So, the fourth night he put on his old duck-shooting clothes and took his favorite shotgun, Learned Seldon, and went down to a blind at the mouth of Green Harbor River, to see what he could see. He didn't tell anybody else about his intentions, because he still felt kind of sensitive about the whole affair.

Well, there was a fine moon that night, and sure enough, about eleven o'clock, the sea serpent showed up, steaming in from ocean, all one continuous wave length, like a giant garden hose. She was quite a handsome sight, all speckled with the moonlight, but Dan'l Webster couldn't rightly appreciate it. And just as she came to the blind, she lifted her head and looked sorrowfully in the direction of Marshfield and let out a long low soulful hoot like a homesick train.

Dan'l Webster hated to do it. But he couldn't have a sea serpent living in Green Harbor River and scaring the stock—not to speak of the universal consternation and panic there'd be in the countryside when such a thing was known. So he lifted Learned Selden and gave her both barrels for a starter, just a trifle over her head. And as soon as the gun exploded, the sea serpent let out a screech you could hear a mile and headed back for open sea. If she'd traveled fast before, she traveled like lightning now, and it wasn't any time before she was just a black streak on the waters.

Dan'l Webster stepped out of the blind and wiped his brow. He felt sorry, but he felt relieved. He didn't think she'd be back, after that sort of scare, and he wanted to leave everything shipshape before he went down to Washington, next morning. But next day, when he told Seth Peterson what he'd done, he didn't feel so chipper. For, "You shouldn't have done that, Mr. Webster," said Seth Peterson, shaking his head, and that was all he would say except a kind of mutter that sounded like "Samanthy was always particular set in her likes." But Dan'l didn't pay any attention to that, though he remembered it later, and he was quite short with Seth for the first time in their long relationship. So Seth shut up like a quahog, and Dan'l took the cars for Washington.

When he got there he was busy enough, for the British treaty was on the boil, and within twenty-four hours he'd forgot all about the sea serpent. Or thought he had. But three days later, as he was walking home to his house on Lafayette Square, with a senator friend of his, in the cool of the evening, they heard a curious noise. It seemed to come from the direction of the Potomac River.

"Must have got a new whistle for the Baltimore night boat," said the senator. "Noisy too."

"Oh, that's just the bullfrogs on the banks," said Dan'l Webster steadily. But he knew what it was, just the same, and his heart sank within him. But nobody ever called Dan'l Webster a coward. So, as soon as he'd got rid of the senator, he went down to the banks of the Potomac. Well, it was the sea serpent, all right.

She looked a little tired, as well she might, having swum from Plymouth Bay. But as soon as she saw Dan'l Webster, she stretched out her neck and gave a long low loving hoot. Then Dan'l knew what the trouble was and, for once in his life, he didn't know what to do. But he'd brought along a couple of roe herring, in a paper, just in case; so he fed them to her and she hooted, affectionate and grateful. Then he walked back to his house with his head bowed. And that very night he sent a special express letter to Seth Peterson at Marshfield, for, it seemed to him, Seth must know more about the business than he let on.

Well, Seth got to Washington as fast as the cars would bring him, and the very evening he arrived Dan'l sent him over to interview the serpent. But when Seth came back, Dan'l could see by his face that he hadn't made much progress.

"Could you talk to her, Seth?" he said, and his voice was eager. "Can she understand United States?"

"Oh, she can understand it all right," said Seth. "She's even picking up a few words. They was always a smart family, those Rock Ledge serpents, and she's the old maid of the lot, and the best educated. The only trouble with 'em is, they're so terrible set in their ways."

"You might have warned me, Seth," said Dan'l Webster, kind of reproachful, and Seth looked uncomfortable.

"Well, to tell you the truth," he said, "I thought all of 'em was dead. Nor I never thought she'd act up like this—her father was as respectable a serpent as you'd see in a long summer's day. Her father—"

"Bother her father!" said Dan'l Webster and set his jaw. "Tell me what she says."

"Well, Mr. Webster," said Seth, and stared at his boots, "she says you're quite a handsome man. She says she never did see anybody quite like you," he went on. "I hate to tell you this, Mr. Webster, and I feel kind of responsible, but I think you ought to know. And I told you that you oughtn't to have shot at her—she's pretty proud of that. She says she knows just how you meant it. Well, I'm no great hand at being embarrassed, Mr. Webster, but, I tell you, she embarrassed me. You see, she's been an old maid for about a hundred and fifty years, I guess, and that's the worst of it. And being the last of her folks in those particular waters, there's just no way to restrain her–her father and mother was as sensible, hard-working serpents as ever gave a feller a tow through a fog, but you know how it is with those old families. Well, she says wherever you go, she'll follow you, and she claims she wants to hear you speak before the Supreme Court–"

"Did you tell her I'm a married man?" said Dan'l. "Did you tell her that?"

"Yes, I told her," said Seth, and you could see the perspiration on his forehead. "But she says that doesn't signify–her being a serpent and different–and she's fixing to move right in. She says Washington's got a lovely climate and she's heard all about the balls and the diplomatic receptions. I don't know how she's heard about them, but she has." He swallowed. "I got her to promise she'd kind of lie low for two weeks and not come up the Potomac by daylight–she was fixing to do that because she wants to meet the President. Well, I got her to promise that much. But she says, even so, if you don't come to see her once an evening, she'll hoot till you do, and she told me to tell you that you haven't heard hooting yet. And as soon as the fish market's open, I better run down and buy a barrel of flaked cod, Mr. Webster–she's partial to flaked cod and she usually takes it in the barrel. Well, I don't want to worry you, Mr. Webster, but I'm afraid that we're in a fix."

"A fix!" said Dan'l Webster. "It's the biggest fix I ever was in in my life!"

"Well, it's kind of complimentary, in a way, I guess," said Seth Peterson, "but–"

"Does she say anything else?" said Dan'l Webster, drawing a long breath.

"Yes, Mr. Webster," said Seth Peterson, his eyes on his boots. "She says you're a little shy. But she says she likes that in a man."

Dan'l Webster went to bed that night, but he didn't sleep. He worked and worked those great brains of his till he nearly wore out the wheels, but he still couldn't think of a way to get rid of the sea serpent. And just about the time dawn broke, he heard one long low hoot, faithful and reminiscent, from the direction of the Potomac.

Well, the next two weeks were certainly bad ones for him. For, as the days wore on, the sea serpent got more and more restive. She wanted him to call her Samanthy, which he wouldn't, and she kept asking him when he was going to introduce her into society, till he had to feed her Italian sardines in olive oil to keep her quiet. And that ran up a bill at the fish market that he hated to think of—besides, her continually threatening to come up the Potomac by day. Moreover, and to put the cap on things, the great Webster-Ashburton treaty that was to make his name as Secretary of State had struck a snag and England didn't seem at all partial to admitting the American claims. Oh, it was a weary fortnight and a troublesome one!

The last afternoon of the fortnight, he sat in his office and he didn't know where to turn. For Lord Asburton was coming to see him for a secret conference that night at nine, and he had to see the sea serpent at ten, and how to satisfy either of them he didn't know. His eyes stared wearily at the papers on his desk. He rang the bell for his secretary.

"The corvette Benjamin Franklin reports—" he said. "This should have gone to the Navy Department, Mr. Jones." Then he glanced at the naval report again and his eyes began to glow like furnaces. "By the bones of Leviathan! I've got it!" he said, with a shout. "Where's my hat, Mr. Jones. I must see the President at once!"

There was a different feeling about the house on Lafayette Square that evening, for Dan'l Webster was himself again. He cracked a joke with Seth Peterson and took a glass of Madeira and turned it to the light. And when Lord Ashburton was announced—a nice, white-haired old gentleman, though a little stiff in his joints—he received him with all the courtesy of a king.

"I am glad to see you so much restored, Mr. Webster," said Lord Ashburton, when the greetings had been exchanged. "And yet I fear I bring you bad news. Concerning clauses six and seven of the proposed treaty between Her Majesty's Government and the United States of America, it is my duty to state—"

"My lord, let us drop the clauses for a moment and take the wider view," said Dan'l Webster, smiling. "This is a matter concerning the future welfare and peace of two great nations. Your government claims the right to search our ships; that right we deny. And our attitude seems to you preposterous. Is that not so?"

"I would hesitate to use the word 'preposterous,'" said Lord Ashburton cautiously. "Yet—"

"And yet," said Dan'l Webster, leaning forward, "there are things which may seem preposterous, and yet are not. Let me put a case. Let us say that Great Britain has the strongest navy afloat."

"Britannia rules the waves," said Lord Ashburton, with a noble smile.

"There were a couple she didn't rule in 1812," said Dan'l Webster, "but let that pass. Let me ask you, Lord Ashburton, and let me ask you solemnly, what could even the power and might of Britain's navy avail against Leviathan?"

"Leviathan?" said Lord Ashburton, rather coldly. "Naturally, I understand the Biblical allusion. Yet—"

"The sea serpent," said Dan'l Webster, kind of impatient. "What could all Britain's navy do against the sea serpent out of the Scriptures?"

Lord Ashburton stared at him as if he had gone mad. "God bless my soul, Mr. Secretary!" he said. "But I fail to see the point of your question. The sea serpent doesn't exist!"

"Doesn't he—I mean she?" said Dan'l Webster, calmly. "And suppose I should prove to you that it does exist?"

"Well, 'pon my word! God bless my soul!" said Lord Asburton, kind of taken aback. "Naturally—in that case—however—but even so—"

Dan'l Webster touched a bell on his desk. "Lord Ashburton," he said, kind of solemn, "I am putting my life, and what is dearer to me, my honor and reputation, in your hands. Nevertheless, I feel it necessary, for a better understanding between our two countries."

Seth Peterson came into the room and Dan'l nodded at him.

"Seth," he said, "Lord Ashburton is coming with us to see Samanthy."

"It's all right if you say so, Mr. Webster," said Seth Peterson, "but he'll have to help carry the sardines."

"Well, 'pon my word! Bless my soul! A very strange proceeding!" said Lord Ashburton, but he followed along.

Well, they got to the banks of the Potomac, the three of them, and when they were there, Seth whistled. Samanthy was lying mostly under water, behind a little brushy island, but when she heard the whistle, she began to heave up and uncoil, all shining in the moonlight. It was what you might call a kind of impressive sight. Dan'l Webster looked at Lord Ashburton, but Lord Ashburton's words seemed sort of stuck in his throat.

Finally he got them out. "Bless my soul!" he said. "You Americans are very extraordinary! Is it alive?"

But then all he could do was goggle, for Samanthy had lifted her head, and giving a low friendly hoot, she commenced to swim around the island.

"Now, is that a sea serpent or isn't it?" said Dan'l Webster, with a kind of quiet pride.

"Indubitably," said Lord Ashburton, staring through his eyeglass. "Indubitably," and he kind of cleared his throat. "It is, indeed and in fact, a serpent of the sea. And I am asleep and in bed, in my room at the British Embassy." He pinched himself. "Ouch!" he said. "No, I am not."

"Would you call it sizable, for a sea serpent?" persisted Dan'l Webster.

Lord Ashburton stared again through his eyeglass. "Quite," he said. "Oh, yes, quite, quite!"

"And powerful?" asked Dan'l.

"I should judge so," said Lord Ashburton, faintly, as the sea serpent swam around and around the island and the waves of its wake broke crashing on the bank. "Yes, indeed, a very powerful engine of destruction. May I ask what it feeds upon?"

"Italian sardines, for preference," said Dan'l. "But that's beside the point." He drew a long breath. "Well, my lord," he said, "we're intending to commission that sea serpent as a regular and acknowledged war vessel in the United States Navy. And then, where's your wooden walls?"

Lord Ashburton, he was a diplomat, and his face didn't change expression as he stared first at the sea serpent and then at the face of Dan'l Webster. But after a while, he nodded. "You need not labor the point,

Mr. Secretary," he said. "My government, I am sure, will be glad to reconsider its position on the last two clauses and on the right of search."

"Then I'm sure we can reach an agreement," said Dan'l Webster, and wiped the sweat from his brow. "And now, let's feed Samanthy."

He whistled to her himself, a long musical whistle, and she came bounding and looping in toward shore. It took all three of them to heave her the barrel of sardines, and she swallowed it down in one gulp. After that, she gave a hoot of thanks and gratitude, and Lord Ashburton sat down on the bank for a minute and took snuff. He said that he needed something to clear his mind.

"Naturally," he said, after a while, "Her Majesty's Government must have adequate assurances as to the good conduct of this—this lady." He'd meant to say "creature" at first, but Samanthy rolled her eye at him just then, and he changed the word.

"You shall have them," said Dan'l Webster, and whistled Samanthy even closer. She came in kind of skittish, flirting her coils, and Lord Ashburton closed his eyes for a minute. But when Dan'l Webster spoke, it was in the voice that hushed the Senate whenever he rose.

"Samanthy," he said, "I speak to you now as Secretary of State of the United States of America." It was the great voice that had rung in the Supreme Court and replied to Hayne, and even a sea serpent had to listen respectful. For the voice was mellow and deep, and he pictured Samanthy's early years as a carefree young serpent, playing with her fellows, and then her hard life of toil and struggle when she was left lone and lorn, till even Seth Peterson and Lord Ashburton realized the sorrow and tragedy of her lonely lot. And then, in the gentlest and kindest way you could ask, he showed her where her duty lay.

"For, if you keep on hooting in the Potomac, Samanthy," he said, "You'll become a public menace to navigation and get sat upon by the Senate Committee for Rivers and Harbors. They'll drag you up on land, Samanthy, and put you in the Smithsonian Institution; they'll stick you in a stagnant little pool and children will come to throw you peanuts on Sundays, and their nurses will poke you with umbrellas if you don't act lively enough. The U.S. Navy will shoot at you for target practice,

Samanthy, and the scientists will examine you, and the ladies of the Pure Conduct League will knit you a bathing suit, and you'll be bothered every minute by congressmen and professors and visitors and foreign celebrities till you won't be able to call your scales your own. Oh, yes, it'll be fame, Samanthy, but it won't be good enough. Believe me, I know something about fame and it's begging letters from strangers and calls from people you don't know and don't want to know, and the burden and wear and tear of being a public character till it's enough to break your heart. It isn't good enough, Samanthy; it won't give you back your free waters and your sporting in the deep. Yes, Samanthy, it'd be a remarkable thing to have you here in Washington, but it isn't the life you were meant for and I can't take advantage of your trust. And now," he said to Seth Peterson, "just what does she say?"

Seth Peterson listened, attentive, to the hootings.

"She says the Washington climate isn't what she thought it was," he said. "And the Potomac River's too warm; it's bad for her sciatica. And she's plumb tired of sardines."

"Does she say anything about me?" asked Dan'l Webster, anxiously.

"Well," said Seth Peterson, listening, "she says—if you'll excuse me, Mr. Webster—that you may be a great man, but you wouldn't make much of a sea serpent. She says you haven't got enough coils. She says—well, she says no hard feelings, but she guesses it was a mistake on both sides."

He listened again. "But she says one thing," he said. "She says she's got to have recognition and a husband, if she has to take this Lord Ashburton. She says he doesn't look like much, but he might get her introduced at Court."

A great light broke over Dan'l's face and his voice rang out like thunder. "She shall have them both," he said. "Come here, Samanthy. By virtue of the authority vested in me as Secretary of State, and by special order of the President of the United States and the Secretary of the Navy, as witness the attached commission in blank which I now fill in with your name, I hereby attach you to the United States Navy, to rank as a forty-four-gun frigate on special duty, rating a rear admiral's flag and a salute of the appropriate number of guns, wherever encountered in American waters. And, by virtue of the following special order, I hereby order you to the South Seas, there to cruise until further orders for the purpose of seeking a suitable and proper husband, with all the rights, privileges, duties and appurtenances pertaining to said search and said American citizenship, as aforesaid and Hail Columbia. Signed John Tyler, President. With which is subjoined a passport signed by Daniel Webster, Secretary of State, bidding all foreign nations let pass without hindrance the American citizen, Samanthy Doe, on her lawful journeys and errands." He dropped his voice for a moment and added reflectively, "The American corvette, Benjamin Franklin, reports sighting a handsome young male sea serpent on February third of the present year, just off the coast of the Sandwich Islands. Said serpent had forty-two coils by actual count, and when last sighted was swimming SSW at full speed."

But hardly had he spoken when Samanthy, for the last time, lifted her head and gave out a last long hoot. She looked upon Dan'l Webster as she did so, and there was regret in her eye. But the regret was tinctured with eagerness and hope.

Then she beat the water to a froth, and, before they really saw her go, she was gone, leaving only her wake on the moonlit Potomac.

"Well," said Dan'l Webster, yawning a little, "there we are. And now, Lord Ashburton, if you'll come home with me, we can draw up that treaty."

"Gladly," said Lord Ashburton, brushing his coat with his handkerchief. "Is it really gone? 'Pon my soul! You know, for a moment, I imagined that I actually saw a sea serpent. You have a very vivid way of putting things, Mr. Webster. But I think I understand the American attitude now, from the–er–analogy you were pleased to draw between such a–er–fabulous animal and the young strength of your growing country."

"I was confident that you would appreciate it, once it was brought to your attention," said Dan'l Webster. But he winked one eye at Seth Peterson, and Seth Peterson winked back.

And I'll say this for Dan'l Webster, too–he kept his promises. All through the time he was Secretary of State, he saw to it that the forty-four-gun frigate, Samanthy Doe, was carried on a special account on the books of the Navy. In fact, there's some people say that she's still so carried, and that it was her give Ericsson the idea for building the Monitor in the Civil War—if she wasn't the Monitor herself. And when the White Fleet went around the world in Teddy Roosevelt's time—well, there was a lookout in the crow's nest of the flagship, one still calm night, as they passed by the palmy isles of the South Seas. And all of a sudden, the water boiled, tremendous and phosphorescent, and there was a pair of sea serpents and seven young ones, circling, calm and majestic, three times around the fleet. He rubbed his eyes and he stared, but there they were. Well, he was the only one that saw it, and they put him in the brig for it next morning. But he swore, till the day he died, they were flying the Stars and Stripes.

If you turn P. J. O'Rourke loose on a topic, he's sure to come up with scintillating humor. In this story he tackles fly-fishing, poking fun at just about everything connected to the sport. O'Rourke, former editor of National Lampoon, *is a brilliant satirist. He has written several books, notably* Age and Guile Beat Youth, Innocence and a Bad Haircut *(1995). Other favorites are* Modern Manners *(1989),* Give War a Chance *(1992), and* Eat the Rich *(1998). O'Rourke's essays have appeared in* Rolling Stone, The American Spectator, *and* Sports Afield.

P. J. O'Rourke

FLY-FISHING (1987)

I'D NEVER FLY-FISHED. I'd done other kinds of fishing. I'd fished for bass. That's where I'd get far enough away from the dock so that people couldn't see there was no line on the pole, then drink myself blind in the rowboat. And I'd deep-sea fished. That's where the captain would get me blind before we'd even left the dock and I'd be the one who couldn't see the line. But I'd never fly-fished.

I'd always been of two minds about the sport. On the one hand, here's a guy standing in cold water up to his liver throwing the world's most expensive clothesline at trees. A full two-thirds of his time is spent untangling stuff, which he could be doing in the comfort of his own home with old shoelaces, if he wanted. The whole business costs like sin and requires heavier clothing. Furthermore it's conducted in the middle of blackfly season. Cast and swat. Cast and swat. Fly-fishing may be a sport invented by insects with fly fishermen as bait. And what does the truly sophisticated dry fly artist do when he finally bags a fish? He lets the fool thing go and eats baloney sandwiches instead.

On the other hand, fly-fishing did have its attractions. I love to waste time and money. I had ways to do this most of the year—hunting, skiing, renting summer houses in To-Hell-and-Gone Harbor for a Lebanon hostage's ransom. But, come spring, I was limited to cleaning up the yard. Even with a new Toro every two years and a lot of naps by the compost heap, it's hard to waste much time and money doing this. And then there's the gear needed for fly-fishing. I'm a sucker for anything that requires more equipment than I have sense. My workshop is furnished with the full panoply of Black & Decker power tools, all from one closet shelf I installed in 1979.

When I began to think about fly-fishing, I realized I'd never be content again until my den was cluttered with computerized robot fly-tying vises, space-age Teflon and ceramic knotless tapered leaders, sterling silver English fish scissors, and thirty-five volumes on the home life of the midge. And there was one other thing, I'm a normal male who takes an occasional nip; therefore, I love to put funny things on my head. Sometimes it's the nut dish, sometimes the spaghetti colander, but the hats I'd seen fly fishermen wear were funnier than either and I had to have one.

I went to Hackles & Tackles, an upscale dry fly specialty shop that also sells fish print wallpaper and cashmere V-neck sweaters with little trout on them. I got a graphite rod for about the price of a used car and a reel made out of the kind of exotic alloys that you can go to jail for selling to the Soviet Union. I also got one of those fishing vests that only comes down to the top of your beer gut and looks like you dressed in the dark and tried to put on your ten-year-old son's three-piece suit. And I purchased lots of monofilament and teensy hooks covered in auk down and moose lint and an entire L. L. Bean boat bag full of fly-fishing do-whats, hinky-doovers, and watchamajigs.

I also brought home a set of fly-fishing how-to videotapes. This is the Eighties, I reasoned, the age of video. What better way to take up a sport than from a comfortable armchair? That's where I'm at my best with most sports anyway.

There were three tapes. The first one claimed it would teach me to cast. The second would teach me to "advanced cast." And the third would tell me where trout live, how they spend their weekends, and what they'd order for lunch if there were underwater delicatessens for fish. I started the VCR and a squeaky little guy with an earnest manner and a double-funny hat came on, began heaving fly line around, telling me the secret to making beautiful casting loops is . . .

Whoever made these tapes apparently assumed I knew how to tie backing to reel and line to backing and leaders to line and so on all the way out to the little feather and fuzz fish snack at the end. I didn't know how to put my rod together. I had to go to the children's section at the public library and check out *My Big Book of Fishing* and begin with how to open the package it all came in.

A triple granny got things started on the spool. After twelve hours and help from pop rivets and a tube of Krazy Glue, I managed an Albright knot between backing and line. But my version of a nail knot in the leader put Mr. Gordian of ancient Greek knot legend fame strictly on the shelf. It was the size of a hamster and resembled one of the Woolly Bugger flies I'd bought except in the size you use for killer whales. I don't want to talk about blood knots and tippets. There I was with two pieces of invisible plastic, trying to use fingers the size of a man's thumb while holding a magnifying glass and a Tensor lamp between my teeth and gripping nasty tangles of monofilament with each big toe. My girlfriend had to come over and cut me out of this with pinking shears. Personally, I'm going to get one of those nine-year-old Persian kids that they use to make incredibly tiny knots in fine Bukhara rugs and just take him with me on all my fishing trips.

What I really needed was a fly-fishing how-to video narrated by Mister Rogers. This would give me advice about which direction to wind the reel and why I should never try to drive a small imported car while wearing boot-foot waders. (Because when I stepped on the accelerator I also stepped on the brake and the clutch.)

I rewound Mr. Squeaky and started over. I was supposed to keep my rod tip level and keep my rod swinging in a ninety-degree arc. When I snapped my wrist forward I was giving one quick flick of a blackjack to the skull of a mugging victim. When I snapped my wrist back I was sticking my thumb over my shoulder and telling my brother-in-law to get the hell out of here and I mean right now, Buster. Though it wasn't explained with quite so much poetry.

Then I was told to try these things with a "yarn rod." This was something else I'd bought at the tackle shop. It looked like a regular rod tip from a two-piece rod but with a cork handle. You run a bunch of bright orange yarn through the guides and flip it around. It's supposed to imitate the action of a fly rod in slow motion. I don't know about that, but I do know you can catch and play a nine-pound house cat on a yard rod, and it's great sport. They're hard to land, however. And I understand cat fishing is strictly catch and release if they're under twenty inches.

Then I went back to the television and heard about stance, loop control, straight line casts, slack line casts, stripping, mending, and giving myself enough room when practicing in the yard so I wouldn't get tangled in my neighbor's bird feeder.

After sixty minutes of videotape, seven minutes of yarn rod practice, twenty-five minutes of cat fishing, and several beers, I felt I was ready. I picked up the fin tickler and laid out a couple of loops that weren't half bad if I do say so myself. I'll bet I cast almost three times before making macramé out of my weight forward Cortland 444. This wasn't so hard.

I also watched the advanced tape. But Squeaky had gone grad school on me. He's throwing reach casts, curve casts, roll casts, steeple casts, and casts he calls squiggles and stutters. He's writing his name with the line in the air. He's making his dry fly look like the Blue Angels. He's pitching things forehand, backhand, and between his wader legs. And, through the magic of video editing, every time his hook-tipped dust kitty hits the water he lands a trout the size of a canoe.

The videotape about trout themselves wasn't much use either. It's hard to get excited about where trout feed when you know that the only way you're going to be able to get a fly to that place is by throwing your fly box at it.

I must say, however, all the tapes were informative. "Nymphs and streamers" are not, as it turns out, naked mythological girls decorating the high school gym with crepe paper. And I learned that the part of fly-fishing I'm going to be best as is naming the flies:

Wooly Hatcatcher
Blue-Wing Earsnag
Overhanging Brush Muddler
Royal Toyota Hatchback
O'Rourke's Ouchtail
P.J.'s Live Worm-'n-Bobber

By now I'd reached what I think they call a "learning plateau." That is, if I was going to catch a fish with a fly rod, I either had to go get in the water or open the fridge and toss hooks at Mrs. Paul's frozen haddock fillets.

I made reservations at a famous fishing lodge on the Au Sable River in Michigan. When I got there and found a place to park among the Saabs and Volvos the proprietor said I was just a few days early for the Hendrikson hatch. There is, I see, one constant in all types of fishing, which is when the fish are biting, which is almost-but-not-quite-now.

I looked pretty good making false casts in the lodge parking lot. I mean no one laughed out loud. But most of the other 2,000 young professionals fishing this no-kill stretch of the Au Sable were pretty busy checking to make sure that their trout shirts were color coordinated with their Reebok wading sneakers.

When I stepped in the river, however, my act came to pieces. My line hit the water like an Olympic belly flop medalist. I hooked four "tree trout" in three minutes. My back casts had people ducking for cover in Traverse City and Grosse Pointe Farms. Somebody ought to tie a dry fly that looks like a Big Mac. Then there'd be an excuse for the hook winding up in my mouth instead of the fish's. The only thing I could manage to get a drag-free float on was me after I stepped in a hole. And the trout? The trout laughed.

The next day was worse. I could throw tight loops. I could sort of aim. I could even make a gentle presentation and get the line to lay right every so often. But when I tried to do all of these things at once, I went mental. I looked like Leonard Bernstein conducting "Flight of the Bumblebee" in fast forward. I was driving tent pegs with my rod tip. My slack casts wrapped around my thighs. My straight line casts went straight into the back of my neck. My improved surgeon's loops looked like full windsors. I had wind knots in everything including my Red Ball suspenders. And two hundred dollars worth of fly floatant, split shot, Royal Coachmen, and polarized sunglasses fell off my body and were swept downstream.

Then, mirabile dictu, I hooked a fish. I was casting some I-forget-the-name nymph and clumsily yanking it in when my rod tip bent and my pulse shot into trade deficit numbers. I lifted the rod, the first thing I'd done right in two days, and the trout actually leaped out of the water as if it were trying for a *Field & Stream* playmate centerfold. I heard my voice go up three octaves until I sounded like my little sister in the middle of a puppy litter, "Ooooo that's-a-boy, that's-a-baby, yesssssss, come to daddy, wooogie-woogie-woo." It was a rainbow and I'll bet it was seven inches long. All right, five. Anyway, when I grabbed the thing some of it stuck out both ends of my hand. I haven't been so happy since I passed my driver's license exam.

So I'm a fly fisherman now. Of course I'm not an expert yet. But I'm working on the most important part of fly-fishing technique—boring the hell out of anybody who'll listen.

The Brothers Grimm fairy tales are among the most famous ever written down. One of their very best is this classic fish story. More accurately, it is a parable on greed. Jacob (1785–1863) and Wilhelm (1786–1859) spent their lives collecting folk tales. They wrote their stories in German, and various translations of Grimm's Fairy Tales *have been handed down over the years. This one is by Margaret Hunt, as revised by James Stern.*

Jacob and Wilhelm Grimm

THE FISHERMAN AND HIS WIFE (1815)

THERE WAS ONCE UPON A TIME a fisherman who lived with his wife in a pig-stye close by the sea, and every day he went out fishing; and he fished and he fished. And once he was sitting with his rod, looking at the clear water, and he sat and he sat. Then his line suddenly went down, far down below, and when he drew it up again, he brought out a large Flounder. Then the Flounder said to him: "Hark, you Fisherman, I pray you, let me live, I am no Flounder really, but an enchanted prince. What good will it do you to kill me? I should not be good to eat, put me in the water again, and let me go." "Come," said the Fisherman, "there is no need for so many words about it—a fish that can talk I should certainly let go, anyhow." And with that he put him back again into the clear water, and the Flounder went to the bottom, leaving a long streak of blood behind him. Then the Fisherman got up and went home to his wife in the pig-stye.

"Husband," said the woman, "have you caught nothing to-day?" "No," said the man, "I did catch a Flounder, who said he was an enchanted prince, so I let him go again." "Did you not wish for anything first?" said the woman. "No," said the man, "what should I wish for?" "Ah," said the woman, "it is surely hard to live always in this pig-stye which stinks and is so disgusting; you might have wished for a little hut for us. Go back and call him. Tell him we want to have a little hut, he will certainly give us that." "Ah," said the man, "why should I go there again?" "Why," said the woman, "you did catch him, and you let him go again; he is sure to do it. Go at once." The man still did not quite like to go, but did not like to oppose his wife either, and went to the sea.

When he got there tFhe sea was all green and yellow, and no longer so smooth; so he stood and said:

> "Flounder, flounder in the sea,
> Come, I pray thee, here to me;
> For my wife, good Ilsabil,
> Wills not as I'd have her will."

Then the Flounder came swimming to him and said: "Well, what does she want, then?" "Ah," said the man, "I did catch you, and my wife says I really ought to have wished for ssomething. She does not like to live in a pig-stye any longer; she would like to have a hut." "Go, then," said the Flounder, "she has it already."

When the man went home, his wife was no longer in the stye, but instead of it there stood a hut, and she was sitting on a bench before the door. Then she took him by the hand and said to him: "Just come inside. Look, now isn't this a great deal better?" So they went in, and there was a small porch, and a pretty little parlor and bedroom, and a kitchen and pantry, with the best of furniture, and fitted up with the most beautiful things made of tin and brass, whatsoever was wanted. And behind the hut there was a small yard, with hens and ducks, and a little garden with flowers and fruit. "Look," said the wife, "is not that nice!" "Yes," said the husband, "and so it shall remain–now we will live quite contented." "We will think about that," said the wife. With that they ate something and went to bed.

Everything went well for a week or a fortnight, and then the woman said: "Hark you, husband, this hut is far too small for us, and the garden and yard are little; the Flounder might just as well have given us a larger house. I should like to live in a great stone castle; go to the Flounder, and tell him to give us a castle." "Ah, wife," said the man, "the hut is quite good enough; why should we live in a castle?" "What!" said the woman, "just go there, the Flounder can always do that." "No, wife," said the man, "the Flounder has just given us the hut, I do not like to go back so soon, it might make him angry." "Go," said the woman, "he can do it quite easily, and will be glad to do it; just you go to him."

The man's heart grew heavy, and he would not go. He said to himself: "It is not right," and yet he went. And when he came to the sea the water was quite purple and dark-blue, and grey and thick, and no longer so green and yellow, but it was still quiet. And he stood there and said:

> "Flounder, flounder in the sea,
> Come, I pray thee, here to me;
> For my wife, good Ilsabil,
> Wills not as I'd have her will."

"Well, what does she want, now?" said the Flounder. "Alas," said the man, half scared, "she wants to live in a great stone castle." "Go to it, then, she is standing before the door," said the Flounder.

Then the man went away, intending to go home, but when he got there, he found a great stone palace, and his wife was just standing on the steps going in, and she took him by the hand and said: "Come in." So he went in with her, and in the castle was a great hall paved with marble, and many servants, who flung wide the doors; and the walls were all bright with beautiful hangings, and in the rooms were chairs and tables of pure gold, and crystal chandeliers hung form the ceiling, and all the rooms and bedrooms had carpets, and food and wine of the very best were standing on all the tables, so that they nearly broke down beneath it. Behind the house, too, there was a great court-yard, with stables for horses and cows, and the very best of carriages; there was a magnificent large garden, too, with the most beautiful flowers and fruit-trees, and a park quite half a mile long, in which were stags, deer, and hares, and everything that could be desired. "Come," said the woman, "isn't that beautiful?" "Yes, indeed," said the man, "now let it be; and we will live in this beautiful castle and be content." "We will consider about that," said the woman, "and sleep upon it;" thereupon they went to bed.

Next morning the wife awoke first, and it was just daybreak, and from her bed she saw the beautiful country lying before her. Her husband was still stretching himself, so she poked him in the side with her elbow, and said: "Get up, husband, and just peep out of the window. Look you, couldn't we be the King over all that land? Go to the Flounder, we will be the King." "Ah, wife," said the man, "why should we be King? I do not want to be King." "Well," said the wife, "if you won't be King, I will; go to the Flounder, for I will be King." "Ah, wife," said the man, "why do you want to be King? I do not like to say that to him." "Why not?" said the woman; "go to him this instant; I must be King!" So the man went, and was quite unhappy because his wife wished to be King. "It is not right; it is not right," thought he. He did not wish to go, but yet he went.

And when he came to the sea, it was quite dark-gray, and the water heaved up from below, and smelt putrid. Then he went and stood by it, and said:

> "Flounder, flounder in the sea,
> Come, I pray thee, here to me;
> For my wife, good Ilsabil,
> Wills not as I'd have her will."

"Well, what does she want, now?" said the Flounder. "Alas," said the man, "she wants to be King." "Go to her; she is King already."

So the man went, and when he came to the palace, the castle had become much larger, and had a great tower and magnificent ornaments, and the sentinel was standing before the door, and there were numbers of soldiers with kettle-drums and trumpets. And when he went inside the house, everything was of real marble and gold, with velvet covers and great golden tassels. Then the doors of the hall were opened, and there was the court in all its splendor, and his wife was sitting on a high throne of gold and diamonds, with a great crown of gold on her head, and a sceptre of pure gold and jewels in her hand, and on both sides of her stood her maids-in-waiting in a row, each of them always one head shorter than the last.

Then he went and stood before her, and said: "Ah, wife, and now you are King." "Yes," said the woman, "now I am King." So he stood and looked at her, and when he had looked at her thus for some time, he said: "And now that you are King, let all else be, now we will wish for nothing more." "No, husband," said the woman quite anxiously, "I find time passes very heavily, I can bear it no longer; go to the Flounder—I am King, but I must be Emperor, too." "Oh, wife, why do you wish to be Emperor?" "Husband," said she, "go to the Flounder. I will be Emperor." "Alas, wife," said the man, "he cannot make you Emperor; I may not say that to the fish. There is only one Emperor in the land. An Emperor the Flounder cannot make you! I assure you he cannot."

"What!" said the woman, "I am the King, and you are nothing but my husband; will you go this moment? go at once! If he can make a king he can make an emperor. I will be Emperor; go instantly." So he was forced to go. As the man went, however, he was troubled in mind, and thought to himself: "It will not end well; it will not end well! Emperor is too shameless! The Flounder will at last be tired out."

With that he reached the sea, and the sea was quite black and thick, and began to boil up from below, so that it threw up bubbles, and such a sharp wind blew over it that it curdled, and the man was afraid. Then he went and stood by it, and said:

> "Flounder, flounder in the sea,
> Come, I pray thee, here to me;
> For my wife, good Ilsabil,
> Wills not as I'd have her will."

"Well, what does she want, now?" said the Flounder. "Alas, Flounder," said he, "my wife wants to be Emperor." "Go to her," said the Flounder; "she is Emperor already."

So the man went, and when he got there the whole palace was made of polished marble with alabaster figures and golden ornaments, and soldiers were marching before the door blowing trumpets, and beating cymbals and drums; and in the house, barons, and counts, and dukes were going about as servants. Then they opened the doors to him, which were of pure gold. And when he entered, there sat his wife on a throne, which was made of one piece of gold, and was quite two miles high; and she wore a great golden crown that was three yards high, and set with diamonds and carbuncles, and in one hand she had the sceptre, and in the other the imperial orb; and on both sides of her stood the yeomen of the guard in two rows, each being smaller than the one before him, from the biggest giant, who was two miles high, to the very smallest dwarf, just as big as my little finger. And before it stood a number of princes and dukes.

Then the man went and stood among them, and said: "Wife, are you Emperor now?" "Yes," said she, "now I am Emperor." Then he stood and looked at her well, and when he had looked at her thus for some time, he said: "Ah, wife, be content, now that you are Emperor." "Husband," said she, "why are you standing there? Now, I am Emperor, but I will be Pope too; go to the Flounder." "Oh wife," said the man, "what will you not wish for? You cannot be Pope; there is but one in Christendom; he cannot make you Pope." "Husband," said she, "I will be Pope; go immediately, I must be Pope this very day." "No, wife," said the man, "I do not like to say that to him; that would not do, it is too much; the Flounder can't make you Pope." "Husband," said she, "what nonsense! if he can make an emperor he can make a pope. Go to him directly. I am Emperor, and you are nothing but my husband; will you go at once?"

Then he was afraid and went; but he was quite faint, and shivered and shook, and his knees and legs trembled. And a high wind blew over the land, and the clouds flew, and towards evening all grew dark, and the leaves fell from the trees, and the water rose and roared as if it were boiling, and splashed upon the shore; and in the distance he saw ships which were firing guns in their sore need, pitching and tossing on the waves. And yet in the midst of the sky there was still a small patch of blue, though on every side it was as red as in a heavy storm. So, full of despair, he went and stood in much fear and said:

> "Flounder, flounder in the sea,
> Come, I pray thee, here to me;
> For my wife, good Ilsabil,
> Wills not as I'd have her will."

"Well, what does she want, now?" said the Flounder. "Alas," said the man, "she wants to be Pope." "Go to her then," said the Flounder; "she is Pope already."

So he went, and when he got there, he saw what seemed to be a large church surrounded by palaces. He pushed his way through the crowd. Inside, however, everything was lighted up with thousands and thousands of candles, and his wife was clad in gold, and she was sitting on a much higher throne, and had three great golden crowns on, and round about her there was much ecclesiastical splendor; and on both sides of her was a row of candles the largest of which was as tall as the very tallest tower, down to the very smallest kitchen candle, and all the emperors and kings were on their knees before her, kissing her shoe. "Wife," said the man, and looked attentively at her, "are you now Pope?" "Yes," said she, "I am Pope." So he stood and looked at her, and it was just as if he was looking at the bright sun. When he had stood looking at her thus for a short time, he said: "Ah, wife, if you are Pope, do let well alone!" But she looked at stiff as a post, and did not move or show any signs of life. Then said he: "Wife, now that you are Pope, be satisfied, you cannot become anything greater now." "I will consider about that," said the woman.

Thereupon they both went to bed, but she was not satisfied, and greediness let her have no sleep, for she was continually thinking what there was left for her to be.

The man slept well and soundly, for he had run about a great deal during the day; but the woman could not fall asleep at all, and flung herself from one side to the other the whole night through, thinking always what more was left for her to be, but unable to call to mind anything else. At length the sun began to rise, and when the woman saw the red of dawn, she sat up in bed and looked at it. And when, through the window, she saw the sun thus rising, she said: "Cannot I, too, order the sun and moon to rise?" "Husband," she said, poking him in the ribs with her elbows, "wake up! go to the Flounder, for I wish to be even as God is." The man was still half asleep, but he was so horrified that he fell out of bed. He thought he must have heard amiss, and rubbed his eyes, and said: "Wife, what are you saying?" "Husband," said she, "if I can't order the sun and moon to rise, and have to look on and see the sun and moon rising, I can't bear it. I shall not know what it is to have another happy hour, unless I can make them rise myself." Then she looked at him so terribly that a shudder ran over him, and said: "Go at once; I wish to be like unto God." "Alas, wife," said the man, falling on his knees before her, "the Flounder cannot do that; he can make an emperor and a pope; I beseech you, go on as you are, and be Pope." Then she fell into a rage, and her hair flew wildly about her head, she tore open her bodice, kicked him with her foot, and screamed: "I can't stand it, I can't stand it any longer! will you go this instant?" Then he put on his trousers and ran away like a madman. But outside a great storm was raging, and blowing so hard that he could scarcely keep his feet; houses and trees toppled over, the mountains trembled, rocks rolled into the sea, the sky was pitch black, and it thundered and lightened, and the sea came in with black waves as high as church-towers and mountains, and all with crests of white foam at the top. Then he cried, but could not hear his own words:

> "Flounder, flounder in the sea,
> Come, I pray thee, here to me;

For my wife, good Ilsabil,
Wills not as I'd have her will."

"Well, what does she want, now?" said the Flounder. "Alas," said he, "she wants to be like unto God." "Go to her, and you will find her back again in the pig-stye." And there they are still living to this day.

In this story, an old man meets a young married woman whose husband fancies the daughter of the old man's deceased rival. This may sound a little complex, but it's really the old love triangle dressed up in Montana fishing clothes. Can the heroine catch a big trout to impress her husband? The story is from Paul Hyde Bonner's book Aged in the Woods *(1958). He also wrote novels, including* Hotel Talleyrand *(1953) and* The Art of Llewellen Jones *(1959).*

Paul Hyde Bonner

JOHN MONAHAN (1958)

WHEN GRETA FIRST SAW THE old man, he was wobbling precariously, clinging to a long pole, a willow sapling which he had obviously cut to use as a staff against the surge of the current in the stream, his short fishing rod waving like a conductor's baton as he struggled to keep his balance. She ran down the bank and waded out to him as quickly as she could, being none too steady herself on the round, slippery rocks in that fast water. By the time she reached him he was back on balance, shuffling slowly forward, jabbing the sapling ahead of him to feel out the boulders and get a firm stance.

"Here, let me carry that," she said, taking the rusty metal casting rod from his left hand and clutching his elbow to help him. At least, that was her purpose, but the contact also helped her to keep her own balance.

The old man emitted a short grunt. "Seems like you need help, too," he said, as her grip on his arm tightened when her foot edged around a large rock.

"There! now the going's easy," she said, when they had reached the shallows. But the old man still edged forward slowly, feeling out each step after poking his staff until he had found a firm hold for it.

Greta took her first good look at him and was more surprised than ever that he had risked the thigh-deep current of midstream. He was really old. His shrunken face was lined and seamed like the skin of a cantaloupe, and his scrawny neck, protruding from a faded grey shirt, was hung with pendants of loose skin, like the neck of a tortoise. A moustache that might have been silver had it not been stained with tobacco and coffee to a disorderly brown hung scraggily over his mouth. His small, watery, colorless eyes peered through a pair of steel-rimmed spectacles. His clothes, except for his khaki-colored hipboots, were old too, threadbare and patched.

Greta noticed that he was wheezing from the exertion of fighting the stream. "Aren't you getting a little bit old to wade the Gallatin?" she asked.

He stopped and looked at her sternly, one claw-like hand gripping the willow staff. "Been fishin' this river since I was a ten-year-old, that makes nigh onto eighty years, and I ain't quittin' yet awhile." He examined her carefully from wading shoes to felt hat. "You're a dude, ain't you?' he asked.

Greta smiled at him, and she could smile prettily when she wanted to, which was not often of late. "Yes, I'm a dude—a dude from New York."

"Humph! Mighty far to come fishin'. I ain't never been no further than Billings, and that was more'n ten years ago."

They had reached the sandbar of the bank, which was shaded by a row of tall cottonwoods. Greta pointed to a white cottage set in an orchard of apple trees near the rusty iron bridge, about a hundred yards from where they were standing. "You live there?" she asked.

"No'm. My ranch is up yonder a piece." He waved towards the wheat fields that clung to the lower slopes of the Gallatin Range. "'Bout every day I ride me down here an' fish. My son-in-law an' daughter, they run the ranch now that I'm too old to work much." He gave a dry cackle of a laugh. "They're welcome to it. Ranchin' ain't what it used to be. It's all farmin' around here now—plows an' tractors an' wheat an' hay. No place no more for a cattle man. I can recollect . . ." He stopped abruptly and looked again searchingly at Greta. "I thought dudes come here to go ridin' the trails up in the canyon. That's what most of the lady dudes does. I seen 'em time an' agin, a whole passel of 'em followin' along after some kid wrangler all dressed up like he knew how to cut out a steer. Mighty seldom you see women folks tryin' to fish this river. When they does, they usually has a man along to catch 'em if they falls in. Ain't you got no man?"

"Yes, I have," Greta answered factually, coldly. "He's upstream, above the bridge."

"Likes to fish alone, eh? Most men is that way."

"No, it's just that he doesn't like to fish with me. I'm not good enough, I guess. Where's your horse?"

"Up to the road by the bridge. You go on with your fishin'. I'm goin' to set here a mite an' rest my knees. That cold water gets 'em to achin'. Rheumatiz. Come on after I passed eighty." He walked over to where the turf bent over the sandbank and sat down, stretching his legs out in front of him carefully, as if the knee joints were rusted.

Greta followed him, laying his old casting rod down on the grass beside him. She noticed now that it was rigged with a worm and a heavy lead sinker. "Did you have any luck?" she asked.

"No'm, not this mornin'," he replied.

"Neither did I—only a couple of tiddlers that I threw back. Do you mind if I sit here with you?"

"Dirt's free. You kin do as you like. Where's your fish pole?"

She turned and pointed. "Leaning up against the willows there."

He followed her gaze, appraising the light, split-bamboo rod. "Fishin' with them flies, eh?"

"Dry flies. My husband says that's the only way to catch trout."

"You don't look like you was married. Is he the fella fishin' upstream?"

"Yes, he's fishing with Mrs. Sullivan. She's our hostess out here. Maybe you know her, she owns that ranch on Deer Creek, up where the canyon begins."

The old man smiled, nodding his head as if an ancient thought had come to life. "I knowed her since she warn't no bigger'n an April lamb. Jelly they used to call her, 'cause she was always laughin' an' shakin'."

"They call her Johnny now."

"Yeah, I know. Jelly Monahan she was till she married, and danged if she warn't a dead spit of her grandpaw, havin' her own way, gettin' anything she set her heart on."

"Did you know old John Monahan?"

The old man took the willow staff that was lying beside him on the bank and broke it in two with a snap. "I worked for John Monahan for forty years. Ain't no one knowed him better'n I did, knowed how hard he was, hard like a rock, trustin' nobody, not even hisself. Like I say, if he wanted somethin', nothin', nobody would stand in his way till he got it. That's how he come to get all the land from the Gallatin to the Madison. Had the boys homsteadin' for him. Build 'em a cabin, then, when the title was theirn, he'd have 'em deed it to him for a quart of whiskey. But I ain't a drinkin' man, never was, an' that's how I come to own my own section. When he come to me to deed over that land, I handed him one hundred dollars for the cabin an' told him I was quittin' to run my own ranch. Lady, I'm tellin' you he was the maddest Irishman I ever seed. He'd a shot me right there on my own doorstep, only I pulled faster'n he did an' told him to git off my section an' stay off. For three years after that he done his best to run me out, rustled my sheep, burned my hay, but it didn't do no good. For every sheep he rustled, I rustled two of hisn, 'cause the boys warn't none too loyal to him, an' they kinda liked me for standin' up to him."

"Mrs. Sullivan says that her grandfather was fearless," Greta said.

"She's right. He warn't scared of nothin' but his own meanness. That's what killed him, I reckon. He couldn't stand me havin' that section, which he didn't need any more than Jelly Sullivan needs another husband."

"What makes you say that?"

The old man turned his head toward her, his watery eyes twinkling. "What's your name, lady?" he asked.

"Mrs. Livingston, Greta Livingston."

"Well, Greta, I'm gettin' on to ninety an' I seen enough to know when a person ain't happy. Has your man taken a fancy to Jelly Sullivan?"

"She's a wonderful fisherman and he likes that."

"So he sends you off to slap a fly around by yourself, catchin' little ones in the fast water while Jelly is gettin' the big rainbows, makin' him think she's the smartest gal in Montana."

"Maybe she is," Greta murmured.

"Yeah, she's smart all right, too danged smart, just like old John, an' pretty, too."

"You're not very encouraging, Mister . . . What is *your* name, by the way?"

"Will. Will Cross. I was aimin' to warn you."

"That's not necessary."

The old man picked the hook off the bar of his casting reel and scraped off the bits of dead, shrivelled worm. "He wouldn't rise to me this mornin'," he said, as if to himself. "Gettin' too smart, won't grab the hook the way he used to, jest nibbles off the ends as it's wrigglin'. Mighty cute old brown, that one. As cute as old John Monahan."

"Is it your special trout?" Greta asked.

"Yes'm. I don't go foolin' around with them ignorant fish they throw in from the hatchery. I only go after the big ones. This one I was talkin' about, this John Monahan, he real big, go nigh onto five pounds. I've had him on twicet, but each time he broke me. But I'll git him yet, leastwise, I will if you don't happen to take him."

Greta laughed bitterly. "No chance of that. I never catch anything but tiddlers. Besides, he's your fish and I wouldn't think of taking him from you."

"Would you take him if it would show your man you was as good as Jelly Sullivan?" Will Cross asked.

Greta could feel an involuntary flush on her cheeks and she was ashamed and annoyed. "I don't even know where he lies," she said.

"He wouldn't take no dry fly," the old man said speculatively. "He's a deep feeder as don't like to show hisself on the top. That's why he's took over the hole and chased all the other fish out."

"Then he's safe from me. All I have are dry flies."

"Lemme see the one you got on."

Greta got up, fetched her rod and brought it back, sitting down again on the bank beside Will Cross. She unhooked the fly from one of the guides and handed it to him, still attached to a leader tapered to 3X.

Will examined it carefully. "What kind of a thing do you call that?" he asked.

"Out here they call it an Irresistible, but in the East it's known as a Rat-Faced McDougal."

The old man burst into a cackle of laughter. "Ratface McDougal, eh? That's a right smart name for him. By gum, if we could get him down fur enough, I believe old John'd take a fancy to him."

"He floats like a feather," Greta said. "You can't sink him."

"Mebbe there's a way to get him under." Will reached into his trouser pocket and brought out an ancient clasp knife with a bone handle that was worn smooth and yellow. When he opened it the blade, which was six inches long, shone clean and bright. "Hand me one of them flat rocks," he commanded, pointing to the water's edge.

Greta slid down on the sand and brought him one of the wet stones. "What are you going to do with my fly?" she asked.

"Never you mind." He placed his big, pear-shaped sinker on the stone and slowly carved a small slice of soft lead from its side. Taking the slice in his grimy fingers he rolled it skillfully around Greta's leader, about a foot above the fly. When he had it wound to his satisfaction, he laid the leader on the rock and pounded the lead gently with the handle of his knife until it was tight enough to the nylon not to slip. "Now, if that gut of yourn will holt, you might have a chance for him," he said, handing the fly back to Greta.

"You know I'll never catch him, that's why you're doing this," she said.

"Looky here, Greta, I want you should catch him," the old man said sternly.

"Why?"

"Never you mind why."

"Because Johnny's a Monahan?"

"Because she is fishin' in water as ain't hers." He gripped her arm so hard that she could feel his fingers like little steel bands through her fishing jacket. "See over yonder where that dead cottonwood stump sticks out over the river? See where underneath it there's a deep hole of black water? That's where he's lyin', right down on the bottom, near the bank."

"If I cast in there, it will only frighten him. The water is as still as a pond."

"Listen to me. Don't go castin' into that hole. Stand up this side of it an' flop your line into the fast water, lettin' it float down by itself. The current there takes a kind of a curl, like a rope on a saddle horn. If you leave it, it'll curl itself right down to the bottom where he can see it."

"I've got to wade across the middle of the river to get there," Greta said apprehensively.

"If I kin do it, you kin in them high waders," the old man urged. "Tain't nothin' to it if you take it slow." He picked up the stouter half of the long willow stick he had broken in two. "Take this to steady yourself."

Greta, gazing at the rushing river, was still fearful. "If by some wild chance I did hook him, I'd never be able to land him standing in that torrent," she said.

"Don't go horsin' him like he was a calf on a rope. That's my trouble, I keep callin' him John an' jerkin' him so hard I bust the line. Just keep enough holt on him to let him know who's boss. Bein' a brown he'll head upstream, an' that'll tire him quicker than it would one of them rainbows what runs downstream an' jumps."

"You talk as if I could really hook him."

"I'm tellin' you, you durn well better if . . ."

"If I want to keep my husband," Greta finished the sentence for him, then laughed bitterly. "Well, there's no harm trying. But if I fall in, I'm going to blame you, Will Cross."

She picked up her rod and the willow stick and waded out into the stream. Will watched her as she moved cautiously into the fast water, feeling for each step, leaning her weight against the force of the stream. As he knew, the worst, the swiftest and deepest part was the first she would encounter. After that the river was less than knee deep, flowing smoothly in a fast, but not violent, glide. He held his breath when he saw her wobble once, clinging to the willow staff, but she regained her balance, rising at last to the shallow glide where she stopped to rest before moving on.

I'll never be able to get back to that bank, she thought. Negotiating the rapids once was enough. Whatever happens I'll get out on the bank that's nearest me. She examined the water ahead, concluding that above the pool where the old man said the big brown lay it was shallow enough to reach the shore. She decided that she had been an idiot to fall into the old man's plot. To begin with, the story of the monster trout was probably senile imagination, and, furthermore, why should she, Greta Livingston, be a party to an old cowpuncher's revenge on the long-dead grandfather of Johnny Sullivan? Johnny was a swell girl and she had been inclined to like her from the very moment they had arrived at Deer Creek Ranch. It had not been Johnny's fault that Tim Sullivan, who had invited them to come out for three weeks of fishing and who had been a classmate of Bob's at Yale, had had to rush back to San Francisco on some important business deal.

She and Bob had heard three years before that Tim had scored a bullseye when he had married the rich, beautiful and talented Johnny Monahan. But they had not known then that one of her accomplishments was an exceptional ability to present a dry fly invitingly on the fast waters of a mountain stream. That was what had captivated Bob. Ever since they had arrived he had been singing the praises of her prowess as a fisherman until Greta thought that she might have to throw up. Then Tim had left and Bob had informed his wife politely but firmly that she would have to fish on her own, as she could not be expected to spoil the sport of professionals. That was all right by her, she liked being alone on a stream. It was the reunions at lunch and at quitting time that infuriated her, when Bob, his face beaming like a fifth form schoolboy, would say, "Look, Greta! Look at this lunker Johnny caught!" He never once had asked to see the little fish in *her* creel.

She was standing now, full of righteous wrath, at the spot where she could cast into the run above the pool. She turned to look back at the bank she had left. The old man was still sitting there watching her. He waved his arm in an impatient casting gesture. Okay, Will Cross, she said to herself, I'll cast where you told me to, but pray for that trout to take with all the might that's left in that old head of yours.

She got her feet set in a good, comfortable stance, stuck the willow staff under her jacket where she could hold it with her left elbow, and started to false cast. The lead on her leader threw her timing off, causing the fly to hit the fast water behind her. It was awkward, but she got enough line out to reach the run, then, stripping a few yards more for the float, she cast forward. The lead hit the water with a plop. The Rat-Faced McDougal floated barely a foot before it was dragged under. In the gin-clear water she could watch it running down over the rocks until it reached the lip of the deep, dark pool where it disappeared into the depths. Holding her rod horizontal, she let the loose line she had stripped run through the guides. The leader had been swallowed up in the pool, but the greased line floated out over the black surface, the end of it curling backward as it was pulled by the descending fly. The whirlpool he was talking about, she thought. Then the knot that held the leader jerked suddenly downward. Instinctively Greta came up sharply with her rod tip. It was a solid, firm hold that bent her rod as the line came taut. A log, she thought, the same log that old Will Cross has for years mistaken for a huge trout.

She released the pressure, hoping the line would float downstream so that she could pull the hook loose. But instead of floating down, the line shot forward and again she came up sharply with the rod tip. But this time the reel screeched as the line whipped out of the pool and up through the run. Her heart stopped. It was a trout, and a big one. Holding the rod high, she felt for the little button on the reel and tightened the drag. Her small rod was bent double, but the fish swam on against the roaring current and the pull of the line as if nothing was deterring him.

Taking a deep breath, Greta recited to herself all the lore she had learned from Bob and the old man; keep your left hand off the line; hold your rod vertical; don't horse him, let him take his own lead; don't reel unless he stops or swims towards you; keep the pressure on, but never too much; let him kill himself. The line was almost down to the backing when he slowed up. But Greta, intent now on landing that trout even if it took all day, was in no hurry to start reeling. She shot a quick glance across the stream, hoping for the old man's applause, but he had vanished. He never waited to see, thought I'd never hook him, she said to herself.

The trout continued to cruise slowly, crossing back and forth from one side of the stream to the other, sometimes letting the current drift him back, then quickly ascending again in a determined plunge, as if trying to reach the big rock that came out of the river half way between Greta and the bridge. But the pull of the lengthening line was always enough to stop him before he reached his goal.

After twenty minutes Greta's arm was beginning to tire. From time to time she shifted the rod to her left hand in order to ease the aching muscles of her right arm, but she could never do it for long as she had to be instantly prepared to reel in when the trout turned. She had no idea of its size other than the pull of it, for it had bored deep, never once coming near the surface. If I could only once get his head out of water, she moaned to herself, forcing her aching muscles to push the rod higher against her chest. At that moment the trout let the current take him again and she had to reel madly to keep tension on the line. It came drifting down almost directly towards her. Maybe this is it, she thought, wondering how she could reach the net and still keep reeling.

When the fish came in sight of her, it lifted its tail out of water and rushed off into the middle of the stream. She saw it, the whole of it, and the sight made her heart stop again. It looked to her as big as the monsters mounted on the wall of the tackle shop in Bozeman. She almost cried with the pain in her arms, thinking that it would take at least another half hour for a fish as big as that to kill himself.

"You're doin' fine," the old man's voice called from the near bank. "Jest keep on like you was doin'. He's killin' hisself fast now."

"Oh, God, I hope so!" she moaned. "He's not as tired as I am."

"It won't be long. He's about ready to quit."

The trout was thrashing on the surface now, flapping his great tail in a vain effort to keep his head down. Greta switched the rod to her left hand and reached down with her right to unhook the net from her creel.

"Never you mind that net," the old man called. "He'll never fit in that corral. Jest you ease him over to the bank here. We'll beach him."

Reeling slowly, keeping the rod tip high to force the trout's head out of water, Greta inched herself backwards towards the bank. She thought of getting out the willow staff to steady herself, but realized that it had vanished long ago, probably when the trout made its first dash. Then she felt the claw-like fingers of the old man holding her arm.

"Steady now," he said in her ear. "You ain't goin' to fall while I got holt of you."

"How did you get over to this side?" she asked breathlessly.

"When I seed you had him hooked, I come across the bridge."

The trout was in close now, lying on its side gasping, but still strong against the leader.

"Keep acomin' back till you're leanin' agin the bank," the old man said. "Then jest hold him. I ain't goin' to fool with him till he's kilt himself."

Greta did as she was told, and was grateful for the backrest of soft grass. The water in which she stood was only a foot deep and the trout was slowly swinging toward her, gasping and thrashing. When the leader was close to the rod tip, she stopped reeling, taking the rod in her left hand and stretching her right to get the kinks out of it. It seemed a full five minutes that she and Will Cross stood there silently, watching the great trout until it finally shivered and lay still.

"Ease him over to me," the old man whispered, as if afraid to frighten the fish. He squatted down on his haunches, putting his hands under the water so that the dying fish slid over them.

Before Greta could see what had happened he had heaved the trout as far back on the bank as the leader would stretch and scrambled up after it on his knees. Greta followed him, pushing the rod before her. There was no need to give the fish the coup de grace. He was dead—huge and magnificent. They both knelt there on the grass looking at him for a long while.

"Well, you done it," the old man said finally, turning his eyes to Greta. "You done what I been tryin' to do for three years." He returned his gaze to the fish. "Like I said, he'll go to five pounds or more—fat as a valley heifer. Wait till your man sees him."

"He'll never believe that I caught him," Greta said sadly.

"He's goin' to have to, 'cause I ain't goin' to be here." He struggled to his feet, cut a forked stick from a willow bush and hooked it through the trout's gills. "Come on, I'll carry him for you. He wouldn't set in that little basket of yourn, not if you folded him double."

Together they walked up the path to the bridge where Johnny Sullivan's car was parked in the shade of the cottonwoods. Greta opened the rear trunk and, with the help of Will, they laid the trout carefully down on some newspapers and covered it with green leaves.

"When are Jelly and your man fixin' to meet you here?" Will asked.

Greta looked at her watch. It was half past twelve. "In about a half an hour," she said.

"Well, I'll be gittin'. Past my dinner time anyway."

"Can I help you with your horse?" Greta asked, wondering how the old man could ever mount alone.

"No'm. He's most as old as I am an' right steady." He laughed, cackling like an old hen. "I shore would like to be watchin' Jelly's face when she puts her eyes on that brown."

Greta stood in the road and watched him as he crossed the bridge and hobbled into the bushes on the far side, his short rod trailing in the dirt behind him, the bow of this thin legs accentuated by the tight hipboots. In a few minutes he reappeared on the road leading a chunky piebald pony. They stopped on the crown of the road and the pony stood like a statue while the old man hitched the rod to the saddle horn with a halter rope. When this was done, he put both hands under his left knee, lifting his leg slowly until his foot reached the stirrup, then, catching a lock of mane with his left hand and the crupper with his right, he pulled himself halfway up the pony's flank. With another hoist he got his knee on the rump. The third heave got him into the saddle. Then taking the reins deliberately he turned and waved to Greta before kicking the pony and starting up the road in a rolling lope.

Greta went back to the rear of the car to gaze incredulously at the fish she had caught. The whole circumstance seemed to her puzzling and slightly unreal, like something out of a fairy tale. Now that Will Cross had vanished on his steed, she wondered, smiling to herself, if he were not some legendary knight, disguised as an ancient cowhand, who had come to rescue her from the wiles of the blonde Princess Johnny. Perhaps it was all a dream resulting from her apprehensions. She lifted the branch of leaves and touched the trout. It was solid and cool and slimy, and its black disc spots seemed to wink at her, as if to say, "I'm real."

Greta, who had taken off her waders and put on a pair of beaded moccasins which Johnny had lent her, was sitting in the car reading *Phineas Redux* when she heard the voices of Bob and Johnny as they crossed the bridge. She could not distinguish the words, but the tone was gay, bantering. Like a pair of courting magpies, she thought, with a pleasant mixture of bitterness and triumph. She looked at her watch. It was a quarter past one and she had hunger pains as well as the ache in her arms. She closed the novel and stepped out of the car.

"Sorry if we're late," Bob said to her as he strode up to the car, beaming under his battered felt fishing hat. "Johnny got into a big one just as we were about to quit. Wait till you see it!"

Johnny Sullivan, who looked stunning in any costume, with her honey-blonde, waving hair, her trim figure and her china-blue eyes, was particularly fetching in khaki shorts and wading shoes to frame her tanned, graceful legs. "He only weighs a pound and three-quarters on Bob's scales," she said modestly.

"Here, let me show you Johnny's catch," Bob said enthusiastically, propping his rod against the bushes and taking Johnny's creel from her shoulder, which entailed putting his arms around her. As his wife made no move, he had to bring the creel to her where she stood beside the car.

"Hmm. Three nice fish," Greta said, glancing into the creel which Bob held under her nose. "What did you get them on?"

Johnny looked rather surprised at the question, for up to this moment Greta had shown little interest in fly patterns. "The two little cutthroats on an Adam and the big rainbow on a Wulff."

"I caught mine on a Rat-Faced McDougal," Greta said casually.

"So, you got a fish, did you?" Bob said. He was sitting on the grass pulling off his waders. "Good for you," he added patronizingly.

"I actually caught three, but I only kept one," Greta said.

"Good kid!" Bob said, full of well-being. He yanked the waders off, tossed them on the bush, and stood up in his stocking feet. "How's about an ice-cold Gibson? Any takers?"

"I've been waiting for one for three-quarters of an hour," Greta said.

"Coming up!" Bob sang and lifted the rear trunk-cover of the car. His eyes caught sight of the leaves and his hand, reaching for the cocktail shaker, stopped in mid air. "What the hell is this?" His hand descended, lifting up the branch. "God Almighty! who killed that?" he yelled.

"That's the one I kept," Greta said. "Hurry up with that cocktail, I need it."

Bob stared at the trout as if hypnotized. "You actually caught that trout, Greta?" he said hoarsely, his voice trembling with amazement. "On that little three-ounce rod? With a 3X tip? It's a miracle! It's the greatest thing that's ever happened!"

Johnny Sullivan walked over to Bob's side, put an arm over his shoulders and looked at the trout. Her first glance was one of astonishment, but that changed to one of sober contemplation. Finally she turned slowly and looked at Greta. "Did you get him in that deep hole by the dead cottonwood?" she asked.

"Yes," Greta answered, still trying hard to appear casual about her triumph.

Johnny came over and put her arm through Greta's. "Then you got

312

him, you got John Monahan," she said, in a tone which implied that it was a prodigious feat.

Bob pushed Johnny to one side and grabbed his wife. "You're a wonder, sweetie!" he said, hugging and kissing her.

When the outburst was over, Greta straightened her hair and said to Johnny, "Why did you call him John Monahan?"

"Because that's what old Will Cross calls him," Johnny answered. "He does it to tease me. Will's an old man who lives on a ranch back there." She pointed to the mountains. "He has tried to catch that trout for years, but never succeeded."

"What has your grandfather got to do with it?" Bob asked. He was holding the fish on his hand scales and straining to read the marker.

"Oh, that's a long story," Johnny replied, gazing at the great trout.

"Five pounds seven ounces!" Bob exclaimed. "I'm going to have him mounted."

"Oh, no you're not!" Greta said firmly. "I'm going to cook John Monahan myself, poach him and serve him cold in jelly."

Johnny shot her a quick, startled glance. "You win, Greta. He's yours, to do with as you like."

This is the second Philip Wylie story about the charter-boat characters Crunch and Des. Like the first, it sparkles with the magic and romance of saltwater fishing. Captain Crunch takes a troubled but malleable youngster under his wing to teach him good ways. It is a charming and inspiring piece, typical of the fifty-one stories that Wylie wrote for the Saturday Evening Post *between 1939 and 1956. He also wrote such important books as* Finnley Wren *(1934),* Generation of Vipers *(1942), and* Gladiator *(1951).*

Philip Wylie

SPARE THE ROD (1940)

THE EYES OF DEXTER HEATH were the most remarkable feature in a rather dashing ensemble—gray eyes, round, penetrating and vigilant. Next was his hair, which was dark and curly, but curly without pattern, and incredibly unkempt; his hair was like a distant view of some irregular object foundering in a stormy sea. The rest of him was normal for a boy of eleven—snub nose, a voice that was invariably an exclamation, although sometimes hushed, and, under his sun-tanned skin, young muscles of which he was proud to the point of racy braggadocio.

On a late summer afternoon, Crunch Adams, coming down the Gulf

Stream Dock to minister to his fishing cruiser, was struck by the posture and attitude of Dexter. Balanced on a rail at the end of the dock, with his chin in his hand, the young man was staring ferociously at the universe, not seeing it, but not liking it, either. Crunch pondered the spectacle of fury in equilibrium for a moment, and then, with a grin, interrupted it.

"What's eating you, Dexter?"

The young man budged a little, put down a tentative foot, and looked at the captain. All traces of wrath had been erased by those slight movements. He seemed calm—even bored. "Nothing," he replied. "Nothing."

Crunch persisted. "Don't kid me. If there had been a nail between your teeth, you'd have ground it to filings."

"I was just thinkin'," Dexter responded lazily. And, indeed, he began thinking. Hard. His broken reverie was not a subject he could discuss. There had been sadness in it, and frenzy at the injustice of the world. His mind had been clamorous with ideas which were antisocial, hostile, and, even, illegal. Dexter did not wish to have any of his secret thoughts heckled out of him. It was therefore necessary to dissemble. Earlier in the afternoon he had indulged in a different sort of daydream. He recalled it and drew on it for material: "I was just thinkin' what if a brontosorassus came steamin' up the bay."

A what?"

"Brontosorassus. Swimmin' like a submarine! Neck out. Fangs drippin' ooze! You couldn't hang him on any fifty-four-thread. But maybe you could hold him on three-hundred-thread. With a fifty-ought reel. You'd have to fight him night and day—for maybe a couple of weeks!"

"Oh," said Crunch. "A dinosaur." He was still grinning, but he fell in with Dexter's mood. He felt that he now understood the savagery which had been on the young man's face. "I guess you could never hang one. And you certainly couldn't boat an eighty-footer in a forty-foot cruiser."

"You could beach him," Dexter said, pleased at this attention from a great man and yielding his inner sorrow to imagination. "Maybe, if they were still plentiful, you'd have to keep a swassy-cans on the dock."

"Swassy-cans?"

"That's French," said the boy with some small condescension. "My father taught it to me. My father knows most languages, I guess. It's the French word for a seventy-five. A gun. You could have one right here—if you put some cement posts under the dock. Then—Wham! Whang! Zowie! Boy! You'd have to mount her like a antiaircraft gun, too, in case any of those big old peterodackles flew by. Wham! Whacko! Blow a wing off one and steam out and polish her off with a lance! Wham! Boom!"

Crunch chuckled. "Guess you're right. Too bad we didn't live in those days. There'd have been some real fishing, hunh?"

"Fishin'," said Dexter, "and huntin'!"

"Like to wet a line now? I mean—I've got a hand line on the *Poseidon*. And some bait. I'd be glad to rig it for you."

Dexter was grateful, but negative. "No, thanks. I don't care much for this old hand-line stuff. But if I ever had a harpoon in any big old brontosorassus . . ."

Crunch nodded and stepped aboard his boat. He had no precise recollection of his own age of dinosaur hunting, but he felt an indefinite kindredship for it. "Maybe," he said as he picked up a square of sandpaper and tore it into suitable sizes, "you'd like to go out with Des and me some day?"

Dexter's head moved forward from his shoulders and his brow puckered. "You mean you'd really take me out?"

Crunch set up a rasp and sizzle on the varnish. "Sure. Sometimes. If I get a couple of nice customers who don't mind."

The young man gasped. Then he controlled himself. Life had taught him not to count too many unhatched chickens. "How soon—how soon—do you think you might possibly run across a couple of people like that?"

"Oh . . . soon," Crunch answered. "Any day."

Dexter had put in frequent appearances at the Gulf Stream Dock before Crunch had made that astonishing offer. But, thereafter, he was the most regular of all the juvenile buffs—boys who wistfully watched the boats go out and who, when the boats came in, identified various fish for less knowing adults, with a marked air of superiority. Dexter scrutinized every party that chartered the *Poseidon*. Sometimes he knew at a glance that the customers were not the sort who would care for an eleven-year-old supercargo. Sometimes he had great hopes. But no invitation was forthcoming.

The truth was that Crunch had forgotten the conversation. Small boys were ubiquitous, indistinguishable, and, on a busy fishing dock, often in the way. The *Poseidon*'s skipper had noticed Dexter closely enough to like him—to be amused by him—and to make a suggestion which had dropped back into his unconscious mind. Dexter, however, was that rather common but always astounding combination of the dreamer and the man of action. His father, who knew all languages, had told him that one of the cardinal virtues was "initiative." He had explained the word. Dexter eventually enlarged upon its meaning.

In consequence, on one blue and golden morning when the *Poseidon*'s outriggers were trailing balaos down the enameled sea, Crunch went below and was startled by the sight of two medium-sized shoes protruding from beneath a pile of pillows, blankets, canvas and gear on the starboard bunk. He grabbed one of the shoes and pulled forth Dexter.

The young man was alarmed, but in control of himself. "I had to do it!" he said. "You invited me! Besides—Mr. and Mrs. Winton fishing out there are two of the nicest people in Miami. My father said so. I heard them charter you last night—so I sneaked here early . . ."

Crunch remembered his offer, then. His first feeling for his stowaway was one of intense sympathy. Mr. and Mrs. Winton would be amused and pleased by the event. There was no doubt of that. But, on the other hand, it had been presumptive of the boy to steal a trip. Crunch had been rather harshly brought up; he felt that contemporary children were less disciplined and respectful than they should be. His father would have given him a good licking for behavior like young Mr. Heath's. Crunch weighed the situation. The corners of his mouth twitched. He hid that reflex with his hand. Sternly, he eyed the boy. "I suppose you realize that what you've done is a crime on the high seas?"

"I just thought—since you'd asked me already—"

"If I had a brig," Crunch went on, "as captain, I could throw you in it. All stowaways are condemned to hard labor. And bread and water—"

"I got my own lunch—right here!" Dexter produced from his blouse a large and messy-looking sandwich which was inadequately wrapped in newspaper. "And I'll be only too glad to work . . ."

Crunch nodded and cast his eye about. The *Poseidon* was spic and span. "You'll go aloft," he said finally, "where my mate can keep his eye on you. Here's a rag and a can of polish. You can shine all the brass till it's too bright to look at. And you can also keep your eye on the baits. If you see anything—don't scream. Just tell Des."

"Gee!" said Dexter. "Golly!" he added. "I was afraid you'd keep me down here!"

Crunch motioned the boy up the companionway and into the cockpit, where the two Wintons regarded his appearance with moderate surprise.

"This," said the captain, "is Dexter Heath. A stowaway. I'm putting him to work polishing brass."

Mr. Winton, who was a big man with white hair and a white mustache, burst into hearty laughter. His wife only smiled, and she regarded the boy's struggle of jubilance and discomfiture with a certain tenderness. "I'm sure he didn't mean any harm, Crunch. How old are you, son?"

"Eleven," Dexter replied.

"Do you like fishing?"

"My father," Dexter said uncompromisingly, "is the greatest fisherman in the world! Sometimes, he takes me. I will be nearly as good when I get that old."

"Your father's a great fisherman," Mr. Winton mused. "Heath. I don't think I've heard about him."

"You would," the boy said, "if—" He broke off. "You can stand a hundred feet from my father and he can cast a plug into your pocket! I guess he knows mostly where every fish lives in every canal in the Glades. He hooked a water moccasin on a plug, once, and reeled it up and killed it with a stick!"

Mr. Winton whistled and shook his head in awe. Crunch turned away his face. "Go and polish that brass," he said.

Desperate received the newcomer placidly. Crunch had yelled up his name and the conditions of tolerance to be applied to him. The *Poseidon* sailed along. Dexter put elbow grease in his work and the results began to show. His eye attention, however, was largely for the baits. He labored perhaps half an hour before he ventured any conversation. Des had been wondering just how long he would keep that humble silence.

"This is the Gulf Stream, isn't it?" the boy inquired.

Des nodded. "Right here, in this dark-blue water, it is. Over yonder, where the water is paler blue, it isn't. You can see the edge."

"Yeah," Dexter murmured. "Like two kinds of tile in a first-class bathroom."

Des pursed his lips, squinted judiciously at the boy, and nodded again. "If you look at that turning buoy out there, you'll see it has a wake behind it. Just as if it was being hauled through the water. But it's anchored. It's the Stream that makes the wake."

"Sure," the boy assented. "I can see it plain." And then, with every atom of energy, every possible vibration of his vocal chords, he bellowed, "Marlin!"

Crunch dropped a bait and stared. Des whirled from the top controls. Mr. Winton sat up straight. His wife said, "Goodness! Where?"

Dexter was pointing with his polishing rag—pointing palely. His knees were knocking together a little. "Right out there!"

Some fifty feet behind Mr. Winton's bait there was, indeed, a fish. Its length lay yellow under the water. A fin stuck darkly from its back into the air. It was obviously following the bait—following it with a speed not greatly in excess of the *Poseidon*'s and with a peculiar wobbling motion, as if it swam in zigzags.

Crunch stepped toward the canopy and peered at his prisoner with annoyance. "I told you not to yell, Dexter. That's no marlin. It's a lousy hammerhead shark. Speed her up. Des, and we'll get away."

Dexter was not dashed. Instead, he seemed rather more interested. "A hammerhead shark!" he repeated. "A real, live one! Boy, look at her cut around that old bait!"

Des notched up the throttles. The shark began to lose the race.

"A real shark," Dexter went on excitedly. "A man-eater! And I saw it first!"

Then Mr. Winton spoke. Perhaps his words contained the whole truth. But perhaps he understood and shared the feelings of the boy. "What do you say we slow down and let him get the bait? The fishing's slow today, anyhow, and I need a workout. Helen's always telling me to take more exercise."

"Boy!" murmured Dexter, in a low tone, but one that held audible hope.

"If you want to do it . . ." said Crunch, who was not much on fighting hammerheads. Mako sharks, or whites, or threshers, were different. He waved Des to slow down.

Out beyond the *Poseidon*'s wake, the shark was plunging back and forth in an effort to pick up the scent of the bait. When Des slowed the boat, the shark got it, and came boiling through the sea. His ugly, scimitar-shaped foreface broke water as he engulfed the small fish. The line drifted down from the clothespin at the outrigger tip. Mr. Winton reeled until it was taut and he struck hard several times. The shark gradually became aware that there was a thorn in its jaws and a hampering line hitched to the thorn. First he swam off in a logy manner. Then he essayed a short run. After that, he went fast and far.

"I saw him swallow it!" Dexter kept saying.

Mr. Winton screwed up the drag on the side of his reel. The extra tension bent the rod in a bow. The reel kept humming.

"Like a big amberjack," Mrs. Winton said. "Only—not so fast."

"He's got about three hundred and fifty yards," her husband finally muttered. "That's a good deal."

Crunch grinned. "You asked for it."

Presently the run stopped. Hammerheads, as a rule, make one exciting and fairly fast run. After that they merely resist—lunging lazily, throwing their weight around, bracing dead against the angler's pull. They are not sporty fish. They do not jump. They lack flash and fire and heart. But any fish that weighs three or four hundred pounds provides a tussle on twenty-four-thread line.

Mr. Winton worked hard. It was a warm day. Perspiration ran from him. He called for a glass of water. He called for his sun helmet. He dried his slippery hands on this trousers. He rocked back in the fighting chair and winked up at Dexter, who was standing on the edge of the canopy with, as Mr. Winton later said, "his eyes popping and his tongue hanging out."

"I can see him!" the boy presently yelled. "He's turning over on his side!"

And so he was. A moment later, the shark quit. He came in without a struggle—so much dead weight pulled through the water like a boat on a painter. Crunch went to the stern. He picked up a long knife. Dexter was panting—as if he had manipulated the tackle through the whole fight. He saw Crunch grab the leader and shorten it. He saw him reach down to the water. Dexter held his breath. The skipper actually grabbed one of the hideous eye stalks in his bare hand. Then the muscles in his arms and the muscles along his back bulged, and hardened like rocks. He pulled the great fish—a fish which in that instant seemed bigger to Dexter than any "brontosorassus"—at least a third of its length out of water. He hooked one eye stalk over the gunwale and held the other while he plunged the knife deep into the white bellyside. "I hate sharks," he said coldly.

Dexter gasped. The shark trembled as the knife point found its heart. Blood poured from it. But, still calmly, Crunch put down the knife, picked up a pair of pliers, and went after the hook. The curved jaws snapped convulsively inches from the captain's hand. Nevertheless, he got the hook out with a quick, hard wrench, and he let the hammerhead slide back into the water. It sank, trailing crimson, stone dead.

Mr. Winton fanned himself with his helmet. "How'd you like it, son?"

Dexter swallowed. "Gee!" he murmured. "Imagine! Bare-handed! I guess that's about the bravest thing I ever heard of."

Crunch laughed. "Nothing to it—if you know how to handle 'em."

"And," Mrs. Winton added, "if you're as strong as a derrick."

It had been a day for Dexter. A champion day. The fishing had not been much—two bonitos and a mackerel. But they had supplemented his sandwich lunch with a piece of chocolate cake, two pears, three hard-boiled eggs, some pickles and potato chips. They had forgotten, after the fight with the shark, that he was a prisoner. He'd been allowed to troll a feather on a casting rod for more than two hours. He hadn't had a strike, but that did not matter. He'd "fished the Stream." Not many kids could say that. He'd seen a big one take out line by the hundreds of yards. You could tell people that, without adding that the "big one" was just a shark.

As the *Poseidon* came in, the world seemed especially elegant to Dexter. The sun was going down in a yellow sky and the whole bay—the islands, the palms, the buildings, the lawns—was gleaming in amber opulence. It made reality theatrical, and only the sight of the Gulf Stream Dock brought they boy out of the mood. Then he became quiet. His thanks were effusive, but not as effusive as his day-long behavior had been. He apologized for stowing away. He went ashore rather solemnly. He had to get home for supper, he said.

"I like that kid," Mr. Winton chuckled.

His wife agreed. "He's marvelous. Who are his people?"

Crunch shrugged. "Darned if I know. I like him, too. He's here a lot. The fellows let him fish—and sometimes he makes a nickel running an errand. I think I heard somebody say that his mother is dead."

It was on the next morning that Des missed the rod. The casting rod with which Dexter had fished. But he didn't think of Dexter right away. "I put it in its regular place on the rack," he told Crunch. "I remember doing it. Who'd swipe that? If somebody wanted dough, why didn't they take an expensive outfit? I made that rod myself two years ago—and there were rods worth five times as much hanging there!"

Crunch did not think of Dexter, either. Not then.

They did when the skipper of the *Firefly* happened to say, "That kid you took out was down here looking for you fellows last night. At least, I think it was him. When I called to him, he beat it."

"Was he carrying a rod and reel?" Des asked.

"Couldn't say. He was maybe carrying something. Skulking along out of the range of the floodlights. You missing one?"

Neither Des nor Crunch replied to that. They went back to their boat. "I'd have bet a week's charter that kid wouldn't touch anything," Crunch said.

"I guess he didn't. At least, I hope he didn't. As far as that goes, the whole outfit wasn't worth more than twenty-five bucks. I can easily—"

"I don't like kids that steal," the captain interrupted angrily. "Still—what can we do? Ask him? Go to his house and ask his father? When you think how he'd feel if somebody else took the rod?"

There the matter dropped. Or, rather, it drifted. Dexter did not show up for three or four days, which was suspicious, but when he did put in an appearance he was as bland and poised as ever. They saw him often, after that. Sometimes he fished for snappers and grunts. Once he did a job of brass polishing on the *Firefly*. Two or three times he hosed down the *Merdora*. But neither Crunch nor Des were happy about the youngster. If he had taken the rod, something should be done about it. If he had not, they would have given a good deal to be certain of the fact. They discussed the situation occasionally, but to no purpose.

It was Desperate's idea to invite him to go fishing again.

"What'll that prove?" Crunch asked.

"I dunno. We'd get to know him better. Kids are funny. We might find that the rod came back all by itself—which would save us buying a new reel and line and me doing a lot of work. Or we might be able to ask him if he took it—and find out he didn't. Which would make me feel a lot better."

"Yeah," Crunch replied. "Me, too. And I'd also feel free to do a little snooping around the dock. There are four or five guys here dumb enough to think we might not recognize that rod if it was rewound and re-painted."

"I haven't seen it yet, anyhow," Des said. "If I do! . . ."

"If you do," Crunch grinned, "let me start the trouble."

They asked the Graymonds first. The Graymonds were summer visitors from Tennessee. They'd never fished in salt water. They said they'd be delighted to have an "extra" mate.

Then they asked Dexter.

He was sitting on a soap box at the time, cutting out long, thick strips of bonito belly for Red. He looked at them with an expression which neither could quite analyze. They decided it changed—from a sort of alarm to eagerness.

"I thought you were mad at me," Dexter said.

"What for?" Crunch asked that question quickly.

"Stowing away."

"Oh. No. You worked that out. We'll be going tomorrow at nine, if you'd like to come along. Bottom fishing–down the reef a ways. Anchored all day. You may have a chance to fish. Somebody swiped one of our casting rods, but you could use a hand line."

"I'll go."

He did not seem especially pleased. Crunch said as much.

Dexter gazed at him in a hurt manner. "Can't a fellow be overwhelmed?" he asked tremulously.

"He didn't do it," Des said later that evening.

And Crunch nodded. "Guess not. And that's a relief!"

Mrs. Graymond found the "extra" mate shy and rather uncommunicative.

She was a dark-haired, dark-eyed girl and she had a way with boys. A most successful way, as a rule. She simply treated them as if they were twice their age. But Dexter did not seem to have an opinion about the outcome of the World's Series, he was not expecting to play football in the fall, he had no dog, and he was willing to admit that he liked fishing–but not with any emphasis or detail.

Indeed, after a quarter of an hour of lopsided conversation, Dexter embarrassedly asked Crunch if he could go "up topside" and shine a little brass. Crunch sent him up. And Desperate respected the boy's vast quietude.

It was a very tragic quietude. The one thing Dexter had wanted in his whole life more than the friendship of two such dramatic, important persons as Crunch and his mate, was that rod. He had taken it. Stolen it so craftily that even though he had been spotted on the night of the theft, he was positive nobody could testify he had been carrying away the precious tackle. Indeed, when the skipper of the *Firefly* had called to him, the rod, line and reel had been hidden underneath the dock in a spot from which Dexter had later retrieved it by means of a temporarily borrowed dinghy.

Now—they had taken him fishing. As he polished brass—and glanced up occasionally with sadness at the broad back of the best mate on the Gulf Stream—Dexter reflected that he had sort of hoped they might vaguely suspect him and would in consequence merely become negative toward him. They couldn't prove anything. And he would never tell. He would go on lying, even if they tortured him worse than the Indians. But the fact that they had invited him to go out—and even to fish—was an almost unendurable kindness. It showed they trusted him.

If he had known their true anxiety over the suspicion of his deed, Dexter would probably have tried to slip overboard unnoticed. On the other hand, when his conscience smote him with the epithet of "thief," he did not flinch. He merely stuck out his chin and squinted back any dampness in his eyes. Maybe he was a thief, but there are things worse than robbery.

It was in the company of such fierce feelings that he watched them cut the *Poseidon*'s speed, make ready the anchor, pick an exact spot over a favorite patch of rocks after much searching through a glass-bottomed bucket, and come to an easy rest. In the distance were the V-shaped outriggers of boats trolling the Stream, the spindly legs of Fowey Rock Light, a few sails, and the smoke-plumed hulls of a pair of tankers beating south inside the current. Under the *Poseidon*'s keel were the irregular blurs of a coral bottom—lumps and caverns, miniature mountains and dark valleys of a size to hide groupers, jewfish, sharks.

The baits went overboard and Dexter was summoned from the comparative obscurity of his place aloft. He was given a hand line by Crunch, who said, "Now son, hang a whopper!" Desperate grinned at him. He wondered how he could stand it all day long.

They fished with dead shrimp and chunks of balao. Mrs. Graymond used a rod like the one Dexter had stolen. Its twin. Her husband chose a larger rig with a bigger hook, a heavier hunk of bait, and a reel that buzzed instead of clicked. The three lines soaked up salt water.

"Just about like perch fishing, isn't it?" Mrs. Graymond said.

Dexter smiled back at her smile. "Perch?"

"We catch them in Tennessee. And catfish. And bass, sometimes. Quite big ones. Two pounds—even three."

Her husband nodded. "I was thinking the same thing. I'd expected, somehow, that salt-water fishing would be different."

Then—it was different. His rod jerked. His reel whirred. His arms shot up and down. "Whoa!" he shouted. "Must be loose from that anchor! I've got bottom, captain!"

"You've got a fish," Crunch said.

Mr. Graymond opened his mouth as if to make a denial. Then—the grouper really ran. If he'd had bottom, the *Poseidon* would have to have been going at its top speed; even Mr. Graymond could reason that far, although his reasoning processes were seriously compromised by the situation. Crunch set him in the fighting chair and helped to thrust the bucking ferrule of the rod into the gimbal.

It was a pretty fight, though clumsy, and marred by a mild profanity of amazement. Even Dexter almost forgot his burden of trouble. Until Crunch reached over with a gaff and scooped in the fish.

Just an old grouper, Dexter said to himself at that point. His reason was the violent behavior of the Graymonds. *You'd think,* Dexter went on thinking, *it was a blue marlin. Or some kind of swordfish, or something.*

"But it's a monster!" Mrs. Graymond gasped. "A perfect giant! How much does he weigh!"

"Oh," Crunch murmured, "around, say, twenty pounds."

"Why, darling, it's a whale!" She kissed her husband.

Perhaps Mr. Graymond caught sight of Dexter's eyes. "Well, dear . . . it may not be so big for here. You've got to remember, we're pond and stream anglers." He stared, however, into the fishbox, where the grouper displayed its tweedy pattern of browns and its brilliant fins, spread taut. "Still," he said, "it's a doggone big fish! Doggoned big." He glanced at Dexter defiantly.

But Dexter had lost his cynical expression. Something had hit his line. He was pulling it up, hand over hand, with an expert continuum of effort which gave the fish no slack, no chance to escape. He flipped his fish deftly into the box, without benefit of gaff. The enthralled Tennesseans bumped heads lightly in their eagerness to look. Dexter had caught a pork fish—a vivid yellow chap, eight or nine inches long, with a flat surface and black, vertical stripes.

"It's the most gorgeous thing I ever saw!" exclaimed Mrs. Graymond.

"And good to eat," said Dexter.

She turned toward him with surprise. "But—it's *much* too beautiful for that! It ought to be in an aquarium!"

Dexter went to the box for bait.

And the fishing continued. Every fish, it appeared, was too beautiful for Mrs. Graymond to think of eating. Even Dexter, who was a practical individual, began to see the quarry through the lady's eyes. And they were kind of pretty—mighty bright-colored—when you thought of it. Right down to grunts.

The accident happened in the only way it could have happened. And in a place where even the most nervous boatman would hardly expect anything serious to occur. Dexter, liking the Graymonds almost against his will, and passionately eager to do anything to aid Crunch and Des, had undertaken to remove fish from the hooks and to put on baits for the customers. He was perfectly competent for the chore. He had weeks of dock fishing behind him.

Relieved of the duty, Crunch had gone below to prepare a special chowder from the grouper. Desperate had already occupied himself with the rearrangement of gear on the foredeck. Thus the two novices and the youngster were left alone. Mrs. Graymond hooked a fish. Dexter went to her side to give advice. It was a pretty good-sized fish—a snapper, he hoped—and his attention was entirely focussed, on the lady.

Mr. Graymond also hooked a fish. Not wishing to disturb his thrilling wife, and imagining himself by then a fairly proficient fisherman, he fought the creature in silence. It ran and it shook and it bent his rod but he dragged it to the surface. Then, seeing that Dexter was still busy, he undertook to copy the boy's trick of flicking his quarry aboard. He wound the line up to the swivel, blocked the reel spool with his thumb, braced his feet, and gave a tremendous heave. His fish was yanked out of the water. It rose into the air, writhing. It landed in the cockpit. It spat out the hook. And Mr. Graymond yelled.

Crunch and Des, separately, interpreted the yell as evidence of another triumph. It was not. It was a yell of sheer horror.

For the thing in the boat was horrible. A thing like a fat snake, five feet long, a sickly rich green, with a sharp, reptilian mouth, terrible teeth, and brilliant, evil eyes. Even as Mr. Graymond yelled, it slithered into a knot and struck like a rattlesnake, at the support of a chair. It bounced from that and stuck again, biting fiercely on a glove. Dexter wheeled and saw it and turned ash-pale. Mrs. Graymond also saw, and she tried to scream and could not. She tried to move, but her legs would not budge.

"Keep away from it!" Dexter said hoarsely. "It'll bite! It's deadly poison!"

That it would bite was obvious. It was, even then, striking a pail. That the green moray is poisonous is a technical problem, since the toxicology of slimes and fish poisons is an unfinished science. Certainly morays make bad wounds that are slow to heal. Certainly men have suffered fearful infections from their bites, or from bacteria that entered the bites. Certainly all the boatmen in Florida waters would be hard put to choose between a big moray and a rattlesnake, if one had to be let loose in a cockpit.

Dexter's husky advice was heeded by the terrified man. He jumped backwards mechanically and found himself, somehow, standing on one of the couches. But his wife was still transfixed. The moray saw her—and started for her.

Dexter had been standing behind her. He came around in front. In coming, he grabbed the only thing handy—a gaff. The moray turned toward him. As it struck, Dexter clipped it with the gaff. Savagely, the green, repugnant monster plunged again and the boy hit it again, knocking it back. His gaff was too short for such work, and he knew it. He knew that if he missed, the moray would not. But he struck a third time. Mrs. Graymond came to galvanic life. She realized the boy had made a place which would permit her to jump to the side of her husband. She jumped. And, at last, she screamed.

Seeing that the lady was clear, Dexter lost no time in leaping up on one of the fishing chairs.

Then Crunch came, fast. He had recognized the scream as one not of exultation. He snatched up the long-handled gaff—which Dexter hadn't been able to reach—and he broke the moray's back with it.

It took two hours and a half, together with one of the tastiest dishes in all the experience of the Graymonds, to start the fishing again. They called Dexter a hero and the bravest kid they had ever seen and Mr. Graymond patted his back and Mrs. Graymond kissed him. There were long discussions of the venomousness of the big eels, and there was a brief but tense altercation between husband and wife over the uncourageous behavior of the former. Dexter noted a look in Crunch's eye which eased away a full half of his sadness. Then the lines were wet again, no more morays were caught, and Mr. Graymond made no further attempts to fling fish aboard unaided.

It turned out to be a good day, with a fine catch of panfish, and two more groupers. A day marked by An Adventure to Tell People Back Home. The Graymonds began to refer to the battle in that fashion. Dexter slipped back into his melancholy. The sun moved down. The anchor went up. And, in the purpling evening, the *Poseidon* hummed paint-slick down the Government Cut toward home.

Dexter was sitting alone on the canopy top when Mr. Graymond came up beside him. He didn't say anything. He just shook Dexter's hand, and his own head, and went away. But he had left something in Dexter's palm. The boy looked at it. And—for him—the sun shone brightly, the sea was perfumed, there were flowers on every tree. It was a five-dollar bill.

His first impulse was to shout for Crunch. Five dollars was a fortune. It would pay for the rod. But Dexter was a youth accustomed to consideration. Maybe four dollars would foot the bill. Or even three. His ideas about money, in sums larger than ten or fifteen cents, were not merely vague. They scarcely existed. If three were enough . . . what he could do with the other two would be! . . . But he sturdily thrust back temptation. He leaned over the cockpit.

"Captain Adams," he said in a low tone, "would you come here a minute? It's important."

Crunch recognized the tone. He had been hoping to hear it all day. "Take over," he said quickly to his mate. "I'll see the kid."

He climbed up on the canopy. He sat down beside the boy. He was smiling. "O.K., Dexter. What's important?"

Dexter handed him the five dollars. "That's for the rod I stole."

Crunch took the money. "Oh," he said somewhat numbly. "Where'd you?—"

"Mr. Graymond gave it to me. A reward, I guess, for saving that Mrs. Graymond's life, or maybe her leg."

"I see. Yeah. Look, Dex. About swiping the rod. Why?"

Dexter was crying a little, then. Things had broken too well for a man to bear. But he started to talk. Every sentence made the going tougher. Crunch didn't interrupt. He just sat there, watching the causeway slide past, watching the boat swing as Des prepared to back her in.

"I had to," the youngster began. "You gotta believe I had to! If you didn't, I'd about die!" He swallowed. "Look. You know about 'business reverses'? Pop's been having what he calls that. It really means we don't have any money. Until they started, we had enough. We had a wonderful time! We'd get up together, and I'd help get breakfast, and eat lunch at school, and evenings, we'd cook at home and sometimes we'd go out for dinner to a real restaurant! Then . . . when Saturday came . . ."

Dexter had to pull himself together. "When—Saturdays came—he'd take me out in the Glades—fishing in the canal! We'd drive in our car, and I'd fish a jack pole and he'd cast plugs. I–I–I told you he could put one in your pocket a hundred feet away. It's true! Then—when we had to sell the car—we couldn't go so far and we had to fish in places that weren't so good—but we hardly never missed a Saturday! He's—he knows all the birds—and how to catch snakes—and we saw deer and 'coons and possums! And then . . ."

The boy's voice went lower—close to inaudibility. His words ran fast. "School was coming. I had to have shoes and knickers and books and things—and Pop sold his rod and his reel and his tackle box and he had about a million plugs and he sold them and said he didn't care to fish with an old jack pole so we didn't go out together any more. He didn't tell me he sold those things to get my school stuff ready—but I found out from the man that bought them. Pop had a chance to sell—and he knew we'd have to buy all my stuff in a few weeks. I found that out. So I knew."

He didn't get any further than that. He couldn't. But there was no need of it.

The *Poseidon* was edging toward the dock. Crunch jumped to the top controls while Des made fast the bow lines. Crunch didn't particularly want Dexter to see him at that instant, anyway. His jaw was set like steel. When the *Poseidon* was snug, Crunch looked at the hunched back of the boy. Then his eye traveled ashore, and he saw a man standing there. A medium-sized man, an unimportant-looking man, with a good face, full of worry. The man's eyes were hurt, and in his hand was the rod Des had made—the one his son had stolen.

Des helped the passengers ashore. Immediately afterward, the man— Mr. Heath—accosted the mate. He spoke rapidly, nervously. "My boy must have stolen this. He left it in my room a few days ago with a note saying he had found it. As soon as I had time—I traced it—through the tackle shops. Somebody recognized your work . . ."

Des just stood.

But the boy heard his father's voice. He leaped up with a tearing, ecstatic cry. "It's all right, Pop! It's yours! I just paid five bucks for it!"

The man, gray, embarrassed, gazed at his son. He spoke the first words that came into his head—spoke them bitterly. "Five bucks—when it's worth twenty-five! See here, son! . . ."

Dexter slid down into the cockpit. He was not breathing, or even seeing. He was sick. Sicker, perhaps, then he would ever be again in his life. He leaped ashore and eluded Desperate's panicky effort to catch him. He ran away down the dock—to be alone.

Crunch dropped down, also, and came ashore. The Graymonds were waiting for their catch to be put on the fish rack. They realized something was wrong. They stood by, puzzled and unhappy.

Crunch took the gray-faced man by the arm. It was quivering. "Look," he began urgently. "I can't explain now. But you've got to believe me, Mr. Heath! This is a mighty important moment in your kid's life! He's a fine kid, Mr. Heath! I only hope mine grows up half that swell! But I want you to let me handle this my way. I want you to keep that rod—"

"I couldn't, Captain! I—I'm kind of broken up about it. I came home that night to tell my son I had found a job—a good one—and there was the stolen rod and the lying note! I've tried to teach him—about stealing—lying—and it half killed me! I decided not to say a thing about the job, till my boy confessed the theft. He—" Mr. Heath stammered. "He did it—for me. That is—for motives which were decent. If you . . ."

Crunch squeezed the father's arm hard. He also swallowed. "Look, Mr. Heath. I know all that! You keep the rod. Do you hear me? You've gotta! You've got to trust my judgment!" His blistering blue gaze held on the gray eyes of the other man.

"All right," said Mr. Heath, sighing. "All right. I'll trust you. I'm sort of mixed up—anyway . . ."

Crunch raced away—butting into people on the dock. He found Dexter hiding, on the ground, under the truck that took away fish carcasses. Dexter was racked by crying. Crunch seized his foot, pulled him out, and stood him up.

"Go away!" Dexter said in near strangulation. "I don't want any favors! I thought that five bucks was plenty."

Crunch shook him. "Listen!" His own voice was wild and tight. "Listen, Dex! I want you to get square with me! You gave that rod to your dad. He's gotta keep it. You got to pay for all of it. That's what I'm here to tell you."

"How can I? Twenty-five!—"

"I told you to shut up! Now, shut up! I'm doing the talking! You owe me twenty bucks. All right. There's just about twenty days before school begins. From now on—every day—you're working for me all day. A dollar a day. And lunches," Crunch added hastily. "A dollar a day and lunches. If you don't earn all of it—if you're a couple of days short—then you can go out a few Saturdays! You shine brass, and watch baits . . ."

Dexter shook his head miserably. "I—I ain't no good! You know that! I steal, and I think hammerheads are marlins. . . ."

"No good?" The man's voice was incredulous. "No good! Son, you got bait eyes like a hawk's! You can see a fin before even the fish knows he's coming up! You're the rarin'est, tearin'est moray fighter I ever saw milling in a cockpit! No good! Why—you're worth any three eighteen-year-old mates on the Gulf Stream Dock! Now! You working for me—or not?"

Dexter had listened. He wiped a wet sleeve wetter. "Gee!—" He hesitated, and dared it—"Gee, *Crunch*, you're a swell guy!"

Crunch slapped his shoulder and caught up his arm.

They went back along the dock together in a swift, easy lope, taking care not to butt into anybody.

This is another evocative story that is as much about life as it is about catching fish. A vacationer returns to a favorite salmon resort in Nova Scotia. He meets an attractive and interesting young lady. Looks like love may blossom at any moment. It is tantalizingly written, with a nifty conclusion.

Warren Gibson

THE GIRL AT THORP'S (1939)

MY BOAT WAS TO SAIL at twelve o'clock noon and I was hurrying with some last minute packing, odds and ends left over from the night before; all the more important things had been put in, but cases left unstrapped to receive toilet articles and other small pieces which I might need in the morning.

I was off on my annual holiday, going fishing this year again as usual. I often thought of having a different sort of holiday, possibly going to the seashore, taking a long ocean trip or something of the kind, but in the end I usually did the same thing. I withstood the temptations presented by such conventional vacations, packed up my rods and reels and tried my luck with the salmon.

Good Lord! What a relief it was to get away. Tackle had all been looked over days before, fly cases checked and a few especially alluring ones added, a half dozen leaders and I thought my kit was complete; must not forget the tried and true old hat though, no luck without that old soft hat.

I taxied to the dock with all my luggage, plenty of time, found my quarters quite all right, in fact rather familiar, as I had gone north on this same boat on several previous occasions.

There was quite a crowd about the lower decks, so I made my way above to the upper deck, found a quiet corner to sit down in until the steward should come around and I could get a permanent chair.

Almost two whole days of absolute loafing before me. This was Saturday, we should make Halifax Monday morning after breakfast. Then a day spent in some minor shopping and getting my fishing permit, overnight train dropping me off at a little way-station at 5:30 in the morning. There to board a fussy old "chug chug" boat which would take me across the lake to Bedeck, at the wharf would be Joe waiting with the Ford, two hours later I would be on the spot.

Joe and Mrs. Joe have run the place for years, mostly Mrs. Joe really, it is she who does all the managing. Joe himself is usually fishing or just getting ready to go fishing; he can be the busiest man doing nothing you ever saw.

Without Mrs. Joe the place wouldn't get on at all, she really runs things, oversees the kitchen, buys all the supplies, makes out your bill and it's she who accepts your money as you leave. Joe has his job though too: it is his part to greet you when arriving, string out his stock of stories during your stay and to look very sad and downcast at your departure; other than that he fishes. He's a lovable old fraud though. It's Joe as much as the fishing that keeps me coming back year after year.

It was a nice trip up, boat not too crowded, smooth water all the way and no fog. I did my various chores in Halifax on Monday, caught my train in the evening and in due time was put down on the dock where

Joe's boy was waiting with the car. A few hours later I was sitting down close by just about the prettiest little salmon stream in Nova Scotia.

Right off I had my customary bad luck; there had been quite a lot of wet weather and for the first few days water was too high for fishing; we did manage to get a few trout from the meadow brook about a quarter mile back of camp though. By the fourth day the water had gone down and cleared up some and from then on we began to get our fishing. Seven beauties fell to my rod in the next few days and I was content, I don't care to murder the fish. The largest topped eighteen pounds, they get them larger up here but somehow I don't seem to land those big ones. My eighteen pounder gave me plenty of sport though, took me out well above the waist, dragged me nearly half mile and I came to shore thoroughly tired out and with a good part of the Margaree in my waders.

The day I had planned to go out I tramped up above the camp some three miles along the back trails and roads, coming down to the stream by the bridge. Not doing any fishing today, just rambling around and saying goodbye till next year.

The whole valley could be seen from here beautiful in the sunlight, small feathery clouds floating by overhead, the sound of rippling water below me, soft meadowland bordering the stream on both sides and then come the hills which bound the valley, lovely, and now I must leave it all and go back to the city. I stopped on the bridge to enjoy this wonderful picture and to see in the sweep of the stream as it came down, a rare opportunity for a painter. Just at the curve above me I saw a fisherman on the opposite bank making ready to cast. He was perhaps some three or four hundred yards upstream; he waded out well above the knees to make his first cast far out to the middle of the stream. There was a sure and workmanlike sweep to the cast that marked him as no novice, that was certain. I stood there for a time watching; it's a pretty sight to see good casting such as this and I was in a splendid position to watch. Cast after cast he made a good twenty-five yards, coming to water right in the channel where it runs strong and swift and where one usually hooks the big fish.

As I stood there watching he started downstream toward me, working the stream as he came along. As he reached a bit of gravelly beach just above the bridge he waded to shore, turned face toward me and looked up. To my surprise I then saw it was a woman, a young woman perhaps in her early twenties.

She was wearing the usual fishing duds, soft felt hat, canvas jacket, men's trousers and high waders; it was not surprising I had not seen it was a woman. I leaned over the bridge rail and nodded to her, she nodded to me and waved a hand in casual greeting. I wouldn't recognize her again, there was quite a distance between us and I couldn't see very much of her face anyhow.

When I returned to camp I told Joe about seeing the girl fishing up above the bridge.

"Oh yes," he said, "I heard o' her, she been comin' up here fur three to four years now but I never did run into her. Some o' the guides they told me about her, said she was pretty good too."

"Yes, she handles a mean rod, Joe; I watched her quite awhile and it was pretty. Where does she stay, do you know?"

"Thorp's, I hear; Thorp got a place up that way a piece above the bridge. She must be stayin' up there."

I had never seen Thorp's but I knew about where it was located. "Well, you ought to take a day off sometime, Joe, and go up there and look her over, she might give you a few pointers."

Women casting for salmon were not often met with in this country, in fact this was the only time I had encountered one in all the years of coming up here. She made quite an impression upon me.

I did not go out the following day as intended; the weather was so fine I just hated to leave, so decided to give the fish one more try after all. The next afternoon, however, I packed up and got everything ready for an early start in the morning. Joe was to drive to Bedeck, where I would get a boat going back through the lakes to Mulgrave, from there by train to Truro, where I could catch the limited for Montreal. I had some business which would keep me a few hours, perhaps overnight, continuing to New York in the morning.

It might have been more direct and with less changing to drive to Sydney, from there by train back to Halifax and make the same limited, but

I had looked forward to the all day boat trip down the lakes, one of the most beautiful to be had in the Provinces. Also Truro being a junction point on the main line, I would lose no time going out this way.

The boat was late in arriving at Bedeck. It usually is, I fancy, but as there would be several hours wait over at Mulgrave for my train it did not matter. The little boat reached Mulgrave late in the evening, after dark at this time of year, and my train would not come along until midnight, so I had a rather long wait with nothing to do but hang around a deserted railroad station, no pleasing prospect. When it arrived I was fortunate in getting a lower and went to bed at once.

At Truro the next morning reservations were awaiting me in response to my wire from Bedeck.

A cup of coffee and some toast had been my breakfast, so after getting on the train I went in for lunch at the first opportunity. The car steward showed me to a small table with an empty chair opposite. During the next few minutes the car filled rapidly. I had just finished my bouillon when a young woman was shown to the table. I rose and bowed to her as she seated herself, then continued with my lunch.

When I looked up a second or two later I saw her eyes fixed upon my chop, which I had just begun to eat; it was grilled with some bacon and I found it excellent. I thought perhaps she was thinking it might suit her own taste. Now the subject of food might serve as well as any other to start conversation with a charming young woman that a kind fate had put before me, so I began by saying:

"If you are interested, the chop is really very good; I would say you cannot do better."

"It does look good. I think perhaps I will," she replied.

From that opening I carried on, we talked of this and that, quite usual table talk such as people use under these circumstances.

All the while I was casually looking her over. She spoke well in a not unpleasant voice; clothes fitted her well, they were quiet and chosen with taste, dark brown sports type with something of orange tone for vest or under jacket; a soft felt hat with flopped down brim completed the picture and it all had the mark of good taste. She was possibly twenty-five, not more certainly, perhaps less, her features were good. I do not think you would say she was pretty, pleasing surely and she had the loveliest eyes, quite the very best thing about her were the eyes, she had the trick of smiling with her eyes. Large and of the deepest blue, real Irish eyes they were and very good to see. Altogether I decided she must be a person of refinement and one who might prove a very interesting companion on the journey if it could be worked out. I would see what could be done about it.

I managed it so that we should finish lunch about the same time, we paid our individual checks and rose from the table together.

"May I offer you a cigarette?" I asked. "And could we go back to the club car to smoke?"

"Why, yes, I think I should like that," she replied. So we made our way back to the rear of the train for comfortable chairs. As she walked on ahead of me I noted she was somewhat taller than I had thought. I am by no means a tall man, five feet nine to be exact, and I saw she was but slightly below me in height, a matter of a couple of inches perhaps, must be long in the legs I thought. I noticed too that they were very good-looking legs and very trim, nice-looking angles. I did not like her shoes though, not quite right with the rest of the costume, it seemed to me; they were made up of different kinds of leather with little perforations all over and tied with broad ribbon and were high in the heel.

We found chairs, got comfortably fixed and lighted our cigarettes. There was a long dreary train ride ahead and I had hated the thought of this part of the trip home; now here was a diversion which might help a lot, much better than reading and besides I had no book with me; the car library is usually a total loss and the radio grows to be a terrible bore.

These thoughts were running through my head in the second or two as we moved our chairs around facing the windows. I was just turning to say something or other when she asked me whether I had boarded the train at Halifax.

"No, I got on at Truro," I replied. "I have had an all night trip, in fact even longer than that. I came down through the Bras d'Or Lakes the day before."

She seemed interested at hearing me say that. "Why, that's curious, isn't it? I've been up in that part of the country too. I came out another way though. I came by way of Sydney and Halifax to make this train. I thought that the most direct way."

"Yes, that's right it is and probably quicker too, but you see I wanted to come down through the lakes. Ever since I have been coming up here they have been telling me I should go out by the lake route. This time I made up my mind I would. I'm glad I did too, it was a gorgeous trip all the way, marvelous. I enjoyed every minute of it."

"You speak as though you came up here pretty often," she questioned, "what brings you so much to this out-of-the-way part of the world?"

"Oh," I answered, "I belong to the fisherman tribe, they go all over you know; when we find a good stream we stay for awhile but when it grows popular why then we have to move on again."

"So you are a fisherman, are you? Salmon, I suppose, in this country. Where do you find that good stream you are talking about, or is that too inquisitive?"

"No," I replied. "I don't mind telling you, it's no private water and not too much fished as yet. I've been on the Margaree, been going there four or five years now. I like the country and I like the people."

"The Margaree! Why, that's just where I've been. I'm a fisherman too. Isn't it remarkable we should meet on a train like this? What I mean is, we've both come from way up there, sort of end of the world almost and we start home different ways and get on the same train at different stations and then I come and sit down at your table and we get to talking and all these days we've been almost next door to each other, on the same stream anyhow. Oh, I do think it the strangest thing. Don't you?"

As a matter of fact there was even more that she didn't know, if I was right in my surmise. It had come to me like a shot while she had been talking. It was almost a certainty she was the girl I had seen that day from the bridge. Not at all likely there would be more than one woman fishing on the Margaree, so I answered:

"Yes, it is strange, as you say. Now tell me this: Were you by any chance fishing last Sunday morning, just above that old steel bridge by Thorp's?"

"Sunday morning, let me think," she mused. "Why yes I was, that was my last time out. I wanted to try out a Jock Scot but I had no luck at all."

"Well, what do you know about that?" I returned. "Besides all the other strange and remarkable things you have mentioned there is this one more. We are really quite old acquaintances. I was the man on the bridge."

She looked at me in amazement and then we both burst out laughing.

"My dear girl," I continued, "that dining car steward was my good angel all right. I don't know how but somehow he did know you belonged at my table. I'll put him in my prayers tonight and, what he will probably appreciate much more, I'll not forget him at dinner tonight."

After this I am sure neither of us felt we were mere chance acquaintances of little more than an hour. We sat on there talking of one thing and another for a good part of the afternoon. I tried to find out as much about her as I could without being overly inquisitive. By now I was sure that not only was she an interesting companion for a day's journey but also if possible I was not going to say a conventional goodbye when we reached Montreal in the morning.

She told very little of herself or her affairs. I gathered from her talk she had travelled about a good deal, seemed to know a number of cities, had no very extensive knowledge of books, went in little for sports, except the fishing of which she was extremely fond and always did alone. I was curious to know whether she was married or single, divorced or perhaps a widow. I did not think she was a business girl. Men did not appear to be much in her life, at least she didn't mention them. I could not recall any reference to her people and there was strange mixture in her sometimes, there was evidence of refinement and education and then sometimes would come something quite different, a word or expression might be quite coarse and unrefined. It was surprising.

Later on in the afternoon she excused herself with some word about repacking a bag but not before I had arranged to see her at dinner.

We dined late that night. An hour or two afterward in the club car I found her well versed in various sporting topics of the day; spoke in the "right language" and needed no detailed explanations, she was *on* to practically everything. Had a masculine attitude generally and yet she was very feminine, I think I was always quite conscious of the woman of her. We had not touched upon any "sexy" stuff in conversation, nevertheless sex was always very present in her; one could not be near her long without feeling that.

Just before going off to bed we stepped out on to the observation platform for a little air. It was a splendid night, stars blinking away up there in the heavens, the air cool and sweet, here and there a glimpse of the river. We were quite alone out there and it seemed intimate and cozy. She learned a little toward me, I thought, and for a second our bodies touched and her hand rested on my arm. It was a "chumpy" thing to do. I took her quickly in my arms, drew her head down on to my shoulder and kissed her hard, full on the lips.

She was absolutely quiet, no protest, no surprise or exclamation, nothing whatever; just nothing. Certainly no response. I might as well have been kissing a mummy. I was surprised, for I had kissed with passion and desire just as I had felt at that moment and she was never the kind of girl to take it like that, she did not impress me as being the cold type. She might resent it, she might welcome it, but in either case I would bet my life she would be absolutely and fully *alive*.

She turned toward the door without a word to me. I made no protest and we walked in silence through the train. When we reached her section I said good night and continued on to my own car ahead. As I undressed and crawled into the berth I had a distinct feeling that I had rather made a mess of things. I was certainly no hero.

Next morning I breakfasted alone, later in the morning stopping at her seat with the idea of squaring myself if I could. I thought it likely, after all I had not done anything so very terrible, she had no right to have such tempting lips and lovely eyes if she didn't expect to be kissed.

The incident was to be ignored, I found; that was plain from the first, she was in very good humor. Last night was *out*. I thought to myself, I just used the wrong system, that was all. The idea was probably all right. I approached it the wrong way, that was the trouble. Sedative for my vanity.

I was now more sure than ever that this adventure should not come to an end at Montreal. Some way must be found to carry on. This girl was evidently not interested in a kiss in the dark, I should have to evolve something which would interest her. Eyes like hers that promised so much could not possibly have been made all for nothing.

We were nearing the end of the journey now and I had no definite plan or idea. I only knew I was going to make the try somehow.

Perhaps I might suggest her staying over and going on to New York with me the following day. I wondered would that work out. Well, why not? It seemed a wonderful idea to me, why would it not appeal to her also? She was no child, she could decide for herself and despite the lack of response to the kiss, I had a feeling I was not unattractive to her. The whole business of last night did not mean very much really, nerves get a bit ragged on a long trip like this. A good hotel, tub, change into other clothes, a good dinner and comfortable quarters; that should make all the difference in the world. Yes, I would suggest it.

We were by now almost to the terminal, luggage had been carried to the vestibule by the porter and passengers were preparing to leave so time was short. I turned to her and said:

"Here we are at last. Do you plan stopping over in Montreal or are you going through? I am afraid you will have difficulty in getting away today unless you have already made reservations. Now, I have a suggestion, it is this: Stay over. We can dine together, perhaps see a show or anything you like; let's make a party of it. We two have had such a good time I just hate to let you go so soon. Now what do you say?"

She looked at me straight in the eyes for a second and answered:

"No, I have made no reservations as yet." Nothing more and yet she had not failed to understand me, of that I felt sure. I waited a little to give her time but she added nothing.

"Well, then," I persisted, "what do you think of my plan? We must not ignore the blessed fate that brought us together. I very much want you to stay and I'll land you safe and sound in New York."

The train was in the terminal by now, passengers were crowding into the aisles and we had to move along with the others, so there was no chance for anything more at the moment. Still I had an idea it was as good as settled.

At the curb our porters had a taxi waiting, here she held out her hand to me and said, "Thank you a lot for a pleasant journey. It's been nice to know you. Goodbye."

This was not at all what I was expecting, it rather knocked me off my balance. True she had not said *yes* but she had not said *no*. Perhaps I was expected to be more persistent. Very well, my girl, I thought; you shall have it your own way. I handed her into the waiting taxi, insisting I would see her safely to her destination, with the idea of playing up to her whim as we drove along.

It was not to be so simple as all that, however. Instead of going to the far side she sat quickly in the seat next the open door, put forth her hand again and said, "Thank you for everything. Don't spoil it. Goodbye; you've been very kind."

What could I do? Nothing but just what I did do. Have the porter take my luggage off, raise my hat to her and watch her drive away, standing there by the curb feeling very much the fool and then turning in time to find the porter grinning at me. I cursed him and told him to find me another taxi.

Reaching my hotel I took a much needed tub, dressed and went for a walk. A good lunch later on put me in better spirits. I tried to argue that possibly I would not have found her as attractive in town as she had proved on the train, perhaps all was for the best. I could not make it very convincing though.

During the afternoon I attended to the business which had brought me here, spent rather a stupid evening and next morning went on to New York.

Back from my holiday I found things piled up at the office and was kept busy for several days with little or no time for anything else. Once in awhile I would think of beautiful dark blue eyes and all that might have been, but most of all I think my thoughts went back to that strangely unflattering dismissal at the station in Montreal. It was all over now, no good having any regrets at this late day, forget it. Suffering pride I suppose it was, I had thought I was a very devil of a fellow and had taken it on the chin.

One evening several weeks later, walking along Fifty-seventh street after dining uptown with some friends, I reached that neighborhood of the lighted shop windows and picture galleries which occupy several blocks. Particularly was I interested in some of the pictures and had stopped to admire a Venetian of very splendid color when I was conscious of a slight touch on my arm. I paid no attention at first, then it happened again unmistakably this time and I turned to see who was nudging me so persistently.

At my side stood a young woman looking in the window. I saw at once she had all the appearance of a distinct type often to be seen in this neighborhood; they are unmistakably to be recognized, a certain hang of the clothes, kind of walk, an air of going nowhere in particular, in fact the whole atmosphere is indicative of the type and seldom to be mistaken and although this girl was simply standing by me I placed her at once as one of our ladies of the evening.

She went on looking in the window but knew I had turned to observe her, I am sure. I was not at all surprised when I heard her say:

"Hello, are you out for a walk?"

Something about the sound of the voice was familiar to me. Where had I heard that voice before? I looked closely at her face and at that instant she turned toward me and I got a good look at her. There was an immediate recognition by both; I stood speechless, not a word would come out. On her part she was as dumb as I, she dropped her eyes and in a second turned and walked away from me.

Good God! How was such a thing possible? This was my fishing girl, the girl of the Montreal train, the same one I had found such an interesting companion, the girl of such uncompromising morals. Oh there must be some mistake somewhere. I must have been wrong. It wasn't the same. I would hurry after her to make sure there had been a mistake.

Of course that was all just sheer nonsense. It was sure enough, perfectly sure. There had been no mistake, I had recognized her beyond all doubt and she had also recognized me.

So I didn't follow her. I couldn't somehow and there wasn't anything for me to say. I realized that when I thought the thing over. So instead I started off in the opposite direction, turned the next corner and went in at the first place to get something to drink.

Guy de Maupassant (1850–1893) needs no introduction to short-story buffs, since he's one of the world's great practitioners of this literary art form. The scene in this story is Paris during the Franco-Prussian War (1870–1871), and the Huns are knocking at the gate. Two French soldiers decide to slip away to visit an old fishing hole, and one thing leads to another. The Complete Short Stories of Guy de Maupassant (1947) contains his over two hundred stories, including such gems as "The Necklace," "A Passion," "The Piece of String," and "The Wedding Night."

Guy de Maupassant

A FISHING EXCURSION (1874)

PARIS WAS BLOCKADED, DESOLATE, FAMISHED. The sparrows were few, and anything that was to be had was good to eat.

On a bright morning in January, Mr. Morissot, a watchmaker by trade, but idler through circumstances, was walking along the boulevard, sad, hungry, with his hands in the pockets of his uniform trousers, when he came face to face with a brother-in-arms whom he recognized as an old-time friend.

Before the war, Morissot could be seen at daybreak every Sunday, trudging along with a cane in one hand and a tin box on his back. He would take the train to Colombes and walk from there to the Isle of Marante where he would fish until dark.

It was there he had met Mr. Sauvage who kept a little notion store in the Rue Notre Dame de Lorette, a jovial fellow and passionately fond of fishing like himself. A warm friendship had sprung up between these two and they would fish side by side all day, very often without saying a word. Some days, when everything looked fresh and new and the beautiful spring sun gladdened every heart, Mr. Morissot would exclaim "How delightful!" and Mr. Sauvage would answer "There is nothing to equal it."

Then again on a fall evening, when the glorious setting sun, spreading its golden mantle on the already tinted leaves would throw strange shadows around the two friends, Sauvage would say "What a grand picture!"

"It beats the boulevard!" would answer Morissot. But they understood each other quite as well without speaking.

The two friends had greeted each other warmly and had resumed their walk side by side, both thinking deeply of the past and present events. They entered a *café*, and when a glass of absinthe had been placed before each Sauvage sighed.

"What terrible events, my friend!"

"And what weather!" said Morissot sadly; "this is the first nice day we have had this year. Do you remember our fishing excursions?"

"Do I! Alas! when shall we go again!"

After a second absinthe they emerged from the *café*, feeling rather dizzy—that light-headed effect which alcohol has on an empty stomach. The balmy air had made Sauvage exuberant and he exclaimed, "Suppose we go!"

"Where?"

"Fishing."

"Fishing! Where?"

"To our old spot, to Colombes. The French soldiers are stationed near there and I know Colonel Dumoulin will give us a pass."

"It's a go; I am with you."

An hour after, having supplied themselves with their fishing tackle, they arrived at the colonel's villa. He had smiled at their request and had given them a pass in due form.

At about eleven o'clock they reached the advance-guard, and after presenting their pass, walked through Colombes and found themselves very near their destination. Argenteuil, across the way, and the great plains toward Nanterre were all deserted. Solitary the hill of Orgemont and Sannois rose clearly above the plains–a splendid point of observation.

"See," said Sauvage pointing to the hills. "The Prussians are there."

Prussians! They had never seen one, but they knew that they were all around Paris, invisible and powerful; plundering, devastating, and slaughtering. To their superstitious terror they added a deep hatred for this unknown and victorious people.

"What if we should meet some?" said Morissot.

"We would ask them to join us," said Sauvage in true Parisian style.

Still they hesitated to advance. The silence frightened them. Finally Sauvage picked up courage.

"Come, let us go on cautiously."

They proceeded slowly, hiding behind bushes, looking anxiously on every side, listening to every sound. A bare strip of land had to be crossed before reaching the river. They started to run. At last, they reached the bank and sank into the bushes, breathless but relieved.

Morissot thought he heard some one walking. He listened attentively, but no, he heard no sound. They were indeed alone! The little island shielded them from view. The house where the restaurant used to be seemed deserted; feeling reassured, they settled themselves for a good day's sport.

Sauvage caught the first fish, Morissot the second; and every minute they would bring one out which they would place in a net at their feet. It was indeed miraculous! They felt that supreme joy which one feels after having been deprived for months of a pleasant pastime. They had forgotten everything–even the war!

Suddenly, they heard a rumbling sound and the earth shook beneath them. It was the cannon on Mont Valérien. Morissot looked up and saw a trail of smoke, which was instantly followed by another explosion. Then they followed in quick succession.

"They are at it again," said Sauvage shrugging his shoulders. Morissot, who was naturally peaceful, felt a sudden, uncontrollable anger.

"Stupid fools! What pleasure can they find in killing each other!"

"They are worse than brutes!"

"It will always be thus as long as we have governments."

"Well, such is life!"

"You mean death!" said Morissot laughing.

They continued to discuss the different political problems, while the cannon on Mont Valérien sent death and desolation among the French.

Suddenly they started. They had heard a step behind them. They turned and beheld four big men in dark uniforms, with guns pointed right at them. Their fishing-lines dropped out of their hands and floated away with the current.

In a few minutes, the Prussian soldiers had bound them, cast them into a boat, and rowed across the river to the island which our friends had thought deserted. They soon found out their mistake when they reached the house, behind which stood a score or more of soldiers. A big burly officer, seated astride a chair, smoking an immense pipe, addressed them in excellent French. "Well, gentlemen, have you made a good haul?"

Just then, a soldier deposited at his feet the net full of fish which he had taken care to take along with him. The officer smiled and said: "I see you have done pretty well; but let us change the subject. You are evidently sent to spy upon me. You pretended to fish so as to put me off the scent, but I am not so simple. I have caught you and shall have you shot. I am sorry, but war is war. As you passed the advance-guard you certainly must have the password; give it to me, and I will set you free."

The two friends stood side by side, pale and slightly trembling, but they answered nothing.

"No one will ever know. You will go back home quietly and the secret will disappear with you. If you refuse, it is instant death! Choose!"

They remained motionless, silent. The Prussian officer calmly pointed to the river.

"In five minutes you will be at the bottom of this river! Surely, you have a family, friends waiting for you?"

Still they kept silent. The cannon rumbled incessantly. The officer gave orders in his own tongue, then moved his chair away from the prisoners. A squad of men advanced within twenty feet of them, ready for command.

"I give you one minute, not a second more!"

Suddenly approaching the two Frenchmen, he took Morissot aside and whispered: "Quick—the password. Your friend will not know; he will think I changed my mind." Morissot said nothing.

Then taking Sauvage aside he asked him the same thing, but he also was silent. The officer gave further orders and the men leveled their guns. At that moment, Morissot's eyes rested on the net full of fish lying in the grass a few feet away. The sight made him faint and, though he struggled against it, his eyes filled with tears. Then turning to his friend: "Farewell! Mr. Sauvage!"

"Farewell! Mr. Morissot."

They stood for a minute, hand in hand, trembling with emotion which they were unable to control.

"Fire!" commanded the officer.

The squad of men fired as one. Sauvage fell straight on his face. Morissot, who was taller, swayed, pivoted, and fell across his friend's body his face to the sky, while blood flowed freely from the wound in the breast. The officer gave further orders and his men disappeared. They came back presently with ropes and stones, which they tied to the feet of the two friends, and four of them carried them to the edge of the river. They swung them and threw them in as far as they could. The bodies weighted by stones sank immediately. A splash, a few ripples, and the water resumed its usual calmness. The only thing to be seen was a little blood floating on the surface. The officer calmly retraced his steps toward the house muttering. "The fish will get even now."

He perceived the net full of fish, picked it up, smiled, and called, "Wilhelm!"

A soldier in a white uniform approached. The officer handed him the fish saying: "Fry these little things while they are still alive; they will make a delicious meal."

And having resumed his position on the chair, he puffed away at his pipe.

Short stories on fishing reached their peak in the middle decades of the twentieth century, and one of the best writers from this period is Sparse Grey Hackle, really the name of a trout fishing fly. A good-humored fellow, writer Alfred W. Miller adopted this moniker as his pseudonym. Hackle/Miller's knowledge of fishing and his deft hand for writing are evident in this story. A collection of his stories and articles is Fishing Days, Angling Nights *(1971).*

Sparse Grey Hackle

MURDER (1954)

"IF FISHING INTERFERES WITH YOUR business, give up your business," any angler will tell you, citing instances of men who have lost health and even life through failure to take a little recreation, and reminding you that "the trout do not rise in Greenwood Cemetery," so you had better do your fishing while you are still able. But you will search far to find a fisherman to admit that a taste for fishing, like a taste for liquor, must be governed lest it come to possess its possessor; that an excess of fishing can cause as many tragedies of lost purpose, earning power and position as an excess of liquor. This is the story of a man who finally decided between his business and his fishing, and of how his decision was brought about by the murder of a trout.

Fishing was not a pastime with my friend John but an obsession—a common condition, for typically your successful fisherman is not really enjoying a recreation, but rather taking refuge from the realities of life in an absorbing fantasy in which he grimly if subconsciously re-enacts in miniature the unceasing struggle of primitive man for existence. Indeed, it is that which makes him successful, for it gives him that last measure of fierce concentration, that final moment of unyielding patience which in angling so often make the difference between fish and no fish.

John was that kind of fisherman, more so than any other I ever knew. Waking or sleeping, his mind ran constantly on the trout and its taking, and back in 1932 I often wondered whether he could keep on indefinitely doing business with the surface of his mind and fishing with the rest of his mental processes—wondered, and feared that he could not. So when he called me one spring day and said, "I'm tired of sitting here and watching a corporation die; let's go fishing," I know that he was not discouraged with his business so much as he was impatient with its restraint. But I went with him, for maybe I'm a bit obsessed myself.

That day together on the river was like a thousand other pages from the book of any angler's memories. There was the clasp and pull of cold, hurrying water on our legs, the hours of rhythmic casting, and the steady somnambulistic shuffling which characterizes steelworkers aloft and fly fishermen in fast water. Occasionally our heads were bent together over a fly box; at intervals our pipes wreathed smoke, and from time to time a brief remark broke the silence. We were fishing "pool and pool" together, each as he finished walking around the other to a new spot above him.

Late afternoon found me in the second pool below the dam, throwing a long line up the still water. There was a fish rising to some insect so small that I could not detect it, so I was using a tiny gray fly on a long leader with a 5X point. John came by and went up to the dam pool and I lost interest in my refractory fish and walked up to watch, for there was always a chance of a good fish there. I stopped at a safe distance and sat down on a rock with my leader trailing to keep it wet, while John systematically covered the tail of the pool until he was satisfied that there was no fish there to dart ahead and give the alarm, and then stepped into it.

As he did so his body became tense, his posture that of a man who stalks his enemy. With aching slowness and infinite craft he began to inch up the pool and as he went his knees bent more and more until he was crouching. Finally, with his rod low to the water and one hand supporting himself on the bottom of the stream, he crept to a casting position and knelt in mid-current with water lapping under his elbows, his left sleeve dripping unheeded as he allowed the current to straighten his line behind him. I saw that he was using the same leader as mine but with a large No. 12 fly.

"John, using 5X?" I breathed. Without turning his head he nodded almost imperceptibly.

"Better break off and reknot," I counseled softly, but he ignored the suggestion. I spoke from experience. Drawn 5X gut is almost as fine as a human hair, and we both knew that it chafes easily where it is tied to a fly as heavy as No. 12, so that it is necessary to make the fastening in a different spot at frequent intervals in order to avoid breaking it.

I kept silence and watched John. With his rod almost parallel to the water he picked up his fly from behind him with a light twitch and then false-cast to dry it. He was a good caster; it neither touched the surface nor rose far above it as he whipped it back and forth.

Now he began lengthening his line until finally, at the end of each forward cast, his fly hovered for an instant above a miniature eddy between the main current and a hand's breadth of still water which clung to the bank. And then I noticed what he had seen when he entered the pool—the sudden slight dimple denoting the feeding of a big fish on the surface.

The line came back with a subtle change from the wide-sweeping false casts, straightened with decision and swept forward in a tight roll. It straightened again and then checked suddenly. The fly swept round as a little elbow formed in the leader, and settled on the rim of the eddy with a loop of slack upstream of it. It started to circle, then disappeared in a sudden dimple and I could hear a faint sucking sound.

It seemed as if John would never strike although his pause must have been but momentary. Then his long line tightened—he had out fifty feet—as he drew it back with his left hand and gently raised the rod tip with his right. There was slight pause and then the line began to run out slowly.

Rigid as a statue, with the water piling a little wave against the brown waders at his waist, he continued to kneel there while the yellow line slid almost unchecked through his left hand. His lips moved.

"A big one," he murmured. "The leader will never hold him if he gets started. I should have changed it."

The tip of the upright rod remained slightly bent as the fish moved into the circling currents created by the spillway at the right side of the dam. John took line gently and the rod maintained its bend. Now the fish was under the spillway and must have dived down with the descending stream, for I saw a couple of feet of line slide suddenly through John's hand. The circling water got its impetus here and this was naturally the fastest part of the eddy.

The fish came rapidly toward us, riding with the quickened water, and John retrieved line. Would the fish follow the current around again, or would it leave it and run down past us? The resilient rod top straightened as the pressure was eased. The big trout passed along the downstream edge of the eddy and swung over the bank to follow it round again, repeated its performance at the spillway, and again refused to leave the eddy. It was troubled and perplexed by the strange hampering of its progress but it was not alarmed, for it was not aware of our presence or even of the fact that it was hooked, and the restraint on it had not been enough to arouse its full resistance.

Every experienced angler will understand that last statement. The pull of a game fish, up to the full limit of its strength, seems to be in proportion to the resistance which it encounters. As I watched the leader slowly cutting the water, I recalled that often I had hooked a trout and immediately given slack, whereupon invariably it had moved quietly and aimlessly about, soon coming to rest as if it had no realization that it was hooked.

I realized now that John intended to get the "fight" out of his fish at a rate slow enough not to endanger his leader. His task was to keep from arousing the fish to a resistance greater than the presumably weakened 5X gut would withstand. It seemed as if it were hopeless, for the big trout continued to circle the eddy, swimming deep and strongly against the rod's light tension, which relaxed only when the fish passed the gateway of the stream below. Around and around it went, and then at last it left the eddy. Yet it did not dart into the outflowing current but headed into deep water close to the far bank. I held my breath, for over there was a tangle of roots, and I could imagine what a labyrinth they must make under the surface. Ah, it was moving toward the roots! Now what would John do—hold the fish and break off; check it and arouse its fury; or perhaps splash a stone in front of it to turn it back?

He did none of these but instead slackened off until his line sagged in a catenary curve. The fish kept on, and I could see the leader draw on the surface as it swam into the mass of roots. Now John dropped his rod flat to the water and delicately drew on the line until the tip barely flexed, moving it almost imperceptibly several times to feel whether his leader had fouled on a root. Then he lapsed into immobility.

I glanced at my wrist watch, slowly bent my head until I could light my cold pipe without raising my hand, and then relaxed on my rock. The smoke drifted lazily upstream, the separate puffs merging into a thin haze which dissipated itself imperceptibly. A bird moved on the bank. But the only really living thing was the stream, which rippled a bit as it divided around John's body and continually moved a loop of his yellow line in the disturbed current below him.

When the trout finally swam quietly back out of the roots, my watch showed that it had been there almost an hour and a quarter. John slackened the line and released a breath which he seemed to have been holding all that while, and the fish re-entered the eddy to resume its interminable circling. The sun, which had been in my face, dropped behind a tree, and I noted how the shadows had lengthened. Then the big fish showed itself for the first time, its huge dorsal fin appearing as it rose toward the surface and the lobe of its great tail as it turned down again; it seemed to be two feet long.

Again its tail swirled under the surface, puddling the water as it swam slowly and deliberately, and then I thought that we would lose the fish, for as it came around to the downstream side of the eddy it wallowed an instant and then headed toward us. Instantly John relaxed the rod until the line hung limp and from the side of his mouth he hissed, "Steady!"

Down the stream, passing John so closely that he could have hit it with his tip, drifted a long dark bulk, oaring along deliberately with its powerful tail in the smooth current. I could see the gray fly in the corner of its mouth and the leader hanging in a curve under its belly, then the yellow line floating behind. In a moment he felt of the fish again, determined that it was no longer moving, and resumed his light pressure, causing it to swim around aimlessly in the still water below us. The sun was half below the horizon now and the shadows slanting down over the river covered us. In the cool, diffused light the lines on John's face from nostril to mouth were deeply cut and the crafty folds at the outer corners of his lids hooded his eyes. His rod hand shook with a fine tremor.

The fish broke, wallowing, but John instantly dropped his rod flat to the water and slipped a little line. The fish wallowed again, then swam more slowly in a large circle. It was moving just under the surface now, its mouth open and its back breaking water every few feet, and it seemed to be half turned on its side. Still John did not move except for the small gestures of taking or giving line, raising or lowering his tip.

It was in the ruddy afterglow that the fish finally came to the top, beating its tail in a subdued rhythm. Bent double, I crept ashore and then ran through the brush to the edge of the still water downstream of the fish, which now was broad on its side. Stretching myself prone on the bank, I extended my net at arm's length and held it flat on the bottom in a foot of water.

John began to slip out line slowly, the now beaten trout moving feebly as the slow current carried it down. Now it was opposite me and I nodded a signal to John. He moved his tip toward my bank and cautiously checked the line. The current swung the trout toward me and it passed over my net.

I raised the rim quietly and slowly, and the next instant the trout was doubled up in my deep-bellied net and I was holding the top shut with both hands while the fish, galvanized into a furious flurry, splashed water in my face as I strove to get my feet under me.

John picked his way slowly down the still-water, reeling up as he came, stumbling and slipping on the stones like an utterly weary man. I killed the trout with my pliers and laid it on the grass as he came up beside me and stood watching it with bent head and sagging shoulders for a long while.

"To die like that!" he said as if thinking aloud. "Murdered—nagged to death; he never knew he was fighting for his life until he was in the net. He had strength and courage enough to beat the pair of us but we robbed him a little at a time until we got him where we wanted him. And then knocked him on the head. I wish you had let him go."

The twilight fishing, our favorite time, was upon us but he started for the car and I did not demur. We began to take off our wet shoes and waders.

"That's just what this depression is doing to me!" John burst out suddenly as he struggled with a shoelace. "Niggling me to death! And I'm up here fishing, taking two days off in the middle of the week, instead of doing something about it. Come on; hurry up. I'm going to catch the midnight to Pittsburgh; I know where I can get a contract."

And sure enough he did.

PERMISSIONS ACKNOWLEDGMENTS

Grateful acknowledgment is extended to the following authors, publications, and agents.

Jack Gilchrist, "Opening Day," originally published in the *Georgia Review*, Volume XVIII, Number 1 (Spring 1964), ©1964 by the University of Georgia. Reprinted by permission of the *Georgia Review* and Jack Gilchrist.

Philip Wylie, "Light Tackle," originally published in the *Saturday Evening Post*, June 1, 1940. Reprinted by permission of the Lyons Press.

Robert Travers, "The Big Brown Trout," originally published in *Argosy*, 1966.

Bob Shacochis, "Squirrelly's Grouper," from *The Next New World*, ©1989 by Bob Shacochis. Reprinted by permission of Crown Publishers, Inc.

Robert Traver, "The Intruder," from *Trout Madness*, ©1960 by Robert Traver.

Elmer Ransom, "Fishing's Just Luck," from *Fishing's Just Luck* by Elmer Ransom, ©1945 by Mrs. Elmer Ransom. New York: Howell, Soskin, 1945.

Stephen King, "The Man in the Black Suit," originally published in the *New Yorker*, October 31, 1994. Reprinted by permission of Darhansoff and Verrill Literary Agency.

Also available from Chicago Review Press:

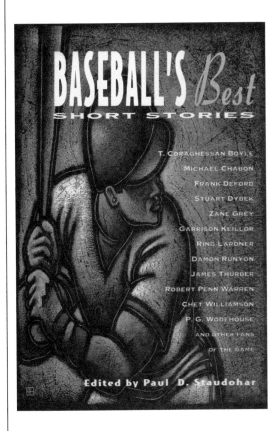

BASEBALL'S BEST SHORT STORIES
Edited by Paul D. Staudohar

"This outstanding anthology is a testament to baseball's enduring drawing power as subject matter for some of our most renowned authors."   *—Booklist*

"Staudohar has hit it out of the park."   *—Publishers Weekly*

Enjoy nostalgic reveries and thoughtful reflections on the great American pastime in this superb collection of 27 short stories and one poem. There's the extra-inning contest, the flamethrower versus the great slugger, the hot prospect who can't keep his mind on the game, the exhilarating win, and the heartbreaking loss. This wonderful anthology attests to baseball's place in our hearts, from "My Roomy," written by Ring Lardner in 1914, to Damon Runyon's "Baseball Hattie," written in the baseball-mad 1930s, to Garrison Keillor's 1988 story "Three New Twins Join Club in Spring."

404 pages, 6 × 9
paper, $16.95
ISBN 1-55652-319-X

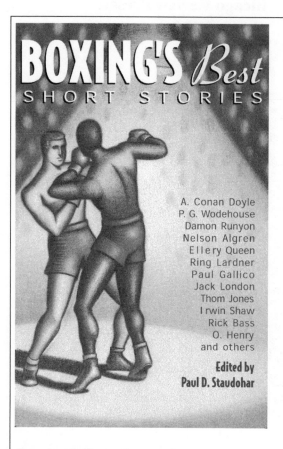

A. Conan Doyle
P. G. Wodehouse
Damon Runyon
Nelson Algren
Ellery Queen
Ring Lardner
Paul Gallico
Jack London
Thom Jones
Irwin Shaw
Rick Bass
O. Henry
and others

Edited by
Paul D. Staudohar

BOXING'S BEST SHORT STORIES
Edited by Paul D. Staudohar

"At once brutish and artistic, primitive and spellbinding, prizefighting provides rich material for talented writers. . . . This collection will delight fight fans, as well as those who just love a good story."   *—School Library Journal*

Boxing has always had its share of violence, disreputable characters, and shattered dreams, but as an inspiration for great writing it is unsurpassed. The bone-jarring crack as a glove smashes into a jaw . . . endless seconds as the referee barks "one, two, three" . . . the roar of the crowd as the winner lifts his pulpy face in victory . . . *Boxing's Best Short Stories* brings the action of the ring to life with 22 classic tales.

352 pages, 6 × 9
cloth, $24.00
ISBN 1-55652-364-5

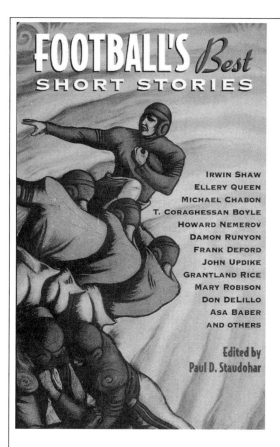

IRWIN SHAW
ELLERY QUEEN
MICHAEL CHABON
T. CORAGHESSAN BOYLE
HOWARD NEMEROV
DAMON RUNYON
FRANK DEFORD
JOHN UPDIKE
GRANTLAND RICE
MARY ROBISON
DON DELILLO
ASA BABER
AND OTHERS

Edited by
Paul D. Staudohar

FOOTBALL'S BEST SHORT STORIES
Edited by Paul D. Staudohar

"An exciting collection of some of the best 20th-century writers venturing into some unexpected venues." —J. C. Martin, *The Arizona Daily Star.*

There are no rookies here—some of America's best writers have penned short stories on football. In this lively anthology of 21 stories and one classic poem about football, fathers and sons tackle their issues, coaches and quarterbacks collide, and ordinary heroes emerge from the blitz. Each decade of the 20th century is tackled, from Ralph D. Paine's 1909 moving story of a down-on-his-luck father who goes to see his son play a big game for Yale, to Ellery Queen's 1940s detective story set in the Rose Bowl, to Frank Deford's spoof on the media hysteria of the Superbowl, written in 1978.

336 pages, 6 × 9
cloth, $22.00, ISBN 1-55652-330-0
paper, $16.95, ISBN 1-55652-365-3

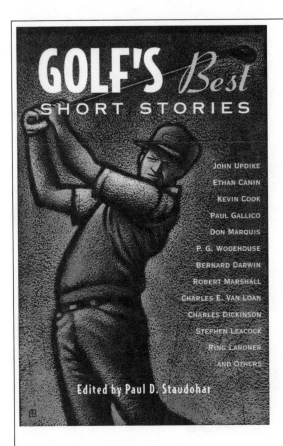

JOHN UPDIKE
ETHAN CANIN
KEVIN COOK
PAUL GALLICO
DON MARQUIS
P. G. WODEHOUSE
BERNARD DARWIN
ROBERT MARSHALL
CHARLES E. VAN LOAN
CHARLES DICKINSON
STEPHEN LEACOCK
RING LARDNER
AND OTHERS

Edited by Paul D. Staudohar

GOLF'S BEST SHORT STORIES
Edited by Paul D. Staudohar

Twenty-four gems from many great writers, including P. G. Wodehouse, Paul Gallico, Don Marquis, and John Updike, are represented in these great tales of golf. British duffers, amateur sleuths, pros, hustlers, plodders, cheaters, starry-eyed lovers, and crass finaglers people these stories, which range from comedy to tragedy, mystery, action, introspection, and romance. Each reveals a true love of the game and a wry understanding of golf's frustrations, perplexities, embarrassments, and moments of pure delight.

416 pages, 6 × 9
cloth, $24.00 ISBN 1-55652-321-1
paper, $16.95 ISBN 1-55652-325-4

HUNTING'S BEST SHORT STORIES
Edited by Paul D. Staudohar

From duck, goose, and grouse hunting to stiffer contests for deer, elk, moose, bear, and big African game—in one case, even a manhunt—all kinds of hunting and all possible outcomes, from the comic to the heartwarming, disastrous, or bizarre, are explored in *Hunting's Best Short Stories*. Against backdrops of ocean, frozen swamp, forest, or jungle, in this powerful collection of 21 classic and contemporary tales we see the deep bonds between father and son, huntsman and dog, and man and nature being forged or shattered as the line between sport and survival blurs.

336 pages, 6 × 9
cloth, $24.00
ISBN 1-55652-402-1

These books are available from your local bookstore or from Independent Publishers Group by calling (312) 337-0747 or (800) 888-4741.